The Architect's Remodeling, Renovation, & Restoration Handbook

The Architect's Remodeling, Renovation, & Restoration Handbook

H. Leslie Simmons
AIA, CSI

VAN NOSTRAND REINHOLD
New York

Printed in the United States of America
Designed by Caliber Studios

Van Nostrand Reinhold
115 Fifth Avenue
New York, New York 10003

Van Nostrand Reinhold International Company Limited
11 New Fetter Lane
London EC4P 4EE, England

Van Nostrand Reinhold
480 La Trobe Street
Melbourne, Victoria 3000, Australia

Nelson Canada
1120 Birchmount Road
Scarborough, Ontario M1K 5G4, Canada

16 15 14 13 12 11 10 9 8 7 6 5 4 3 2 1

Library of Congress Cataloging in Publication Data

Simmons, H. Leslie.
    The architect's remodeling, renovation, and restoration handbook/
  H. Leslie Simmons.
      p. cm.
    Bibliography: p.
    Includes index.
    ISBN 0-442-20574-0
      1. Architecture—United States—Conservation and restoration—Handbooks, manuals,
etc. I. Title.
NA106.S57 1989
720′.28′8—dc19   88-23612
                                                                                CIP

Contents

Preface

For 30 years I have watched a succession of architects struggle with the unique problems associated with documenting changes to existing buildings. For 8 years, I managed a sixty-person drawing production department in an architect's office where I experienced firsthand the problems involved with deciding the best methods to use to produce such documents. Later, my experience broadened during a stint in my own architectural practice.

In 1975, I began my current practice as a specifications consultant. Since then I have produced project manuals for more than fifty major projects and many other small projects for several architect clients. Thirty-five of those major projects and most of the smaller projects included work related to existing construction. They have included commercial, institutional, educational, industrial, and housing projects. There have been projects in both the private and governmental sectors of our economy. Some of them have been prestigious and some lesser known. They have ranged from multistory additions to repair of roof leaks. Many have been challenging. A few have been nightmarish.

While producing those projects, my architect clients and I struggled with two related problems—How to produce effective and accurate construction documents for projects where existing construction is involved and how to realize a profit while producing them. I eventually developed methods of producing project manuals that were both effective and profitable. My architect clients also produced the necessary drawings, of course. Some of them did it both well and profitably. But some of their methods were better than others. Some were not profitable. Some were ineffective and contributed to problems during the construction phase. Over time, I began to realize which methods were the more effective.

So I wrote a series of eight feature articles on the subject which *The Construction Specifier* published between July 1982 and January 1984. We called the series "The 3-Rs of Specifying Restoration, Rehabilitation, and Remodeling." The articles addressed some problems associated with producing the bidding requirements, contract conditions, and general requirements portions of project manuals for projects where existing construction is involved.

But the articles were limited to only a small part of the project manual. They did not complete discussion of Division One, said nothing about Divisions Two through Fourteen, and did not even mention drawing production. This book carries the discussion into those additional subjects and shares what I have learned about them with fellow architects who produce drawings, specifications, or both for remodeling, renovation, and restoration projects.

Acknowledgments

I would like to thank those who helped make this a better book. I especially want to thank Robert B. Molseed, AIA, CSI; Donald Prowler, AIA; David E. Guise, architect; George Stewart, Sr., of Stewart Brothers, Photographers, Rockville, Maryland; and Ronald N. Anderson, architectural photographer, Rockville, Maryland. Special thanks also to Judith R. Joseph, executive editor, architecture and design at Van Nostrand Reinhold; and my wife, Joyce, whose immeasurable help made the book possible.

Introduction

America has always been a land obsessed with the new. We build washing machines, lawn mowers, automobiles, and even buildings to last for limited—sometimes even predetermined—times. Our tax structure is based on expected depreciation. We have made buildings to last for shorter and shorter periods, until today we build some of them out of thin plastic and inflate them with hot air like aerial balloons.

Many Americans live in portable homes. The 1980 census revealed that 3.8 million Americans occupied trailers and mobile homes. That figure may not be startling, but 20 years earlier, portable home dwellers numbered only 700,000—a more than fivefold increase.

Most of the other 76.6 million occupied dwellings in the United States are only temporary, in the historical sense. In 50 years or so, many of them will literally disintegrate.

Only in the last quarter of the nineteenth century did we begin to realize that some new world things might be worth saving. In March of 1872, Yellowstone National Park became the first national park. Forty-four years later, the Act of August 25, 1916, established the National Park Service, and the setting aside of battlefields, national parklands, and historic buildings for preservation began in earnest.

In spite of the new laws, many historic structures fell to the indomitable wrecking ball. Largely to counteract the wholesale destruction of the nation's historic monuments, Congress passed the National Historic Preservation Act of

1966, which created the National Register of Historic Places, state-based historic preservation programs, the Advisory Council on Historic Preservation, and the review procedures necessary to assess the effects of federal actions on historic properties.

Since that time, other laws and tax law revisions have enhanced the market value of preserving our heritage by creating accelerated depreciation allowances and other tax advantages for reusing existing buildings, including those that are not necessarily historic. The advantages have been somewhat eroded in the mid-eighties, but they are still significant.

Even if there were no tax-related incentives for reusing existing buildings rather than building new structures, a major driving force influencing the reuse of older structures is the well-substantiated fact that rehabilitation often costs less for the same space than new construction.

In spite of all that incentive, however, is rehabilitation really that large a part of the market?

You bet it is.

As far back as 1982, *Architectural Record* reported that 96 percent of the architectural firms they surveyed had been involved in some renovation, rehabilitation, or restoration work. In December 1986, the magazine *Commercial Renovation* reported the results of a survey which projected that $90 billion would be spent in 1987 on renovation projects in the commercial markets compared with a projected $66 billion of new commercial construction for the same year. The magazine stated that ''Commercial renovation is now the largest U.S. construction market, and it will remain so for decades to come.''

Over the next several years, if it has not happened already, every architect and consulting engineer in the United States is going to work on a project that involves existing construction.

In spite of the pronounced swing toward reusing existing buildings, the construction industry has been slow to respond with written data intended to help architects and engineers do that work.

There is some data aimed at those who will decide *whether* to reuse or build anew and some directed to the financial aspects of the issue. There are many data available telling architects and building contractors how to actually repair existing materials. A few years ago, the National Park Service produced some comprehensive and useful details and specifications dealing with repairing existing materials. Much of it is still available. Other organizations, such as the Brick Institute of America, have also produced documentation detailing repair methods. Unfortunately much of the needed data are scattered and often difficult to obtain quickly, thereby requiring much research.

By contrast, there is almost nothing in print directed toward helping architects and engineers produce drawings and specifications for projects where existing construction plays a major role. The limited available how-to material is not generally publicized and therefore is not well known among many firms that produce construction documents.

This book fills in some of the gaps in that available data. Its purpose is to suggest means and methods that an architect can use to produce construction drawings and specifications for projects where existing construction plays a part. This material will not solve every problem an architect has when dealing with such projects but should lessen the need to reinvent every schedule form, specifications paragraph, drawing symbol, and note needed for such projects. This book presents an orderly system for producing complete documents. It does not solve specific problems but rather explores and describes methods that an architect can use to solve a multitude of problems.

Definitions

Many words and phrases have been used to describe construction work related to existing buildings. Sometimes it seems that every time another pamphlet is published, a new term springs into existence. Here are some of the terms in use today and their meanings as they apply to this book:

Adaptive reuse: Taken literally, adaptive reuse means "having a tendency toward the act or process of adapting for a further or repeated use." On the other hand, *adapted* reuse would seem to mean to "make fit for future use," which makes more sense. The term "adaptive reuse" is, however, in general use and will undoubtedly continue to be in use, in spite of being grammatically incorrect and regardless of whether the term actually makes any sense.

Addition: A part added to an existing building.

Alteration: The act, process, or result of making different without changing into something else.

Preservation: The noun form of the verb "preserve," which means to keep safe from injury, harm, or destruction. Also: to protect; to maintain.

Reconstruction: The process of rebuilding nonexistent or severely damaged structures and site works as they once existed, according to documented evidence of original condition.

Recycle: The return to a condition such that operation can begin again.

Rehabilitation: The same as restoration, except that new additions and adjacent new construction compatible in scale, materials, and texture are appropriate.

Remodeling: The act of altering the structure of; reconstructing; reassembling; making or forming by recombining parts.

Renovation: Restoration to an earlier state; improvement by cleaning, repair, or rebuilding.

Restoration: The act of bringing back to a former condition; restoring existing work to a condition that existed at some historic time. New construction, such as an addition, is not appropriate in restoration work.

Retrofit: A procedure of furnishing with new parts or equipment not available at the time of manufacture (construction).

The Secretary of the Interior's Standards for Historic Preservation Projects contains broader definitions of some of the terms defined above as they relate specifically to historic preservation projects.

Suggestions for Using this Book

This book contains three parts. The first part discusses the documents that were used to build the existing structure and suggests methods for using them to help produce documents for the current project. It contains checklists designed to help an architect gather needed data about the existing construction.

The second part contains lists of symbols for use in documents for projects where existing construction plays a part and example drawings showing how to use the symbols. It also includes methods for producing drawings for projects with existing construction involvement, including suggestions and examples showing how to produce plans, elevations, and details. It also includes schedule formats and lists of notes for use directly on drawings for remodeling, renovation, and restoration projects.

Part three consists of guide paragraphs that an architect can edit and add to office guide (master) specifications developed for projects where all the work is new to make those guides work for remodeling, renovation, and restoration projects. It does not, however, include guides for landscaping, structural, mechanical, plumbing, or electrical sections.

Each part contains commentary and detailed instructions for using the documents that the part contains.

Throughout the book, the emphasis is on how documents for renovation, remodeling, and restoration projects differ from documents for new projects. The differences between large and small projects are also addressed. Examples show an architect how to expand document production methods and specifications guides developed for projects where all the work is new, to make them usable for renovation, remodeling, and restoration projects of all sizes.

There is a tendency when using a book such as this to turn directly to the part in which you are most interested at the moment and begin to use it without regard to the remainder of the book. You can, of course, do exactly that, since each of the three parts of the book is self-contained; but to use the book more effectively, it would be much better to first become familiar with the contents of the entire book. You may not want to study it as you would a text book, which is not necessary, but you should become generally familiar with the contents. Then go to the part containing the specific data you want. It is important to become familiar with the entire book and not just the part that interests you at the moment, because the book describes a system in which the parts interrelate. The specifications paragraphs in Part Three, for example, are more effective when used with the drawing production methods that Part Two recommends. Reusing existing documentation (discussed in Part One) will affect the drawings discussed in Part Two.

Disclaimer

The example library illustrated in Part Two is purely fictitious. The drawings, notes, and schedules presented are intended to demonstrate production methods and not technical content and are therefore incomplete and may also be technically inaccurate. Neither the author nor the publisher warrants or assumes liability for the drawings, schedules, or other presented material's accuracy, completeness, or suitability for any particular purpose.

The example specifications paragraphs in Part Three were extracted from several of the author's projects and combined into the form presented to show more than one case in each example. The examples are deliberately incomplete as described in the text and may be inaccurate as well. Neither the author nor the publisher warrants the accuracy or completeness of the examples or assumes liability for their use for any particular purpose.

It is the user's responsibility to apply his or her professional knowledge when using this book, to adapt the principles presented here in the best way for the project at hand, to supply data missing from this book, and to correct errors in and adapt the data presented here to suit the use to which he or she puts that data.

PART ONE

Existing Conditions

1

Obtaining Necessary Data

Occasionally, a client will ask an architect to provide professional services for a project that includes an addition to an existing building, or remodeling, renovation, or restoration of an existing building for which the original construction documents no longer exist. Such a situation often happens when the work is historic preservation. When no documents are available, the architect must determine in the field all the data needed to perform those professional services. At least some original construction documents are available for most projects, but it is rare for all of them to be available. Typically, some original documents are available, while others are not.

This chapter includes three checklists, Figure 1-1, "Owner Survey Checklist," Figure 1-2, "Existing Documents Survey Checklist," and Figure 1-3, "Field Conditions Survey Checklist." The checklists will help an architect obtain and record the data necessary to estimate fees and perform professional services for projects where existing construction plays a part.

Obtaining all the data listed in Figures 1-1 to 1-3 will not be possible, or even desirable, before the architect submits a fee proposal for professional services. But it is critical for the architect to obtain all the data necessary to establish a fee. Too often, architects only superficially investigate existing conditions before signing professional service agreements, sometimes with disastrous consequences. Documents for projects with existing construction involvement routinely cost architectural firms twice as much to produce as do projects with all new construction. Expenses four and five times normal are not unusual on historic preservation projects.

Even so, time and cost pressures often cause architects to accept a potential client's statements about existing construction. Verification, if any, often consists of perusing existing building drawings. Due to the extreme nature of the potential problems associated with dealing with existing construction without proper information, caution is in order. Under no circumstances should an architect, or anyone else for that matter, assume without field verification that existing construction documents accurately represent the actual construction. Nor should an architect assume that a potential client's statements about existing conditions are accurate. The potential client may be misinformed. Undocumented changes may have been made during construction. Products used may not be the same as those specified or even the same as those shown on approved shop drawings. Undocumented remodeling may have occurred later. Many buildings have undergone several successive remodelings, making it virtually impossible to ascertain actual field conditions by examining construction documents.

It may be hard to get some of the data in the checklist in Figures 1-1 to 1-3. The owner may think that gathering the data the architect requests is unnecessary. "After all," the owner will say, "I want only a price." An owner who has requested proposals from other professionals as well might add, "No one else is asking for all this stuff." The owner may be reluctant to release so much data before reaching an agreement with the architect, fearing that the information will fall into the hands of competitors or opponents of the project. The owner may be reluctant to give up one-of-a-kind data such as original shop drawings and may balk at the expense of copying so much material.

Calculating the time a project where existing construction occurs will take is difficult even with sufficient data. A proposal made without such information is a wild guess. You might as well pour money into a Las Vegas slot machine.

When unable to ascertain enough data to properly estimate the work involved, an architect should probably propose a contingency fee. The architect could, for example, work by the hour during the early project phases until determining the amount of work and then shift to a flat fee for the remainder of the work.

Whether before or after signing a services agreement, at some point, the architect must obtain the necessary data.

A particular project may require more data than is listed in the checklists in this chapter. The architect should add appropriate checklist questions. No one has ever developed a truly complete checklist for anything.

Some checklist questions may not apply to a particular project. Delete them. Generally, however, an architect will need most of the information listed for every project with existing construction involvement.

The checklists may at first appear more detailed than necessary. For tiny projects that may be the case, but for most projects, even small ones, and especially for large or complicated projects with large fees and correspondingly large potential losses, it is important to learn as much as possible about the project before signing a services agreement. Architects routinely ascertain some of the data in the checklists before offering proposals, though they might not write either the questions or answers on a formalized list. For the sake of clarity, the checklists include some questions architects routinely ask. But most questions an architect would routinely ask even for a project where all the work was new have been omitted for the sake of brevity. An architect using the checklists must, of course, add the missing questions to obtain the full picture.

The checklist forms in this chapter contain enough blank space for the data an architect needs to collect for most small projects. Recording necessary data for large, complicated projects, however, may take more blank space than the presented forms contain. Then the forms in this chapter may be used as guides to developing more voluminous forms.

Owner Survey

An architect must obtain directly from the owner data which is difficult or impossible to ascertain from examining existing documents or existing construction. Figure 1-1 is a convenient form for recording data obtained from a potential client. Some of the information listed in the form may not be available before the architect submits a proposal. It may be possible to ascertain whether a requirement will exist but not possible to determine the extent of the requirement. Sometimes, some questions must be held until later. Under no circumstances, however, can the architect permanently ignore the questions.

For example, it may be adequate for proposal purposes to know that the contractor must disconnect and move items to new locations within the building, and to know the general scope of the architect's related work. At that stage, having a detailed listing of such items might not be important. It is important to know if the architect must survey the equipment to be moved and ascertain connection and service requirements, or the owner will furnish that data. Sooner or later, however, the architect must determine the entire detailed extent of that work.

The need for answers to some checklist questions may not become apparent until the architect's work is well under way. Do not ignore a question because it seems unnecessary, without examining the question closely. For example, the need to know specific requirements for protecting existing construction and non-interference with occupants may not seem important at first glance. But such requirements sometimes force architects to develop extensive schedules, which can be quite time-consuming.

Tips on Using the Owner Survey Checklist

Caution: Take an owner's attempts to avoid answering questions into account when deciding whether to accept that owner as a client, but do not try to force the owner to answer a question. It could be that the owner simply does not know the answer.

Do not consider the checklist complete. Answering one of its questions might trigger additional questions. A particular project may include aspects not anticipated in the checklist.

If you need to ask additional questions for a particular project, add them to the list.

Some checklist items will not apply to every project. Ignore them. Be careful, however, that the deleted items really are not applicable. Sometimes applicability is difficult to determine until you have asked the question.

Use the "Project ID" blank at the top of each checklist page to show the preparer's project identification number or name so that the pages are easy to identify should they become separated. The ID might be the architect's project identification number or name.

If a project has more than one part (building) or site zone, use a separate copy of the checklist for each building or site zone and place the building or site-zone name in the allotted space at the top of each page.

OWNER SURVEY CHECKLIST

(Insert Firm Name Here)

Date:

PROJECT NAME: _____

PROJECT IDENTIFICATION: _____

PROJECT LOCATION: _____

OWNER'S NAME AND ADDRESS: _____

_____

_____

Representative: _____   Phone: (   ) _____

Position: _____

PROJECT SCOPE:

The Project consists of   ☐ A single building   ☐ _____ buildings as follows:

_____

_____

_____

_____

_____

_____

_____

_____

_____

(Use a separate copy of the remainder of this checklist for each separate building or site zone in the Project.)

Figure 1-1. Form for Owner Survey Checklist.

BUILDING OR SITE-ZONE NAME: _____ Project ID: _____

Description: _____

_____

_____

Project work type: ☐ New building   ☐ Addition   ☐ Remodeling   ☐ Renovation
   ☐ Restoration   ☐ Rehabilitation   ☐ Historic preservation   ☐ Alterations   ☐ Repairs

☐ Retrofit   ☐ Cleaning   ☐ _____
(Clarify the meaning of each as it applies to this building or site zone and describe the extent of

each type of work): _____

_____

_____

Extent (dimensions or square footage of each Project work type, or other appropriate designation of

scope): _____

_____

Number of building stories: _____

_____

Describe the extent and type of existing construction: _____

_____

_____

_____

Existing construction is to be   ☐ Left in place as is   ☐ Remodeled and left in place
   ☐ Renovated and left in place   ☐ Restored to an earlier condition   ☐ Demolished,
removed from the site, and wasted   ☐ Moved to another location on the site
☐ Moved to another site

☐ _____

Clarify and give extents: _____

_____

_____

_____

Owner Survey Checklist—Page 2

BUILDING OR SITE-ZONE NAME: Project ID:

Hazardous material: Removal of   ☐ Asbestos   ☐ Other hazardous material

   (specify) _____   ☐ Is not required

   ☐ Is required to the following extent: _____

_____

_____

_____

_____

_____

Existing building use during construction: ☐ Building   ☐ Adjacent site   ☐ Site zone (in
each case describe extent):   ☐ Will be vacated by Owner during the construction period _____

_____

_____

_____

☐ Will remain   ☐ Totally   ☐ Partly in use by the Owner as follows: _____

_____

_____

_____

While work under this Contract is under way, Owner will   ☐ Not perform other work at the site

   ☐ Perform other work at the site as follows: _____

_____

_____

_____

While work under this Contract is under way, other Contractors will   ☐ Not perform other work at
the site   ☐ Perform other work at the site as follows: _____

_____

_____

_____

BUILDING OR SITE-ZONE NAME: _____   Project ID: _____

Construction phasing: ☐ Not required   ☐ Required as follows: (specify scope of each phase;

use additional pages if necessary): _____ ____

_____

_____

_____

The Contractor will be required to relocate the following existing items: _____

_____

_____

_____

The Contractor will be required to disconnect the following existing items for removal

by the Owner: _____

_____

_____

_____

_____

_____

Because of its special nature, this Project will require the following special procedures (include
special security, access, salvage, and materials handling and storage procedures, as well as
special requirements related to protection of existing construction, noninterference with
occupants and the public, and unusual special hazards):

_____

_____

_____

_____

_____

_____

_____

_____

_____

BUILDING OR SITE-ZONE NAME: _____   Project ID: _____

The Owner will permit the Contractor to use existing   ☐ Electric power   ☐ Water   ☐ Heating

and cooling systems for construction purposes subject to the following conditions: _____

_____

_____

_____

_____

Special support of existing construction will be required to the following extents:

☐ Underpinning   ☐ _____

_____

New elevators: (For existing elevators see Figure 1-3, "Field Conditions Survey Checklist.")
☐ Passenger   ☐ Hydraulic   ☐ Electric
☐ May use for construction purposes
☐ Do not use for construction purposes

☐ Freight   ☐ Hydraulic   ☐ Electric
☐ May use for construction purposes
☐ Do not use for construction purposes

Measured drawings of existing construction: ☐ Do not exist   ☐ Are not available   ☐ Are
available and have been requested   ☐ Have been received   ☐ Have been reviewed
☐ Are part of the architect's work under this contract (refer to Figure 1-3, "Field Conditions
Survey Checklist.")

☐ No new documents have been prepared for this part of the Project.
The following new documents have been prepared for this part of the Project:

☐ Program: ☐ Requested date: _____   ☐ Received date: _____

                    ☐ Reviewed date: _____

☐ Soil reports: ☐ Requested date: _____   ☐ Received date: _____

                    ☐ Reviewed date: _____

☐ Measured drawings: ☐ Requested date: _____   ☐ Received date: _____

                    ☐ Reviewed date: _____

☐ Owner sketches: ☐ Requested date: _____   ☐ Received date: _____

                    ☐ Reviewed date: _____

BUILDING OR SITE-ZONE NAME: Project ID:

☐ Design drawings: ☐ Requested date: _____   ☐ Received date: _____

                             ☐ Reviewed date: _____

☐ Environmental impact statement:

                             ☐ Requested date: _____   ☐ Received date: _____

                             ☐ Reviewed date: _____

☐ _____: ☐ Requested date: _____   ☐ Received date: _____

                             ☐ Reviewed date: _____

The existing building   ☐ Was   ☐ Was not designed to   ☐ Support   ☐ Accept the
proposed new construction. Extent of existing preparations for new work: ☐ Structural
system designed to support extension   ☐ Knockout panels provided   ☐ HVAC systems
designed to support new work   ☐ Other building systems designed to support new work

as follows: _____

_____

_____

_____

_____

_____

Existing Documents Survey

Existing construction documents are excellent sources of data that an architect needs to produce documents for a remodeling, renovation, or restoration project. Figure 1-2 lists most existing documents one would ordinarily find. Unfortunately, many of them may not exist for a particular project.

Some listed documents may seem unnecessary at first. When working with existing buildings, you never know what you are going to run into until you run into it. So you never know when some obscure data will become critical. It is best to obtain all available data as soon as possible and then review it. Some situations that might require an architect's time, or even delay the project, are not apparent until the architect examines the existing documents. For example, an existing building is built on spread footings. The owner logically assumes that the addition will also be on spread footings. But close examination of soil borings made before the existing structure was built reveals a sandy silt layer and a corresponding decrease in blow count at one corner of the building, suggesting a fill layer made before the original building was built. The fill did not affect the existing building but seems to extend beneath the planned addition. New borings are needed to determine the extent of the fill and its effect on support of the addition. New borings are always a good idea, of course, but it is not always possible to persuade an owner to pay for them without good evidence that they are needed. Detailed examination of existing borings and the related soils report can offer that persuasive evidence.

An architect can use existing documents in several ways. The obvious one is to help determine existing conditions. But they can also be used directly as working drawings for new work. We will address that subject more fully later in this book.

Tips on Using the Existing Documents Survey Checklist

Do not consider the checklist complete. A particular project may include aspects not anticipated in the checklist.

If additional data exist for a particular project, add them to the list.

Some checklist items will not apply to every project. Ignore them. Be careful, however, that the items deleted are really not applicable. Sometimes applicability is difficult to determine until you have asked the question.

It may not be necessary to obtain all the details included in the checklist before submitting a proposal. It may be sufficient to know that certain data is available but not necessary to see the data before submitting a proposal. If the owner is dealing with more than one architect in a competition, giving each architect a copy of all the data may not be practicable. Decide which listed data are essential to determining the amount of work necessary to produce the project and be sure to get a look at that data. Ascertain whether the remaining data is available or whether the architect will have to extrapolate it from other sources, which will increase the cost of doing the work.

In the "Project ID" blank at the top of each checklist page, show the preparer's identification number or name for the project so that the pages are easy to identify should they become separated. The ID might be the architect's project identification number or name.

If a project has more than one part (building) or site zone, use a separate copy of the checklist for each building or site zone and place the building or site-zone name in the allotted space at the top of each page.

EXISTING DOCUMENTS SURVEY CHECKLIST

(Insert Firm Name Here)

Date:

PROJECT NAME:

BUILDING OR SITE-ZONE NAME:

Contract drawings of existing construction ☐ Do not exist ☐ Are not available

☐ Are available and have been requested   Date: _____   ☐ Have been received

Date: _____   ☐ Have been reviewed   Date: _____

Bidding Requirements, Contract Forms, and Conditions of the Contract documents for existing construction: ☐ Do not exist   ☐ Are not available

☐ Are available and have been requested   Date: _____

☐ Have been received   Date: _____   ☐ Have been reviewed   Date: _____

Documents available include   ☐ Invitation to Bid   ☐ Instruction to Bidders
☐ Equipment suppliers lists   ☐ Subcontractor list   ☐ General Conditions of the Contract
☐ Supplementary Conditions   ☐ List of Drawings and schedules

☐ _____

Contract specifications for existing construction: ☐ Do not exist   ☐ Are not available

☐ Are available and have been requested   Date: _____   ☐ Have been received

Date: _____   ☐ Have been reviewed   Date: _____

Available Contract documents include   ☐ Finishes Schedule   ☐ Ceiling Heights
Schedule   ☐ Door Schedule   ☐ Window Schedule   ☐ Glazing Schedule   ☐ Louver

Schedule   ☐ Finish Hardware Schedule   ☐ _____

Equipment schedules for: ☐ Library   ☐ Theater and stage   ☐ Laundry and dry
cleaning   ☐ Audiovisual   ☐ Food service   ☐ Residential appliances
☐ Darkroom   ☐ Athletic   ☐ Laboratory   ☐ Medical

☐ _____

Figure 1-2. Form for Existing Documents Survey Checklist.   Page 1

BUILDING OR SITE-ZONE NAME: Project ID:

Addenda prepared for existing construction   ☐ Do not exist   ☐ Are not available   ☐ Are

available and have been requested   Date: _____   ☐ Have been received

Date: _____   ☐ Have been reviewed   Date: _____

As-built documents prepared for existing construction   ☐ Do not exist   ☐ Are not

available   ☐ Are available and have been requested   Date: _____   ☐ Have been

received   Date: _____   ☐ Have been reviewed   Date: _____
As-built documents are in the form of   ☐ Marked-up prints   ☐ Record reproducibles
    ☐ Marked-up specifications

Shop and setting drawings and associated product and technical data and record samples prepared
for existing construction   ☐ Do not exist   ☐ Are not available   ☐ Are available and have

been requested   Date: _____   ☐ Have been received   Date: _____

☐ Have been reviewed   Date: _____

Construction Change Directives prepared for existing construction   ☐ Do not exist   ☐ Are not

available   ☐ Are available and have been requested   Date: _____   ☐ Have been

received   Date: _____   ☐ Have been reviewed   Date: _____

Change Orders prepared for existing construction   ☐ Do not exist   ☐ Are not available

☐ Are available and have been requested   Date: _____   ☐ Have been received

Date: _____   ☐ Have been reviewed   Date: _____

Field Orders and other modifications prepared for existing construction   ☐ Do not exist   ☐ Are

not available   ☐ Are available and have been requested   Date: _____   ☐ Have

been received   Date: _____   ☐ Have been reviewed   Date: _____

Geotechnical data, prepared for existing construction   ☐ including borings logs   ☐ not
including borings logs   ☐ including soil survey report   ☐ not including soils survey
report   ☐ Do not exist   ☐ Are not available   ☐ Are available and have been

requested   Date: _____   ☐ Have been received   Date: _____

☐ Have been reviewed   Date: _____

Environmental impact statement prepared for existing construction   ☐ Does not exist   ☐ Is not

available   ☐ Is available and has been requested   Date: _____   ☐ Has been

received   Date: _____   ☐ Has been reviewed   Date: _____

BUILDING OR SITE-ZONE NAME: Project ID:

Building location survey and floor and wall check records for existing construction   ☐ Do not

exist   ☐ Are not available   ☐ Are available and have been requested   Date: _____

☐ Have been received   Date: _____   ☐ Have been reviewed   Date: _____

Factory and field inspection and test records for existing construction   ☐ Do not exist   ☐ Are

not available   ☐ Are available and have been requested   Date: _____   ☐ Have

been received   Date: _____   ☐ Have been reviewed   Date: _____
Included are test reports for   ☐ Piles   ☐ Caissons   ☐ Earthwork   ☐ Topsoil
     ☐ Pavements   ☐ Site utilities   ☐ Cast-in-place concrete   ☐ Precast concrete
     ☐ Structural steel framing   ☐ Joists   ☐ Roofing   ☐ Doors   ☐ Storefronts
     ☐ Windows   ☐ Curtain walls   ☐ Elevators   ☐ Escalators   ☐ Lifts
     ☐ Hoists   ☐ Cranes   ☐ Equipment
Construction photographs of existing construction   ☐ Do not exist   ☐ Are not available

☐ Are available and have been requested   Date: _____   ☐ Have been

received   Date: _____   ☐ Have been reviewed   Date: _____

As-built documents, for existing construction   ☐ Do not exist   ☐ Are not available   ☐ Are

available and have been requested   Date: _____   ☐ Have been received

Date: _____   ☐ Have been reviewed   Date: _____
Available as-built documents include: ☐ Marked-up contract drawings   ☐ Marked-up
     Project Manual including   ☐ Contract conditions   ☐ Contract requirements
     ☐ Specifications portions   ☐ Record reproducibles

List of subcontractors, fabricators, and manufacturers providing materials and equipment for existing
construction, including names, addresses, and telephone numbers   ☐ Does not exist

☐ Is not available   ☐ Is available and has been requested   Date: _____   ☐ Has

been received   Date: _____   ☐ Has been reviewed   Date: _____

Manufacturers' names, and type, color, and pattern, as applicable, and catalog data, equipment
operation manuals and instructions, maintenance manuals, and spare-parts lists for materials,
products, and equipment used in existing construction. Look for such lists in data submitted
prerequisite to Contract closeout. Such lists   ☐ Do not exist   ☐ Are not available   ☐ Are

available and have been requested   Date: _____   ☐ Have been received

Date: _____   ☐ Have been reviewed   Date: _____
Obtain data for items not listed in Contract closeout material from other Project submittals.
Information is required for the following items (draw a line through items that do not occur in the
existing work. Mark boxes when data has been obtained):
☐ Tunnel lining   ☐ Asphaltic block pavers   ☐ Brick pavers   ☐ Concrete pavers
☐ Stone pavers   ☐ Athletic paving and surfacing   ☐ Subdrainage system piping and

BUILDING OR SITE-ZONE NAME: Project ID:

appurtenances   ☐ Storm sewage system piping and appurtenances   ☐ Site sanitary
system piping and appurtenances   ☐ Water distribution system piping and
appurtenances   ☐ Fuel distribution system piping and appurtenances   ☐ Irrigation system
piping and appurtenances   ☐ Pond and reservoir liners and covers   ☐ Communication
transmission devices such as microwave and shortwave equipment and satellite receivers
☐ Fountains   ☐ Chain link fences and gates   ☐ Wire fences and gates   ☐ Wood fences
and gates   ☐ Ornamental fences and gates   ☐ Bicycle racks   ☐ Guardrails   ☐ Site
signs   ☐ Traffic signals   ☐ Prefabricated planters   ☐ Prefabricated shelters   ☐ Site
seating   ☐ Site tables   ☐ Trash and litter receptors   ☐ Tree grates

☐ Architectural precast concrete

☐ Brick   ☐ Concrete masonry units   ☐ Clay tile unit masonry   ☐ Structural facing
tile   ☐ Ceramic veneer   ☐ Terra-cotta   ☐ Glass unit masonry   ☐ Gypsum unit
masonry   ☐ Adobe masonry   ☐ Simulated stone   ☐ Cast stone   ☐ Marble
☐ Limestone   ☐ Granite   ☐ Sandstone   ☐ Slate

☐ Other stone _____   ☐ Special brick _____

☐ Framing systems such as geodesic structures or space frames   ☐ Steel joists   ☐ Metal
floor deck   ☐ Metal roof deck   ☐ Ornamental railings   ☐ Utility railings   ☐
Prefabricated sheet metal enclosures   ☐ Prefabricated ornamental stairs   ☐ Other

ornamental metal _____

☐ Sheathing   ☐ Wood siding   ☐ Plywood siding   ☐ Plastic siding   ☐ Wood
trusses   ☐ Wood truss joists   ☐ Wood-cord metal joists   ☐ Plywood web joists
☐ Glued-laminated framing and decks   ☐ Plastic laminate   ☐ Prefinished wood
paneling   ☐ Board paneling   ☐ Molded architectural ornamentation   ☐ Wood
preservative treatments   ☐ Wood fire retardant treatment   ☐ Custom wood
casework   ☐ Prefabricated structural plastics   ☐ Glass fiber and resin fabrications
☐ Cast plastic fabrications

☐ Elastomeric sheet membrane waterproofing   ☐ Modified bitumen sheet
waterproofing   ☐ Fluid applied waterproofing   ☐ Bentonite waterproofing   ☐ Metal
oxide waterproofing   ☐ Cementitious waterproofing   ☐ Dampproofing   ☐ Batt and
blanket insulation   ☐ Board insulation   ☐ Foamed-in-place insulation   ☐ Loose fill
insulation   ☐ Sprayed insulation   ☐ Exterior insulation and finish systems
☐ Cementitious fireproofing   ☐ Mineral fiber fireproofing   ☐ Intumescent fireproofing
☐ Magnesium oxychloride fireproofing   ☐ Asphalt shingles   ☐ Glass fiber shingles
☐ Metal shingles   ☐ Mineral fiber-cement shingles   ☐ Porcelain enamel shingles
☐ Slate shingles   ☐ Wood shingles   ☐ Wood shakes   ☐ Clay roofing tile
☐ Concrete roofing tile   ☐ Metal roofing tile   ☐ Mineral fiber-cement roofing tile

☐ Plastic roofing tile   ☐ Preformed wall panels   ☐ Preformed roof panels
☐ Metal siding   ☐ Built-up bituminous membrane roofing   ☐ Elastomeric sheet roofing
☐ Modified bitumen sheet roofing   ☐ Fluid applied roofing   ☐ Protected membrane
roofing   ☐ Traffic topping   ☐ Sheet metal flashing and trim   ☐ Sheet metal roofing
specialties   ☐ Flexible flashings   ☐ Prefabricated copings   ☐ Prefabricated gravel
stops and fascias   ☐ Prefabricated expansion joints   ☐ Prefabricated curbs   ☐ Roof
hatches   ☐ Gravity ventilators   ☐ Ridge vents   ☐ Smoke vents   ☐ Plastic
skylights   ☐ Metal-framed skylights   ☐ Sealants

BUILDING OR SITE-ZONE NAME: Project ID:

☐ Steel doors   ☐ Steel frames   ☐ Aluminum doors and frames   ☐ Bronze doors and frames   ☐ Wood doors   ☐ Plastic doors   ☐ Door opening assemblies   ☐ Access doors   ☐ Sliding glass doors   ☐ Sliding fire doors   ☐ Sliding grills   ☐ Blast-resistant doors   ☐ Security doors   ☐ Metal-clad doors   ☐ Cold storage doors   ☐ Coiling counter doors   ☐ Coiling overhead doors   ☐ Side coiling doors   ☐ Coiling grills   ☐ Accordion folding doors   ☐ Panel folding doors   ☐ Accordion folding grills   ☐ Flexible doors   ☐ Sectional overhead doors   ☐ Vertical lift overhead doors   ☐ Hangar doors   ☐ Sound-retardant doors   ☐ Safety glass doors   ☐ Screen and storm doors   ☐ Flood-barrier doors   ☐ Entrances and storefronts   ☐ Revolving doors   ☐ Automatic door equipment   ☐ Metal windows   ☐ Wood windows   ☐ Clad wood windows   ☐ Roof windows   ☐ Pass windows   ☐ Finish hardware   ☐ Weather stripping and seals   ☐ Door and window accessories   ☐ Glass   ☐ Plastic glazing   ☐ Glazed curtain walls

☐ Prefinished gypsum board   ☐ Ceramic tile   ☐ Quarry tile   ☐ Paver tile   ☐ Glass mosaics   ☐ Plastic tile   ☐ Metal tile   ☐ Terrazzo   ☐ Acoustical ceilings   ☐ Acoustical wall treatment   ☐ Acoustic space units   ☐ Wood strip flooring   ☐ Wood block flooring   ☐ Wood parquet flooring   ☐ Wood composition flooring   ☐ Resilient wood flooring systems   ☐ Flagstone flooring   ☐ Marble flooring   ☐ Granite flooring   ☐ Slate flooring   ☐ Brick flooring   ☐ Pressed concrete unit flooring   ☐ Resilient flooring   ☐ Carpet   ☐ Resinous flooring   ☐ Magnesium oxychloride flooring   ☐ Elastomeric liquid flooring   ☐ Plastic laminate flooring   ☐ Other flooring _____   ☐ Cementitious coatings   ☐ High build glazed coatings   ☐ Fire-resistant coatings   ☐ Protective coatings for concrete   ☐ Other special coatings   ☐ Paint   ☐ Transparent finishes   ☐ Wall coverings

☐ Chalkboards and tackboards   ☐ Toilet compartments   ☐ Shower and dressing compartments   ☐ Cubicles   ☐ Louvers and vents   ☐ Grills and screens   ☐ Service wall systems   ☐ Wall and corner guards   ☐ Access flooring   ☐ Prefabricated fireplaces   ☐ Prefabricated steeples   ☐ Prefabricated spires   ☐ Prefabricated cupolas   ☐ Flagpoles   ☐ Directories   ☐ Bulletin boards   ☐ Plaques   ☐ Exterior signs   ☐ Interior signs   ☐ Lockers   ☐ Fire extinguishers   ☐ Fire extinguisher cabinets   ☐ Walkway covers   ☐ Awnings   ☐ Mail chutes and distribution and collection boxes   ☐ Demountable partitions   ☐ Operable partitions   ☐ Prefabricated storage shelving   ☐ Sun-control devices   ☐ Toilet and bath accessories

☐ Maintenance equipment   ☐ Security and vault equipment   ☐ Teller and service equipment   ☐ Ecclesiastical equipment   ☐ Library equipment   ☐ Theater and stage equipment   ☐ Instrumental equipment   ☐ Registration equipment   ☐ Checkroom equipment   ☐ Mercantile equipment   ☐ Laundry and dry-cleaning equipment   ☐ Vending equipment   ☐ Audiovisual equipment   ☐ Service station equipment   ☐ Parking-control equipment   ☐ Loading dock equipment   ☐ Solid-waste-handling equipment   ☐ Detention equipment   ☐ Water supply and treatment equipment   ☐ Hydraulic gates and valves   ☐ Fluid waste treatment and disposal equipment   ☐ Food service equipment   ☐ Residential appliances   ☐ Unit kitchens   ☐ Darkroom equipment   ☐ Athletic equipment   ☐ Recreational equipment   ☐ Therapeutic equipment   ☐ Laboratory equipment   ☐ Planetarium equipment   ☐ Observatory equipment   ☐ Medical equipment   ☐ Mortuary equipment

BUILDING OR SITE-ZONE NAME: Project ID:

☐ Manufactured casework   ☐ Blinds   ☐ Shades   ☐ Drapery and curtain hardware
☐ Draperies and curtains   ☐ Floor mats and frames   ☐ Auditorium and theater seating
☐ Stadium and area seating   ☐ Pews and benches

☐ Air-supported structures   ☐ Integrated ceilings   ☐ Athletic rooms   ☐ Audiometric
rooms   ☐ Clean rooms   ☐ Cold storage rooms   ☐ Hyperbaric rooms   ☐ Insulated
rooms   ☐ Saunas   ☐ Steam baths   ☐ Vaults   ☐ Sound control devices
☐ Vibration-control devices   ☐ Seismic-control devices   ☐ Radiation protection
☐ Nuclear reactors   ☐ Preengineered buildings   ☐ Metal building systems
☐ Greenhouses   ☐ Grandstands and bleachers   ☐ Observatories   ☐ Fabric
structures   ☐ Swimming pools   ☐ Aquariums   ☐ Hot tubs   ☐ Therapeutic
pools   ☐ Ice rink equipment   ☐ Kennel enclosures, gates, and feeding devices
☐ Incinerators   ☐ Liquid and gas storage tanks   ☐ Digestion tank covers and
assemblies   ☐ Oxygenation systems   ☐ Solar energy collection systems   ☐ Energy
monitoring and control systems   ☐ Environmental control systems   ☐ Communications
systems   ☐ Security systems   ☐ Clock control systems   ☐ Elevator monitoring and
control systems   ☐ Moving stair and walk monitoring and control systems   ☐ Alarm and
detection systems   ☐ Door control systems   ☐ Nurse call systems   ☐ Fire suppression
and supervisory systems

☐ Dumbwaiters   ☐ Elevators   ☐ Escalators   ☐ Moving walks   ☐ People lifts
☐ Wheelchair lifts   ☐ Platform lifts   ☐ Sidewalk lifts   ☐ Vehicle lifts   ☐ Automatic
transport systems   ☐ Hospital transport systems   ☐ Postal transport systems
☐ Baggage conveyors and dispensers   ☐ Conveyors   ☐ Chutes   ☐ Tube systems
☐ Hoists   ☐ Cranes   ☐ Derricks   ☐ Structural turntables   ☐ Permanent
scaffolding   ☐ People mover systems   ☐ Monorail systems

Project closeout record documents for existing construction   ☐ Do not exist   ☐ Are not

available   ☐ Are available and have been requested   Date: _____   ☐ Have been

received   Date: _____   ☐ Have been reviewed   Date: _____
Available closeout documents include   ☐ Warranties   ☐ Guarantees   ☐ Affidavits
☐ Permits   ☐ Bonds   ☐ Certificates including certificates of inspection for plumbing and
drainage, fire protection system, elevator, occupancy, and other items requiring certificates and
certificates of compliance with applicable laws and regulations

Field Conditions Survey

An architect can obtain some data only in the field. Figure 1-3 will help record that data.

Obtaining some of the data in this checklist before submitting a professional services proposal may not be appropriate. The checklist is therefore divided into two phases. Phase 1 contains data one might note on an initial site visit before submitting a proposal. Phase 2 contains more detailed data an architect should obtain over the course of a project.

Which data an architect should look for in the field will be more apparent, locating that data will be easier, and the data will be more meaningful if the architect obtains and becomes familiar with the data included in the "Owner Survey Checklist" and "Existing Documents Survey Checklist" before beginning field survey work.

Field survey work might initially consist of a general walk-around to become familiar with the project. Carrying the existing drawings and specifications, when they are available, will help answer many questions that will occur in the first and later walk-throughs.

After signing the agreement, the architect should make much more involved and detailed site surveys until all needed data has been ascertained.

Tips on Using the Field Conditions Survey Checklist

Use the data obtained from this checklist to produce contract documents.

Do not consider the checklist complete. A particular project may include aspects not anticipated in the checklist.

If additional data exist for a particular project, add them to the list.

Some checklist items will not apply to every project. Ignore them. Be careful, however, that the items you delete are really not applicable. Sometimes applicability is difficult to determine until you have asked a question.

Obtaining some of the data necessary to complete this checklist will require destruction and uncovering of field elements. The architect should be careful to determine enough data before submitting a proposal to ascertain the cost of the architect's services. Where such costs are extensive, the architect should determine the reimbursement method. The architect should also determine who will actually do the work and who will pay the workers.

In the "Project ID" blank at the top of each checklist page, show the preparer's project identification number or name so that the pages are easy to identify should they become separated. The ID might be the architect's project identification number or name.

If a project has more than one part (building) or site zone, use a separate copy of the checklist for each building or site zone and place the building or site zone name at the top of each page in the allotted space.

Complete the phase 1, "Preproposal Walk-Through," part of the checklist before offering a professional services proposal.

Make the surveys which are part of the phase 2, "Predesign Walk-Through," part of the checklist after signing a professional services agreement. Portions of the work listed may be done at different times by different people. The architect should deal with every item in the checklist before completing construction documents, however. Use and mark a different copy of this checklist on each site visit.

FIELD CONDITIONS SURVEY CHECKLIST

(Insert Firm Name Here)

Date:

PHASE 1—PREPROPOSAL WALK-THROUGH

PROJECT NAME:

BUILDING OR SITE-ZONE NAME:

☐ Site visit was made on above date.
☐ Photographs were taken during this visit and Photograph Record was made.
☐ Existing working Drawings   ☐ Were available   ☐ Were not available   ☐ Were
    carried   ☐ Were marked   ☐ Were not marked to show existing conditions
Indicate below those existing conditions observed, and either marked or not marked as stipulated
    above, that differ from those indicated in existing construction documents or discussed with the
    Owner. In the blanks following each item, describe and give locations for the differences.
    ☐ Extent and type of existing construction (major items) that differs from that described in the
        ☐ Owner Survey Checklist,   ☐ Existing Documents Checklist, or   ☐ Both: ☐ None

        ☐ As follows: _____

_____

_____

_____

_____

_____

_____

_____

_____

_____

_____

_____

_____

_____

_____

Figure 1-3. Form for Field Conditions Survey Checklist.

Page 1

BUILDING OR SITE-ZONE NAME: Project ID:

☐ Major items of construction not previously indicated: ☐ None   ☐ As follows: _____

_____

_____

_____

_____

_____

☐ Materials different from those previously indicated or shown on existing construction

documents: ☐ None   ☐ As follows: _____

_____

_____

_____

_____

☐ Spaces used for different purposes than those previously discussed or shown on original

working Drawings: ☐ None   ☐ As follows: _____

_____

_____

_____

_____

_____

☐ No unexpected damage was found.

The following major damage was discovered which was not disclosed in discussions with the Owner or other documentation. (Major damage is damage that will require extensive investigation and design work to rectify. The purpose of this examination is to find existing damage that might not be obvious to the Owner, might not be included in the program, but which will affect the Architect's fee.) In each case indicate whether damage is thought to be serious (affecting the

finish and probably the substrates as well) or cosmetic (affecting only the finish). _____

Field Conditions Survey Checklist—Page 2

BUILDING OR SITE-ZONE NAME: Project ID:

_____

_____

_____

_____

_____

_____

_____

_____

_____

_____

_____

_____

_____

_____

_____

_____

_____

_____

_____

_____

_____

_____

_____

_____

FIELD CONDITIONS SURVEY CHECKLIST

(Insert Firm Name Here)

Date:

PHASE 2—PREDESIGN WALK-THROUGH

PROJECT NAME:

BUILDING OR SITE-ZONE NAME:

Purpose of visit: _____

☐ Photographs were taken during this visit and Photograph Record was made.

☐ Existing working Drawings   ☐ Were available   ☐ Were not available   ☐ Were carried   ☐ Were marked   ☐ Were not marked to show existing conditions

☐ Measurements of existing conditions were made during this visit and recorded on   ☐ Copies of original working Drawings   ☐ Sketches (Use sketches only when original working Drawings are not available. Describe below the location and type of measurements made on this visit.)

_____

_____

_____

_____

_____

_____

Indicate below those existing conditions observed, and either marked or not as stipulated above, that differ from those shown on the existing construction documents or discussed with the Owner. In the blanks following each item, describe the differences and give locations where the differences occur.

☐ Extent and type of existing construction (minor items) that differs from that described in the   ☐ Owner Survey Checklist,   ☐ Existing Documents Checklist, or   ☐ Both   ☐ None

☐ As follows: _____

_____

_____

Field Conditions Survey Checklist—Page 4

BUILDING OR SITE-ZONE NAME: _____   Project ID: _____

☐ Minor items of construction not previously indicated: ☐ None   ☐ As follows: _____

_____

_____

_____

_____

_____

_____

☐ Minor spaces used for different purposes than those previously discussed or shown on

original working Drawings   ☐ None   ☐ As follows: _____

_____

_____

_____

_____

_____

The list on the following pages contains existing items likely to be found. Examine each item in the field, and indicate in the blank space following each item the following:

1. None, when the item does not exist.
2. Condition of the item. Type and extent of damage, if any. In each case, specify whether the damage is major or cosmetic (both as defined in this checklist) and the location(s) where the damage occurs.
3. A detailed description of existing items which were not included in the original construction documents.
4. A detailed description of existing items which are described in the original construction documents but where the actual conditions differ from the original contract documents. Such differences might include use of a somewhat different material or finish; a different manufacturer's product; a different installation method; a different location.
5. Items or conditions of which photographs were taken.
6. At elevators, lifts, hoists, cranes, and similar transportation items, indicate whether construction use is permitted. Be sure to identify exact device where use is permitted.

Where the blanks do not contain enough room to indicate all necessary data, add pages to the checklist. Number each page and name each page with the same title as used in the list below and note in the blank space the number of the additional page containing data.

Where information related to a checklist item is indicated on a copy of an existing, measured, or new design development, or working drawing, so indicate in the blank space behind the item. Include a description of the drawing on which the information is indicated so that the information can be located easily.

BUILDING OR SITE-ZONE NAME: Project ID:

☐ There are items found in the field which are not listed below. See supplemental pages

numbered _____

The following items occur in the existing construction:

Tunnel: _____

Concrete walks: _____

Concrete roadway paving: _____

Concrete curbs and gutters: _____

Asphalt walks: _____

Asphalt roadway paving: _____

Asphalt curbs: _____

Stone paving: _____

Asphaltic block pavers: _____

Brick pavers: _____

Concrete pavers: _____

Stone pavers: _____

Athletic surfacing: _____

Subdrainage system: _____

Storm sewage system: _____

Site sanitary system: _____

Water distribution system: _____

Fuel distribution system: _____

Electric distribution system: _____

Telephone distribution system: _____

Pond: _____

Reservoir: _____

Irrigation system: _____

Fountain: _____

Field Conditions Survey Checklist—Page 6

BUILDING OR SITE-ZONE NAME: _____   Project ID: _____

Chain link fence: _____

Wire fence: _____

Wood fence: _____

Ornamental fence: _____

Bicycle racks: _____

Guardrails: _____

Site sign: _____

Planters: _____

Tree grates: _____

Cast-in-place concrete: _____

Architectural precast concrete: _____

Structural precast concrete: _____

Brick: _____

Concrete masonry units: _____

Clay tile unit masonry: _____

Structural facing tile: _____

Ceramic veneer: _____

Terra-cotta: _____

Glass unit masonry: _____

Gypsum unit masonry: _____

Adobe masonry: _____

Simulated stone: _____

Cast stone: _____

Marble: _____

Limestone: _____

BUILDING OR SITE-ZONE NAME: Project ID:

Granite: _____

Sandstone: _____

Slate: _____

Structural steel: _____

Steel joists: _____

Metal floor deck: _____

Metal roof deck: _____

Ornamental railings: _____

Utility railings: _____

Prefabricated sheet metal enclosures: _____

Other ornamental metal: _____

Expansion control devices: _____

Wood framing: _____

Sheathing: _____

Wood decking: _____

Wood siding: _____

Plywood siding: _____

Wood trusses: _____

Wood truss joists: _____

Wood-cord metal joists: _____

Plywood web joists: _____

Glued-laminated framing and decks: _____

Wood finish cabinetwork: _____

Plastic laminate finished cabinetwork: _____

Plastic laminate finished countertops: _____

Natural finish wood shelving: _____

BUILDING OR SITE-ZONE NAME: _____   Project ID: _____

Painted wood shelving: _____

Prefinished wood paneling: _____

Board paneling: _____

Wood stairs: _____

Wood handrails: _____

Standing and running trim: _____

Wood door frames: _____

Plastic fabrications: _____

Elastomeric sheet membrane waterproofing: _____

Modified bitumen sheet waterproofing: _____

Fluid applied waterproofing: _____

Bentonite waterproofing: _____

Metal oxide waterproofing: _____

Cementitious waterproofing: _____

Dampproofing: _____

Batt and blanket insulation: _____

Board insulation: _____

Foamed-in-place insulation: _____

Loose fill insulation: _____

Sprayed insulation: _____

Exterior insulation and finish systems: _____

Cementitious fireproofing: _____

Mineral fiber fireproofing: _____

Intumescent fireproofing: _____

Magnesium oxychloride fireproofing: _____

Asphalt shingles: _____

BUILDING OR SITE-ZONE NAME: Project ID:

Glass-fiber shingles: _____

Metal shingles: _____

Mineral fiber-cement shingles: _____

Porcelain enamel shingles: _____

Slate shingles: _____

Wood shingles: _____

Wood shakes: _____

Clay roofing tile: _____

Concrete roofing tile: _____

Metal roofing tile: _____

Mineral fiber-cement roofing tile: _____

Plastic roofing tile: _____

Preformed wall panels: _____

Preformed roof panels: _____

Metal siding: _____

Built-up bituminous roofing: _____

Elastomeric sheet roofing: _____

Modified bitumen sheet roofing: _____

Fluid applied roofing: _____

Protected membrane roofing: _____

Traffic topping: _____

Concealed sheet metal flashing: _____

Exposed sheet metal flashing and trim: _____

Valley flashing: _____

Roofing specialties: _____

Flexible flashings: _____

Copings: _____

BUILDING OR SITE-ZONE NAME: Project ID:

Gravel stops and fascias: _____

Expansion joints: _____

Curbs: _____

Roof hatches: _____

Gravity ventilators: _____

Ridge vents: _____

Smoke vents: _____

Plastic skylights: _____

Metal framed skylights: _____

Sealants: _____

Steel doors: _____

Steel frames: _____

Aluminum doors and frames: _____

Bronze doors and frames: _____

Wood doors: _____

Plastic doors: _____

Door opening assemblies: _____

Access doors: _____

Sliding glass doors: _____

Sliding fire doors: _____

Sliding grills: _____

Blast-resistant doors: _____

Security doors: _____

Metal-clad doors: _____

Cold storage doors: _____

Coiling counter doors: _____

BUILDING OR SITE-ZONE NAME: Project ID:

Coiling overhead doors: _____

Side coiling doors: _____

Coiling grills: _____

Accordion folding doors: _____

Panel folding doors: _____

Accordion folding grills: _____

Flexible doors: _____

Sectional overhead doors: _____

Vertical lift overhead doors: _____

Hangar doors: _____

Sound retardant doors: _____

Safety glass doors: _____

Screen and storm doors: _____

Flood barrier doors: _____

Entrances and storefronts: _____

Revolving doors: _____

Automatic door equipment: _____

Metal windows: _____

Wood windows: _____

Clad wood windows: _____

Roof windows: _____

Pass windows: _____

Finish hardware: _____

Weather stripping and seals: _____

Door and window accessories: _____

Glass: _____

Plastic glazing: _____

BUILDING OR SITE-ZONE NAME: Project ID:

Glazed curtain walls: _____

Plaster: _____

Stucco: _____

Gypsum board: _____

Ceramic tile: _____

Quarry tile: _____

Paver tile: _____

Glass mosaics: _____

Plastic tile: _____

Metal tile: _____

Terrazzo: _____

Acoustical ceilings: _____

Acoustical wall treatment: _____

Acoustic space units: _____

Wood strip flooring: _____

Wood block flooring: _____

Wood parquet flooring: _____

Wood composition flooring: _____

Resilient wood flooring systems: _____

Flagstone flooring: _____

Marble flooring: _____

Granite flooring: _____

Slate flooring: _____

Brick flooring: _____

Pressed concrete unit flooring: _____

Resilient flooring: _____

BUILDING OR SITE-ZONE NAME: Project ID:

Carpet: _____

Resinous flooring: _____

Magnesium oxychloride flooring: _____

Elastomeric liquid flooring: _____

Plastic laminate flooring: _____

Cementitious coatings: _____

High build glazed coatings: _____

Fire resistant coatings: _____

Protective coatings for concrete: _____

Paint: _____

Transparent finishes: _____

Wall coverings: _____

Chalkboards and tackboards: _____

Toilet compartments: _____

Shower and dressing compartments: _____

Cubicles: _____

Louvers and vents: _____

Grills and screens: _____

Service wall systems: _____

Wall and corner guards: _____

Access flooring: _____

Fireplaces: _____

Steeples: _____

Spires: _____

Cupolas: _____

Flagpoles: _____

BUILDING OR SITE-ZONE NAME: Project ID:

Directories: _____

Bulletin boards: _____

Plaques: _____

Signs: _____

Lockers: _____

Fire extinguishers: _____

Fire extinguisher cabinets: _____

Walkway covers: _____

Awnings: _____

Mail chutes: _____

Mail distribution and collection boxes: _____

Demountable partitions: _____

Operable partitions: _____

Prefabricated storage shelving: _____

Toilet and bath accessories: _____

Equipment:

    Maintenance: _____

    Security and vault: _____

    Teller and service: _____

    Ecclesiastical: _____

    Library: _____

    Theater and stage: _____

    Checkroom: _____

    Mercantile: _____

    Laundry and dry cleaning: _____

    Vending: _____

    Audiovisual: _____

BUILDING OR SITE-ZONE NAME: Project ID:

Parking control: _____

Loading dock: _____

Solid waste handling: _____

Detention: _____

Water supply and treatment: _____

Fluid waste treatment and disposal: _____

Food service: _____

Darkroom: _____

Athletic: _____

Recreational: _____

Therapeutic: _____

Laboratory: _____

Planetarium: _____

Observatory: _____

Medical: _____

Mortuary: _____

Residential appliances: _____

Unit kitchens: _____

Manufactured casework: _____

Blinds: _____

Shades: _____

Draperies and curtains: _____

Floor mats and frames: _____

Auditorium and theater seating: _____

Stadium and area seating: _____

Pews and benches: _____

BUILDING OR SITE-ZONE NAME: _____   Project ID: _____

Air supported structures: _____

Integrated ceilings: _____

Athletic rooms: _____

Audiometric rooms: _____

Clean rooms: _____

Cold storage rooms: _____

Hyperbaric rooms: _____

Insulated rooms: _____

Saunas: _____

Steam baths: _____

Vaults: _____

Sound control devices: _____

Vibration control devices: _____

Seismic control devices: _____

Radiation protection: _____

Preengineered building: _____

Metal building system: _____

Greenhouse: _____

Grandstands and bleachers: _____

Observatory: _____

Fabric structure: _____

Swimming pool: _____

Aquariums: _____

Hot tubs: _____

Therapeutic pools: _____

Ice rink equipment: _____

Kennel enclosures, gates, and feeding devices: _____

BUILDING OR SITE-ZONE NAME: _____   Project ID: _____

Incinerators: _____

Liquid and gas storage tanks: _____

Solar energy collection system: _____

Energy monitoring and control system: _____

Environmental control system: _____

Communications system: _____

Security system: _____

Clock control system: _____

Elevator monitoring and control system: _____

Moving stair and walk monitoring and control system: _____

Alarm and detection system: _____

Door control system: _____

Nurse call system: _____

Fire suppression and supervisory system: _____

Dumbwaiters: _____

Passenger elevators

    ☐ Electric: _____

    ☐ Hydraulic: _____

Freight elevators

    ☐ Electric: _____

    ☐ Hydraulic: _____

Escalators: _____

Moving walks: _____

People lifts: _____

Wheelchair lifts: _____

Platform lifts: _____

BUILDING OR SITE-ZONE NAME: Project ID:

Sidewalk lifts: _____

Vehicle lifts: _____

Automatic transport system: _____

Hospital transport system: _____

Postal transport system: _____

Conveyors: _____

Chutes: _____

Tube system: _____

Hoists: _____

Cranes: _____

Derricks: _____

Monorail systems: _____

2

Photographing Existing Work

Photography has become a strong tool in the design process in recent years. Architects use photographs for many purposes. Among those uses are

1. To make a permanent record of conditions before remodeling, renovation, and restoration work.
2. To use during design and construction document production to convey field conditions to office personnel and consultants. Visualizing a condition is much easier when one can look at a picture.

Architects do not need elaborate cameras to make photographs for those two purposes. An instant-development camera is quite satisfactory for many record and design-use pictures. A major drawback of such cameras, however, is that they do not produce negatives. When a negative is required, a 35-mm single-lens reflex camera, with appropriate lenses, is quite satisfactory. Negatives are necessary for making multiple copies, for consultant's use, for example, or for making blow-ups, for depicting conditions that are hard to see without elaborate scaffolding. A single-lens reflex camera is also better when overall photographs are desirable, such as that for an entire building facade.

Figure 2-1. Existing conditions an architect might photograph. (Photograph by Stewart Bros., courtesy of Mid-City Financial Corp.)

Record of Photographs Taken

It is not possible to take too many photographs of existing conditions. Even for small projects, keeping track of existing conditions photographs can become a problem. The best way to store the actual photographs is in an album. The breakdown of photographs within the album depends on the project. Sometimes, sorting photographs by damage type is better. Sometimes, storing them by building location is better.

Recalling which building portion each photograph shows and recording the weather, time, date, and other conditions when the photograph was taken can be a major problem. The form in Figure 2-4 offers a simple solution.

Tips on Using the Photograph Record

Mark each photograph's location and direction immediately, as shown by the numbers and arrows in Figure 2-3. Do not trust to memory even for a short time. If you are interrupted, you may forget which photograph number you took last and what the photograph was showing. Fill out the rest of the form as soon as possible at the building site. Waiting until you return to the office may result in recording mistakenly remembered data. Save time and aggravation by filling in data unrelated to individual photographs before going to the field.

When using an instant-development camera, copy the photograph number from the form on the photograph itself.

Figure 2-2. Existing conditions an architect had better photograph. (Photograph by Stewart Bros., courtesy of Sigal Construction Corporation.)

If you take several photographs within a particular space, or of a particular condition, it is sometimes a good idea to make a separate record form just for that space or condition. If you do not, general sketches such as that shown in Figure 2-3 can become crowded with information and hard to read.

The ''ID NO.'' item in the form is for the architect's normal identifying number (job number).

The ''Film Roll No.'' space is for the number of the film roll used to make the photographs shown on the sketch. It may be a continuing number for all photographs taken during the year, all photographs taken for the particular project, or just for the rolls taken during this particular site visit.

Slabon Grade, Architect
13011 Suffolk Drive
Pester, PA 22222
(888) 555-1234

PHOTOGRAPH RECORD

Date: JUNE 23, 1990

PROJECT NAME: EISENHOWER LIBRARY

ID No.: 2437

BUILDING OR SITE-ZONE NAME:

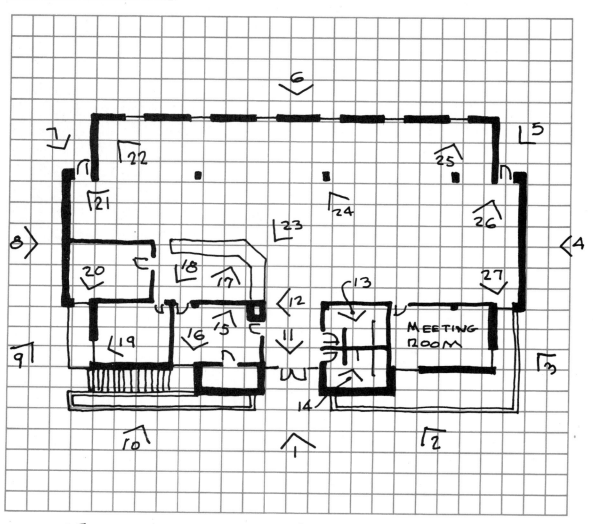

CAMERA: 35 MM   FILM ROLL NO.: 104   PAGE NO. FOR THIS ROLL: 1 OF 1

TIME: 10-11:45 AM   WEATHER: CLOUDY

REMARKS: BUILDING UNOCCUPIED

MEETING ROOM locked & INACCESSIBLE

Figure 2-3. Example Photograph Record.

(Insert
Firm Name
Here)

PHOTOGRAPH RECORD

Date:

PROJECT NAME: ID No.:

BUILDING OR SITE-ZONE NAME:

CAMERA: FILM ROLL NO.:   PAGE NO. FOR THIS ROLL:

TIME: WEATHER:

REMARKS:

Figure 2-4. Blank Form for Photograph Record.

PART TWO

Drawings and Schedules

Construction documents for projects where existing construction plays a part are different from comparable documents for projects where all the work is new. Projects where existing construction is involved are more complex, which dictates that documents for them must show more data. Their documents must represent existing work the characteristics of which will be at least partially unknown until uncovered during the construction phase. Often, they must include disclaimers, such as "Existing brick *is believed to be* Uptown Corporation's Blue Boy series." Sometimes multiple instructions, such as "If "A" is found, instruction "B" applies. If "C" is found instead of "A," then "D" applies" are necessary. They must show both new and existing construction. Often, they must show requirements for reworking existing construction and for new work on the same drawings. They must tell the contractor not only what must be but also what already is.

Part 2 of this book includes detailed discussions of the ways in which construction documents for projects with existing work in place differ from projects where all the work is new. It then suggests methods and shows the means an architect can use to show the differing requirements in construction documents. The discussion includes suggestions for drawings and schedules, and the abbreviations, notes, and symbols used on those drawings and schedules. To illustrate the discussions, Part 2 includes recommended abbreviations, notes, symbols, blank schedule forms, and examples. The examples include working drawings and filled-in schedules and accompanying notes and drawings required to make the schedules complete.

The example drawings and schedules in book Part 2 are for a hypothetical small-town public library project. The examples are intended solely to show means and methods of producing construction documents for projects where existing construction plays a part. No attempt has been made to make the drawings, notes, or schedules complete, or to ensure that they reflect current or past construction methodology. The building design does not necessarily reflect the best or latest in library science.

Our hypothetical project is the Eisenhower Library in Smalltown, U.S.A. The library was built in 1953. The low-roof areas of the building are of wall-bearing construction with composite walls of brick and concrete masonry units. The center (high-roof) portion of the building is framed with structural steel columns and beams. Flat roofs are built-up bituminous roofing over insulation on steel deck supported by steel bar joists. Sloped roofs are asphalt shingles fastened to plywood, fastened through rigid insulation to steel decking supported by steel bar joists. Interior partitions are painted concrete masonry units. Ceilings are gypsum plaster in toilets and lay-in acoustical panels elsewhere. Interior finishes are as shown in Figure 6-2A, "Left Half of Example Existing Interior Finishes Schedule," Figure 6-2B, "Right Half of Example Existing Interior Finishes Schedule," and Figure 6-3, "Example Existing Interior Finish Material and Color Code Schedule." Exterior finishes are shown in Figure 6-10, "Example Existing Exterior Finish Material and Color Schedule." The building is heated by an oil-fired hot water boiler serving unventilated convection units throughout the building. The boiler and other system components are located in a basement accessible only by exterior areaway.

The town council has appropriated funds to upgrade the existing building and build an addition to

Increase the number of library shelves

Change the library's catalog system from cards to microform

Refine the book-handling system, separating returns and deliveries from charging

Air condition the library and make it energy efficient

Add a larger meeting room accessible from the exterior during times when the library is closed

Small-scale drawings of the existing library are shown in Figures 4-4 and 4-5. Small-scale drawings showing the new work are shown in Figures 5-2 and 5-4.

3

Abbreviations, General Notes, and Symbols for Drawings and Schedules

Abbreviations

Architects use abbreviations to reduce repetitive work and to keep drawings and schedules uncluttered and easier to read.

It is possible to include a project's list of abbreviations in the project manual, but the better idea is to type the list and place it on the drawings so that a person reading the drawings will be able to find the abbreviations easily.

Abbreviations List

Figure 3-1 is a list of abbreviations for use with projects where existing construction occurs. The list is representative, but does not include all possible construction industry abbreviations for the following reasons:

A list of possible abbreviations would contain most English words, some foreign words, and many phrases. Compiling such a list would be a thankless job. Including it here would serve no useful purpose. One could argue that the list in Figure 3-1 is already too long.

It includes only abbreviations used by architects when producing architectural drawings. It omits abbreviations used primarily by the architect's civil, structural, mechanical, and electrical consultants.

It excludes acronyms for construction industry organizations such as BIA (Brick Institute of America), AIA (American Institute of Architects), and UL (Underwriter's Laboratories). *Masterspec*'s Section 01090, "Definitions and Standards" contains a comprehensive and quarterly updated list of organization acronyms in general use.

It omits rarely used abbreviations.

It excludes common abbreviations, such as lb (pound) and E (east).

It omits abbreviations for toilet accessories, assuming that the architect will use the preferred method of numbering accessories and providing a schedule which contains no abbreviations. Because the industry cannot seem to agree on the names of toilet accessories, much less their abbreviations, abbreviating the names of toilet accessories has been a continuing source of confusion in the construction industry for years.

Some abbreviations that apply only to schedules and are not often used on the drawings are shown in additional lists adjacent to the schedules.

Some abbreviations, such as ACP (acoustical plaster), in Figure 3-1 are seldom or never used today. The products those abbreviations represent may no longer be available, but an architect might find the products in existing buildings.

Tips on Using Abbreviations

The abbreviations in Figure 3-1 are from construction industry sources. Use care when creating abbreviations. Use those which are already in general use. Before using abbreviations not generally recognized in the industry, consider that there may be a not-too-obvious reason that a particular abbreviation is not generally accepted.

Always follow the adage "when in doubt, spell it out."

Use abbreviations sparingly and only when the meaning is absolutely clear.

Avoid strings of abbreviations. "PNT CONT EXIST PLAS MLD, except ASC, U.O.N." is hard to read.

Delete from the abbreviations list for each project those abbreviations not used in the set of drawings for that project.

Do not use abbreviations in specifications. It saves little ink and even less time.

LIST OF ABBREVIATIONS

AB	Anchor bolt		C	Course (masonry)
ABR	Abrasive		CAB	Cabinet
AC	Air conditioning		CALK	Caulk(ing)
ACC	Access		CEM	Cement
ACOUS	Acoustical, acoustic		CER	Ceramic
ACP	Acoustical plaster		CHAN	Channel
ADD	Additive		CI	Cast Iron
ADD'N	Addition		CJ	Control joint
ADJ	Adjustable		CG	Corner guard
AFF	Above finish floor		CL	Center line
AGGR	Aggregate		CLG	Ceiling
ALT	Alternate		CLO	Closet
ALTN	Alteration		CLR	Clear
ALUM	Aluminum		CMU	Concrete masonry unit
ANCH	Anchor		CNTR	Counter
AP	Access panel		COL	Column
APP	Approved		COM	Combination
APPLIC	Applicable		COMP	Composition
APPROX	Approximate		CONC	Concrete
ARCH	Architectural		CONN	Connection
ASB	Asbestos		CONST	Construction
ASC	Above suspended ceiling		CONT	Continue, continuous
ASPH	Asphalt		CORR	Corridor
ATC	Architectural terra cotta		CORRU	Corrugated
ATT	Attach(ment)		CPT	Carpet(ed)
AUTO	Automatic		CRC	Cold rolled channel
AV	Audiovisual		CSMT	Casement
			CT	Ceramic tile
BC	Brick course		CTC	Center to center
BD	Board		CTR	Center
BE	Baked enamel		CTSK	Countersunk
BF	Barrier free		CUST	Custodian
BITUM	Bituminous		CW	Casework
BJ	Bed joint			
BKT	Bracket		d	Penny (nail size)
BL	Blinds		DA	Double acting
BLDG	Building		DBL	Double
BLK	Block		DEM	Demolish(ed), demolition
BLK C	Block course		DEP	Depressed
BLKG	Blocking		DEPT	Department
BLKT	Blanket		DET	Detail
BM	Beam		DF	Drinking fountain
B.M.	Bench mark		DG	Double glaze(d)
B.N.	Bullnose		DH	Double hung
BTB	Back to back		DIA	Diameter
BRG	Bearing		DIAG	Diagonal
BRK	Brick		DIM	Dimension
BRK C	Brick course		DL	Dead load
BOT	Bottom		DMT	Demountable
BUR	Built up roofing		DN	Down

Figure 3-1. List of Abbreviations.

DP	Dampproofing
DR	Door
DS	Downspout
DSA	Double strength A glass
DSB	Double strength B glass
DT	Dovetail
DWG	Drawing
DWR	Drawer
EA	Each
E.F.	Exhaust fan
EJ	Expansion joint
EL	Elevation (height)
ELEC	Electric, electrical
ELEV	Elevation (illustration)
ENCL	Enclose, enclosure
ENT	Entrance
EQ	Equal
EQUIP	Equipment
EXH	Exhaust
EXIST	Existing
EXP	Exposed
EXPAN	Expansion
EXT	Exterior
EXTR	Extruded
EWC	Electric water cooler
FAB	Fabricate(d) (tion)
FD	Floor drain
FDN	Foundation
FE	Fire extinguisher
FEC	Fire extinguisher cabinet
FF	Finish floor
FHC	Fire hose cabinet
FIN	Finish(ed)
FL	Floor(ing), floor type
FLASH	Flashing
FLUOR	Fluorescent
FM	Floor mat
FOC	Face of concrete
FOF	Face of finish
FOM	Face of masonry
FOS	Face of studs
FP	Fireproofing
FS	Full size
FT	Foot, feet
FTG	Footing
FURR	Furred, furring
FUT	Future
GAGE	Gauge
GALV	Galvanized

GB	Gypsum board
GL	Glazing, glazing type
GND	Ground
GMU	Glazed masonry units
GR	Grade
GYP	Gypsum
HC	Hollow core
HDWD	Hardwood
HM	Hollow metal
HORIZ	Horizontal
HP	Horsepower
HR	Hour
HGT	Height
HVAC	Heating, ventilating, air conditioning
HW	Hardware
ID	Inside diameter, inside dimension
INCL	Include(d), including
INSUL	Insulate(d), insulation
INT	Interior, internal
IPS	Iron pipe size
JAN	Janitor
JST	Joist
JT	Joint
KAL	Kalamein
KCP	Keene's cement plaster
KIT	Kitchen
KD	Knocked down
KO	Knock out
KPL	Kick plate
L	Angle
LAB	Laboratory
LAM	Laminate(d)
LAV	Lavatory
LG	Long
LKR	Locker
LP	Low point
LT	Light
MAT	Material
MAX	Maximum
MDF	Modify, modified
ME	Match existing
MECH	Mechanical
MEMB	Membrane
MET	Metal

MC	Mineral core
MFGR	Manufacture(r), manufactured, manufacturing
MIN	Minimum
MISC	Miscellaneous
MLD	Moulding
MO	Masonry opening
MOD	Modification
MT	Metal threshold
MTD	Mounted, mounting
MTL	Metal
MUL	Mullion
MW	Millwork
NAT	Natural, natural finish type
NIC	Not in contract
NO.	Number
NOM	Nominal
NRC	Noise reduction coefficient
NTS	Not to scale
OA	Overall
OC	On center
OD	Outside diameter
OFF	Office
OH	Overhead
O.H.	Overhang
OPG	Opening
OPP	Opposite
PC	Precast concrete
PE	Porcelain enamel
PL	Plastic laminate
P.L.	Property line
PLAS	Plaster
PLAST	Plastic
PLYWD	Plywood
POL	Polished
PNL	Panel
PR	Pair
PREFAB	Prefabricate(d)
PREFIN	Prefinish(ed)
PRE-ENGR	Preengineered
PROT	Protection
PSI	Pounds per square inch
PSF	Pounds per square foot
P.T.	Pressure-treated
PT	Paint(ed), paint type
PTN	Partition
PVA	Polyvinyl acetate
PVC	Polyvinyl chloride
PVF	Polyvinyl fluoride

QT	Quarry tile
QTY	Quantity
R	Riser
RAD	Radius
RB	Resilient base, resilient base type
RD	Roof drain
REFR	Refrigerator
REINF	Reinforced
REQD	Required
RESIL	Resilient
REV	Revision
RFG	Roofing
RL	Rain leader
RM	Room
RO	Rough opening
Rx	Remove existing
SAC	Suspended acoustical ceiling, suspended acoustical ceiling type
SC	Solid core
SCH	Schedule
SECT	Section
SF	Square foot, square feet
SFT	Structural facing tile
SH	Shelf, shelf type
SHR	Shower
SHT	Sheet
SIM	Similar
SMP	Solid masonry pier
SPEC	Specification, specified
SQ	Square
SS	Stainless steel
STC	Sound transmission coefficient
STD	Standard
STL	Steel
STOR	Storage
STRUCT	Structural
SUSP	Suspended
SVF	Sheet vinyl flooring
SYM	Symmetrical
T & G	Tongue and groove
TEMP	Tempered
TER	Terrazzo
THR	Threshold
THK	Thick(ness)
TOC	Top of curb
TOIL	Toilet
TOS	Top of steel

TOSL	Top of slab		WC	Wall covering
TOW	Top of wall		W.C.	Water closet
TR	Tread		W/C	Wainscot, wainscot type
TRANS	Transformer		WD	Softwood
TYP	Typical		WH	Weep hole
			WI	Wrought iron
UNFIN	Unfinished		W/O	Without
U.O.N.	Unless otherwise noted		WP	Waterproof(ing)
			WR	Water resistant
VAT	Vinyl asbestos tile		WSCT	Wainscot
VB	Vinyl base		WT	Weight
VCT	Vinyl composition tile		WWF	Welded wire fabric
VERT	Vertical			
VEST	Vestibule		X	Existing, when used as a prefix (XCONC)
VWC	Vinyl wall covering			
W/	With		Z	Zee (bar)

General Notes

In spite of CSI's recommendations in its *Manual of Practice* to use notes sparingly, if at all, on drawings, architects use general notes extensively on many kinds of projects with good results. Using general notes on projects where existing construction occurs is different only in the content of the notes.

If, as CSI's recommends, duplication of data on drawings and in specifications is avoided, putting notes on the drawings is often the best way to describe some requirements common to projects where existing buildings play a part. CSI's *Manual of Practice* instructs architects, in effect, to not put comprehensive notes on the drawings. But nowhere in CSI's recommendations, or in *Masterformat,* is there a hint about where to locate many of the kinds of requirements this book discusses.

List of General Notes

The notes in Figure 3-2 give a general idea of the types of notes an architect might use to convey general requirements to a contractor. It is not a complete list of every general note an architect will need to produce any project with existing construction involvement. Even if it were possible to produce such a list, this book would not be long enough to print it.

Tips on Using General Notes

Consider using a general note when a note must be repeated more than three times on a set of drawings.

Place the general notes on the cover sheet or a sheet immediately following the cover.

On smaller projects, include all notes in one list and put it in one place in the drawings, preferably on, or near, the cover or title sheet.

On larger projects, put general notes (applicable to the entire set) on, or near, the cover or title sheet. When a note applies to only one, or only a few, drawings (floor plans, for example) and not the entire project, consider putting that note on the affected drawing, while still keeping notes which apply to the entire project on, or near, the cover or title sheet.

The list in Figure 3-2 does not include notes needed for projects where all the work is new, even when those same notes are also needed for projects where existing construction occurs. An example is: "Where different ceiling heights occur in the same room, the vertical surface connecting them shall be gypsum board." The assumption here is that architects already know that those notes are necessary and will add them by rote. Such notes vary considerably with individual preference and project type. A complete list of general notes for an actual project must, of course, include the same kinds of notes an architect would ordinarily use on new projects.

Requirements vary from project to project and preferences vary from office to office. The list does not include options. Note 9, for example, says, "Existing brick coursing is based on five courses equals 16". New brick coursing shall match existing." In a real project, *six* courses may be equal to 16 inches; new brick may not be the same size as the existing brick; there might not even be new brick. Each architect must reword the listed notes as necessary to reflect the particular project and that architect's preferences.

GENERAL NOTES

1. Before beginning Work at the site, where possible, and throughout the course of the Work, inspect and verify the location and condition of every item affected by the Work under this Contract and report discrepancies to Architect before doing Work related to that being inspected.

2. Before beginning Work at the site, inspect the existing building and determine the extent of existing finishes, specialties, casework, equipment, and other items which must be removed and reinstalled in order to perform the Work under this Contract.

3. The architectural drawings show principal areas where Work must be accomplished under this Contract. Incidental Work may also be necessary in areas not shown on the architectural drawings due to changes affecting existing mechanical, electrical, plumbing, or other systems. Such incidental Work is also a part of this Contract. Inspect those areas, and ascertain Work needed, and do that Work in accord with the Contract requirements, at no additional cost.

4. Trade, product, or manufacturer's names or catalog numbers shown on the drawings for new products are to establish quality required. In each case add, by inference, after trade, product, or manufacturer's name, the phrase ''or approved equal.''

5. Trade, product, or manufacturer's names or catalog numbers, and indications of product types, such as ''glass fiber insulation,'' shown on the drawings for

Figure 3-2. General Notes.

existing products are believed to be accurate. If they are discovered to be inaccurate, notify Architect immediately and do not proceed without instructions.

6. Determine location of partitions not dimensioned by their relation to column face or center, window jamb or mullion, or other similar fixed item.

7. Dimensions to existing surfaces are to finished face. Dimensions to new masonry are to rough face of units. Masonry dimensions are nominal. Dimensions to new channel stud partitions are to finished face in corridors and to face of studs in other locations. Channel stud partition dimensions are nominal.

8. Existing masonry block coursing is based on two courses equals 16″. New block coursing shall match existing.

9. Existing brick coursing is based on five courses equals 16″. New brick coursing shall match existing.

10. Undimensioned new unit masonry partitions shall be no less than 6″ thick (nominal).

11. Do not drill or cut existing floor joists, beams, columns, or other structural elements, unless specifically indicated. Drill slabs where approved. Core drill circular openings through slabs. Line drill for rectangular openings. Make openings of proper size for conduits, ducts, pipes, and other items passing through openings.

12. Prepare, submit, and receive approval of sleeve and opening drawings before locating sleeves and openings in new construction and before drilling existing structure. Show each opening and sleeve in the entire project.

13. Protect existing work to remain from damage.

14. Repair, patch, and finish, or refinish as applicable, to match adjacent existing finishes, those existing surfaces damaged or newly exposed during performance of the Work under this Contract.

17. Where permanent removal of existing millwork, casework, cabinetwork, accessories, equipment or furnishings is required, and previously concealed surfaces are to remain exposed, patch previously concealed surfaces to match adjacent exposed surfaces. Where such surfaces are scheduled to receive new finishes, prepare the surfaces to receive the new finishes.

18. Where cutting of existing surfaces or removal of existing finishes is required to perform the Work under this Contract, and a new finish is not indicated, fill resulting openings and patch the surface after doing the work, and finish to match adjacent existing surfaces.

19. Except in spaces where no Work under this Contract is required, enclose existing and new conduits, ducts,

pipes, and similar items in furring where such items pass through finished spaces whether or not furring is indicated.

20. Where conduits, ducts, pipes, and similar items are shown to be installed in existing walls or partitions, neatly chase the walls or partitions, install the items, and patch the walls or partitions to make the installation not discernible in the finished Work.

21. Seal tight and protect with fire safing existing and new sleeves and openings through floors.

22. Where a new ceiling is not scheduled, install new conduits and pipes in every case, and new ducts where possible, above the existing ceiling. Remove existing ceiling as necessary. After installation of concealed work, reinstall removed ceiling and patch and refinish to match adjacent unremoved ceilings.

23. Furr to conceal horizontal ducts passing through existing or new spaces where it is not possible to install the ducts above the ceiling. Use gypsum board for such furring.

24. Provide lintels over every new opening in both new and existing walls and partitions.

25. Refer to demolition drawings, Existing Interior Finish Schedule, Existing Interior Finish Material and Color Code Schedule, and Existing Exterior Finish Material and Color Schedule for existing finishes.

26. Where match existing (ME) is indicated, new construction or finishes, as appropriate to the note, shall match the existing in every particular.

27. Use saw cuts to remove masonry where remaining masonry is to be exposed.

28. Junctures between existing masonry and patches or extensions shall be made to clean-cut lines or neatly toothed in.

29. New partitions are type 1A unless otherwise indicated.

30. Work shown is new unless specifically noted or otherwise indicated as existing.

31. Where ''X'' precedes a reference to a material or product (XConcrete or XConc), the ''X'' means that the indicated material or product is existing.

32. Salvage removed BRK1; clean and reuse approved units for filling in openings in BRK1 surfaces and building new BRK1 walls. Do not use damaged brick. Provide new matching brick where approved brick is not available in sufficient quantities to carry out the new Work.

33. Salvage removed CMU; clean and reuse approved units for filling in openings in CMU and for building new CMU walls and partitions. Do not use damaged CMU. Provide new CMU where approved salvaged CMU is not available in sufficient quantity to carry out the new Work.

Symbols

Using symbols saves time and by reducing clutter on drawings, makes them easier to read. Architects are often too cryptic when adding notes to their drawings, leaving out important details for the sake of time or expediency. They also tend to omit notes they should write out when the same note occurs sixteen other times on the same drawing sheet. Using symbols alleviates such problems.

Architects accustomed to using symbols on drawings for projects where all the work is new will find them even more useful when existing construction occurs.

List of Symbols

Figure 3-3 includes symbols for use on demolition drawings, and symbols for use on drawings prepared to illustrate requirements for remodeling, renovation, restoration, and new work. Figure 3-3 excludes symbols mostly used by the architect's civil, structural, mechanical, and electrical consultants, and does not include materials indication symbols or line weight recommendations, both of which are well covered in many other sources.

Tips on Using Symbols

Use a symbol wherever a note would unduly clutter the drawings, where it is difficult to show enough detail because of drawing scale to fully describe requirements, and where notes must be repeated many times to describe the requirements fully.

Use a symbol by preference over a written explanation whenever the symbol is adequate for the purpose.

Never use the same symbol to indicate different information or different symbols to indicate the same information in a single set of documents. An architect who uses the symbols in Figure 3-3 will not have that happen. But it might be convenient sometime to use a symbol not included in Figure 3-3. Invented symbols should be readily discernible and unique.

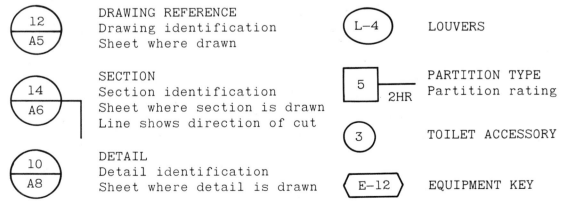

LIST OF SYMBOLS

DRAWING REFERENCE
Drawing identification
Sheet where drawn

LOUVERS

SECTION
Section identification
Sheet where section is drawn
Line shows direction of cut

PARTITION TYPE
Partition rating

TOILET ACCESSORY

DETAIL
Detail identification
Sheet where detail is drawn

EQUIPMENT KEY

Figure 3-3. List of Symbols.

⬭ 6 / A14 ▷	ELEVATION (drawing) Elevation identification Sheet where elevation is drawn
W–6	WINDOWS
S–12	STOREFRONT
CW–5	CURTAIN WALL
◐–·–	MATCH LINE (black portion is side considered)
⊕	ELEVATION (height)
EL+55.1′	SPOT ELEVATION (in plan)
OFFICE / 101	SPACE IDENTIFICATION Space name Space designation (1 = Floor no.; 01 = space no.)
OFFICE / 101 / NF–1	SPACE IDENTIFICATION Space name Space designation (1 = Floor no.; 01 = space no.) Finish designation
EF–1	EXISTING FINISH (Type 1)
NF–1	NEW FINISH IN EXISTING SPACE (Type 1)
F–1	NEW FINISH IN NEW SPACE (Type 1)

◇ 7	DEMOLITION OR REPAIR NOTE
⬡ 5	NUMBERED REMARK (in schedules)
△ 2	REVISION
○ 6 –·–	COLUMN NUMBER
▬▬▬	EXISTING MATERIALS TO REMAIN (plan or section)
– – – –	REMOVE EXISTING WALL OR PARTITION
[– – –]	REMOVE EXISTING ITEM
	EXISTING DOOR TO REMAIN
	REMOVE EXISTING DOOR
	REMOVE EXISTING DOOR AND JAMB
	NEW DOOR IN EXISTING WALL OR PARTITION

4

Demolition Drawings

Demolition requirements vary with project size, project type, percentage of existing work to be demolished, and extent of the new work. There are several basic methods an architect can use to convey those requirements to a contractor. The method selected depends on the extent of the requirements that must be conveyed.

Some demolition requirements are best conveyed using annotated photographs of the existing construction. We will discuss that process in detail in this chapter in paragraphs entitled "Photographs as Demolition Drawings."

Most demolition requirements, however, are best conveyed by drawings, notes, and specifications paragraphs.

Methods of Producing Demolition Drawings

An architect can either include demolition requirements on the same drawings with new-work requirements or produce separate documents that show only demolition. To decide which is best for a particular project, the architect must first analyze the project.

Separate documents are usually best where demolition is large in scope when compared with project size. Separate documents are also usually best when demolition is complex in nature.

Separate demolition drawings are usually not necessary when demolition is limited in scope. Separate demolition drawings might be unnecessary, for example, where demolition consists primarily of removing existing partitions. It might be appropriate to show demolition and new work on the same drawings on small projects, but the decision should not be based on project size alone. The library example in this book is a small project where the demolition–new-work combination is complex and begs for separate documents, which we have provided. A single document here would become unduly cluttered, even if we used symbols extensively.

Combined Demolition and New-Work Drawings

The only satisfactory method for producing combined demolition and new-work drawings is to draw them from scratch. Tracing original drawings, when they are available, is useful if the original drawings are at proper and accurate scale and their content reflects actual conditions. It is easy to correct inaccuracies and omit unwanted data while tracing. Tracing prints is usually less satisfactory, however. Even when the original drawings are to proper scale, the printing process distorts the drawings.

Using reproducible copies of existing drawings as new working drawings is sometimes possible but seldom satisfactory because the original drawings almost never reflect actual field conditions in every respect. In addition, transparencies will include much superfluous data. The time necessary to verify data and delete inaccurate and unnecessary information is better spent elsewhere. Chapter 5 covers this subject in greater detail.

Separate Demolition Drawings

There are two basic methods for producing separate demolition drawings. The first method is to make new drawings. Obviously, making new drawings is necessary when there are no existing drawings. Even when drawings do exist, making new drawings may be desirable where demolition occurs in only a small portion of a large existing building. New drawings are also necessary where existing drawings are so untrustworthy as to require extensive modifications to accurately reflect field conditions. Producing new drawings to show demolition requirements permits including only cogent information and easy use of desirable schedule types regardless of the types used on the original drawings. There are two ways to make new drawings.

Draw them from scratch. This is the only possible method when working from measured drawings. It is also the method to use when the original drawings prove to be grossly inaccurate or out of scale. An advantage of developing demolition drawings from scratch is that they can become the basis for new-work drawings. This is particularly advantageous if the architect is using overlay drafting or CADD systems. The demolition drawing becomes the first background overlay for the entire set and as many subsequent overlays as is necessary to produce the demolition drawing.

Trace existing drawings. This method is useful for overlay drafting or conventional drafting methods when the project is small, or when the new project involves only a small portion of a large existing structure. Tracing part of an existing drawing may be worthwhile where a portion of the existing drawing is grossly inaccurate but other portions are accurate.

The second basic method of producing separate demolition drawings is to alter reproducible copies of existing drawings. If they are sufficiently accurate to permit doing so, altering reproducibles may be best when dealing with large projects where the new work involves major portions of the existing building. Using reproducibles may also make sense where the amount of work involved in producing new drawings is larger than that involved in working with the reproducibles. Where changes are extensive, eradicating and restoring dashed lines may be more work than drafting the drawings anew. Using reproducibles has the advantage of making available all the data shown on the existing drawings without the necessity to hand-copy it. It will be necessary, however, to remove much of the data to avoid confusion. For example, as we will discuss in Chapter 6, finish, door, and other schedule marks used on the existing drawings are not easily usable on demolition drawings.

Information Required on Demolition Drawings

Whether an architect produces separate demolition drawings or includes demolition requirements on the new-work drawings, the information required is the same. Strictly speaking, demolition drawings need only show the extent of the demolition, but it is a shame to stop there, because demolition drawings are a natural way to designate existing conditions. Architects often use demolition drawings to convey demolition requirements but do not include in them the data necessary for a contractor to determine what is actually in place in the existing structure.

One way to inform a contractor about existing conditions is to include a copy of the original construction documents in the bid set. Even though few architects would consider such an approach, what they do is often just as inappropriate. They withhold data from the construction documents. They do so for several reasons. One is that they do not trust contractors. Many architects expect to have a confrontational relationship with contractors and act accordingly. They think that if they include information in the construction documents that turns out to be inaccurate, the contractor will request an extra and, if the extra is denied, will try to collect from the architect, claiming that the architect provided misleading information.

Even though a confrontational relationship between a project's architect and its building contractor is sometimes unavoidable, it is not reasonable for architects to approach every project under the assumption that a confrontational relationship will exist on that project. An architect may require that a contractor confirm data in the field before proceeding and even state that the data shown is questionable and may be used only at the contractor's risk. Such disclaimers will not absolve the architect of responsibility for the architect's own negligence. Neither will they ensure that the contractor will not file claims for extra payment due to unforeseen conditions. In fact, an architect should not try to prevent a contractor from submitting legitimate claims. It is often not possible to determine concealed conditions before the demolition work begins. In the face of the many uncertainties that will always exist with any project where existing conditions play a part, there is no excuse for deliberately withholding known information from the contractor.

Of course, architects who knowingly withhold necessary information from contractors do not always do so solely to protect themselves from lawsuit and their clients from claims. Some architects withhold data because they feel that the contractor does not need to know everything about existing conditions and that much of that existing data is superfluous and useless to the contractor and would simply confuse the issue. In the end, decisions about what to show and what to omit are subjective and depend almost solely on the architect's judgment based on experience.

Even when all the work is new, omission of needed data can have serious consequences. Where existing construction plays a part, the consequences can be much more severe.

Of course, many architects instinctively do what all architects should do. They tell the contractor everything they know about a project that might affect costs or construction methods.

In Chapters 1 and 2, we discussed some means and methods an architect can use to gather the information necessary to design and produce construction documents for a project where some of the work involves existing construction. Once the architect has done the research, the next problem is to find ways to convey the gathered information to the contractor.

The process begins with demolition drawings. Demolition drawings should show everything the architect knows about the existing structure which will be useful to the contractor in carrying out the work under the new contract. They should show existing materials, finishes, dimensions, and relationship of elements. Demolition drawings should be as accurate as any other contract document. Too often, demolition requirements are hazy and drawings are out of scale and unclear about the extent of removals. Demolition drawings are too often neglected by architects who are too busy to do them properly, or are more interested in getting on to the exciting part, the new work.

Photographs as Demolition Drawings

Architects can sometimes use photographs as demolition drawings. A photograph of a small building to be demolished, for example, might make drawings unnecessary, reduce the need to take measurements, and still effectively convey the extent of the work required to the demolition contractor.

Photographs can also effectively convey demolition requirements for a project where the extent of an element requiring demolition is difficult to define in writing, or which would require extraordinary effort to measure and draw to scale. Perhaps the building's articulation is complex and there are no existing drawings. Perhaps height or other features make the building hard to measure. A photograph might eliminate the need to measure the building and even to make drawings.

The magic ingredient is a process known as "rectified photography," in which an existing building's elevations are produced to scale. Rectified photography is not complicated, but it does require expertise and equipment not owned by most architects. Rectified photography may be expensive, depending on the problems associated with taking the photographs.

The rectified photography process starts when a photographer photographs an existing building using a large format camera with special lenses designed to produce a flat image with parallel surfaces in the same plane. The shot is made from as near the center of the building elevation as the photographer can position the camera. Tall buildings are photographed from other buildings, scaffolds, or even cranes. Long and very tall elevations are photographed in several shots which the photographer then combines into a single composite photograph. Having made the photograph, the photographer then produces a print to scale using field measurements of building elements as a guide and delivers the print to the architect.

The architect then fastens the to-scale photograph in the desired location on a bordered drawing sheet and sends it to a properly equipped print shop.

The print shop then makes a mylar transparency of the entire sheet using a halftone screen over the photograph to make an image that standard print machines can clearly reproduce. Unfortunately, not all print shops can make the necessary transparencies. An architect who does not have local access to a well-equipped print shop might have to ship the work to an out-of-town shop.

The process results in a photograph of the building printed to scale on a transparency which the architect can alter or add notes to. Figure 4-1 is a rectified photograph of two existing buildings made by photographer Ronald N. Anderson of Rockville, Maryland, who specializes in architectural photography.

The photograph in Figure 4-1, reduced to fit onto a book page, is not at ⅛-inch scale as noted on the drawing's title. The photograph would ordinarily appear at the full ⅛-inch scale on a drawing sheet with borders and title block. The borders and title block do not show in Figure 4-1 in the interest of clarity.

The buildings in Figure 4-1 are as nearly in flat elevation as was possible given the available camera locations. The scale is reasonably consistent throughout. Actually, no photograph can ever produce a true flat elevation. As would be true for most rectified photographs used as elevations, the photograph in Figure 4-1 is acceptably close to a flat image. Using a rectified photograph, in this instance, saved much drafting time.

Figure 4-2 is a blown up portion of Figure 4-1 with demolition notes added. The blowup is at approximately ⅛-inch scale. In actual practice, a separate blowup would probably not be used. Instead, the entire photograph in Figure 4-1 would be produced at ⅛-inch scale and used as a demolition drawing.

Refer to Figure 4-3 for the demolition notes referred to by numbered symbols in Figure 4-2.

Figure 4-2 is a simple use of rectified photography as a demolition drawing. It might not make economic sense to make a rectified photograph solely to tell a contractor to demolish the building in the example. We had the rectified photograph made to use as a new-work drawing (see Figure 5-1) and decided to also use it as a demolition drawing. In practice, the only limits to using rectified photographs are those imposed by the architect's imagination. The more complex the problem, the more useful is the rectified photography technique.

Whether rectified photography costs or saves money depends to a large extent on the complexity and accessibility of the existing building to be photographed. Before deciding to use rectified photography, an architect should determine the availability of a photographer and a print shop capable of producing the photograph in usable form. Then the architect should compare the cost of the photograph against the cost and inconvenience of having to measure and draw the elevations. Costs are affected by the accessibility of a platform for the camera at the proper elevation.

On the other hand, measuring buildings can be expensive, and sometimes almost impossible. On balance, rectified photographs are often cheaper than is measuring and drawing the same elevations, when all costs are taken into account.

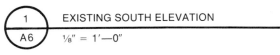

1 / A6   EXISTING SOUTH ELEVATION
⅛″ = 1′—0″

Figure 4-1. Rectified photograph. (Photograph © Ronald N. Anderson, Rockville, Maryland.)

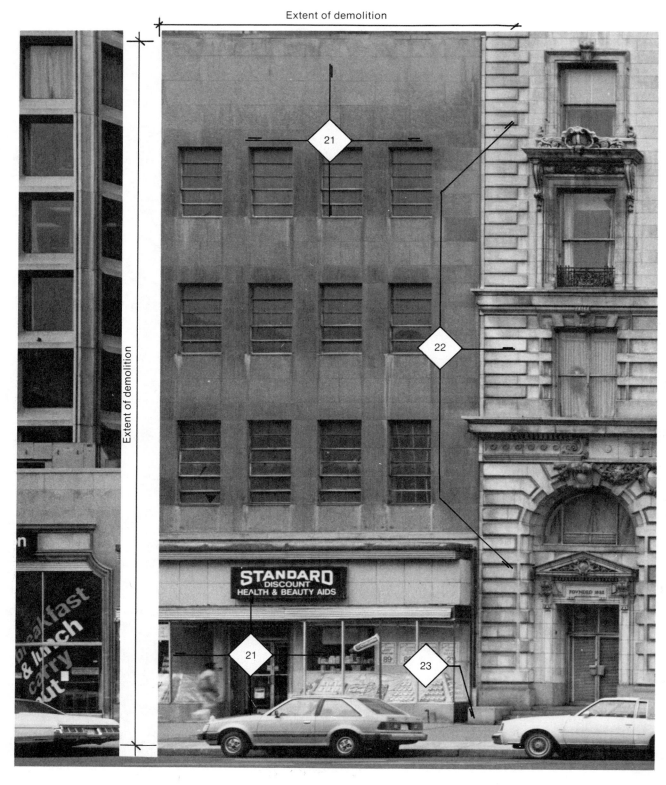

Figure 4-2. Rectified photograph used as a demolition drawing. (Photograph © Ronald N. Anderson, Rockville, Maryland.)

Demolition and Repair Notes

Architects tend to be too cryptic when adding notes to drawings. They also tend to leave out notes they should include when that note already occurs sixteen times on the same drawing sheet. Using a list of notes keyed to the drawings by numbers in a standard symbol alleviates that problem.

The notes in Figure 4-3, which follows these explanations, give a general idea of demolition and repair note types that an architect might use to convey requirements to the contractor. Figure 4-3 is not a complete list of every demolition note an architect might need to produce demolition documents. Such a list would be so long as to be unusable.

Figure 4-3 excludes notes that the architect's civil, structural, mechanical, and electrical consultants might use on their drawings.

Figure 4-9 contains demolition and repair notes applicable to the example library drawings.

Tips on Using Demolition and Repair Notes

Consider using a demolition or repair note when a note must be repeated more than three times on a set of drawings.

Use a symbol and note wherever writing a note on the drawing itself would unduly clutter the drawing, where it is difficult to show enough detail because of drawing scale to fully describe the requirements, and where notes must be repeated many times to fully describe the requirements.

Place demolition and repair notes on the demolition drawings. If there are several demolition drawings, place the notes on the first demolition drawing sheet and reference the other sheets to that one. Alternatively, place the demolition and repair notes on each sheet of the demolition drawings. Place a cross-reference note on new-work drawings on which repair notes occur, referring to the demolition and repair notes list. Alternatively, place a copy of the demolition and repair notes on one or more new-work drawings.

Do not use more than one list of demolition and repair notes or the same note number for two different notes in the same set of documents. If you want the demolition and repair notes to appear on every demolition sheet, repeat the entire list.

Combine several notes when appropriate. Notes 8 and 11 together might read, "Remove existing window. Enlarge opening to receive new door." Notes 8 and 15 might read, "Remove existing door. Existing frame to remain." When combining several notes, either place both numbers on the drawing or combine the notes into a third note and give it a different number.

Use generalized notes, such as Note 5, "Remove and discard," when it is clear which item the contractor must remove. Otherwise modify such notes to make them more specific. Note 5, for example, might become "Remove and discard existing cabinet."

Do not use passive constructs such as "to be removed" or "to be modified." Such terms lead to confusion about who is responsible. If the contractor must carry out the action described, it is enough to say just "remove" or "modify." Of course, the project manual should state that the contractor is to add "the contractor shall" by inference and that any time the documents do not state specifically who is to carry out an instruction, the contractor is responsible. If someone other than the contractor is to carry out an instruction, say who is responsible. "The owner will remove kitchen equipment," for example.

DEMOLITION AND REPAIR NOTES

1. Existing (fill in name of item).
2. Carefully remove without damage and deliver to Owner at designated location.
3. Disconnect, remove, store, and reinstall in new location indicated when construction progress permits.
4. Clean without damage.
5. Remove and discard.
6. Demolish in accord with Contract document requirements.
7. To remain property of Owner.
8. Remove existing (fill in name of item to be removed).
9. Owner will remove existing (fill in name of item) before Contractor begins work at the site.
10. Connect to existing (fill in name of utility, such as 6" PVC drain pipe).
11. Enlarge (modify) opening to receive new (fill in item, such as door or window).
12. No work is required in this space.
13. Demolish entire existing (fill in name of structure, such as Storage Shed) structure, including foundations, walls, interior construction, and roof, and remove debris from Owner's property.
14. Provide new opening in existing surface to receive new (fill in item to be received, such as louver).
15. Existing (fill in item name) to remain.
16. Extend removal to (fill in distance) below existing grade.
17. Fill in opening with brick or CMU to match existing.
18. Provide new (fill in item, such as stone sill) to match existing.
19. Blank off shaded portion of existing louver using concealed insulated metal panel.
20. Remove existing (fill in name of item, such as food service equipment) and store on Owner's property in location as directed by Owner for future use by Owner.
21. Demolish entire structure by suitable means in accordance with the Contract documents. Refer to specifications for list of salvage items.
22. Do not damage existing stone.
23. Remove existing carved cornerstone and time capsule. Deliver to Owner. Do not open.
24. Repair cracked water table.
25. Clean all stone surfaces.
26. Remove damaged flashing. Snap-lock new lead-coated copper flashing into existing receiver and seal with Sealant Type 1.
27. Remove, clean, and reset loose pediment stone.

Figure 4-3. Demolition and Repair Notes.

Examples

Figures 4-4 through 4-9 assume use of the abbreviations, symbols, notes, schedules, and recommendations in this book.

Figure 4-4 is a small-scale drawing showing the existing floor plan of the library building which is the subject of all the drawing and schedule examples that follow. The building is described at the beginning of book Part 2.

Figure 4-5 consists of small-scale elevations and a small-scale cross-section of the same existing library.

Figure 4-6 is a portion of the original working drawing floor plan for the library. Some details and notes one might expect to find on a set of working drawings have been omitted for the sake of clarity. For example, only detail keys which will appear as other illustrations are shown, and the original door, window, and room numbers do not show. When viewed together with Figure 4-7, Figure 4-6 illustrates some types of data that might appear on an existing building's original working drawing but be omitted from a demolition drawing. An actual set of contract documents for a remodeling, renovation, or restoration project would not usually include a drawing such as Figure 4-6.

Figures 4-7 to 4-9 illustrate a method for preparing demolition drawings and related notes and show the types of information demolition drawings and related notes might contain.

Figure 4-7 is a portion of the demolition floor plan for the existing example library.

Figure 4-8 is a demolition elevation for a portion of the existing example library.

Figure 4-9 is a list of demolition and repair notes applicable to the demolition drawings in Figures 4-7 and 4-8. These notes do not include requirements for doors and frames or for windows. Demolition requirements for those are included in Chapter 6 where their respective schedules occur. Additional demolition requirements related to finishes are also addressed in Chapter 6 where the finish schedules occur.

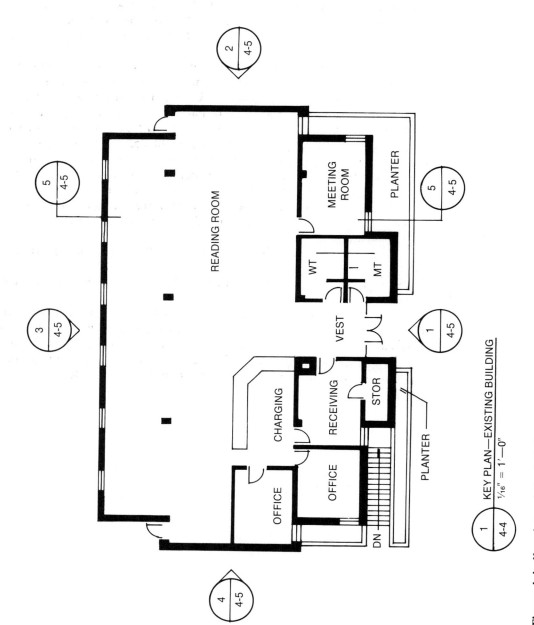

Figure 4-4. Key plan: existing building.

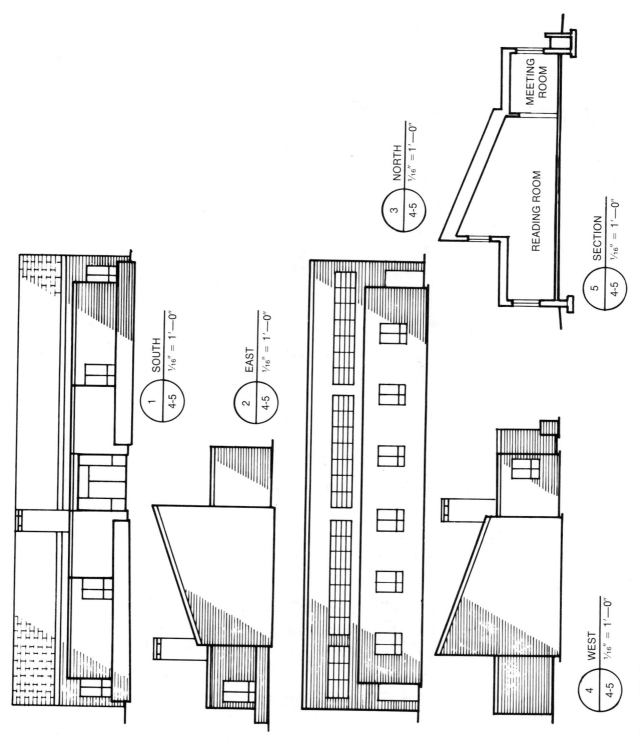

Figure 4-5. Elevations: existing building.

SOUTH
1/16" = 1'—0"

1
4-5

EAST
1/16" = 1'—0"

2
4-5

NORTH
1/16" = 1'—0"

3
4-5

WEST
1/16" = 1'—0"

4
4-5

SECTION
1/16" = 1'—0"

5
4-5

MEETING ROOM

READING ROOM

69

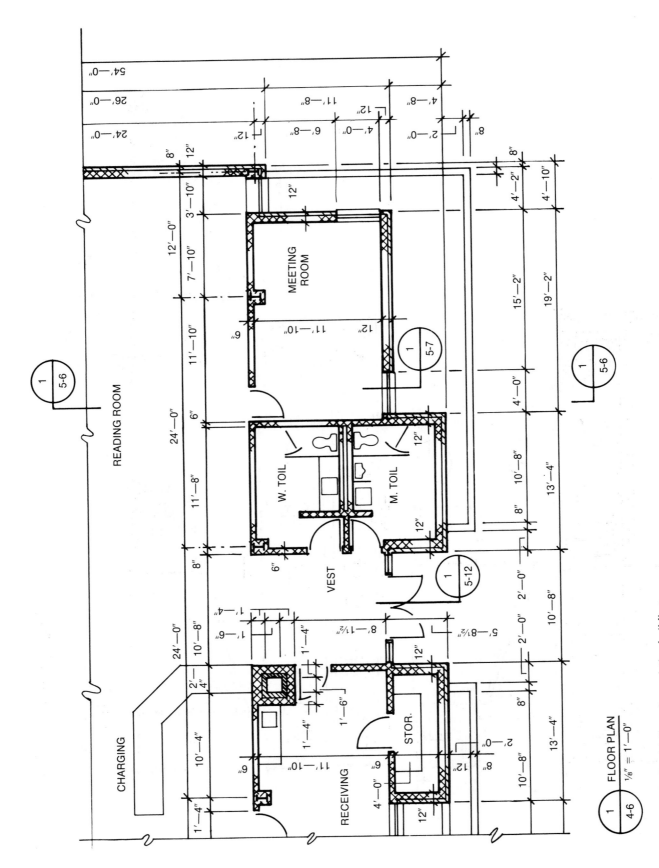

Figure 4-6. Partial floor plan: existing building.

70

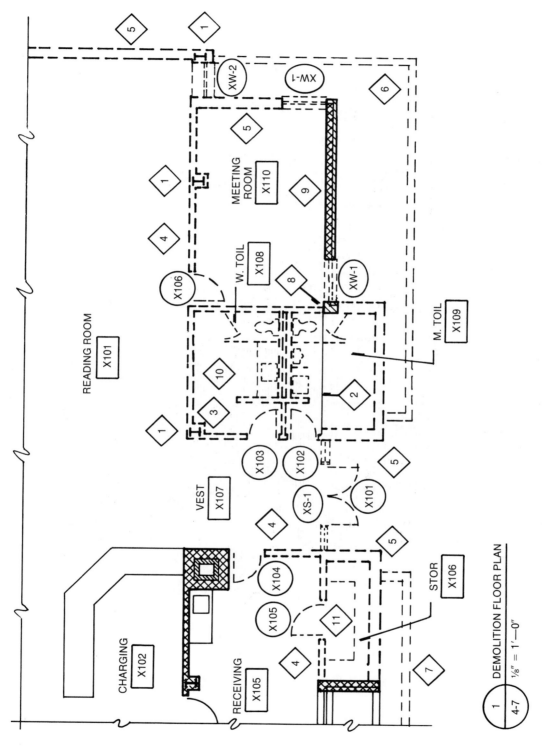

Figure 4-7. Demolition drawing: part floor plan.

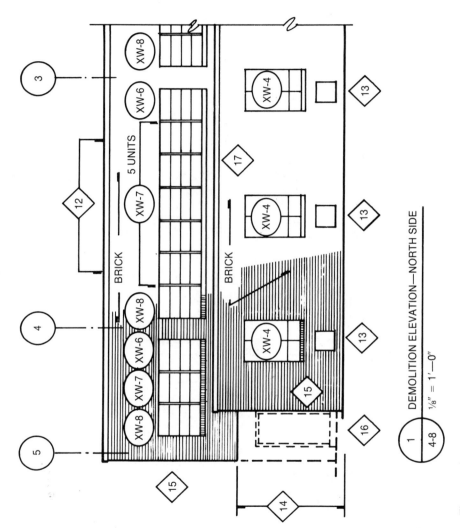

Figure 4-8. Demolition drawing: part elevation.

DEMOLITION AND REPAIR NOTES

1. Existing steel column to remain. Remove and discard covering masonry and anchors.
2. Remove existing 4″ thick slab-on-grade and 4″ thick porous stone fill to limit shown.
3. Remove and discard existing ceramic floor tile, marble thresholds, and setting beds in Men's and Women's Toilets.
4. Remove existing 6″ thick CMU partition to slab line where partition is supported by slab. Remove to 8″ below top of slab where partition penetrates slab.
5. Remove existing 12″ thick composite (4″ brick and 6″ CMU) cavity wall to 8″ below top of floor slab. Refer to structural drawings for temporary roof support requirements.
6. Remove 8″ thick brick planter walls to 8″ below top of future floor slab.
7. Remove 8″ thick brick planter walls and related footings.
8. Existing 12″ by 16″ solid masonry pier to remain.
9. Existing 12″ thick composite (4″ brick and 6″ CMU) cavity bearing wall to remain.
10. Remove, from both Men's and Women's Toilet rooms, and discard existing plumbing fixtures, accessories, counter top, toilet partitions, and urinal screen.
11. Remove existing wood shelving and standards. Protect, and store in Library basement where directed, for Owner's use.
12. Remove and discard damaged existing gravel stop and fascia section (approximately 12 feet long) and provide new matching gravel stop and fascia of same material and gage as existing. Existing gravel stop and fascia are believed to be 20-oz. lead-coated copper. Lap new section 6″ over existing at each end and seal using two beads of Sealant Type 1 at each lap. Set roof flange in a bed of plastic roofing cement and nail at 3″ o.c. through roofing to existing wood nailer. Have flange stripped in by roofer.
13. Remove existing face brick and CMU backup and prepare opening for new fresh air intake. See Figures 5-5 and 5-12 for additional requirements.
14. Remove existing face brick and CMU composite cavity wall to make way for new construction. Remove wall from 8″ below top of future floor slab to underside of existing ledger angle.
15. Remove sufficient brick and CMU to permit toothing new brick and CMU into existing.
16. Remove existing door and frame for reinstallation in another location. See Door and Frame Schedule for requirements.
17. Remove existing gravel stop and fascia to permit installing new standing seam metal mansard.

Figure 4-9. Demolition and Repair Notes.

18. Tooth new brick and CMU into existing.
19. Fill 1-1/2" deep depression left when existing ceramic floor tile and setting beds were removed. Use specified concrete topping and mesh. Leave top flush with top of adjacent slabs. Finish as specified to receive carpet.
20. Fill existing window opening with CMU. Tooth new CMU into existing at jambs.
21. Tooth new masonry into existing.
22. Remove existing gravel stop and fascia, nailers, 3" by 3" by 1/4" angle, tapered cant, and roof edge flashing. Remove existing stone ballast and BUR sufficiently to strip in new BUR.
23. Remove existing brick and cavity wall insulation sufficiently to place new bond beam and CMU course.
24. Remove existing window (see Window Schedule), slate stool, brick rolock sill, and sill flashing. Clean remaining masonry before laying new brick or CMU.
25. Cut existing metal flashing at top of existing CMU bond beam.
26. Remove and discard existing gravel stop and fascia, top nailer, and tapered cant. Remove existing stone ballast and BUR sufficiently to strip in new BUR and bituminous flashing.
27. Remove existing CMU, brick, and cavity wall insulation. Provide new louver, lintels, brick rolock sill, and flashing as shown. Remove additional brick and CMU as necessary to support opening and install new louver. Re-lay removed brick and CMU when construction progress permits.

5

New-Work Drawings

New-work drawings for projects where existing construction plays a part are more complex than are drawings for projects where all the work is new. Not only must they convey all the requirements needed for any new-work project, they must show existing conditions as well.

An architect can produce working drawings for projects where existing construction occurs using existing drawings or photographs, or produce new drawings from scratch.

Existing Drawings

Using existing drawings as new working drawings seems a good idea at first glance. The idea is especially attractive for small projects and projects where little change takes place within the walls of the existing building. Second thought, however, exposes the idea as a bad one.

There is little assurance that the existing working drawings for any project will be accurate. If there is so little work as to make using them worthwhile, then there is too little work to warrant all the field checking necessary to ensure the accuracy of all the superfluous data a set of working drawings for the existing building will contain.

Photographs as Working Drawings

In Chapter 4, where we discussed using photographs as demolition drawings, we said that rectified photographs can save an architect time and effort when making demolition drawings. The advantages are much greater when using photographs as construction drawings.

An architect should examine every remodeling, renovation, and restoration project to determine whether using rectified photography would make sense. Some projects and some problems lend themselves more to the use of photographs than do others. Projects where existing conditions are hard to define in writing, where existing documents are not available, and where measurement and production of measured drawings would be extensive lend themselves to use of photography.

Cost is certainly important when deciding whether to use rectified drawings, but it is not the only consideration. Often, rectified photographs show existing conditions more clearly than they can be shown by any other means.

Architects can apply notes, window marks, and even dimensions where appropriate to rectified photographs. In fact, any data an architect would place on a drawn elevation are appropriate on a rectified photograph.

Figure 5-1 is part of the rectified photograph in Figure 4-1 reproduced at about ⅛-inch scale. Sometimes, architects blow up part of a rectified photograph to show damage that does not show clearly in the overall photograph. Here we are using the blowup only because of the size limitation of this book. As was true for demolition drawings, the actual working drawing would be the full photograph shown in Figure 4-1 reproduced at ⅛-inch scale. Just as was true in our example of a demolition drawing (Figure 4-2) the notes on the blowup in Figure 5-1 illustrate a method of showing work to be done. Refer to Figure 4-3 for the demolition notes referred to by numbered symbols in Figure 5-1.

New Drawings

The best way to produce new work drawings is to draw them from scratch. Sometimes, tracing all, or part, of an existing drawing will save time if the original drawing is accurate. As we mentioned earlier, prints are usually too inaccurate to trace. Using reproducibles of existing drawings is seldom satisfactory. They contain too much data and much of the data they do contain is inaccurate or superfluous. All the data shown on them must be checked to ensure accuracy. New drawings, on the other hand, need contain only necessary data. When new drawings are made, it is necessary to field-check only data that affects the work.

The requirements that must be shown on new-work drawings include the same data needed for a project where all the work was new. In addition, new-work drawings for projects where existing construction plays a part must show existing conditions in sufficient detail to permit the contractor to determine what exists and to carry out the new work. The best way to show methods for indicating the requirements is with examples.

Examples

Figures 5-2 through 5-12, which follow these explanations, are plans, elevations, and details of the example library described at the beginning of this book part.

These figures assume use of the abbreviations, symbols, notes, schedules, and recommendations in this book. Numbers and marks shown for finishes,

Figure 5-1. Photograph as a working drawing. (Photograph © Ronald N. Anderson, Rockville, Maryland.)

doors, windows, entrances, storefronts, and louvers are those included in the appropriate schedule in Chapter 6. Figure 4-9 includes demolition and repair note applicable to the examples.

Figures 5-6 , 5-8, and 5-11 are existing working drawings. They have been included to offer a comparison for the corresponding new-work drawings (Figures 5-7, 5-9, 5-10, and 5-12), and to show some types of data that might appear on an existing building's original working drawing but be omitted from a new-work drawing. Working drawings of existing conditions, such as those shown in Figures 5-6, 5-8, and 5-11 would not appear in the contract drawings for an actual project.

The drawings in Figures 5-3, 5-5, 5-7, 5-9, 5-10, and 5-12 collectively illustrate a method for preparing demolition drawings and show the types of information demolition drawings might contain.

Plans

Figure 5-2 is a small-scale drawing showing the new floor plan of the example library building.

Figure 5-3 is a portion of the new working drawing floor plan for the library. Some details and notes one might ordinarily expect to find on a set of working drawings have been omitted for the sake of clarity. For example, only details which appear in other illustrations in this book have been keyed. Demolition and repair notes keyed in Figure 5-3 are shown in Figure 4-9.

Elevations

Figure 5-4 consists of small-scale elevations of the example library showing the new work in place.

Figure 5-5 is a portion of an elevation of the example library showing the new work. The scope of the elevation in Figure 5-5 is limited by book page size. The actual working drawings would include all of every exterior elevation on which work occurred. Refer to Figure 4-9 for demolition and repair notes keyed in Figure 5-5.

Wall Sections

Figure 5-6 is an existing wall section.

Figure 5-7 shows the same condition as Figure 5-6 but with new work added. Note the method of showing existing conditions in Figure 5-7.

Details

Figure 5-8 is an existing detail at the top of the exterior wall shown in Figure 5-6.

Figure 5-9 shows new work at the top of the existing exterior wall shown in Figure 5-8, where the addition occurs.

Figure 5-10 shows new work at a different location along the top of the exterior wall shown in Figure 5-8.

Figure 5-11 is a detail at the bottom of the exterior wall shown in Figure 5-6.

Figure 5-12 is a new condition at the existing location shown in Figure 5-11.

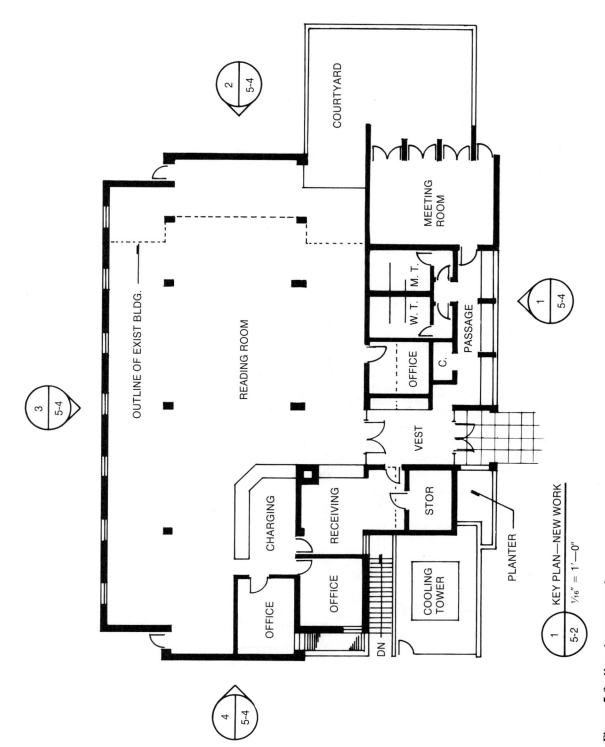

Figure 5-2. Key plan: new work.

79

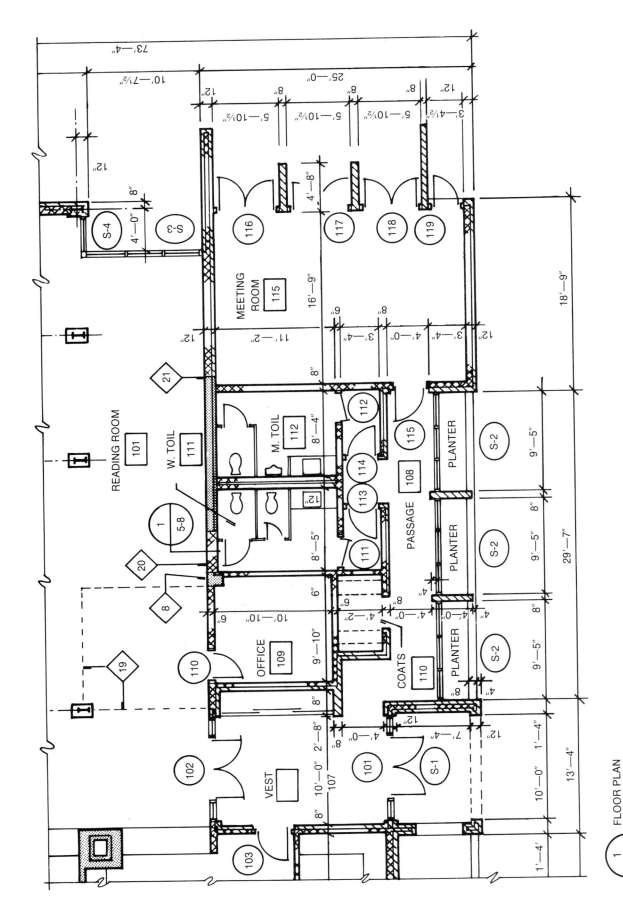

Figure 5-3. Part floor plan: new work.

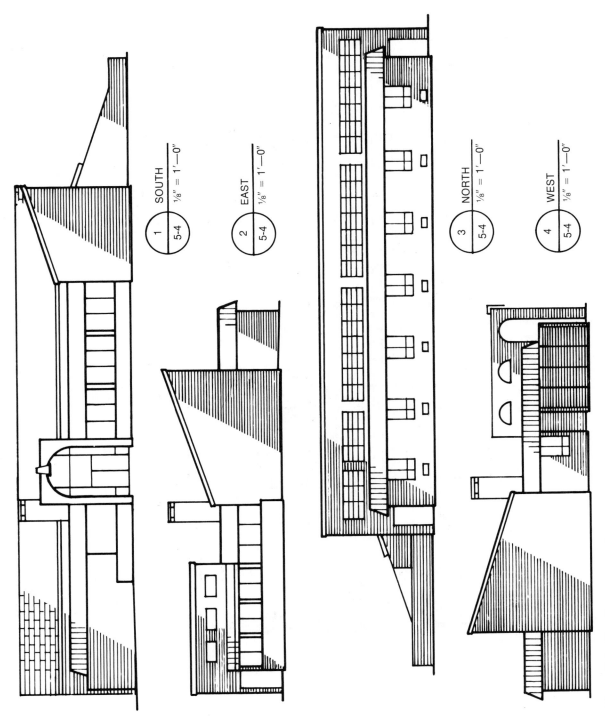

Figure 5-4. Elevations: new work.

1 / 5-4   SOUTH   ⅛" = 1'—0"

2 / 5-4   EAST   ⅛" = 1'—0"

3 / 5-4   NORTH   ⅛" = 1'—0"

4 / 5-4   WEST   ⅛" = 1'—0"

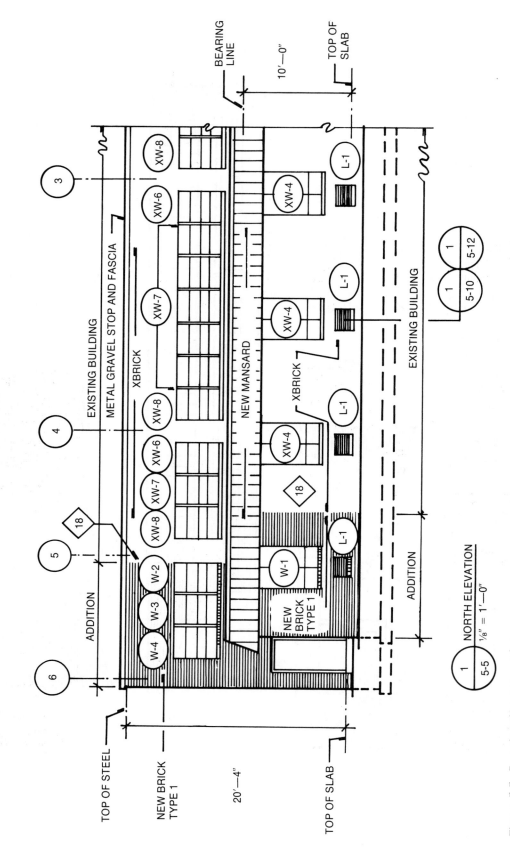

Figure 5-5. Part elevation: new work.

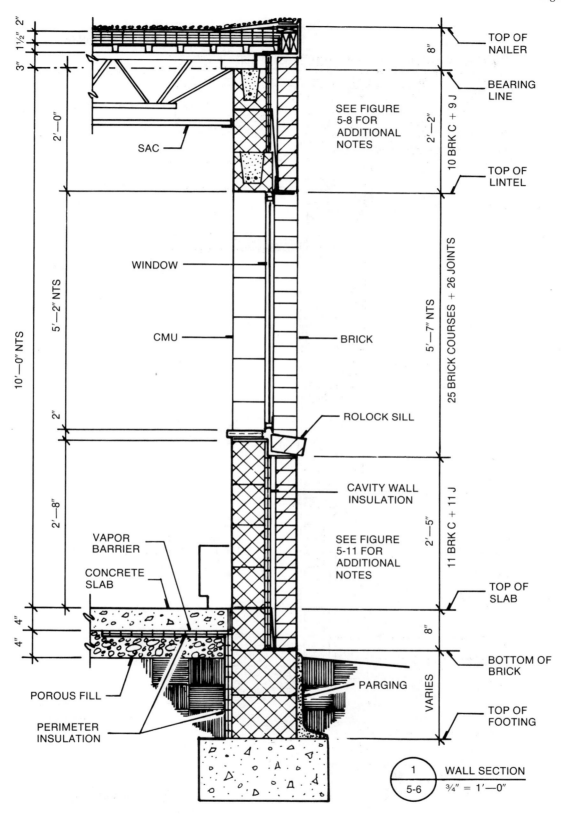

Figure 5-6. Wall section: existing building.

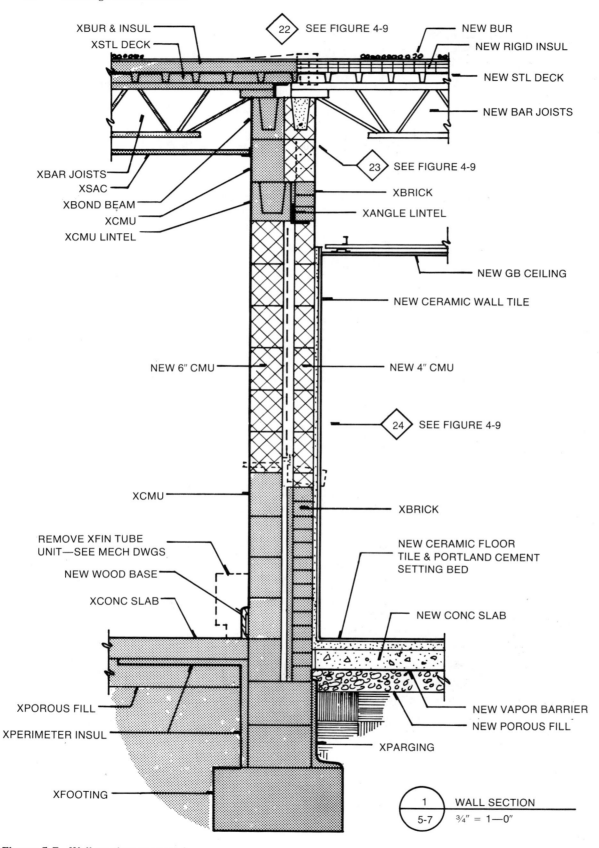

Figure 5-7. Wall section: new work.

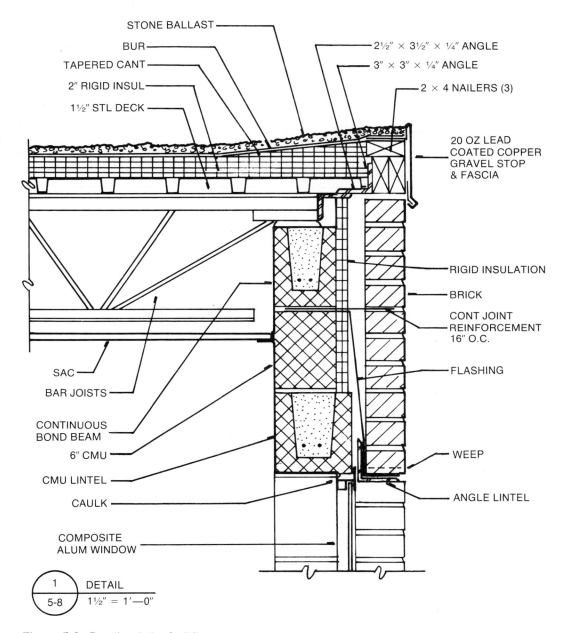

STONE BALLAST

BUR

TAPERED CANT

2" RIGID INSUL

1½" STL DECK

2½" × 3½" × ¼" ANGLE

3" × 3" × ¼" ANGLE

2 × 4 NAILERS (3)

20 OZ LEAD
COATED COPPER
GRAVEL STOP
& FASCIA

RIGID INSULATION

BRICK

CONT JOINT
REINFORCEMENT
16" O.C.

FLASHING

SAC

BAR JOISTS

CONTINUOUS
BOND BEAM

6" CMU

CMU LINTEL

CAULK

WEEP

ANGLE LINTEL

COMPOSITE
ALUM WINDOW

1
5-8
DETAIL
1½" = 1'—0"

Figure 5-8. Detail: existing building.

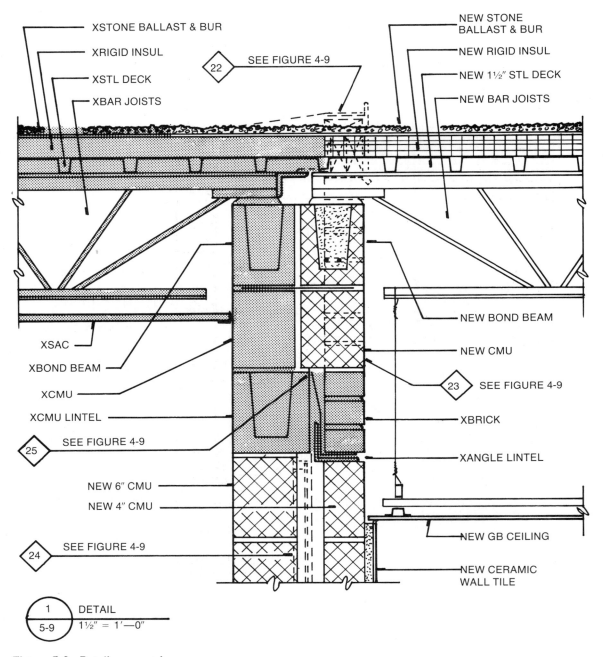

XSTONE BALLAST & BUR

XRIGID INSUL

XSTL DECK

XBAR JOISTS

⟨22⟩ SEE FIGURE 4-9

NEW STONE BALLAST & BUR

NEW RIGID INSUL

NEW 1½″ STL DECK

NEW BAR JOISTS

XSAC

XBOND BEAM

XCMU

XCMU LINTEL

⟨25⟩ SEE FIGURE 4-9

NEW 6″ CMU

NEW 4″ CMU

⟨24⟩ SEE FIGURE 4-9

NEW BOND BEAM

NEW CMU

⟨23⟩ SEE FIGURE 4-9

XBRICK

XANGLE LINTEL

NEW GB CEILING

NEW CERAMIC WALL TILE

1 / 5-9 DETAIL 1½″ = 1′—0″

Figure 5.9. Detail: new work.

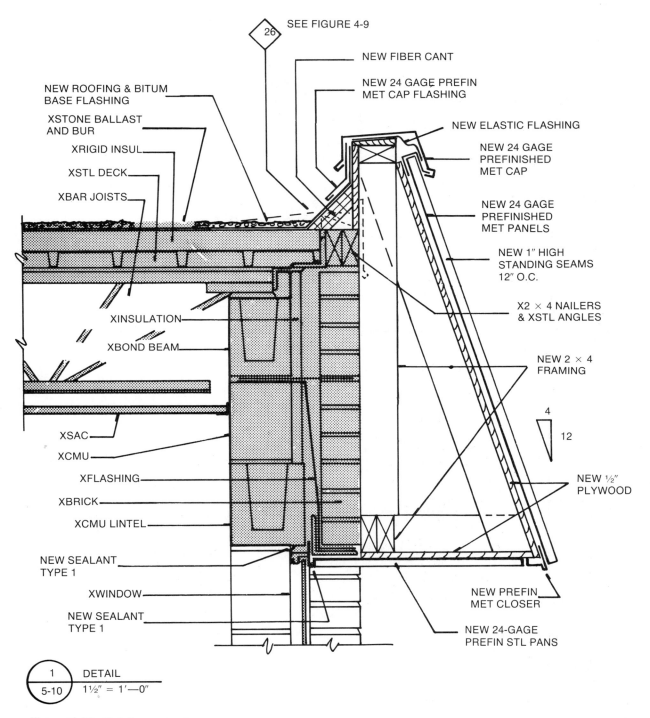

SEE FIGURE 4-9

NEW FIBER CANT

NEW 24 GAGE PREFIN MET CAP FLASHING

NEW ROOFING & BITUM BASE FLASHING

XSTONE BALLAST AND BUR

XRIGID INSUL

XSTL DECK

XBAR JOISTS

NEW ELASTIC FLASHING

NEW 24 GAGE PREFINISHED MET CAP

NEW 24 GAGE PREFINISHED MET PANELS

NEW 1" HIGH STANDING SEAMS 12" O.C.

XINSULATION

XBOND BEAM

X2 × 4 NAILERS & XSTL ANGLES

NEW 2 × 4 FRAMING

XSAC

XCMU

XFLASHING

XBRICK

XCMU LINTEL

NEW SEALANT TYPE 1

XWINDOW

NEW SEALANT TYPE 1

4

12

NEW ½" PLYWOOD

NEW PREFIN MET CLOSER

NEW 24-GAGE PREFIN STL PANS

1
5-10

DETAIL
1½" = 1'—0"

Figure 5-10. Detail: new work.

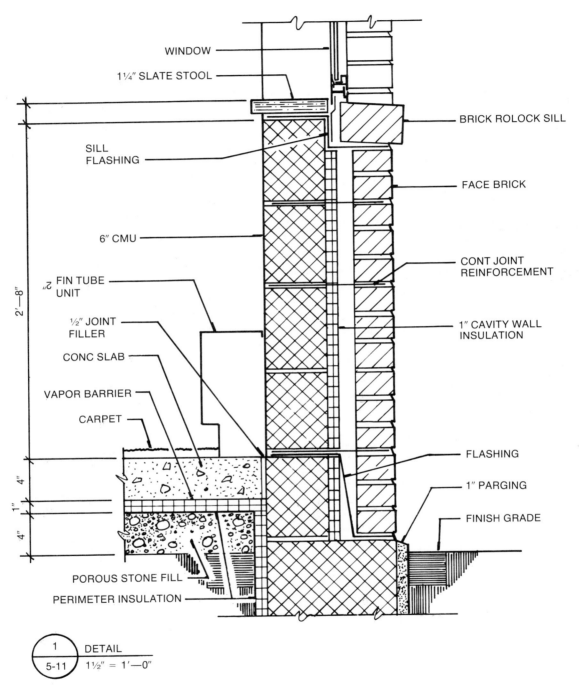

Figure 5-11. Detail: existing building.

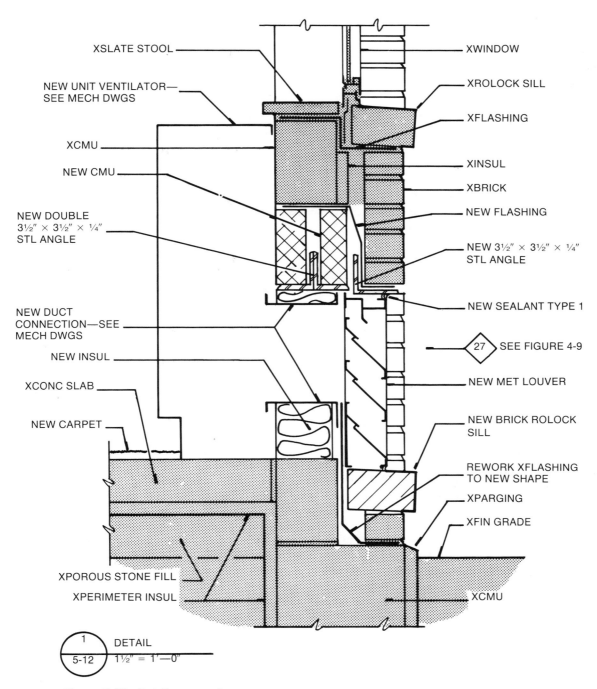

XSLATE STOOL

NEW UNIT VENTILATOR—
SEE MECH DWGS

XCMU

NEW CMU

NEW DOUBLE
3½″ × 3½″ × ¼″
STL ANGLE

NEW DUCT
CONNECTION—SEE
MECH DWGS

NEW INSUL

XCONC SLAB

NEW CARPET

XPOROUS STONE FILL

XPERIMETER INSUL

XWINDOW

XROLOCK SILL

XFLASHING

XINSUL

XBRICK

NEW FLASHING

NEW 3½″ × 3½″ × ¼″
STL ANGLE

NEW SEALANT TYPE 1

27 SEE FIGURE 4-9

NEW MET LOUVER

NEW BRICK ROLOCK
SILL

REWORK XFLASHING
TO NEW SHAPE

XPARGING

XFIN GRADE

XCMU

1
5-12   DETAIL
1½″ = 1′—0″

Figure 5-12. Detail: new work.

6

Schedules

Schedules are effective tools for indicating requirements which cannot be shown clearly on drawings. Often, requirements are easier to describe and more clearly delineated when scheduled rather than drawn. Adding too many notes to drawings can make the drawings unduly cluttered and hard to read. Because of the increased number of necessary data resulting from having to deal with both new and existing conditions, schedules are even more effective on projects where existing construction plays a part.

Chapter 6 contains effective blank forms for finish, door, window, glazing, louver, and equipment schedules for projects where existing construction plays a part. Accompanying the blank forms are filled-in examples of each form using the hypothetical library drawn in Chapters 4 and 5. Supporting the filled-in examples are drawings and notes necessary to make the schedules complete.

The examples in this chapter are representative only. They do not include every item needed for any building other than our sample library. In most cases, they do not even include all data necessary for the example library. Architects must develop schedules independently for each particular project.

The examples are intended to show technique only. Data in them is not necessarily technically accurate or complete and is not applicable to other projects. Do not copy data contained in the examples in this book into the documents for actual projects without careful examination for suitability. Any use of data in the examples is completely at the user's risk.

Manufacturers' names, product names, and catalog numbers used in the examples are fictitious. Any similarity between names and numbers in the schedules and those of actual manufacturers is purely coincidental.

The schedules in this chapter were initially developed on a microcomputer using a spread sheet. The final forms, as they appear in this book, were typeset. It is possible to develop these forms by conventional drafting techniques with hand lettering, by computer using a word processor, with or without the vertical and horizontal lines, and even by use of CADD overlays.

The blank forms in this chapter assume use of the abbreviations, general notes, and symbols in Chapter 3 and code prefixes, drawings, notes, and coded remarks similar to those that accompany the examples in each case.

The column widths in the schedules in this chapter will, in most cases, accept the maximum number of characters required in that column, based on using the abbreviations and codes in this book. Select column widths in your schedules to suit the requirements of each particular project.

Some schedules in this chapter have been broken into more than one piece. Sometimes all the parts appear on a single page. Other times, the parts appear on different pages. The breaks are solely to accommodate the restriction of book size and have no other significance or purpose. Give them no consideration when developing schedules for actual projects. Schedules on actual projects should be unbroken.

The number of rows in the schedules in this chapter is arbitrary. Use the number of rows necessary for the project at hand.

Interior Finishes

Except on the smallest of projects, architects should, and most of the time do, delineate finishes using schedules. On small residential projects, architects will sometimes list finishes directly on the floor plans. Doing that saves little time and forces the architect to leave out necessary data, which can lead to unfortunate experiences in the field. Where existing construction is involved, writing finishes directly on the plans is not satisfactory, regardless of the project's size.

In fact, on projects where existing construction plays a part, architects often use two sets of schedules to designate finish materials and colors. They use one set to show existing conditions and a second to show final conditions expected at construction contract completion. Where an addition occurs, especially if the addition is large or complex, three sets of finish material and color schedules may be appropriate; one to show existing conditions, a second to show new finishes in the existing building, and a third for work in the addition.

There are several ways to construct finish materials and color schedules. Most architects use one of the following types.

Conventional All-Spaces Schedules

In conventional all-spaces schedules each space in a project is listed on a separate line. The finishes associated with that space are then listed on the same line in separate columns. Conventional all-spaces schedules are, by definition, limited to interior work. There are several variations of conventional all-spaces schedules in general use.

All-spaces schedules work well for projects where all the work is new, particularly for small projects and for projects with many different finishes. Some architects insist that all-spaces schedules are the only proper way to identify finishes.

Conventional all-spaces schedules can be made to work on projects where existing construction occurs, but for that use, many notes must be added to cover all likely conditions.

It is possible to add columns to conventional all-spaces finish schedules for colors, textures, and materials quality requirements, but the schedules then tend to become unwieldy. More often, architects using all-spaces schedules generate separate schedules to delineate colors and materials quality requirements.

All-spaces finish schedules in most conventional formats do not contain the detail necessary in finish schedules for projects where existing construction plays a major roll.

Conventional Coded Schedules

In a conventional coded schedule, groups of finishes are identified by codes, usually called "finish types." A code (finish type) includes all the finishes in a particular space. All spaces with identical finishes are given the same code (finish type). Because they include only finish types, conventional coded finish schedules apply only to interior work. There are two major types of conventional coded finish schedules.

In the first type, all necessary data is listed in a single schedule, in a format similar to that used in conventional all-spaces finish schedules, with all the finishes associated with a particular code on the same schedule line. The only code usually used is the finish type. The single advantage of this type of conventional coded finish schedule is that it tends to be shorter than conventional all-spaces finish schedules, especially where a project has many finished-alike spaces. Otherwise, this type of conventional coded finish schedule has all the disadvantages of conventional all-spaces finish schedules and none of the advantages. One major disadvantage is that it does not show each space on a separate line, which forces the architect to add many notes to make the schedule effective. This type of coded schedule is adequate for some projects where the work is all new and there are many spaces and few finishes. It is not adequate for projects where existing construction plays a part, except when augmented with many notes and clarifications.

The second type of coded schedule is actually two schedules. The first, a finishes schedule, lists each finish type on a separate line and identifies the finishes included in that finish type on the same line using materials codes. The second schedule, a materials and color schedule, lists the material codes and identifies the material or product, including finish and color, for each coded material. For example, in the finish schedule, in the "Finish Types" column, in a row (horizontal) labeled "F2" (Finish Number 2), under a column headed "Floors" might appear the code "FL4." In the materials and color schedule, a column labeled "Floors" would define the code "FL4" as "vinyl composition tile." In another finish type (F6) the "Floors" column might contain "FL6." The materials and color schedule would then define "FL6" as "sheet vinyl."

Conventional coded finish schedules consisting of a finish schedule and a materials and color schedule have several advantages over the other types mentioned above. They permit listing much detail, especially in the materials and color schedule where the coded finishes are identified. Identification of coded finishes can go as far as the architect wants it to go, even as far as listing manufacturers' and product names, catalog numbers, and colors and finishes.

Conventional coded schedules consisting of a finish schedule and a materials and color schedule work well for projects where all the work is new, especially for large projects and for both large and small projects where many spaces have the same finish.

A major drawback of conventional coded finish schedules is that they do not permit listing each space in a building. Listing each space is important when spaces are likely to be different, as often happens when existing buildings are remodeled, renovated, or restored.

All-Spaces Coded Schedules

Effectively scheduling interior finishes and colors where existing construction occurs requires combining and expanding several generally used conventional schedule types. Figures 6-1 through 6-9, which follow these explanations, illustrate such a combination.

Figure 6-1 is a list of code prefixes used in the schedules in Figures 6-2A, 6-2B, 6-3, 6-5A, 6-5B, and 6-6. It also applies to the schedules in Figures 6-10 and 6-12 which are explained in the section of this chapter entitled "Exterior Finishes."

Figures 6-2A, 6-2B, and 6-3 are example Existing Interior Finishes and example Existing Interior Finish Material and Color Code Schedules for our hypothetical library using the blank forms in Figures 6-8 and 6-9.

Figure 6-4 is a list of notes and numbered remarks to accompany the examples in Figures 6-2A, 6-2B, and 6-3. It also contains notes and remarks not applicable to the examples to further illustrate the types of notes and remarks an architect might need for existing finishes schedules.

Figures 6-5A, 6-5B, and 6-6 are example New Interior Finishes and example New Interior Finish Material and Color Code Schedules for our hypothetical library using the blank forms in Figures 6-8 and 6-9.

Figure 6-7 is a list of notes and numbered remarks to accompany the examples in Figures 6-5A, 6-5B, and 6-6. It also contains notes and remarks not applicable to the example to further illustrate the types of notes and remarks an architect might need for new finishes schedules for projects where existing construction plays a part.

Figures 6-8 and 6-9 are the blank forms used in the examples. Figure 6-8 is an all-spaces coded interior finish schedule. Figure 6-9 is the accompanying Interior Finish Material and Color Code Schedule. The forms in Figures 6-8 and 6-9 have the positive attributes of all three of the finish schedule types mentioned earlier in this chapter. The Interior Finishes Schedule shows every space in the building on a separate line. The Finish Materials and Color Code Schedule permits as much detail as any of the other schedules discussed. Even so, as the examples make clear, the spaces allowed in the schedules in Figures 6-8 and 6-9 are still not adequate to cover every condition. In addition, many notes are required. The notes are fewer, however, than would be necessary to convey the same information using conventional schedules.

Interior Finishes Schedule Blank Form

The Interior Finishes Schedule blank form (Figure 6-8) is only effective when used with the Interior Finish Material and Color Code Schedule form in Figure 6-9, and accompanied by a list of code prefixes similar to that in Figure 6-1 as well as notes and numbered remarks similar to those in Figures 6-4 and 6-7.

The first column in the form is left blank. Use it to denote the location of spaces within the building (first floor, second floor, etc.) or buildings within a project (Library, Administration Building, Gymnasium, etc.).

Some general subjects have been subdivided to permit showing needed data. Every element, except "Doors" and "Door Frames" has a subdivision labeled "Mat." (Material) and a subdivision labeled "Fin." (Finish). Including the

"Mat." heading permits listing the substrate condition when the substrate is existing. Indicating the substrate material can save time and error by helping to avoid selection of inappropriate finishes—the wrong paint, for example—by the architect and clarifying the intent of the finish selection to the contractor and workers in the field. The "Mat." heading does not appear under the "Doors" or "Door Frames" headings because the door and frame schedule covers materials data for doors and frames. "Wainscot" and "Ceilings" headings have additional subdivisions labeled "Hgt." (Height).

The "Walls" heading has subheadings labeled "North," "West," "South," and "East," because different finishes or amounts of work are often required on different walls within the same space in remodeling, renovation, and restoration projects.

Interior Finish Material and Color Code Schedule Blank Form

The Finish Material and Color Code Schedule blank form (Figure 6-9) is effective only when used with the Interior Finishes Schedule form in Figure 6-8 and accompanied by a list of code prefixes similar to that in Figure 6-1 as well as notes and numbered remarks similar to those illustrated in Figures 6-4 and 6-7.

Examples

Colors are listed in the Interior Finish Material and Color Code Schedule and not in the Interior Finishes Schedule, which establishes a pattern for the entire project. The only other schedule where colors are listed is the Exterior Finish Materials and Color Schedule. Colors are not listed in other schedules in spite of temptation to the contrary, because doing so would scatter color selections over many project drawing sheets and make coordinating colors more difficult. So the Interior Finish Material and Color Code Schedule lists all interior colors, and the Exterior Finish Materials and Color Schedule lists all the exterior colors for the entire project.

In an actual project there will probably be more paint colors than the examples show. Each color will require a separate line in the schedule.

The examples do not list many items requiring finish and color selection that will occur in an actual project. Among them are

Cabinets and casework
Lockers
Shelving
Shower and dressing compartments
Blinds
Floor mats and frames
Interior anodized aluminum items
Wall coverings
Paneling
Other specialties
Other equipment

Tips on Using All-Spaces Coded Interior Finish Schedules

Use the forms in Figures 6-8 and 6-9 for both existing and new finishes on projects where existing construction plays a part. This may seem like bad advice when many spaces initially appear to have the same finish. If many spaces were actually identical, that advice would not be sound. Very seldom, however, will existing spaces in which renovation, restoration, or remodeling takes place be identical in every way. Using a conventional coded finish schedule for them will necessitate using many notes listing exceptions or almost as many finish types as there are spaces. The sole exception is the case of an addition where many spaces are identical. Using three finish schedules there, as we mentioned earlier, might make sense. Then the two schedules associated with existing finishes and work in existing spaces might be the all-spaces coded schedule type while the schedules for the addition might be a conventional coded schedule. Take care in such an instance to use the same codes throughout the project. To change Figure 6-8 into a conventional coded schedule, simply delete the first (unlabeled) column, change the title of the "Space No." column to "Finish Type," and delete the column labeled "Space Name." Then use the second form of space designation shown in the symbols list (Figure 3-3).

Refer to the examples (Figures 6-2A, 6-2B, 6-3, 6-5A, 6-5B, and 6-6) for additional guidance in using the forms in Figures 6-8 and 6-9.

Most code prefixes in Figure 6-1 are the same as the abbreviations listed in Chapter 3. Figure 6-1 contains a few additional abbreviations, however, to cover conditions that apply only to the schedules. Examples are "AS," meaning "as scheduled," and "N," meaning "none." Place the code prefixes on the drawings near the schedules even though most of the abbreviations used are already included in the abbreviations list applicable to the entire project. Otherwise, individuals referring to the schedules will expend a lot of effort flipping through the drawings or simply will not bother. They will, instead, rely on memory, which could lead to errors that might otherwise be avoided.

The codes listed in Figure 6-1 are representative only. In the actual list used, include every abbreviation and only abbreviations used in the actual schedules.

Include in existing finishes schedule every space which shows in a drawing. Include spaces where architectural work occurs and spaces where structural, mechanical, plumbing, electrical, or other nonarchitectural work occurs, even when there is no architectural work in those spaces. It is very difficult to determine where work will lap over into adjacent spaces due to unforeseen conditions. An exception to this rule might be spaces shown merely to complete a plan when the contractor has been explicitly denied access to those spaces, but the better way is to not show those spaces at all.

In general, in interior finish material and color code schedules, stipulate the entire item, including color, when it is factory finished, but the finish only when the item is field finished. Do not, under any circumstance, repeat data listed in other schedules, which could result in copying errors, and coordination errors as well, if a product change is made during document production.

FINISH CODE PREFIXES

ALUM	= Aluminum	NW	= No work required
AS	= As scheduled. When in Finish Schedule this refers to Code Schedule and vice versa	PL	= Plastic laminate
		PLAS	= Plaster
		PT	= Paint type
		RB	= Resilient base type
BE	= Baked enamel	SAC	= Suspended acoustical ceiling type
BRK	= Brick		
CMU	= Concrete masonry units	SCH	= Schedule
		SH	= Shelf type
CONC	= Concrete	T	= Trim type
CPT	= Carpet type	TF	= Two finishes
CT	= Ceramic tile type	TP	= Toilet partitions and urinal screens
EQUIP	= Equipment		
FL	= Floor type		
GB	= Gypsum board	VAT	= Vinyl asbestos tile
HDWD	= Hardwood		
INTER	= Integral	VCT	= Vinyl composition tile
ME	= Match existing		
N	= None	W	= Wall type
NA	= Not applicable	W/C	= Wainscot type
		WD	= Softwood
NAT	= Natural finish type	X	= Existing, when used as a code prefix (XCONC)
NO.	= Number		
NS	= No substitutions		

Figure 6-1. Finish Code Prefixes.

EXISTING INTERIOR FINISHES SCHEDULE

| Space No. | Space Name | Floor | | Base | | Walls | | | | | | | | | | | |
| | | | | | | North | | West | | South | | East | |
		Mat.	Fin.	Mat.	Fin.	Mat.	Fin.	Mat.	Fin.	Mat.	Fin.	Mat.	Fin.
X101	Boiler Room	Conc	PT1	N	NA	Conc	PT2	Conc	PT2	Conc	PT2	Conc	PT2
X101	Reading Room	Conc	CPT1	WD	PT4	CMU	PT3	CMU	PT3	CMU	PT3	CMU	PT3
X102	Charging	Conc	CPT1	WD	PT4	N	NA	CMU	PT3	CMU	PT3	N	NA
X103	Office	Conc	CPT1	WD	PT4	CMU	PT3	CMU	PT3	CMU	PT3	CMU	PT3
X104	Office	Conc	CPT1	WD	PT4	CMU	PT3	CMU	PT3	CMU	PT3	CMU	PT3
X105	Receiving	Conc	VAT	RB1	AS	CMU	PT3	CMU	PT3	CMU	PT3	CMU	PT3
X106	Storage	Conc	VAT	RB1	AS	CMU	PT7	CMU	PT7	CMU	PT7	CMU	PT7
X107	Vestibule	Conc	CPT1	WD	PT4	CMU	PT3	CMU	PT3	CMU	PT3	CMU	PT3
X108	Women's Toilet	Conc	CT1	CT2	AS	PLAS1	PT5	PLAS1	PT5	TF1	AS	CT2	AS
X109	Men's Toilet	Conc	CT1	CT2	AS	TF1	AS	PLAS1	PT5	PLAS1	PT5	CT2	AS
X110	Meeting Room	Conc	CPT1	WD	PT4	CMU	PT3	CMU	PT3	CMU	PT3	CMU	PT3

First Floor

Figure 6-2A. Left half of example Existing Interior Finishes Schedule.

EXISTING INTERIOR FINISHES SCHEDULE

Columns		Wainscot			Trim		Doors	Door Frames	Ceilings			Remarks
Mat.	Fin.	Mat.	Fin.	Hgt.	Mat.	Fin.	Fin.	Fin.	Mat.	Fin.	Hgt.	
N	NA	N	NA	NA	N	NA	PT2	PT2	Conc	PT2	8'–6"	
											·	
PLAS1	PT8	N	NA	NA	WD	PT7	PT4	PT4	SAC1	INTER	Varies	④
CMU	PT3	N	NA	NA	WD	PT7	NA	NA	SAC1	INTER	9'–1"	
CMU	PT3	N	NA	NA	WD	PT7	PT4	PT4	SAC1	INTER	9'–1"	
N	NA	N	NA	NA	WD	PT7	PT4	PT4	SAC1	INTER	9'–1"	
CMU	PT3	N	NA	NA	WD	PT7	PT4	PT4	SAC1	INTER	9'–1"	
N	NA	N	NA	NA	N	NA	PT4	PT4	SAC1	INTER	9'–1"	⑤
CMU	PT3	N	NA	NA	WD	PT7	PT4	PT4	SAC1	INTER	9'–1"	
PLAS1	PT5	CT2	AS	48"	N	NA	PT4	PT4	PLAS1	PT6	7'–6"	
N	NA	CT2	AS	48"	N	NA	PT4	PT4	PLAS1	PT6	7'–6"	
CMU	PT3	N	NA	NA	WD	PT7	PT4	PT4	SAC1	INTER	9'–1"	

Figure 6-2B. Right half of example Existing Interior Finishes Schedule.

98

EXISTING INTERIOR FINISH MATERIAL AND COLOR CODE SCHEDULE

Code	Material	Manufacturer	Product	Catalog No.	Finish	Color	Remarks
CPT1	Broadloom	Acme	Wanderlust	AW-37	–	Coffee	⬡1
CT1	Mosaic tile	Softtile	Earthglow	SE12	Unglazed	Canary	1" x 2"
CT2	Glazed tile	Softtile	Starshine	SS31	Matt	Canary	4" x 4"
PLAS1	Cement plaster	Unknown	Unknown	Unknown	AS	AS	
PT1	Floor paint	Unknown	Enamel	Unknown	High gloss	Crimson	⬡2 ⬡3
PT2	Oil paint	Unknown	Enamel	Unknown	High gloss	White	⬡2 ⬡3
PT3	Latex paint	The Paint Co.	Latex-Flo	L-F345	Semi-gloss	Beige	
PT4	Alkyd paint	The Paint Co.	Mor-Flo	M-F456	Semi-gloss	Chocolate	
PT5	Alkyd paint	The Paint Co.	Hi-Flo	H-F234	High gloss	Light gray	
PT6	Alkyd paint	The Paint Co.	Flat-Flo	F-F567	Flat	Off white	
PT7	Alkyd paint	The Paint Co.	Mor-Flo	M-F456	Semi-gloss	Beige	
RB1	Vinyl base	Unknown	Set-on style	Unknown	Gloss	Chocolate	With cove
SAC1	Lay-in panels	Unknown	Mineral fiber	Unknown	Fissured	White	24" x 48" x 3/4"
SH1	Oak	*	*	*	Factory	Natural	*See Equip Sch
TF1	PLAS1 & CT2	Unknown & AS	Unknown & AS	Unk & SS31	PT5 & Matt	AS	
VAT	Smooth tile	QRX, Inc.	Master Tile	MT123	Waxed	Solid beige	12" x 12" x 1/8"
TP	Metal	BeanCo	Florset	None	Enamel	Light gray	

Figure 6-3. Example Existing Interior Finish Material and Color Code Schedule.

EXISTING INTERIOR FINISHES NOTES

Notes in this list apply generally throughout the existing building.

1. Existing finishes were taken from original documents for the existing building as prepared by (fill in architect's name) and dated (fill in date), and verified in the field.
2. Colors are shown only where they are to be exactly matched and the name of the actual color (manufacturer's product or paint name) is known.
3. Refer to demolition floor plans for extent of finishes when two occur on the same surface.
4. Resilient bases have premolded corners.
5. Except where noted otherwise, the existing building has been painted within the past 5 years using the paints scheduled.
6. Throughout the project, existing materials names are preceded by an "X" denoting that they are existing. Each finish listed in the Existing Interiors Finishes Schedule or in the Existing Finish Materials and Color Code Schedule is an existing finish. The "X" preceding those finishes has been omitted from the schedules, however, for the sake of clarity. In each case, add the "X" by inference. For example, read CPT1 in the Existing Finishes Schedule as XCPT1.

NUMBERED REMARKS

Notes in this list apply where noted in schedule Remarks columns.

⟨1⟩ Tackless installation with pad.

⟨2⟩ Paint is in poor condition; has probably not been repainted since building was new.

⟨3⟩ Paint is probably linseed oil based.

⟨4⟩ Library stack shelves shall be SH1.

⟨5⟩ Paint shelves with PT7.

Figure 6-4. Existing Interior Finishes Notes and Numbered Remarks.

NEW INTERIOR FINISHES SCHEDULE

Space No.	Space Name	Floor Mat.	Floor Fin.	Base Mat.	Base Fin.	North Mat.	North Fin.	West Mat.	West Fin.	South Mat.	South Fin.	East Mat.	East Fin.
B01	Boiler Room	XConc	PT1	N	NA	XConc	PT2	XConc	PT2	XConc	PT2	XConc	PT2
101	Reading Room	XConc	CPT1	ME	PT4	ME	PT3	XCMU	PT3	ME	PT3	CMU	PT3
102	Charging	XConc	CPT1	XWD	PT4	N	NA	XCMU	PT3	XCMU	PT3	N	NA
103	Office	XConc	CPT1	XWD	PT4	XCMU	PT3	XCMU	PT3	XCMU	PT3	XCMU	PT3
104	Office	XConc	CPT1	XWD	PT4	XCMU	PT3	XCMU	PT3	XCMU	PT3	XCMU	PT3
105	Receiving	ME	CPT1	WD	PT4	XCMU	PT3	ME	PT3	CMU	PT3	CMU	PT3
106	Storage	Conc	VCT1	RB1	AS	CMU	PT7	CMU	PT7	CMU	PT7	CMU	PT7
107	Vestibule	Conc	BRK3	BRK2	INTER	XDR&GL	AS	BRK2	INTER	DR&GL	AS	BRK2	INTER
108	Passage	Conc	BRK3	BRK2	INTER	BRK2	INTER	BRK2	INTER	HM&GL	AS	BRK2	INTER
109	Office	Conc	CPT1	WD	PT4	CMU	PT3	CMU	PT3	CMU	PT3	CMU	PT3
110	Coats	Conc	BRK2	WD	PT4	GB	PT3	GB	PT3	GB	PT3	CMU	PT3
111	Women's Toilet	Conc	CT1	CT2	AS	CT2	AS	CT2	AS	CT2	AS	CT2	AS
112	Men's Toilet	Conc	CT1	CT2	AS	CT2	AS	CT2	AS	CT2	AS	CT2	AS
113	Vestibule	Conc	CT1	CT2	AS	CMU	PT3	CMU	PT3	CMU	PT3	CMU	PT3
114	Vestibule	Conc	CT1	CT2	AS	CMU	PT3	CMU	PT3	CMU	PT3	CMU	PT3
115	Meeting Room	Conc	CPT1	WD	PT4	BRK1	INTER	GB	PT3	GB	PT3	BRK1	INTER

First Floor

Figure 6-5A. Left half of example New Interior Finishes Schedule.

NEW INTERIOR FINISHES SCHEDULE

Columns		Wainscot			Trim		Doors	Door Frames	Ceilings			Remarks
Mat.	Fin.	Mat.	Fin.	Hgt.	Mat.	Fin.	Fin.	Fin.	Mat.	Fin.	Hgt.	
N	NA	N	NA	NA	N	NA	PT8	PT8	XConc	PT2	8'-6"	⑥ ⑦
GB	PT3	N	NA	NA	ME	PT7	PT5	PT5	ME	INTER	Varies	②
XCMU	PT3	N	NA	NA	XWD	PT7	NA	NA	XSAC	INTER	9'-1"	
XCMU	PT3	N	NA	NA	XWD	PT7	PT5	PT5	XSAC	INTER	9'-1"	
N	NA	N	NA	NA	XWD	PT7	PT5	PT5	XSAC	INTER	9'-1"	
CMU	PT3	N	NA	NA	ME	PT7	PT5	PT5	SAC1	INTER	9'-1"	
N	NA	N	NA	NA	N	NA	PT5	PT5	GB	PT6	9'-1"	⑤
N	NA	N	NA	NA	WD	PT7	PT5	PT5	SAC1	INTER	9'-1"	①
N	NA	N	NA	NA	N	NA	PT5	PT5	SAC1	INTER	9'-1"	
N	NA	N	NA	NA	N	NA	PT5	PT5	SAC1	INTER	9'-1"	
N	NA	N	NA	NA	N	NA	NA	NA	GB	PT6	9'-1"	⑤
N	NA	N	NA	NA	N	NA	PT5	PT5	GB	PT6	7'-6"	③ ④
N	NA	N	NA	NA	N	NA	PT5	PT5	GB	PT6	7'-6"	③ ④
N	NA	N	NA	NA	N	NA	PT5	PT5	GB	PT6	7'-6"	
N	NA	N	NA	NA	N	NA	PT5	PT5	GB	PT6	7'-6"	
N	NA	N	NA	NA	N	NA	PT8	PT8	SAC1	INTER	Varies	

Figure 6-5B. Right half of example New Interior Finishes Schedule.

NEW INTERIOR FINISH MATERIAL AND COLOR CODE SCHEDULE

Code	Material	Manufacturer	Product	Catalog No.	Finish	Color	Remarks
BRK1	Face brick	Crafty, Inc.	Craftline (NS)	CI-3 (NS)	ME	Red to ME	Size to ME
BRK2	Face brick	Crafty, Inc.	Craftline (NS)	CI-4 (NS)	Integral	Terra cotta	Size to ME
BRK3	Paver brick	Pavers, Inc.	Flat brick	FB6	Unglazed	Terra cotta	4" x 8"
CPT1	Nylon carpet	PDQ Carpets	Rapidline	456-RL	NA	Slate tweed	
CT1	Mosaic tile	Certile Corp.	Grid Mosaic	M11	Unglazed	Salmon	1" x 2"
CT2	Glazed tile	Certile Corp.	Glazed Tile	G44	Matt	Salmon	4" x 4"
PL1	Plastic lam.	PL, Inc.	PL Executive	PL-33	Smooth	Mist gray	
PT1	Deck enamel	The Paint Co.	Deck-Flo	D-F123	High gloss	Redglow	
PT2	Alkyd paint	The Paint Co.	Hi-Flo	H-F234	High gloss	Near white	
PT3	Latex paint	The Paint Co.	Latex-Flo	L-F345	Semi-gloss	Salmon	
PT4	Alkyd paint	The Paint Co.	Mor-Flo	M-F456	Semi-gloss	Slate	
PT5	Alkyd paint	The Paint Co.	Hi-Flo	M-F234	High gloss	Terra cotta	
PT6	Alkyd paint	The Paint Co.	Flat-Flo	F-F567	Flat	Off white	
PT7	Alkyd paint	The Paint Co.	Mor-Flo	M-F456	Semi-gloss	Salmon	
PT8	Alkyd paint	The Paint Co.	Hi-Flo	M-F234	High gloss	Charcoal	
RB1	Vinyl base	MDD. Inc.	Vinyl Base	VB4	Gloss	Slate	With cove
SAC1	Lay-in panels	Monitor Corp.	Monitype	MT14	Fissured	White	24" x 24" x 3/4"
TP1	Plastic lam.	Overlay Co.	Excellent	OE-47	Smooth	Light gray	
VCT1	Smooth tile	MDD. Inc.	Silver Series	MDD678	Smooth	Pearl gray	12" x 12" x 1/8"

Figure 6-6. Example Interior Finish Material and Color Code Schedule.

NEW INTERIOR FINISHES NOTES

1. Unless specifically indicated otherwise, products scheduled indicate quality standard required, but are not intended to limit competition. Listed colors and finishes establish color and finish required. Except for products noted "NS" or "no substitutions," approved equal products of approved equal manufacturers will be considered. Colors and finishes shall match samples available for view by Contractor at Architect's office. Match of manufacturer's samples other than those on hand in Architect's office is not adequate unless such other samples exactly match Architect's samples. Architect is sole judge of equality and of color and finish match.

2. Refer to large-scale plans and interior elevations for extent of finishes when two occur on the same surface.

3. Refer to reflected ceiling plans for extent and height of varying ceiling heights.

4. When more than one space designation is scheduled on the same line (101/107), the slash means "and all numbers that follow, up to and including."

5. Where match existing (ME) is indicated, provide new material as necessary to patch or extend existing material. Unless an exception is specifically noted, new material shall match existing in all particulars.

6. Where Contract documents require color match, but existing color's name is unknown, match colors as nearly as practicable by field comparison. Architect is sole judge of color match accuracy. Mismatched colors where match is required will be rejected.

7. Except where marked as existing (X), scheduled items are new.

8. Where new finish floor is scheduled, completely remove existing flooring and install completely new finish floor.

9. Where existing substrate is concrete slab-on-grade, existing flooring is ceramic or quarry tile, and new ceramic tile, quarry tile, or resilient flooring is scheduled, completely remove existing fill and flooring and provide new fill to proper level before installing resilient material. Finish new surfaces smooth and in same plane with adjacent flooring.

10. In existing above-grade-floor spaces where substrate is supported concrete, existing flooring is ceramic or quarry tile, and new ceramic or quarry tile is scheduled, completely remove existing setting beds and flooring and provide new setting beds and flooring.

11. In existing above-grade-floor spaces where substrate is supported concrete, existing flooring is ceramic or quarry tile, and new resilient flooring is scheduled, completely remove existing setting beds and flooring, clean slab, and patch substrate as specified for new resilient flooring.

Figure 6-7. New Interior Finishes Notes and Numbered Remarks.

12. Refer to specifications for requirements where new resilient flooring is specified in existing spaces where existing finish is resilient flooring.
13. Refer to specifications for requirements where new carpet is specified in existing spaces.
14. Where existing construction is removed and remaining walls are exposed, refinish surfaces as necessary to receive new finishes scheduled.
15. Where existing wall finish is ceramic tile and new finish is scheduled, completely remove existing tile and setting beds and prepare substrates to receive new finishes.
16. In existing spaces finished with ceramic tile, where existing toilet partitions or plumbing fixtures are removed, remove damaged tile and provide new tile to match existing. Where tile is not available to match existing, remove tile and setting bed and provide new tile in entire space.
17. Where new ceiling is scheduled in a space with an existing ceiling, completely remove existing ceiling, unless otherwise shown or specified. Refer to specifications for requirements for reusing existing suspension systems. Install complete new ceiling at scheduled height.
18. Where existing ceilings are to remain as structure fire protection, repair openings and damage as soon as possible using same construction as in existing ceiling.
19. Refer to Section 09900, "Painting," for list of existing surfaces requiring painting and list of existing items not to be painted.

NUMBERED REMARKS

1. Loose entrance mat will be furnished by Owner.

2. Refinish existing charging desk. Refer to specifications for materials and methods.

3. Use plastic laminate Type 1 (PL1) on vanity cabinets. Use specified simulated marble tops with marbelized pattern and salmon color.

4. Toilet partitions and urinal screens shall match TP1.

5. Paint shelves using PT7.

6. Library stack shelves are SH1.

7. Paint exterior doors and frames using PT8.

8. Seal exposed concrete slab with a chemical hardener of the type indicated in the specifications.

9. Use PT9 below chair rail and PT11 above chair rail.

10. Use NAT2 on chair rail; PT8 on crown mold.

11. Use PL2 on casework.

INTERIOR FINISHES SCHEDULE

Space No.	Space Name	Floor		Base		Walls							
						North		West		South		East	
		Mat.	Fin.	Mat.	Fin.	Mat.	Fin.	Mat.	Fin.	Mat.	Fin.	Mat.	Fin.

Columns		Wainscot			Trim		Doors	Door Frames	Ceilings			Remarks
Mat.	Fin.	Mat.	Fin.	Hgt.	Mat.	Fin.	Fin.	Fin.	Mat.	Fin.	Hgt.	

Figure 6-8. Right and left halves of blank form for Interior Finishes Schedule.

Code	Material	Manufacturer	Product	Catalog No.	Finish	Color	Remarks

INTERIOR FINISH MATERIAL AND COLOR CODE SCHEDULE

Figure 6-9. Blank form for Interior Finish Material and Color Code Schedule.

Exterior Finishes

Architects often note exterior finishes directly on elevation drawings. Where existing construction is involved, materials notes must compete with instructions about work to be done, which can clutter the drawings, making them more difficult to read. When such a thing happens, it is often better to provide a schedule to indicate exterior finishes. A properly constructed schedule can include colors also, thus eliminating the need for a separate color schedule and making the material and color information easier to coordinate than is likely when two separate schedules are used.

Exterior Finish Materials and Color Schedule

The schedule illustrated in Figures 6-10 through 6-14, which follow these explanations, works well for exterior finishes, materials, and colors. It can be used for both existing and new work, as illustrated by the examples.

Figure 6-10 is an Existing Exterior Finish Materials and Color Schedule for our hypothetical library using the blank form in Figure 6-14.

Figure 6-11 is a list of notes and numbered remarks to accompany the example in Figure 6-10. It also contains notes and remarks not applicable to the example to further illustrate the types of notes and remarks an architect might need for existing finish materials and color code schedules.

Figure 6-12 is a New Exterior Finish Materials and Color Schedule for our hypothetical library using the blank forms in Figure 6-14.

Figure 6-13 is a list of notes and numbered remarks to accompany the example in Figure 6-12. It also contains notes and remarks not applicable to the example to further illustrate the types of notes and remarks an architect might need for new exterior finish materials and color schedules for projects where existing construction plays a part.

Figure 6-14 is the blank form used in the examples.

The Exterior Finish Materials and Color Schedule blank form (Figure 6-14) is effective only when accompanied by a list of code prefixes similar to that in Figure 6-1, and notes and numbered remarks similar to those illustrated in Figures 6-11 and 6-13.

Tips on Using the Exterior Finish Materials and Color Schedule

Use the same blank form to generate separate existing and new finishes schedules.

Refer to the examples in Figures 6-10 and 6-12 for guidance in filling out the forms.

List on the forms all exterior items requiring color and finish selection, including paving and site works.

In general, stipulate the entire item when factory finished and the finish only where field finished.

Where more than one of a finish type occurs, give each a number and note locations on the drawings. In the example in Figure 6-12 there are two different brick types, BRK1 and BRK2. The locations of each should be noted on the elevations.

EXISTING EXTERIOR FINISH MATERIAL AND COLOR SCHEDULE

Material	Location	Manufacturer	Product	Catalog No.	Finish	Color	Remarks
Face brick	All	Arty, Inc.	Artline	ART42	Weathered	Red	
Mortar	All	Unknown	Type S Cem	Unknown	Natural	Natural	
Joint sealers	All	Unknown	Oil based calk	Unknown	NA	White	
Roof shingles	All	BK Roofs	Deep Line	BK102	Standard	Medium gray	①
Doors	HM	Unknown	Hollow metal	Unknown	Enamel paint	Red	②
Door frames	HM	Unknown	Hollow metal	Unknown	Enamel paint	Charcoal	②
Doors	ALUM	*	*	*	Anodized	Natural	See Storefront Sch
Door frames	ALUM	*	*	*	Anodized	Natural	See Storefront Sch
Windows	Combination	*	*	*	Anodized	Natural	See Window Sch
Windows	Awning	*	*	*	Anodized	Natural	See Window Sch
Fascias	All	Unknown	Galv. metal	None	Enamel paint	Charcoal	②
Handrails	All	Unknown	Steel pipe	None	Enamel paint	Charcoal	②
Louvers	All	Unknown	Sheet steel	Unknown	Enamel paint	Match red BR	②
Grating	All	Unknown	Steel bar	Unknown	Galvanized	Natural	

Figure 6-10. Example Existing Exterior Finish Material and Color Schedule.

EXISTING EXTERIOR FINISHES NOTES

1. Existing finishes were taken from original documents for the existing building as prepared by (fill in architect's name) and dated (fill in date), and verified in the field.
2. Colors are shown only where they are to be exactly matched and the name of the actual color (manufacturer's product or paint name) is known.
3. The existing building has been painted within the past 5 years using the paints indicated in the numbered remarks list below.
4. Throughout the project, existing materials names are preceded by an "X" denoting that they are existing. Each finish listed in the Existing Exterior Finishes Schedule is an existing finish. The "X" preceding those finishes has been omitted from the schedules, however, for the sake of clarity. In each case, add the "X" by inference. For example, read "Roof shingles" in the Existing Exterior Finishes Schedule as "XRoof shingles."

NUMBERED REMARKS

$\langle 1 \rangle$ Original shingles were removed within the past 5 years and the scheduled shingles installed.

$\langle 2 \rangle$ Painted within the past 5 years using The Paint Co.'s Alkyd "Hi-Flo," high gloss enamel in the color scheduled.

Figure 6-11. Existing Exterior Finishes Notes and Numbered Remarks.

NEW EXTERIOR FINISH MATERIAL AND COLOR SCHEDULE

Material	Location	Manufacturer	Product	Catalog No.	Finish	Color	Remarks
Face brick 1	Where shown	Crafty, Inc.	Craftline (NS)	CI-3 (NS)	ME	ME	①⑥
Face brick 2	Where shown	Crafty, Inc.	Craftline (NS)	CI-4 (NS)	Integral	Terra cotta	
Mortar	New brick work	No restriction	Type S	None	Natural	ME	
Joint sealers	All sealed jts	Sealitup	Elasto	S-E14	Smooth	②	③
Roof shingles	New & exist	BK Roofs	Deep Line	BK102	Standard	ME	④
HM Dr & Fr Fin	New & exist	The Paint Co.	Hi-Flo	M-F234	High gloss	Charcoal	
Window finish	Existing	The Paint Co.	Hi-Flo	M-F234	High gloss	Charcoal	⑤
Stl Windows	New	*		*	Baked enamel	Charcoal	See Window Sch
Alum Windows	New	*		*	Baked enamel	Charcoal	See Window Sch
Fascia finish	New & exist	The Paint Co.	Hi-Flo	M-F234	High gloss	Match shingles	
Handrail fin	Exist (no new)	The Paint Co.	Hi-Flo	M-F234	High gloss	Charcoal	
Air intake fin	New & exist	The Paint Co.	Hi-Flo	M-F234	High gloss	Charcoal	
Louvers	New (no exist)	Raveon	Vertical	RL81	Fluorocarbon	Charcoal	
Grating finish	Exist (no new)	Unknown	Steel bar	Unknown	Galvanized	As is	
Stucco	New soffits	Porcem Corp	Porcem	P12	Standard	Light gray	
Mansard	New (No exist)	Metals, Inc.	Gridline	MG48P	Fluorocarbon	Match exist BR	
Storefront	New	*	*	*	Fluorocarbon	Charcoal	See Storefront Sch

Figure 6-12. Example New Exterior Finish Material and Color Schedule.

111

NEW EXTERIOR FINISHES NOTES

1. Unless specifically indicated otherwise, scheduled products indicate quality standard required, but are not intended to limit competition. Listed colors and finishes establish color and finish required. Except for products noted "NS" or "no substitutions," approved equal products of approved equal manufacturers will be considered. Colors and finishes shall match samples available for view by Contractor at Architect's office. Match of manufacturer's samples other than those on hand in Architect's office is not adequate unless such other samples exactly match architect's samples. Architect is sole judge of equality and of color and finish match.

2. Where match existing (ME) is indicated, provide new material as necessary to patch or extend existing material. Unless an exception is specifically noted, new material shall match existing in all particulars.

3. Where Contract documents require color match, but existing color's name is not known, match colors as nearly as practicable by field comparison. Architect is sole judge of color match accuracy. Mismatched colors where match is required will be rejected.

4. Unless marked as existing (X), scheduled items are new.

NUMBERED REMARKS

⟨1⟩ Substitutions will not be permitted.

⟨2⟩ Match brick color when sealant is in contact with brick. In other locations, match color of adjacent materials.

⟨3⟩ Remove existing caulking and sealants in every location and provide new sealant.

⟨4⟩ Do not disturb existing shingles except as necessary to install new shingles.

⟨5⟩ Clean and paint existing aluminum windows to match new windows.

⟨6⟩ Match existing brick size.

Figure 6-13. New Exterior Finishes Notes and Numbered Remarks.

EXTERIOR FINISH MATERIAL AND COLOR SCHEDULE

Material	Location	Manufacturer	Product	Catalog No.	Finish	Color	Remarks

Figure 6-14. Blank form for Exterior Finish Material and Color Schedule.

113

Doors and Frames

Regardless of project size or type, architects almost always schedule doors and frames. There are several types of door and frame schedules in general use today, and dozens of variations of each of them. Many of them, unfortunately, do not contain all the data they should. In this chapter we will discuss the several types and recommend a schedule that works well for projects where existing construction plays a part.

Coded Door and Frame Schedules

A coded door and frame schedule is one in which a separate and distinctive code is given to each group of framed openings that have frames, and doors if any, that are alike in every respect. The code may be alphabetic, numeric, or alphanumeric. The codes are usually written on the plans adjacent to the door, often inside a symbol, such as a circle. The codes are then listed in a schedule which also delineates all the characteristics of that door and frame type. No attempt is made to list the doors or frames consecutively or to relate the codes identifying them to the spaces in which the frames occur. Schedules in which openings are numbered consecutively or in which each opening is given a separate and distinctive number or letter are not coded schedules for our purposes here, even when they use codes to identify the characteristics of the doors and frames listed.

Of the several forms that door and frame schedules can take, coded schedules are the least effective. They save the architect time during contract document production, but much of that time can be lost during the construction phase because of increased time needed to check a shop drawing based on coded schedules. Coded schedules can also lead to confusion among door, frame, and hardware suppliers and make their jobs more complicated than is necessary. All these shortcomings can lead to errors that could be prevented by using a different type schedule.

All-Openings Door and Frame Schedules

In all-openings door and frame schedules, each opening containing a frame, whether or not it holds a door, is identified by a distinctive designation, which may be numbers, letters, or a combination of numbers and letters.

It is possible to configure all-openings door and frame schedules in several ways. A common form lists the openings by number in a vertical column and the characteristics of the door and frame within that opening in additional columns. The columns list each characteristic in groups. For example, a group labeled "Door Opening Size" might contain a separate column for each size. One column could be labeled "3'–0" × 6'–8" × 1'–¾"." Another column under "Door Opening Size" could be labeled "Pair 2'–6" × 6'–8" × 1'–¾"." Under a group called "Door Material" one column might be labeled "Hollow Metal" and another "Wood—Solid Core." A dot, slash, or some other symbol is then placed in the box formed by the intersection of the row labeled with a door number and the column labeled with the characteristic. The symbol would be placed in the box in the row called "101" in the column labeled "Hollow Metal" indicating that door number 101 is a hollow metal door.

There is nothing wrong with scheduling doors and frames using that kind of form, especially for projects where all construction is new. It does not work as well for projects where existing construction plays a part, however, because of the large number of variables. It is one thing to use grouped columns of characteristics when there are three or so characteristics in each group. When the number of characteristics grows larger, as is likely in projects with existing construction involved, this type of schedule becomes long and unwieldly.

The schedule illustrated by Figures 6-15 through 6-22, which follow these explanations, works well for projects with existing construction involvement. The example schedule is incomplete without all the parts contained in Figures 6-15 through 6-22.

Figure 6-15 is a legend listing abbreviations used in the door and frame schedule.

Figures 6-16A and 6-16B constitute a combined existing and new door schedule for our hypothetical library using the blank form in Figure 6-22.

Figure 6-17 is a drawing showing the scheduled frame elevations.

Figure 6-18 is a drawing showing the scheduled door elevations.

Figure 6-19 is a drawing showing scheduled frame configurations.

Figure 6-20 is a drawing showing scheduled frame installation details.

Figure 6-21 is a list of notes and numbered remarks to accompany the example schedule.

Figure 6-22 is the blank form used in the example.

Door and Frame Schedule Blank Form

The Door and Frame Schedule blank form (Figure 6-22) is only effective when accompanied by a Door and Frame Schedule Legend similar to that illustrated in Figure 6-15, drawings similar to those in Figures 6-17 through 6-20 and notes and numbered remarks similar to those in Figure 6-21.

The first column in the form is blank. Use it to denote the location of doors within the building (first floor, second floor, etc.) or buildings within a project (Library, Gymnasium, Administration Building, etc.). Add more columns at the beginning of the schedule to separate building phases or other subdivisions as necessary for clarity.

General subjects are sometimes subdivided to permit display of needed data. Which data a door schedule should contain is controversial. There is no intent here to enter that controversy in any way. Our intent is to demonstrate a method for handling existing conditions, not to persuade anyone to change their minds about which data door schedules should contain.

With that in mind, an explanation for including certain data in the schedule seems in order. Some of the data in the schedule in this book is there to head off errors caused by the supplier not being able to find, or properly interpret, data scattered throughout the documents. The acuteness of the problem is in direct proportion to the amount of data suppliers must have to provide a project's doors, frames, and builders' hardware. Projects where there are existing doors and frames require more data than projects where all doors and frames are new.

To survive in practice, architects must hold down document production costs. Some architects save time by omitting requirements from their door schedules, with the excuse that putting all that information in there is doing someone else's job. In reality, filling in the schedule itself is not that time-consuming. The real problem lies in knowing what to fill in. Too many people in architects' offices who fill out door schedules are not knowledgeable enough to do the job properly. Many decisions that should be delineated in the schedule are left to the specifications to call out, forcing the need to have knowledge onto the specifications writer. Splitting requirements in the contract documents can lead to errors during construction that could have been prevented by proper schedules.

Checking shop drawings is a time-consuming chore. Having the proper data in a door schedule can save time during that checking. Time supposedly saved in filling out a schedule can be spent many times over when someone must check a stop drawing prepared using insufficient data. Not only must the preparer search through the documents to find requirements—door material gages, for example—but the shop drawing checker must repeat the process to see if the shop drawings are correct. More important are errors that occur solely because of emission of information from the door and frame schedule. Installing frames backward so that the door would swing the wrong way is a typical example. Manufacturing frames with the loose stops on the wrong side is another.

Example

Methods for numbering openings are so controversial that one might conclude that there is no proper way to do it. We have elected to name the openings in the example using a sequential numerical form of door numbering arranged by building floor. Some architects do not like to number openings serially because developing a logical sequence is difficult, expecially for large or complicated projects, and because adding doors or frames late in the document production process creates havoc.

We could have named the openings in our example using sequential letters, which would work for our small library but not well for large projects.

We could have used room numbers to designate openings, which would work for our library. On larger projects, even though the method makes the supplier's work more difficult, which can tend to lead to errors, some architects tie opening numbers to room numbers because the method is quick and simple to use.

Using opening codes, however, as we mentioned earlier, is a bad idea. Using opening codes is questionable even on projects with all new construction. Codes are difficult to use and can cause many problems on projects where existing construction plays a part, because of the large number of variables involved.

The schedule's "Location" column is there to head off difficulties that contractors and door, frame, and hardware suppliers and installers face when the key-side location is unclear or when they cannot determine from the drawings which side of a frame is to receive the loose stops. Figure 6-21 includes a note describing the use of the "Location" column.

Some scheduled openings do not show on the new-work floor plan (Figure 5-3), which may appear to violate the suggestion in the paragraph titled "Tips On Generating Door Schedules" to schedule doors that show on the drawings. It actually does not violate the rule, because the contract documents would include the entire floor plan for the library and not just the portion shown in Figure 5-3.

Conversely, since only enough doors and frames are scheduled to show the method, some doors and frames which show on Figure 5-3 are not scheduled.

Frame head and jamb details keys (1/6-20) in the schedule refer to figures in this book. The number (6-20) to the right of the slash (/) is the figure number. The number (1) to the left of the slash (/) is the detail number in that figure. On an actual project, use the numbers of the applicable details. Since this book includes only sufficient details to demonstrate the method, some of the details keyed in the schedule do not exist. Nonexistent details have 13-1 to the right of the slash.

Tips for Generating Door Schedules

Include both existing and new doors in a single schedule.

Refer to the example (Figures 6-15 through 6-21) for additional guidance in filling out the form in Figure 6-22.

Most abbreviations in the Door and Frame Schedule Legend (Figure 6-15) are the same as the abbreviations listed in Chapter 3. A few additional abbreviations

have been added, however, to cover conditions that apply only to the schedules. Place the Door and Frame Schedule Legend on the drawings near the
Door and Frame Schedule, even though most of the abbreviations used are
already included in the abbreviations list applicable to the entire project.
Otherwise, individuals referring to the schedules will need to spend a lot of
effort flipping back and forth in the drawings set. The problem, of course, is
that they will not bother to do so. They will, instead, rely on memory, which
could result in errors that could otherwise be avoided.

Some abbreviations listed in the Door and Frame Schedule Legend (Figure 6-15)
do not occur in the example schedule so that the list will better represent
abbreviations that might occur on other projects. The list does not, however, include every abbreviation needed for all door and frame schedules.
Add items as necessary for each particular project. The list for a particular
project should include every abbreviation used in that project's frame and
door schedule and none that are not used.

Number on the demolition plans and list in the Door and Frame Schedule all
openings where the door or frame is to be removed. Include those to be
discarded and those to be reinstalled in a different location. Do not give
existing (X prefix) numbers on the demolition plans to doors or frames to
remain undisturbed except for refinishing. Prefix with an "X" (X101) the
numbers assigned to doors or frames that are to be removed and discarded
or relocated to show that the doors and frames so labeled are existing items
requiring action by the contractor. Listing doors and frames that are to be
removed and discarded is clearer than noting removal on the drawings and
is apparent in the schedule even to persons who do not need to look at the
demolition drawings. Listing the old number and location for doors and
frames that are to be relocated as well as the new number and location helps
avoid errors caused by lack of coordination between demolition drawings
and new-work drawings. A typical example is that of telling the contractor
on the demolition drawing to salvage a particular door for reuse and then
scheduling a new door for that location.

Number on the new-work plans and include in the Door and Frame Schedule
every door and frame that shows on any new-work drawing. Include doors
and frames in spaces where architectural work occurs as well as doors and
frames occurring in spaces where structural, mechanical, plumbing, electrical, or other nonarchitectural work occurs, even where there is no architectural work. It is difficult to determine where work will lap over into adjacent
spaces due to unforeseen conditions. An exception to this rule might be
spaces shown merely to complete a plan when the contractor has been
explicitly denied access to those spaces, but the better way is to omit those
spaces from the new-work drawings. Numbering and listing every door that
shows, even when that door and frame are to remain unaltered, eliminates
confusion and makes it absolutely clear at a glance whether work is required
on a particular door or frame.

Develop a new set of door numbers. Trying to work the required new numbers
into the system used on the original working drawings accomplishes nothing
useful and is not worth the effort.

Do not reproduce the original door schedule. Much of the data it contains will be
inaccurate and much of it is superfluous for the new work. The effort needed
to correct it is better spent elsewhere. Instead, verify the characteristics of
every existing door in the field and generate a new schedule that includes
only the pertinent data.

Use nominal door opening sizes. "Qty" (Quantity) defines the number of doors of the size listed that occur in the opening scheduled. If more than one door opening occurs in the same frame, use a separate number for each door opening, fill in the frame data in the row with the first door, and cross-reference the frame in the row with the second number. Do not fill in frame data more than once for the same frame.

The same principle holds for doors or frames that are to be relocated. Show pertinent characteristics only once to avoid duplication and copying errors.

Where several glazed frames of the same configuration but different sizes occur, either (1) Draw duplicate frame elevations for each size and give each a separate frame type designation; (2) add multiple dimension rows to a single elevation and give each dimension string a new frame type designation; or (3) add "Width" and "Height" columns to the schedule under "Frame."

Door elevation types shown in Figure 6-18 are those recommended by the Steel Door Institute and shown for years in industry standard publications such as *Architectural Graphic Standards.*

DOOR AND FRAME SCHEDULE LEGEND

ALUM	=	Aluminum	PL	=	Plastic laminate
CA	=	Carpet accessory	PT	=	Paint
Config	=	Configuration	Qty	=	Quantity
Const	=	Construction	RH	=	Right hand
Elev	=	Elevation	SC	=	Solid core
Ent	=	Entrance	SCH	=	Schedule
Fin	=	Finish	Thk	=	Thickness
HC	=	Hollow core	UNK	=	Unknown
HDWD	=	Hardwood	WD	=	Wood
HM	=	Hollow metal	WK	=	Work
HW	=	Hardware	X	=	Existing when used alone, or as a code prefix (XPT), or as a schedule column head
KAL	=	Kalamein			
LH	=	Left hand			
MAR	=	Marble			
Mat	=	Material			
ME	=	Match existing			
MC	=	Mineral core			
NA	=	Not applicable	XNC	=	Existing, make no changes
NAT	=	Natural			
ND	=	No detail has been drawn	*	=	Refer to note marked * in "Remarks" column
NS	=	No substitutions			
NW	=	No work required			

Figure 6-15. Door and Frame Schedule Legend.

DOOR AND FRAME SCHEDULE

Opening Number	Location	Qty	Width	Height	Thk	X	New	Mat.	Gage	Elev.	Jamb	Head	LH Jamb	RH Jamb	Head	Fin.	High	Low
			Door Opening Size					Frame			Config.		Installation Details				Glazing Type	
X101	Exterior	*	*	*	*	X		ALUM	*	*	*	*	*	*	*	*	*	*
X102/X103	X Vestibule	1	3'-0"	6'-8"	1-3/4"	X		HM	UNK	A	E1	A1	1/6-20	1/6-20	2/6-20	XPT	NA	NA
X104	X Vestibule	1	3'-0"	6'-8"	1-3/4"	X		HM	UNK	A	E1	A1	1/6-20	1/6-20	2/6-20	XPT	NA	NA
X105	X Receiving	1	3'-0"	6'-8"	1-3/4"	X		HM	UNK	A	E1	A1	1/6-20	1/6-20	2/6-20	XPT	NA	NA
X106	X Reading Room	1	3'-0"	6'-8"	1-3/4"	X		HM	UNK	A	E1	A1	1/6-20	1/6-20	2/6-20	XPT	NA	NA
X107	Exterior	1	3'-0"	6'-8"	1-3/4"	X		HM	UNK	A	F2	B2	1/13-1	2/13-1	6/6-20	XPT	NA	NA
101	Exterior	*	*	*	*		o	ALUM	*	*	*	*	*	*	*	*	*	*
102	Vestibule 107	2	3'-0"	7'-0"	1-3/4"		o	HM	14	B	E1	A1	3/13-1	5/6-20	4/13-1	PT	GL-1	GL-3
103	Vestibule 107	*	*	*	*	X		*	*	*	*	*	3/6-20	3/6-20	4/6-20	PT	NA	NA
104	Receiving 105	*	*	*	*	X		*	*	*	*	*	1/6-20	1/6-20	2/6-20	PT	NA	NA
105/107	See floor plan	1	3'-0"	6'-8"	1-3/4"	X		HM	UNK	A	E1	A1	ND	ND	ND	PT	NA	NA
108	Exterior	1	3'-0"	6'-8"	1-3/4"	X		HM	UNK	A	F2	B2	2/13-1	1/13-1	6/6-20	PT	NA	NA
109	Exterior	*	*	*	*	X		*	*	*	*	*	*	*	*	PT	NA	NA
110	Reading Room 101	*	*	*	*	X		*	*	*	*	*	*	*	*	PT	NA	NA
111	Vestibule 113	1	3'-0"	6'-8"	1-3/4"		o	HM	16	A	E1	A1	1/6-20	1/6-20	2/6-20	PT	NA	NA
112	Vestibule 114	1	3'-0"	6'-8"	1-3/4"		o	HM	16	A	E1	A1	1/6-20	1/6-20	2/6-20	PT	NA	NA

First Floor

Figure 6-16A. Left half of example Door and Frame Schedule.

X	New	Doors Mat.	Doors Gage Const	Doors Elev.	Doors Fin.	Glazing Type	Louvers Fresh Air (sq. ft.)	Louvers Fin.	Fire Rating UL Label	Fire Rating Label Const	Under Cut	Sill	HW Set No.	Remarks
X		ALUM	*	*	*	*	None	NA	None	None	*	*	*	*See Alum Ent & Storefront Sch
X		WD	SC	F	XPT	None	None	NA	None	C	1"	MAR	X	(1)
X		WD	SC	F	XPT	None	None	NA	None	C	None	None	X	(2)
X		WD	SC	L	XPT	None	X1.0	XPT	B-1hr	None	None	None	X2	(3)
X		WD	SC	N	XPT	XGL-1	None	NA	None	None	None	None	X3	(4)
X		HM	XNC	N	XPT	XGL-1	None	NA	None	None	None	XALUM	X4	(5)
	o	ALUM	*	*	*	*	None	NA	None	None	None	*	*	*See Alum Ent & Storefront Sch
	o	HM	14	FG	PT	GL-3	None	NA	None	None	None	CA	2	
X		*	*	*	PT	*	*	*	*	*	*	CA	3	*See X104 (6)
X		*	*	*	PT	*	*	PT	*	*	*	CA	*	*See X105 (7)(8)
X		WD	SC	F	PT	None	None	NA	None	None	None	None	XNC	(9)
X		HM	XNC	N	PT	XGL-1	None	NA	None	None	None	XNC	XNC	(9)
X		*	*	*	PT	XNC	*	*	*	*	*	*	*	*See X107 (10)
X		*	*	*	PT	XNC	*	*	*	*	*	*	*	*See X106 (11)
	o	WD	SC	L	PT	None	1.0	PT	None	None	None	MAR	4	(7)
	o	WD	SC	L	PT	None	1.0	PT	None	None	None	MAR	4	(7)

Figure 6-16B. Right half of example Door and Frame Schedule.

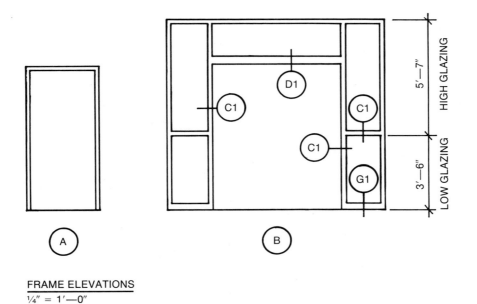

<u>FRAME ELEVATIONS</u>
¼″ = 1′—0″

Figure 6-17. Frame elevations.

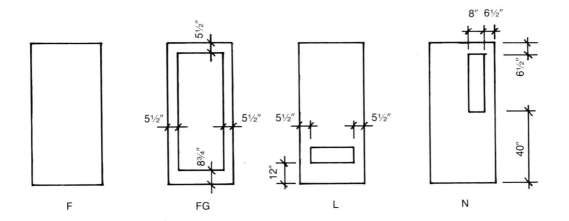

<u>DOOR ELEVATIONS</u>
¼″ = 1′—0″

Figure 6-18. Door elevations.

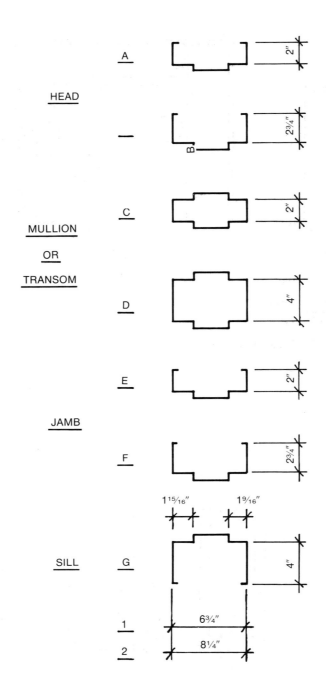

HEAD

MULLION

OR

TRANSOM

JAMB

SILL

FRAME CONFIGURATIONS
$1\frac{1}{2}'' = 1'—0''$

Figure 6-19. Frame configurations.

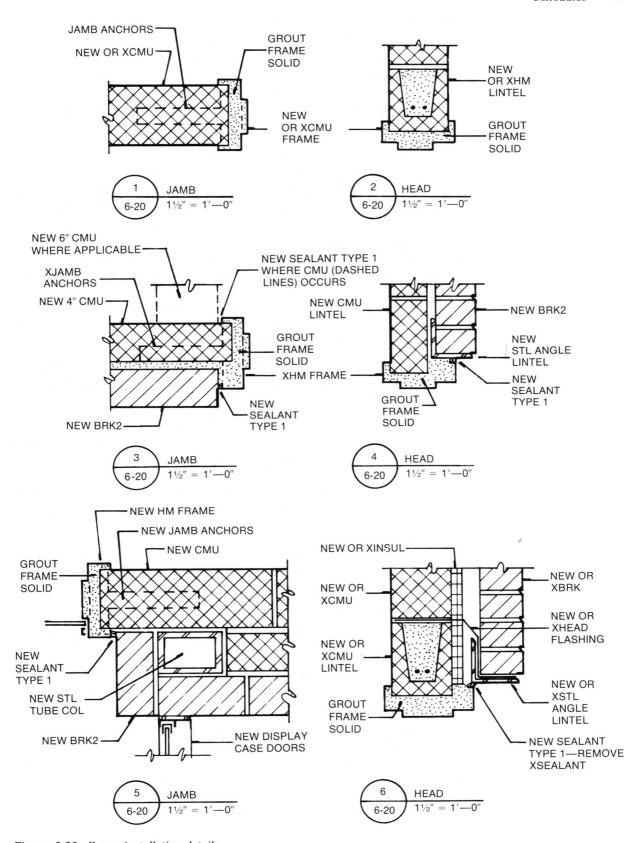

Figure 6-20. Frame installation details.

DOOR AND FRAME SCHEDULE NOTES

1. Data shown for existing doors and frames were taken from original documents for the existing building as prepared by (fill in architect's name) and dated (fill in date), and verified in the field.
2. Refer to demolition floor plans for location of existing doors and frames to be relocated or removed and discarded.
3. Spaces indicated in "Location" column are security side. Security side is defined as key side on doors with locks and side from which glazing cannot be removed (fixed stops side) on glazed doors and frames. Where security is not a requirement and doors and frames are not glazed, location shown is space into which door swings.
4. When more than one door number is shown in same schedule row (101/106), the slash means "and all door numbers that follow up to and including."
5. Unless specifically noted as existing (X), scheduled finishes are new. Refer to New Finishes Schedule and New Finish Material and Color Code Schedule for additional requirements, including colors.
6. Unless specifically noted as existing (X), scheduled glazing types are new. Refer to Glazing Schedule for description of glazing types.
7. When more than one glazing type is scheduled, refer to frame elevation for extent of each type.
8. Unless marked as existing (X), items in the following columns are new: "Fin;" "Louvers;" "Undercut," "Sill;" and "HW Set No."
9. On existing doors and frames, all items are existing unless noted otherwise.
10. On new doors and frames, all items are new unless noted otherwise.
11. Left- and right-hand door and frame conditions are determined as viewed from side of door listed in "Location" column.

NUMBERED REMARKS

⟨1⟩ Remove existing door, hardware, and threshold and discard.

⟨2⟩ Remove existing door, frame, and hardware. Discard hardware. Salvage door and frame for relocation in Opening Number 103.

⟨3⟩ Remove existing door, frame, and hardware and salvage for relocation in Opening Number 104.

⟨4⟩ Remove existing door, frame, and hardware and salvage for relocation in Opening Number 110.

Figure 6-21. Door and Frame Schedule Notes and Numbered Remarks.

⟨5⟩ Remove existing door, frame, hardware, and threshold and salvage for relocation in Opening Number 109.

⟨6⟩ Prepare existing door and frame from Opening Number X104 to receive new hardware and install in new opening.

⟨7⟩ Paint louver to match door.

⟨8⟩ Install existing frame, door, and hardware from Opening Number X105 in new opening.

⟨9⟩ Existing frame, door, and hardware. Do not disturb except to repaint.

⟨10⟩ Install existing frame, door, and hardware from Opening Number X107 in new opening.

⟨11⟩ Install existing frame, door, and hardware from Opening Number X106 in new opening.

DOOR AND FRAME SCHEDULE

Opening Number	Location	Door Opening Size			Frame									
		Qty	Width	Height	Thk	X New	Mat.	Gage	Elev.	Config.		Installation Details			Fin.	Glazing Type	
										Jamb	Head	LH Jamb	RH Jamb	Head		High	Low

Doors						Louvers		Fire Rating		Under Cut	Sill	HW Set No.	Remarks
X New	Mat.	Gage Const	Elev.	Fin.	Glazing Type	Fresh Air (sq. ft.)	Fin.	UL Label	Label Const				

Figure 6-22. Right and left halves of blank form for Door and Frame Schedule.

Windows

Architects seldom attempt to indicate window requirements directly on plans or elevations, preferring instead to identify each window using a code mark on the plans and elevations and show their detailed requirements in a single central location. Sometimes the vehicle for listing those requirements is a schedule. More often it consists of a series of drawings showing the window types. In this part of the book we will discuss the advantages and disadvantages of using drawings to convey window requirements on projects where existing construction plays a part and recommend a true schedule that works well for such projects.

Probably the most prevalent procedure for indicating window requirements today does not involve using a schedule at all. This procedure consists of drawing an elevation of each window type and noting the requirements for that type directly on the elevations. Using drawings to convey window requirements works for most projects, especially for very small projects and projects where most of the windows are of a single type, and most especially when all the construction is new.

Window requirements for most all-new-work projects are simple and repetitive. The number of special conditions are few. The number of window types and sizes are also few. With little information to show, a single elevation of each window type, even at a scale of ¼ inch to the foot, is adequate to show all the information required. Even on projects where varying conditions make more requirements necessary, it is usually adequate to simply add a few more window types, generating another elevation or two.

Using drawings to convey window requirements also works, though not as well, for small, simple projects where existing construction is involved. That method could be made to work for projects of the scope and complexity of our example library. But for larger and more complex projects where existing construction plays a major part, the number of conditions grows to such an extent that indicating window requirements without some sort of schedule becomes cumbersome. Even for our example library, conveying window requirements using drawings alone would require more elevations and more notes and would result in cluttered, hard to read drawings. Worst of all, working without a schedule makes it much more difficult to develop and record the requirements. In fact, it is often necessary to schedule the information in some form just to keep it straight. And the window manufacturer will have the same problem. It makes the most sense to go ahead and include the schedule in the documents.

Window Schedules

In a window schedule, list the code (here called a mark) identifying each window or window type in the schedule. Place each mark in a separate row. In the same row, in a separate column for each characteristic, show all the characteristics of each window, or group of windows, represented by the mark heading that row. Except where each window has a distinctive mark, make no attempt to list the windows consecutively or to relate the codes identifying them to the spaces in which the windows occur.

The schedule illustrated by Figures 6-23 through 6-26, which follow these explanations, works well for projects with existing construction involvement. The example schedule is incomplete without all the parts contained in Figures 6-23 through 6-25, and requires some drawings as well.

Figure 6-23 is a legend listing abbreviations used in the window schedule.

Figures 6-24A and 6-24B constitute a combined existing and new window schedule for our hypothetical library using the blank form in Figure 6-26.

Figure 6-25 is a list of notes and numbered remarks to accompany the example schedule.

Figure 6-26 is the blank form used in the example.

Window Schedule Blank Form

The Window Schedule blank form (Figure 6-26) is effective only when accompanied by a Window Schedule Legend similar to those in Figure 6-23, notes and numbered remarks similar to those in Figure 6-25, and window elevations and detailed drawings.

The first column in the form is blank. Use it to denote the location of windows within a building (first floor, second floor, etc.) or buildings within a project (Library, Gymnasium, etc.). Add more columns at the beginning of the schedule to separate building phases or other subdivisions as necessary for clarity.

General subjects are sometimes subdivided to permit display of needed data. Which data a window schedule should contain is somewhat controversial. There is no attempt here to enter that controversy. Our intent is to suggest a method for handling existing conditions, not to persuade anyone to change office practices regarding which information to list in window schedules.

Example

Few architects would give each individual window a separate and distinct mark when using drawings to convey window requirements for projects where all the work was new, because it would increase the work considerably for little or no gain. The same is generally, but not always, true when existing windows occur in a project.

Some projects are so complex that the work required related to each window is really different from all others. An historic preservation project, for example, might have varying types and degrees of damage to its wood windows. The windows might have been handmade and thus be all different in size. Some might have the original hardware. Others might have replacement hardware. When the differences are many, an architect might want to give each window a separate mark.

Weigh whether to use window types or to number each window separately against the time involved in developing the schedule and the time involved in checking the shop drawings. Schedules using window types take less time to develop, but such schedules require more time of a shop drawing checker. The problem is similar to, though not nearly as severe as, that for door and frame schedules.

Much of the time, however, using window types is adequate. In our example, we have used types. Our schedule would otherwise be the same if each window had a distinctive mark.

We have chosen alphanumeric window marks for our example, but marks used to identify window types may be alphabetic, numeric, or alphanumeric.

Window marks are usually written on the building elevations adjacent to, or within, the window, but may also be placed on the floor plans. In our example, the marks are shown on both plans and elevations. The mark is usually placed inside a symbol, such as an ellipse, as they are in our example.

Many of our scheduled windows do not show on the new-work floor plan (Figure 5-3), which may appear to violate the suggestion in the "Tips On Generating Window Schedules" section, which suggests scheduling windows that show on the drawings. It actually does not violate the rule because the contract documents would include the entire floor plan and all the elevations for the library and not just the portion shown in Figure 5-3, which is restricted by book page size.

Installation detail keys (1/5-11) in the schedule refer to figures in this book. The number (5-11) to the right of the slash (/) is the figure number. The number (1) to the left of the slash is the detail number in that figure. On an actual project, use the numbers of the appropriate details shown on the drawings. Since this book contains details sufficient only to demonstrate methods, many details keyed in the schedule do not exist. All nonexistent details have 14-1 to the right of the slash.

Tips For Generating Window Schedules

Include both existing and new windows in a single schedule.

Refer to the example (Figures 6-23 through 6-26) for additional guidance in filling out the form in Figure 6-26.

Most abbreviations in the Window Schedule Legend (Figure 6-23) are the same as the abbreviations listed in Figure 3-1. A few additional abbreviations have been added, however, to cover conditions that apply only to the schedules. Place the Window Schedule Legend on the drawings near the Window Schedule, even though most of the abbreviations used are already included in the abbreviations list applicable to the entire project. Otherwise, people referring to the schedules must spend a lot of time flipping back and forth in the drawings set. The problem, of course, is that they will not bother to do so. They will, instead, rely on memory, which could result in errors that might otherwise be avoided.

Some abbreviations not used in the sample schedule are listed in the Window Schedule Legend (Figure 6-23) so that the list will better represent abbreviations that might occur on other projects. The list does not, however, include every abbreviation needed for all window schedules. Add items as necessary for each particular project. The list for a particular project should include every abbreviation used in that project's window schedule and none that are not used.

Number on the demolition plans and elevations and list in the Window Schedule all windows that are to be removed. Include those that are to be discarded and those that are to be reinstalled in a different location. Do not give existing (X prefix) numbers on the demolition plans or elevations to windows to remain undisturbed except for refinishing. Prefix with an "X" (XW-1) the numbers assigned to windows which are to be removed and discarded or relocated to show that they are existing items requiring action by the contractor. Listing windows that are to be removed and discarded is clearer than noting removal on the drawings and is apparent in the schedules even to those who have no need to look at the demolition drawings. Listing the old number and location for windows that are to be relocated and the new number and location helps avoid coordination errors between demolition drawings and new-work drawings. A typical example is that of telling the contractor on the demolition drawing to salvage a particular window for reuse and then scheduling a new window for that location.

Number on the new-work drawings and include in the window schedule every window that shows on a new-work drawing. Include windows in spaces where architectural work occurs and windows in spaces where structural, mechanical, plumbing, electrical, or other nonarchitectural work occur, even where there is no architectural work. It is difficult to determine where work will lap over into adjacent spaces due to unforeseen conditions. An exception to this rule might be spaces shown merely to complete a plan when the contractor has been explicitly denied access to those spaces, but the better way is to omit those spaces from the new-work drawings. Numbering and listing every window that shows, even when that window is to remain unaltered, eliminates confusion and makes it absolutely clear at a glance whether work is required on a particular window.

Develop a new set of window marks. Trying to work the required new marks into the system used on the original working drawings accomplishes nothing useful and is not worth the effort.

Do not reproduce the original window schedule. Much of the data it contains will be inaccurate and much of it is superfluous for the new work. The effort needed to correct it is better spent elsewhere. Instead, verify the characteristics of every existing window in the field and generate a new schedule including only the pertinent data.

Do not repeat data. For windows to be relocated, show pertinent characteristics only once to avoid duplication and copying errors.

Be sure that all windows with the same type mark are actually identical in every characteristic.

Draw window elevations and configuration and installation details as necessary to convey all requirements. Use techniques shown earlier in this chapter for doors and frames.

```
                    WINDOW SCHEDULE LEGEND
```

ALUM	= Aluminum	RH	= Right hand
BE	= Baked enamel	SD	= See detail
Elev	= Elevation	STL	= Steel
Fin	= Finish	UNK	= Unknown
FL	= Fluorocarbon	WD	= Wood
GL	= Glazing Type	X	= Existing when
HDWD	= Hardwood		used alone, or
LH	= Left hand		as a code or
Mat	= Material		abbreviation
ME	= Match existing		prefix (XW-1
NA	= Not applicable		or XGL-1), or
NAT	= Natural		as a schedule
ND	= No detail has		column head
	been drawn	XNC	= Existing, make
NS	= No		no changes
	substitutions	*	= Refer to note
NW	= No work		marked * in
	required		"Remarks"
PT	= Paint		column

Figure 6-23. Window Schedule Legend.

WINDOW SCHEDULE

Mark	Type	X	New	Mat.	Fin.	Manufacturer		
						Name	Product	Cat No.
XW-1	Combination	X		Alum	X	Harvey's	Bettermade	ALC45
XW-2	Combination	X		Alum	X	Harvey's	Bettermade	ALC45
XW-3	Combination	X		Alum	PT	Harvey's	Bettermade	ALC45
XW-4	Combination	X		Alum	PT	Harvey's	Bettermade	ALC45
XW-5	Combination	X		Alum	X	Harvey's	Bettermade	ALC45
XW-6	Awning	X		Alum	PT	Harvey's	Bettermade	ALA34
XW-7	Awning	X		Alum	PT	Harvey's	Bettermade	ALA34
XW-8	Awning	X		Alum	PT	Harvey's	Bettermade	ALA34
W-1	Combination		o	Alum	BE	Harvey's Son's	Bestmade	HBC45
W-2	Awning		o	STL	BE	B. Jones, Inc.	Oldways	AW314
W-3	Awning		o	STL	BE	B. Jones, Inc.	Oldways	AW314
W-4	Awning		o	STL	BE	B. Jones, Inc.	Oldways	AW314
W-5	Fixed		o	Alum	BE	Harvey's Son's	Bestmade	FIX42
W-6	Fixed		o	WD	PT	Custom Sash Co.	Circles	CSC42

Figure 6-24A. Left half of example Window Schedule.

Elev	Size			Installation Details				Glazing Type	Remarks
	Width	Height	Depth	Sill	LH Jamb	RH Jamb	Head		
A	4'–3"	5'–3"	1–5/8"	1/5–11	1/14–1	2/14–1	1/5–8	XGL–3	①
A	3'–6"	5'–3"	1–5/8"	1/5–11	1/14–1	2/14–1	1/5–8	XGL–3	①
A	4'–3"	5'–3"	1–5/8"	1/5–11	1/14–1	2/14–1	1/5–8	GL–7	② ③
A	4'–3"	5'–3"	1–5/8"	1/5–11	1/14–1	2/14–1	1/5–8	GL–7	② ③
A	3'–6"	5'–3"	1–5/8"	1/5–11	1/14–1	2/14–1	1/5–8	GL–7	② ③
B	3'–1"	3'–11"	1–5/8"	3/14–1	4/14–1	5/14–1	6/14–1	GL–7	② ③ ④
B	3'–1"	3'–11"	1–5/8"	3/14–1	4/14–1	4/14–1	6/14–1	GL–7	② ③ ④
B	3'–1"	3'–11"	1–5/8"	3/14–1	5/14–1	4/14–1	6/14–1	GL–7	② ③ ④
A	4'–3"	5'–3"	1–5/8"	1/5–12	1/14–1	2/14–1	1/5–10	GL–7	
B	3'–1"	3'–11"	1–5/8"	3/14–1	4/14–1	5/14–1	6/14–1	GL–7	⑤
B	3'–1"	3'–11"	1–5/8"	3/14–1	4/14–1	4/14–1	6/14–1	GL–7	⑤
B	3'–1"	3'–11"	1–5/8"	3/14–1	5/14–1	4/14–1	6/14–1	GL–7	⑤
C	4'–3"	1'–11"	1–5/8"	9/14–1	8/14–1	8/14–1	7/14–1	GL–7	
D	4'–2"	2'–0"	SD	12/14–1	11/14–1	11/14–1	10/14–1	GL–7	

Figure 6-24B. Right half of example Window Schedule.

WINDOW SCHEDULE NOTES

1. Data shown for existing windows were taken from original documents for the existing building as prepared by (fill in architect's name) and dated (fill in date), and verified in the field.
2. Unless specifically indicated otherwise, scheduled products indicate quality standard required, but are not intended to limit competition. Except for products noted "NS" or "no substitutions," approved equal products of approved equal manufacturers will be considered.
3. Unless specifically noted as existing (X), scheduled finishes are new. Refer to New Exterior Finish Material and Color Schedule for additional requirements including colors.
4. Unless specifically noted as existing (X), scheduled glazing types are new. Refer to the Glazing Schedule for description of glazing types.
5. On existing windows, all items are existing unless noted otherwise.
6. On new windows, all items are new unless noted otherwise.
7. Left-hand and right-hand window jamb conditions are determined as viewed from exterior.

NUMBERED REMARKS

⟨1⟩ Remove existing window and discard.

⟨2⟩ Existing window sash and frames are natural anodized aluminum. Clean and paint to match new windows.

⟨3⟩ Existing glass is GL-3. Remove existing glass, clean rebates, and provide scheduled new glazing material.

⟨4⟩ Existing remote geared manual operator for each window bank. Provide four new electric motors (one for each existing hand crank) and convert each existing manual device to function as a motorized operator. Provide remote switches in location indicated.

⟨5⟩ Provide single new remote motorized operator for new bank of windows (marks W-2, W-3, and W-4). Locate switch where indicated.

Figure 6-25. Window Schedule Notes and Numbered Remarks.

WINDOW SCHEDULE

	Mark	Type	X	New	Mat.	Fin.	Manufacturer		
							Name	Product	Cat No.

Elev	Size			Installation Details				Glazing Type	Remarks
	Width	Height	Depth	Sill	LH Jamb	RH Jamb	Head		

Figure 6-26. Right and left halves of blank form for Window Schedule.

Aluminum Entrances and Storefronts

In this book, the term "aluminum entrance" refers to glazed entrance doors and their frames fabricated from extruded or shop-formed aluminum, bronze, or other decorative metal (not steel) sections manufactured by companies who identify their products as aluminum (or other metal) entrances.

In this book, the term "aluminum storefront," or just "storefront," refers to glazed walls framed with aluminum, bronze, or another decorative (not steel) metal sections manufactured by companies who call their product "storefront."

The word "aluminum" is used here for convenience only and does not imply a limit on applicable materials. In an actual project, change aluminum to the name of the metal used.

This book calls glazed entrances and walls constructed of hollow metal (steel) sections "doors and frames" and includes them in the Door and Frame Schedule.

Glazed walls framed with sections identified by their manufacturers as curtain wall components are not aluminum entrances or storefronts. Do not schedule their requirements in an aluminum entrance and storefront schedule. An architect faced with many variables, or many different existing conditions requiring description, might generate a glazed curtain wall schedule similar to the Aluminum Entrance and Storefront Schedule suggested in this book. Only large and complex projects require glazed curtain wall schedules, however. Usually, typical panel elevations and spandrel and other glazing panel schedules keyed to the elevations are sufficient to convey necessary requirements.

Wood-framed glazed walls are also not usually included in entrance and storefront schedules. Depending on the complexity of a project's wood-framed glazed walls and entrances, an architect might develop a schedule for them or simply detail them and show the needed information on the drawings. Projects with wood-framed glazed walls are seldom large enough to present the magnitude of problems aluminum framed walls generate. A glazing schedule for wood-framed glazed walls is, however, necessary. Key the glazing schedule to the building elevations or to typical panel elevations.

There are almost as many systems for listing aluminum entrance and curtain wall requirements in contract documents as there are architectural firms. There seems to be no identifiable "normal" method.

Aluminum entrances and storefronts share characteristics with both doors and their frames and with windows. Often, entrances consist only of doors and their frames, with sidelights and transoms. Occasionally, storefronts include operable windows, but for scheduling purposes, entrances and storefronts are more like doors and frames than they are like windows.

As is true with doors and their frames and with windows, architects seldom show aluminum entrance and storefront requirements directly on plans or elevations. They usually identify each entrance and storefront section using a code mark on the plans and elevations and state their detailed requirements in a single central location. Sometimes the vehicle for listing requirements is a schedule. More often it consists of a series of elevation drawings showing the entrances and storefronts. In this chapter, we will discuss the advantages and disadvantages of using drawings to convey aluminum entrance and storefront requirements on projects where existing construction plays a part and recommend a true schedule that works well for such projects.

Probably the most prevalent procedure for indicating aluminum entrance requirements today is that of scheduling the aluminum entrances in the door and frame schedule. When aluminum entrances are few and not complex, such a method can be satisfactory, particularly when all the work is new.

Unfortunately, the procedures that some architects use for showing aluminum entrance and storefront requirements are inefficient and ineffective. They scatter entrance and storefront requirements haphazardly through the construction documents as if they were sowing grass seed. They might schedule doors in a door and frame schedule and show overall dimensions on storefront elevations, or even on building elevations. Then they scatter details, which are sometimes sketchy and inadequate in number, throughout the drawings in no particular order. They place additional requirements in the specifications. Such methods are poor at best, even when the problems are simple. On projects where existing construction is extensive, such a loosely controlled system can cause havoc in the field.

Entrance and Storefront Schedules

A better way to convey entrance and storefront requirements is to use a schedule. Identify each aluminum entrance and storefront section using a code (here called a mark). List the marks in a schedule with the marks all in the same column but in separate rows. Then, in the same row with each mark, in a series of columns, list the characteristics of the entrance or storefront section listed in that row. Except where each entrance and storefront section has a distinctive mark, do not try to list entrance and storefront sections consecutively or relate the marks to the spaces in which the entrances or storefront sections occur.

The schedule illustrated by Figures 6-27 through 6-30, which follow these explanations, works well for projects with existing construction involvement. The example schedule is incomplete without all the parts contained in Figures 6-27 through 6-29. The example schedule is also incomplete without elevations of each door, entrance, and storefront bank, and the installation details scheduled. The elevations and details are not illustrated in this book, however, since in every case in the example the elevations and details would show only new conditions. Should existing conditions requiring details occur, use the methods suggested in this book for doors and frames.

Figure 6-27 is a legend listing abbreviations used in the entrance and storefront schedule.

Figures 6-28A and 6-28B constitute a combined existing and new Aluminum Entrance and Storefront Schedule for our hypothetical library using the blank form in Figure 6-30.

Figure 6-29 is a list of notes and numbered remarks to accompany the example schedule.

Figure 6-30 is the blank form used in the example.

Aluminum Entrances and Storefront Schedule Blank Form

The Aluminum Entrance and Storefront Schedule blank form (Figure 6-30) is effective only when accompanied by a legend similar to that in Figure 6-27, notes and numbered remarks similar to those in Figure 6-29, door and frame elevations, and installation details.

The first column in the form is blank. Use it to denote the location of entrances and storefront banks within a building (first floor, second floor, etc.) or buildings within a project (Library, Gymnasium, Administration Building, etc.). Add more columns at the beginning of the schedule to separate building phases or other subdivisions as necessary for clarity.

General subjects are sometimes subdivided to permit display of needed data. Which data to include in entrance and storefront schedules is somewhat controversial. There is no attempt here to enter that controversy. Our intent is to suggest a method for handling existing conditions, not to persuade anyone to change office practices regarding which information to include in entrance and storefront schedules.

Example

Few architects would give each individual storefront panel a separate and distinct mark for scheduling purposes for new projects, because it would increase the work considerably for little or no gain. The same is generally, but not always, true when existing entrances or storefront work occurs in a project.

Some projects are so complex that the work related to each entrance or storefront section is really different from all others. When such is the case, an architect might want to give each entrance and storefront section a separate mark. The decision relates to the number of different marks to use. Many projects require only a few marks, but in any case, an architect should use a separate mark for each condition that cannot be described in the schedule. Including information in the schedule reduces the number of separate marks and therefore the work of drawing separate elevations for each mark or keying different marks to the same elevation, which clutters up the drawings and makes them hard to read. Regardless of the number of marks used, the schedule should otherwise be the same.

We have chosen alphanumeric marks for our example, but marks used to identify entrance and storefront section types may be alphabetic, numeric, or alphanumeric.

Entrance and storefront marks are usually written on the building elevations adjacent to, or within, the entrance or storefront section, but may also be placed on the floor plans. In our example, the marks are on the plans. The marks are usually placed inside a symbol such as an ellipse, as in our example.

The main entrance door in our example has a door number (101) and an entrance and storefront mark (S-1). The purpose is to make clear to the steel door and frame supplier the extent of that supplier's work. Every door in the project appears in the Door and Frame Schedule, but the requirements for the aluminum entrance door and its frame show in the Aluminum Entrance and Storefront Schedule (Figures 6-28A and 6-28B) and are cross-referenced in the Door and Frame Schedule (Figures 6-16A and 6-16B).

Elevations and installation details keyed in the Aluminum Entrance and Storefront Schedule have not been drawn in this book, because they are all new conditions. The purpose of including details in this book is to suggest methods of showing the interface between existing and new conditions. Including details of entirely new conditions would serve no useful purpose. On an actual project, use the numbers for details shown in the drawings.

Tips for Generating Aluminum Entrance and Storefront Schedules

Include both existing and new aluminum entrances and storefront sections in a single schedule.

Refer to the example (Figures 6-27 through 6-29) for additional guidance in filling out the form in Figure 6-30.

Most abbreviations in the Aluminum Entrance and Storefront Schedule Legend (Figure 6-27) are the same as the abbreviations listed in Figure 3-1. A few additional abbreviations have been added, however, to cover conditions that apply only to the schedules. Place the Aluminum Entrances and Storefront Schedule Legend on the drawings near the Aluminum Entrance and Storefront Schedule, even though most of the abbreviations used are already included in the abbreviations list applicable to the entire project. Otherwise, people referring to the schedules will have to spend a lot of effort flipping back and forth in the drawings set. The problem, of course, is that they will not bother to do so. They will, instead, rely on memory, which could result in errors that could otherwise be avoided.

Some abbreviations not used in the sample schedule are listed in the Aluminum Entrance and Storefront Schedule Legend (Figure 6-27) so that the list will better represent abbreviations that might occur on other projects. The list does not, however, include every abbreviation needed for all entrance and storefront schedules. Add items as necessary for each particular project. The list for a particular project should include every abbreviation used in that project's entrance and storefront schedule and none that are not used.

Number on the demolition plans and elevations and list in the Aluminum Entrance and Storefront Schedule all entrances and storefront sections that are to be removed. Include those to be discarded and those that are to be reinstalled in a different location. Do not give existing (X prefix) numbers on the demolition plans or elevations to entrances or storefront sections that are to remain undisturbed except for refinishing. Prefix with an "X" (XS-1) the numbers assigned to entrances and storefronts which are to be removed and discarded or relocated to show that the entrances and storefront sections so labeled are existing items requiring action by the contractor. Listing entrances and storefront sections that are to be removed and discarded is clearer than noting removal on the drawings and is apparent in the schedules even to those who have no need to look at the demolition drawings. Listing the old number and location for entrances and storefronts that are to be relocated and the new number and location helps avoid errors caused by lack of coordination between demolition drawings and new-work drawings.

Number on the demolition drawings and include in the entrance and storefront schedule every entrance and storefront which shows on any new-work drawing. Numbering and listing every entrance and storefront that shows, even when that entrance or storefront is to remain unaltered, eliminates confusion and makes it absolutely clear at a glance whether work is required related to a particular entrance or storefront.

Develop a new set of entrance and storefront marks. Trying to work the required new marks into the system used on the original working drawings accomplishes nothing useful and is not worth the effort.

Do not reproduce the original entrance and storefront schedule. Much of the data it contains will be inaccurate and much of it is superfluous for the new work. The effort needed to correct it is better spent elsewhere. Instead, verify the characteristics of every existing entrance and storefront section in the field and generate a new schedule that includes only the pertinent data.

Use nominal door opening sizes. "Qty" (Quantity) defines the number of doors of the size listed that occur in the opening scheduled. If more than one door opening occurs in the same frame, use a separate number for each door, fill in the frame data in the row with the first door and, cross-reference the frame in the row with the second number. Do not repeat data.

The same principle holds for entrances and storefronts that are to be relocated. Show pertinent characteristics only once to avoid duplication and copying errors.

Be sure that all entrance and storefront sections with the same type mark are actually identical in every way.

Draw aluminum entrance and storefront elevations and configuration and installation details as necessary to convey all requirements. Use techniques shown earlier in this chapter for doors and frames.

ALUMINUM ENTRANCE AND STOREFRONT SCHEDULE LEGEND

ALUM	= Aluminum	SD	=	See detail
BE	= Baked enamel	UNK	=	Unknown
Elev	= Elevation	X	=	Existing when used alone, or as a code or abbreviation prefix (XS-1 or XGL-4), or as a schedule column head
Fin	= Finish			
FL	= Fluorocarbon			
GL	= Glazing type			
LH	= Left hand			
Mat	= Material			
ME	= Match existing			
NA	= Not applicable			
ND	= No detail has been drawn	XNC	=	Existing, make no changes
NS	= No substitutions	*	=	Refer to note marked * in "Remarks" column
NW	= No work required			
RH	= Right hand			

Figure 6-27. Aluminum Entrance and Storefront Schedule Legend.

ALUMINUM ENTRANCE AND STOREFRONT SCHEDULE

Mark	X	New	Mat.	Fin.	Manufacturer Name	Product	Cat No.	Elev.	Glazing Type High	Glazing Type Low	Width	Height	Depth
											\multicolumn{3}{c}{Overall Frame Size}		
XS-1	X		ALUM	X	Unknown	Unknown	Unknown	ND	XGL-4	XGL-4	10'-8"	9'-1"	4-1/2"
S-1		o	ALUM	FL	Breaker Corp	Stickline	BCS412	A	GL-5	GL-6	10'-0"	14'-5"	4-1/2"
S-2		o	ALUM	FL	Breaker Corp	Stickline	BCS412	B	GL-5	NA	9'-5"	5'-2"	4-1/2"
S-3		o	ALUM	FL	Breaker Corp	Stickline	BCS412	C	GL-5	GL-6	3'-4"	8'-0"	4-1/2"
S-4		o	ALUM	FL	Breaker Corp	Stickline	BCS412	B	GL-5	GL-6	11'-0"	8'-0"	4-1/2"

Installation Details Sill	LH Jamb	RH Jamb	Head	Opening Number	X	New	Mat.	Fin.	Manufacturer Name	Product	Cat No.
ND	ND	ND	ND	X101	X		ALUM	XNW	Unknown	Unknown	Unknown
1/15-1	2/15-1	2/15-1	3/15-1	101		o	ALUM	FL	Breaker Corp	Highline	BCH9
4/15-1	5/15-1	5/15-1	6/15-1	None	None		NA	NA	NA	NA	NA
7/15-1	8/15-1	9/15-1	6/15-1	None	None		NA	NA	NA	NA	NA
7/15-1	9/15-1	8/15-1	6/15-1	None	None		NA	NA	NA	NA	NA

Figure 6-28A. Left and center one-thirds of example Aluminum Entrance and Storefront Schedule.

Elev.	Glazing Type	Qty	Width	Height	Sill	HW Set No.	Remarks
		\multicolumn{3}{c}{Door Opening Size}				
ND	XGL-2	2	3'-0"	7'-0"	XALUM	XNW	①
D1	GL-5	2	3'-0"	7'-0"	ALUM	S1	
NA	NA	NA	NA	NA	NA	NA	
NA	NA	NA	NA	NA	NA	NA	
NA	NA	NA	NA	NA	NA	NA	

Figure 6-28B. Right one-third of example Aluminum Entrance and Storefront Schedule.

ALUMINUM ENTRANCE AND STOREFRONT SCHEDULE NOTES

1. Data shown for existing aluminum entrances and storefront sections were taken from original documents for the existing building as prepared by (fill in architect's name) and dated (fill in date), and verified in the field.
2. Refer to demolition floor plans for location of existing aluminum entrances and storefront sections to be relocated or removed and discarded.
3. Unless specifically indicated otherwise, scheduled products indicate quality standard required, but are not intended to limit competition. Except for products noted "NS" or "no substitutions," approved equal products of approved equal manufacturers will be considered.
4. Unless specifically noted as existing (X), scheduled finishes are new. Refer to New Exterior Finish Material and Color Schedule for additional requirements including colors.
5. Unless specifically noted as existing (X), scheduled glazing types are new. Refer to the Glazing Schedule for description of glazing types.
6. Where more than one glazing type is scheduled, refer to frame type elevation for locations.
7. On existing aluminum entrances and storefront sections, all items are existing unless noted otherwise.
8. On new aluminum entrances and storefront sections, all items are new unless noted otherwise.
9. Left-hand and right-hand aluminum entrances and storefront jamb conditions are determined as viewed from exterior.

NUMBERED REMARKS

⟨1⟩ Remove existing aluminum door, hardware, threshold, glazing, and storefront framing and discard.

Figure 6-29. Aluminum Entrance and Storefront Schedule Notes and Numbered Remarks.

ALUMINUM ENTRANCE AND STOREFRONT SCHEDULE

Mark	X	New	Mat.	Fin.	Frame				Elev.	Glazing Type		Overall Frame Size		
					Manufacturer					High	Low	Width	Height	Depth
					Name	Product	Cat No.							

Installation Details				Opening Number	X	New	Mat.	Fin.	Doors		
									Manufacturer		
Sill	LH Jamb	RH Jamb	Head						Name	Product	Cat No.

Elev.	Glazing Type	Door Opening Size			Sill	HW Set No.	Remarks
		Qty	Width	Height			

Figure 6-30. Left, center, and right one-thirds of blank form for Aluminum Entrance and Storefront Schedule.

Glazing

Too often, architects say little on their drawings about glazing, relying on the specifications to state not only installation methods and material types but also glazing locations. Not only does indicating locations in the specifications violate the generally accepted wisdom of the day, the practice can also result in confusion and overlooked conditions, especially on projects with existing construction involvement. The methods presented in this book are an attempt to alleviate those difficulties. The blank forms for the Door and Frame Schedule in Figures 6-22A and 6-22B, the Window Schedule in Figure 6-26, and the Aluminum Entrance and Storefront Schedule in Figure 6-30 all have columns for listing glazing types. The implication, of course, is that there will be a schedule listing the characteristics of those glazing types.

Glazing Schedule

Some architects disdain schedules and show glazing types directly on elevation drawings accompanying the Door and Frame Schedule, Window Schedule, and Aluminum Entrance and Storefront Schedule. That method may be satisfactory for simple projects where all the work is new and there are few glazing types or conditions. One must be careful to indicate glazing materials for locations that do not show on those schedules, but such is the case regardless of the method used to indicate glazing types. Glazing schedules work better for complicated projects with many glazing types, however. A schedule makes the various conditions easier to keep track of and delineate in the construction documents.

The schedule illustrated by Figures 6-31 through 6-34, which follow these explanations, works well for projects with existing construction involvement. The example schedule is incomplete without all the parts contained in Figures 6-31 through 6-33.

Figure 6-31 is a legend listing abbreviations used in the glazing schedule.

Figure 6-32 is a list of notes to accompany the example schedule. If numbered remarks were needed, they should also be included in Figure 6-32.

Figure 6-33 is a combined existing and new Glazing Schedule for our hypothetical library using the blank form in Figure 6-34.

Figure 6-34 is the blank form used in the example.

Glazing Schedule Blank Form

The Glazing Schedule blank form (Figure 6-34) is only effective when accompanied by a legend similar to that in Figure 6-31 and notes similar to those in Figure 6-32.

General subjects are sometimes subdivided to permit display of needed data. Columns for requirements related to transmission, reflectance, and similar characteristics do not appear in the schedule. Include that data in the specifications.

Tips for Generating Glazing Schedules

Include both existing and new glazing in a single schedule.

Refer to the example (Figures 6-31 through 6-33) for additional guidance in filling out the form in Figure 6-34.

Most abbreviations in the Glazing Schedule Legend (Figure 6-31) are the same as the abbreviations listed in Figure 3-1. A few additional abbreviations have been added, however, to cover conditions that apply only to the schedules.

Place the Glazing Schedule Legend on the drawings near the Glazing Schedule, even though most of the abbreviations used are already included in the abbreviations list applicable to the entire project. Otherwise, people referring to the schedules will have to spend a lot of effort flipping back and forth in the drawings set. The problem, of course, is that they will, instead, rely solely on memory, which could result in errors.

Some abbreviations not used in the sample schedule are listed in the Glazing Schedule Legend (Figure 6-31) so that the list will better represent abbreviations that might occur on other projects. The list does not, however, include every abbreviation needed for all glazing schedules. Add items as necessary for each particular project. The list for a particular project should include every abbreviation used in that project's glazing schedule and none that are not used.

List in the Glazing Schedule glazing types noted on the drawings, or in the glazing schedule itself, or in any other schedule. Include both existing and new glazing types, even when the existing glazing types are to be removed. A well-informed contractor will bid lower and do a better job in the field. Note that some glazing types listed may occur only in the project as part of another glazing type. In our library example (see Figure 6-33) for instance, GL-2, ⅛-inch-thick clear float glass occurs only in GL-7 insulating glass. GL-2 has been listed and numbered separately so that it can be used in GL-7 without repeating GL-2's characteristics. Suppose, for example, that there were four ½-inch-thick insulating glass types that contained GL-2 as one light and some other glass type as the other light. If there were no GL-2 listing, it would be necessary to repeat the name and requirements for ⅛-inch-thick clear float glass four times.

Develop a new set of glazing types. Trying to work the required new types into the system used on the original working drawings accomplishes nothing useful and is not worth the effort.

Do not reproduce the original glazing schedule. Much of the data it contains will be inaccurate and much of it is superfluous for the new work. The effort needed to correct it is better spent elsewhere. Instead, verify the characteristics of existing glazing in the field and generate a new schedule that includes only pertinent data.

Be sure that all glazing with the same type mark are actually identical in every characteristic.

GLAZING SCHEDULE LEGEND

Air	=	Air-space thickness	Thk	=	Thickness
AS	=	As scheduled in Glazing Schedule	UNK	=	Unknown
			X	=	Existing when used alone, or as a code or abbreviation prefix (XGL-1)
GL	=	Glazing type			
Inbd	=	Inboard light			
Mid	=	Middle light	XNC	=	Existing, make no changes
ME	=	Match existing			
NA	=	Not applicable	*	=	Refer to note marked * in "Remarks" column
NS	=	No substitutions			
NW	=	No work required			
Outbd	=	Outboard light			

Figure 6-31. Glazing Schedule Legend.

GLAZING SCHEDULE NOTES

1. Data shown for existing glazing were taken from original documents for the existing building as prepared by (fill in architect's name) and dated (fill in date), and verified in the field.

Figure 6-32. Glazing Schedule Notes.

GLAZING SCHEDULE

Type	Material	Thk	Color	Insulating Glass			Plys	Safety Glass			Remarks
				Inbd	Air	Outbd		Inbd	Mid	Outbd	
XGL-1	Wire glass	1/4"	Clear								
XGL-2	Tempered plate glass	1/4"	Clear								
XGL-3	Sheet glass	DSB	Clear								
XGL-4	Polished plate glass	1/4"	Clear								
GL-1	Float glass	1/4"	Clear								
GL-2	Float glass	1/8"	Clear								
GL-3	Tempered float glass	1/4"	Clear								
GL-4	Wire glass	1/4"	Clear								
GL-5	Insulating glass	1"	AS	GL-1	1/2"	GL-1					
GL-6	Insulating glass	1"	AS	GL-3	1/2"	GL-3					
GL-7	Insulating glass	1/2"	AS	GL-2	1/4"	GL-2					

Figure 6-33. Example Glazing Schedule.

146

GLAZING SCHEDULE

| Type | Material | Thk | Color | Insulating Glass | | | Safety Glass | | | | Remarks |
				Inbd	Air	Outbd	Plys	Inbd	Mid	Outbd	

Figure 6-34. Blank form for Glazing Schedule.

Louvers

Where there are few louvers, it may make sense to give each a distinctive mark. Where there are many louvers of the same type, as happens with the new unit ventilator fresh air intakes for our example library, it makes more sense to give each louver type a mark rather than to list each louver separately. On projects where existing construction is involved, the number of different conditions, even at existing louvers, may make using individual marks for each louver advantageous. It is generally better to add rows on a schedule than to show multiple details on the same louver elevation in order to hold down the number of different marks. When each louver has a different mark, there is far less chance of missing requirements when preparing the drawings.

Regardless of the manner of marking louvers, the best way to include the requirements for louvers in a set of construction documents is to put them in a schedule.

Louver Schedule

The schedule illustrated in Figures 6-35 through 6-37, which follow these explanations, works well for projects with existing construction involvement. The example schedule is incomplete without all the parts contained in Figures 6-35 through 6-37, and requires some drawings as well.

Figure 6-35 is a legend listing abbreviations used in the louver schedule.

Figure 6-36 is a combined existing and new louver schedule for our hypothetical library using the blank form in Figure 6-38.

Figure 6-37 is a list of notes to accompany the example schedule.

Figure 6-38 is the blank form used in the example.

Louver Schedule Blank Form

The Louver Schedule blank form (Figure 6-38) is effective only when accompanied by a legend similar to that in Figure 6-35, notes similar to those in Figure 6-37, louver elevations, and configuration and installation details.

The first column in the form is blank. Use it to denote the location of louvers within a building (first floor, second floor, etc.) or buildings within a project (Library, Gymnasium, Administration Building, etc.). Add more columns at the beginning of the schedule to separate building phases or other subdivisions as necessary for clarity.

General subjects are sometimes subdivided to permit display of needed data.

Example

Louver marks are usually written on the building elevations adjacent to, or within, the louver, but may also be placed on the floor plans. In our examples, the marks are shown on the elevations. The mark is usually placed inside a symbol such as an ellipse, as they are in our example.

Many of our scheduled louvers do not show on the new-work floor plan (Figure 5-3), which may appear to violate the suggestion in "Tips On Generating Louver Schedules" to schedule louvers that show on the drawings. It actually does not violate the rule because the contract documents would include the entire first floor plan, basement floor plan, and all the elevations for the library and not just the portion shown in Figure 5-3, which is restricted by book-page size.

Installation detail keys (1/5-12) in the schedule refer to figures in this book. The number (5-10) to the right of the slash (/) is the figure number. The number (1) to the left of the slash (/) is the detail number in that figure. On an actual project, use the numbers of details shown on the drawings. Since this book includes details sufficient only to suggest methods, some of the details keyed in the schedule do not exist. Nonexistent details have 16-1 to the right of the slash.

Tips For Generating Louver Schedules

Include both existing and new louvers in a single schedule.

Refer to the example (Figures 6-35 through 6-37) for additional guidance in filling out the form in Figure 6-38.

Most abbreviations in the Louver Schedule Legend (Figure 6-35) are the same as the abbreviations listed in Figure 3-1. A few additional abbreviations have been added, however, to cover conditions that apply only to the schedules. Place the Louver Schedule Legend on the drawings near the Louver Schedule, even though most of the abbreviations used are already included in the abbreviations list applicable to the entire project. Otherwise, people referring to the schedules must spend a lot of effort flipping back and forth in the drawings set. The problem, of course, is that they will not bother to do so and will, instead, rely solely on memory, which could result in errors that might otherwise be avoided.

Some abbreviations not used in the sample schedule are listed in the Louver Schedule Legend (Figure 6-35) so that the list will better represent abbreviations that might occur on other projects. The list does not, however, include every abbreviation needed for all louver schedules. Add items as necessary for each particular project. The list for a particular project should include every abbreviation used in that project's louver schedule and none that are not used.

Number on the demolition plans and elevations, and list in the Louver Schedule all louvers that are to be removed, including those that are to be discarded and those that are to be reinstalled in a different location. Do not give existing (X prefix) numbers on the demolition plans or elevations to louvers to remain undisturbed except for refinishing. Prefix with an ''X'' (XL-2) the numbers assigned to louvers which are to be removed and discarded or relocated to show that the louvers so labeled are existing items requiring action by the contractor. Listing louvers that are to be removed and discarded is clearer than noting removal on the drawings and is apparent in the schedules even to those who have no need to look at the demolition drawings. Listing the old number and location for louvers that are to be relocated and the new number and location helps avoid errors caused by lack of coordination between demolition drawings and new-work drawings. A typical example is that of telling the contractor on the demolition drawing to salvage a particular louver for reuse and then scheduling a new louver for that location.

Number on the demolition drawings and include in the louver schedule every louver which shows on any new-work drawing. Include louvers in spaces where architectural work occurs and louvers in spaces where structural, mechanical, plumbing, electrical, and other nonarchitectural work occur, even where there is no architectural work. It is very difficult to determine where work will lap over into adjacent spaces due to unforeseen conditions.

An exception to this rule might be spaces shown merely to complete a plan when the contractor has been explicitly denied access to those spaces, but the better way is to omit those spaces from the new-work drawings. Numbering and listing every louver that shows, even when that louver is to remain unaltered, eliminates confusion and makes it absolutely clear at a glance whether work is required related to a particular louver.

Develop a new set of louver marks. Trying to work the required new marks into the system used on the original working drawings accomplishes nothing useful and is not worth the effort.

Do not reproduce the original louver schedule. Much of the data it contains will be inaccurate or superfluous for the new work. The effort needed to correct it is better spent elsewhere. Instead, verify every existing louver's characteristics in the field and generate a new schedule that includes only the pertinent data.

Do not repeat data. For louvers to be relocated, show pertinent characteristics only once to avoid duplication and copying errors.

Be sure that all louvers with the same type mark are actually identical in every characteristic.

Draw louver elevations and configuration and installation details as necessary to convey all requirements. Use techniques shown earlier in this chapter for doors and frames.

LOUVER SCHEDULE LEGEND

ACOUS	= Acoustic	Reqd	= Required
ALUM	= Aluminum	RH	= Right hand
BE	= Baked enamel	SD	= See detail
CONT	= Continuous	SGTP	= Sightproof
Elev	= Elevation	SP	= Stormproof
Fin	= Finish	STD	= Standard
FL	= Fluorocarbon	STL	= Steel
HC	= High capacity	UNK	= Unknown
HDWD	= Hardwood	WD	= Wood
INV	= Inverted	X	= Existing when used alone, or as a code or abbreviation prefix (XL-1), or as a schedule column head
LH	= Left hand		
Mat	= Material		
ME	= Match existing		
NA	= Not applicable		
NAT	= Natural		
ND	= No detail has been drawn	XNC	= Existing, make no changes
NS	= No substitutions	*	= Refer to note marked * in "Remarks" column
NW	= No work required		
OPER	= Operating		
PT	= Paint		

Figure 6-35. Louver Schedule Legend.

LOUVER SCHEDULE

Mark	X	New	Mat	Fin	Elev	Overall Size			Performance		Blade Type
						Width	Height	Depth	Free Air	Rating Reqd	
XL–1	X		STL	PT	ND	11'–8"	6'–4"	4"	XNC	NA	SP
L–1		o	ALUM	FL	A	2'–0"	1'–3–1/2"	4"	50%	No	SP
L–2		o	ALUM	FL	B	15'–8"	8'–8"	6"		Yes	STD

Installation Details				Screen Type		Insul Blank-off Panel Reqd	Remarks
Sill	LH Jamb	RH Jamb	Head	Insect	Bird		
ND	ND	ND	ND	XNC	None	None	
1/5–12	1/16–1	2/16–1	1/5–12	None	o	None	
3/16–1	4/16–1	5/16–1	6/16–1	None	None	None	

Figure 6-36. Left and right halves of example Louver Schedule.

LOUVER SCHEDULE NOTES

1. Data shown for existing louvers were taken from original documents for the existing building as prepared by (fill in architect's name) and dated (fill in date), and verified in the field.

2. Unless specifically noted as existing (X), scheduled finishes are new. Refer to New Exterior Finish Material and Color Schedule for additional requirements including colors.

3. On existing louvers, all items are existing unless noted otherwise.

4. On new louvers, all items are new unless noted otherwise.

5. Left-hand and right-hand louver jamb conditions are determined as viewed from exterior.

6. Refer to specifications for detailed requirements where performance ratings are scheduled as required.

7. Free air requirements are based on a 48″ by 48″ unit. Where performance rating is indicated as required, free air requirements are included with performance rating requirements in the specifications.

Figure 6-37. Louver Schedule Notes.

LOUVER SCHEDULE

Mark	X	New	Mat	Fin	Elev	Overall Size			Performance		Blade Type
						Width	Height	Depth	Free Air	Rating Reqd	

Installation Details				Screen Type		Insul Blank-off Panel Reqd	Remarks
Sill	LH Jamb	RH Jamb	Head	Insect	Bird		

Figure 6-38. Left and right halves of blank form for Louver Schedule.

Equipment

On projects, such as hospitals and schools, that have large amounts of equipment, architects almost always give each equipment item a mark on the drawings and schedule the equipment in some manner. Usually, on such projects, architects produce separate equipment drawings.

On smaller projects, there is a tendency to skip the schedule and try to cover the needed requirements directly on the architectural drawings or in the specifications. That procedure, though questionable on any project, might suffice for a small project with little equipment, when all the equipment is new. Because of the many variables, trying to delineate equipment requirements without an equipment schedule and equipment drawings is a bad idea, even on small projects, where it is necessary to alter or relocate existing equipment.

Equipment Schedules

The schedule illustrated by Figures 6-39 through 6-44, which follow these explanations, works well for projects with existing construction involvement. The example schedule is incomplete without all the parts contained in Figures 6-39 through 6-43.

Figure 6-39 is a legend listing abbreviations used in the equipment schedule.

Figure 6-40 is an existing equipment plan showing a portion of the existing example library floor plan. The existing equipment scheduled in Figures 6-42A and 6-42B is shown on the plan in Figure 6-40.

Figure 6-41 is a new equipment plan showing a portion of the example library's new floor plan. New and existing-to-remain equipment scheduled in Figures 6-42A and 6-42B is shown in Figure 6-41.

Figures 6-42A and 6-42B constitute a combined existing and new equipment schedule for our hypothetical library using the blank form in Figure 6-44.

Figure 6-43 is a list of notes and numbered remarks to accompany the example schedule.

Figure 6-44 is the blank form used in the example.

Equipment Schedule Blank Form

The Equipment Schedule blank form (Figure 6-44) is effective only when accompanied by a legend similar to that in Figure 6-39, equipment plans similar to those shown in Figures 6-40 and 6-41, and notes and numbered remarks similar to those in Figure 6-43.

Use the first blank column in the form to note equipment location within a building or buildings within a project. Add more columns at the beginning of the schedule to separate building phases or other subdivisions as necessary for clarity.

Example

Equipment marks, especially for projects where the work involves existing equipment, should be shown on separate equipment drawings, adjacent to, or within, the equipment items. Where elevations are necessary to convey equipment requirements, equipment marks should also show on the elevations. In our example, the marks are shown on equipment plans. The marks are usually placed inside a symbol, as they are in our example.

The equipment plans shown in Figures 6-40 and 6-41 are only a small portion of the drawings needed to show all the equipment in our example library. In actual practice, because equipment occurs in most spaces, existing and new equipment floor plans of the entire library would probably be required.

Tips for Generating Equipment Schedules

Include both existing and new equipment in a single schedule.

Refer to the example (Figures 6-39 through 6-43) for additional guidance in filling out the form in Figure 6-44.

Most abbreviations in the Equipment Schedule Legend (Figure 6-39) are the same as the abbreviations listed in Figure 3-1. Additional abbreviations have been included, however, to cover conditions that apply only to the schedule. Place the Equipment Schedule Legend on the drawings near the Equipment Schedule, even though most of the abbreviations used are already included in the abbreviations list applicable to the entire project. Otherwise, people referring to the schedules will have to spend a lot of effort flipping back and forth in the drawings set. The problem, of course, is that they will, instead, rely solely on memory, which could lead to errors that could otherwise be avoided.

Some abbreviations not used in the sample schedule are listed in the Equipment Schedule Legend (Figure 6-39) so that the list will better represent abbreviations that might occur on other projects. The list does not, however, include every abbreviation needed for all equipment schedules. Add items as necessary for each particular project. The list for a particular project should include every abbreviation used in that project's equipment schedule and none that are not used.

Number on existing equipment plans, using "X" prefix marks, and list in the Equipment Schedule every piece of existing equipment in every area of the existing building where work under the contract is to take place, even in spaces where there is no architectural work. Include equipment to remain in place, whether any work related to the equipment is required or not. Also mark and schedule equipment that is to be removed, including items that are to be discarded and those that are to be reinstalled in a different location. Listing all existing equipment is the only sure way to avoid missing necessary work and of conveying to the contractor which work is required. When a complete schedule exists, there can be no mistake about who owns each existing equipment item and no later quarrel about disposition of any listed item. To properly prepare contract documents, an architect must identify each equipment item in any case. There is no valid reason for not conveying that information to the contractor and heading off later disputes.

Develop a new set of equipment marks. Trying to work the required new marks into the system used on the original working drawings accomplishes nothing useful and is not worth the effort.

Do not reproduce the original equipment schedule. Much of the data it contains will be inaccurate or superfluous for the new work. The effort to correct it is better spent elsewhere. Instead, verify every existing equipment item's characteristics in the field and generate a new schedule including only the pertinent data.

List each equipment item only once, to avoid duplication and copying errors.

EQUIPMENT SCHEDULE LEGEND

ACOUS	=	Acoustic	PL	=	Plastic laminate
ALUM	=	Aluminum	PT	=	Paint
BE	=	Baked enamel	Reqd	=	Required
BG	=	Beaded glass	RH	=	Right hand
CONT	=	Continuous	SD	=	See detail
CONTR	=	Contractor	SGTP	=	Sightproof
Elev	=	Elevation	STD	=	Standard
Fin	=	Finish	STL	=	Steel
GF	=	Glass fiber	UNK	=	Unknown
HDWD	=	Hardwood	WD	=	Wood
INT	=	Integral	X	=	Existing when used alone, or as a code or abbreviation prefix (XL–1), or as a schedule column head
INV	=	Inverted			
LH	=	Left hand			
Mat	=	Material			
ME	=	Match existing			
NA	=	Not applicable			
NAT	=	Natural			
ND	=	No detail has been drawn	XNC	=	Existing, make no changes
NS	=	No substitutions	*	=	Refer to note marked * in "Remarks" column
NW	=	No work required			
OPER	=	Operating			

Figure 6-39. Equipment Schedule Legend.

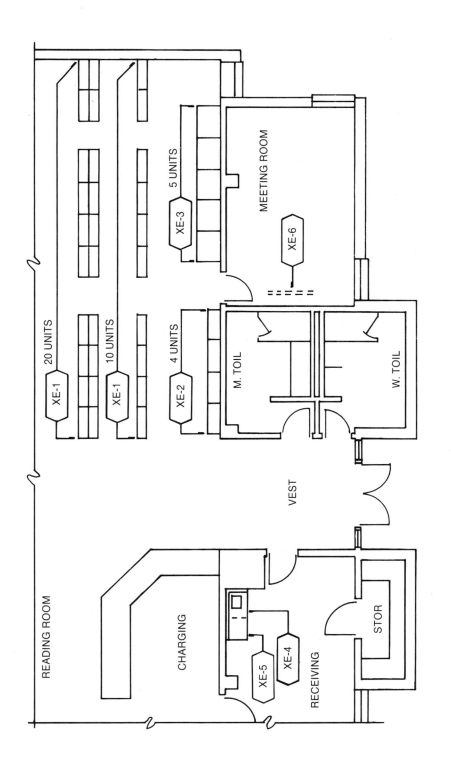

Figure 6-40. Existing equipment plan.

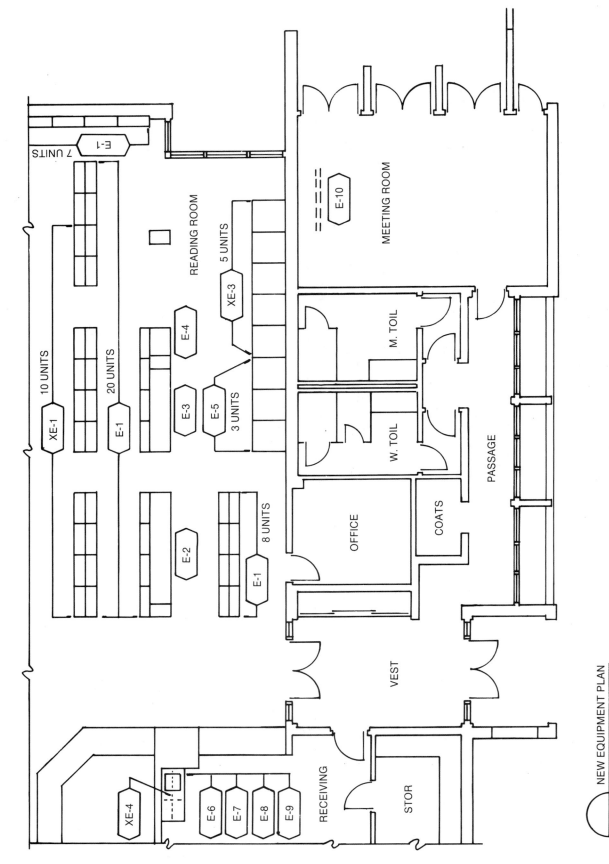

Figure 6-41. New equipment plan.

EQUIPMENT SCHEDULE

Mark	Item	Location	X	New	Mat.	Fin.	Manufacturer Name	Manufacturer Product	Cat No.
XE-1	Library shelving	Reading Room	X		Oak	XNAT	Rodman, Inc.	Wood Shelving	WS3682
XE-2	Card catalogs	Reading Room	X		Oak	XNAT	Rodman, Inc.	Card Holder	CH3648
XE-3	Study carrels	Reading Room	X		Oak	XNAT	Rodman, Inc.	Carrels	RSCC-1
XE-4	Unit kitchen	Receiving	X		PL	XINT	Buxom Co.	Unlimited	ULB60
XE-5	Refrigerator	XE-4	X		X	X	Buxom Co.	Colaun	COB-6
XE-6	Projection screen	Meeting Room	X		UNK	UNK	Rollit, Inc.	Beaded Baby	RUB9
E-1	Library shelving	Reading Room		O	Oak	NAT	Rodman Sons	Wood Shelving	WS3682
E-2	Microfiche Counter	Reading Room		O	Oak	NAT	Rodman Sons	Counter	RSCM1
E-3	Microfiche Counter	Reading Room		O	Oak	NAT	Rodman Sons	Counter	RSCM1
E-4	Microfiche Counter	Reading Room		O	Oak	NAT	Rodman Sons	Counter	RSCM1
E-5	Study carrels	Reading Room		O	Oak	NAT	Rodman Sons	Carrels	RSCC-3
E-6	Wall cabinet	Above XE-4		O	PL	INT	Buxom Co.	Unlimited	ULB39
E-7	Backsplash	Below E-6		O	PL	INT	Buxom Co.	Guard Duty	ULB111
E-8	Exhaust hood	E-6		O	MET	BE	Nature, Inc.	Blowout	NIB17
E-9	Refrigerator	XE-4		O	MET	ME	Pretty Boy	Undercounter	PBU41
E-10	Projection screen	Meeting Room		O	GF	BG	Bigadun	Glassface	BBG70

Figure 6-42A. Left half of example Equipment Schedule.

159

	Size			Furnish By	Install By	Services				Remarks
	Width	Height	Depth			HW	CW	San	Elec	
	36"	82"	12"	X	X	NA	NA	NA	NA	①
	36"	48"	14"	X	NA	NA	NA	NA	NA	②
	36"	52"	26"	X	X	NA	NA	NA	NA	③
	60"	42"	24"	X	X	*	*	*	*	④ *⑪
	24"	31"	24"	X	NA	NA	NA	NA	o	⑤
	50"	50"	NA	X	NA	NA	NA	NA	NA	⑥
	36"	82"	12"	CONTR	CONTR	NA	NA	NA	NA	⑦
	128"	28"	24"	CONTR	CONTR	NA	NA	NA	*	⑦ *⑪
	96"	28"	24"	CONTR	CONTR	NA	NA	NA	*	⑦ *⑪
	32"	28"	24"	CONTR	CONTR	NA	NA	NA	*	⑦ *⑪
	36"	52"	26"	CONTR	CONTR	NA	NA	NA	NA	⑦
	60"	30"	14"	CONTR	CONTR	NA	NA	NA	NA	⑧
	*	*	*	CONTR	CONTR	NA	NA	NA	NA	⑧ *⑩
	24"	9"	14"	CONTR	CONTR	NA	NA	NA	*	⑨ *⑪
	24"	31"	24"	CONTR	CONTR	NA	NA	NA	*	*⑪
	70"	70"	NA	Owner	CONTR	NA	NA	NA	*	Recessed *⑪

Figure 6-42B. Right half of example Equipment Schedule.

EQUIPMENT SCHEDULE NOTES

1. Data shown for existing equipment were taken from original documents for the existing building as prepared by (fill in architect's name) and dated (fill in date), and verified in the field.
2. Unless specifically indicated otherwise, scheduled products indicate quality standard required, but are not intended to limit competition. Except for products noted "NS" or "no substitutions," approved equal products of approved equal manufacturers will be considered.
3. Unless specifically noted as existing (X), scheduled finishes are new. Refer to New Interior Finishes Schedule and New Interior Finish Material and Color Code Schedule for additional requirements including colors.
5. On existing equipment, all items are existing unless noted otherwise.
6. On new equipment, all items are new unless noted otherwise.

NUMBERED REMARKS

⟨1⟩ Existing shelving to remain in present location. Remove if necessary to protect from harm or make way for new Work, and reinstall in same location from which removed when construction progress permits.

⟨2⟩ Remove and discard existing card catalog units.

⟨3⟩ Remove existing study carrels and relocate where indicated.

⟨4⟩ Existing unit kitchen contains burner top and sink which require no work.

⟨5⟩ Remove and discard existing refrigerator.

⟨6⟩ Remove and discard existing projection screen.

⟨7⟩ Match existing furniture in type and finish.

⟨8⟩ Match existing base cabinet finish and color.

⟨9⟩ Provide duct and external exhaust fan. See mechanical drawings.

⟨10⟩ Refer to detail (show detail number here) for dimensions.

⟨11⟩ Services are required. Refer to specifications and mechanical and electrical drawings for characteristics and other requirements.

Figure 6-43. Equipment Schedule Notes and Numbered Remarks.

EQUIPMENT SCHEDULE

Mark	Item	Location	X	New	Mat.	Fin.	Manufacturer			Size			Furnish By	Install By	Services				Remarks
							Name	Product	Cat No.	Width	Height	Depth			HW	CW	San	Elec	

Figure 6-44. Left and right halves of blank form for Equipment Schedule.

PART THREE

Project Manual

In the old days, architects called the written portion of construction documents "Specifications," even though those documents often included much more than specifications. Today, we call volumes containing written construction documents "project manuals." The 1987 version of AIA Document A201, *General Conditions of the Contract for Construction* defines "Project Manual" as "the volume usually assembled for the Work which may include the bidding requirements, sample forms, Conditions of the Contract and Specifications." The term "project manual" in this book refers to every document AIA says belongs in project manuals. When this chapter uses the term "project manual," it means all such documents, even when they were not originally bound in the existing building's specifications volume.

We cannot emphasize too strongly an architect's need to obtain a valid copy of the project manual for the existing construction, if it is available, before beginning professional services for an associated project. Such documents often permit an architect to know something about concealed conditions before tearing into the building. Project manuals always contain data not shown on the drawings.

Existing project manuals are not infallible, however.

7

Using Existing Project Manual Parts

Specifications and other project manual documents and sections written for an existing building are often excellent guides for producing a new project manual for remodeling, renovating, or restoring the building for which they were originally written. Unfortunately, it is seldom possible to use such project manual documents and sections in the new project manual without extensive modifications.

Existing Project Manual Updating

A specifications writer must be cautious when using specifications and other documents from an existing building's project manual in a new project manual, even when the new project manual is for work related to the same existing building. For example, the specifier must examine, with an eye toward revision if necessary, the following.

Cross-References

Cross-references in the original specifications will almost certainly not be usable in the new project manual, even if there are no new products. References will change because different production methods will be used, and there will be differences between office guides and specifications numbering procedures from one architect's office to another. Reference changes will also occur because some project manual documents and sections in the original project will not be used in the remodeling, renovation, or restoration work because there is no work by that trade, or too little work related to that product, to justify an entire section to describe it.

Format

The new project manual's format may not be the same as the original's for many reasons, including, but by no means limited to, the architect or specifications writer's personal preferences. The architect may have adopted a later version of CSI's page and section formatting recommendations than that used in the original documents. If the documents are very old, they may not even follow *Masterformat*'s sixteen-division format.

Standards

Standards used in project manuals include

Government standards including Federal Standards and Specifications (Fed. Spec.); Military Specifications and Standards (Mil. Specs.), Product Standards (PS) of the National Bureau of Standards (NBS), and many others. *Masterspec* Section 01090 has a detailed listing including addresses, telephone numbers, and acronyms which specifications often use when referring to government standards setting agencies and their standards.

Private sector standards setting body standards including ASTM; ANSI; TCA; BIA; UL; and others. Refer to *Masterspec* Section 01090 for a more complete listing including addresses, telephone numbers, and acronyms by which standards setting organizations and their standards are often referenced in specifications. Alternatively, obtain associations names and addresses from the *Encyclopedia of Associations* published by Gale Research Co.

It will probably be necessary to revise references to applicable documents and standards because

The standard has been abandoned or replaced, sometimes by a standard of another organization. For example, a PS may have been replaced by an ASTM standard.

The listed date may not be the latest version of the standard.

The standard may have applied to the original project but not to the remodeling, renovation, or restoration work.

Manufactured Products

Some products used in the existing building may no longer be manufactured. Others may be manufactured but not in the same model. Current colors may not match those existing. The appearance of new models may be radically different from the older version. Replacement parts may not be available. Matching may be impossible.

Construction Methods

The construction methods category somewhat overlaps the standards category but bears specific mention because it is an area in which an architect is likely to run into the most difficult to handle problems. For example,

Tile Council of America, Inc. TCA Method F102-80 was valid in 1980 but the TCA Method F102 detail may have changed by now. To find out what exists, examine the detail in the 1980 *TCA Handbook for Tile Installation*. To determine which number to use in describing requirements for extending the tile, consult the latest *TCA Handbook for Tile Installation*.

The materials or methods used in the original building may no longer be desirable. An architect needing to specify a product and method for restoring deteriorated sand-lime plaster on a 200-year-old tavern would not use the original specifications for that plaster, even if the specifications were readily available. Deciding which methods to use to repair or extend surfaces constructed with outdated or inferior methods or materials may require great research.

Terminology

In the construction industry, as in all other facets of life, the way people speak of things and the words they use change with time. The quite proper word "retort," meaning a vessel in which substances are distilled or decomposed by heat, is today usually replaced by the less descriptive, but more generally understood, "vat." A "rod" is still 16.5 feet, but most of us would not use the word, or the measure, today. Abbreviations become words in their own right, at least in restricted usage. "Caulk," for example, becomes "calk" and "gauge" becomes "gage."

Field Conditions

It is necessary to compare the products, methods, and other requirements specified in the original documents with those used in the actual construction. This investigation requires review of shop drawings, products literature, change orders, field orders, as-built drawings, and specifications, and an all-important field visit to confirm the paperwork.

8

Project Manual Guide Paragraphs

Many specifications guides lack adequate provisions to cover existing construction. Some commercial (for sale) guides, such as *Spectext* and *Masterspec,* contain some existing-construction provisions but often just state that a problem may exist and instruct the user to determine the requirements and fill in the missing data. Most government agency specifications guides do not adequately cover existing conditions either. So architects must invent their own existing-conditions provisions. It is as if a new computer purchaser were to find a blurb in the manual stating that there may be some additional steps necessary to have the computer drive a printer, but there are too many possibilities to cover them all in the manual. So the user must figure it out independently and write the missing manual portions without guidance.

This chapter contains paragraphs excerpted from the author's project manuals for more than thirty-five major remodeling, renovation, and restoration projects. The paragraphs presented do not contain every provision from all those projects that was specific to existing construction. They are offered to stir the reader's mind and act as a checklist for necessary provisions. Do not assume the paragraphs presented to be accurate or usable for any project other than the author's project for which they were originally written. They may be now out of date. Products in them may no longer be produced. Manufacturers listed may no longer be in business. Methods may have been since outdated by better ones. The examples may not be usable in any current project. They may even do harm if used without updating and modification to make them suit actual project conditions.

Coordination with Drawings

It is important to coordinate drawings and project manual requirements for every project. The requirement is, if anything, more important when part of the project involves an existing building. When existing construction enters the picture, there are more drawings and project manual documents and sections to coordinate. There will be more drawing notes than is usual for projects where all the work is new, as evidenced by the examples in Part 2 of this book. Sometimes, the drawing notes will be invented by persons who are not as familiar as they ought to be with project manual provisions. Besides doing normal review, a specifier should pay particular attention to drawing notes.

Format for Adding Existing Conditions Provisions

Rudyard Kipling (1865–1936) wrote,

There are nine and sixty ways
   of constructing tribal lays,
And every single one of them
            is right.

There are not quite that many ways to adapt project manual guide documents and specifications sections intended for new construction so that they work for projects where existing buildings play a part, but however many there are, every single one of them is right.

Fortunately, each of the many ways can be placed in one of three categories.

Write each document and specifications section as though there were no existing building involved. Then write additional paragraphs to cover existing conditions. The additional paragraphs can be tacked onto the end of each of the three parts of the CSI format or placed within the body of each of the three parts.

Write the entire section as a unit, integrating new and existing work requirements in the same paragraphs, often in the same sentences.

Combine the first two options, writing some documents and sections with tacked-on paragraphs and other documents and sections with requirements for new and existing work integrated throughout.

First decide which of those three methods to use for a particular project. Then decide how to handle minor conditions that do not seem to warrant their own separate document or section. In almost every project where an existing building is involved, there will be existing conditions that must be modified where no similar new work will be done. There might be, for example, a marble toilet partition to remove and later reinstall but no new marble partitions, no new stone of other kinds, and no new toilet partitions at all. Is it necessary to write a section to cover that condition or is there another, perhaps easier, way to specify that work?

Organizing Project Manual Documents and Sections

The correct way to organize project manual documents and specifications sections for projects where existing buildings are involved depends on the type of project. For this purpose, there are four basic project types.

Type 1 includes projects where all the work is in or on the existing building. This type includes restoration.

Type 2 includes projects where work in an existing building is a majority, but not necessarily all, of the work. It includes rehabilitation and projects where an existing building is converted to a new use with no, or at most very little, space added.

Type 3 includes projects where new construction outside the existing building constitutes the major portion of the work. It includes major additions.

Type 4 includes any combination of the other three types.

In each type, the problem is to decide whether to write a given project manual document or specifications section as a unit, integrating new work with existing work in the same paragraphs, or to write the new-work requirements first and then tack on paragraphs related to existing conditions.

When all the work is related to existing conditions (type 1 projects) there is no decision to make. Writing each section in the integrated fashion is the only legitimate way.

With respect to the other three types, however, the answer may not be so clear-cut. Decisions there are influenced by the following factors:

- How extensive the new work is relative to existing similar work. For instance, if the ceramic floor tile in one small existing toilet must be regrouted and there will be twelve new toilets with ceramic tile wall and floor finishes, it might be appropriate to write Section 09310, "Ceramic Tile," as a standard new work section and tack on paragraphs about regrouting tile. On the other hand, if there is much existing tile and it requires extensive reworking and extensions, while new ceramic tile is limited (maybe one new toilet), it would probably be better to write an integrated section.

- Whether there is a clean break, either in time or physical separation, between new work and the work related to existing construction. If there is a clean break, the tack-on method would probably work best. If not, then the integrated method is probably the one to use.

- Whether all, or most, of the work is within or on the existing building. The more directly related to the existing construction the new work is, the more likely it is that the integrated method is best.

- What type guides specifications the architect's office is using. If the architect is using a commercial master specifications series such as *Spectext* or *Masterspec,* the tack-on method may work best. Using tack-on paragraphs permits easier updating. When updates of the masters arrive, it is necessary only to excerpt the added paragraphs and append them to the new masters. If, on the other hand, the architectural firm has its own masters, it might be easier to have them integrated. The decision is subjective, dependent on the architect's personal preference.

It is not important to be consistent about using the tack-on or integrated method, even from section to section on the same project. It is much better to let the circumstances dictate than to strive for an artificial consistency meaningful only to the specifier. Purists may say, "it ought to be all the same," but in this case, each situation is different and ought to be handled in whatever manner will produce the clearest document or specifications section.

Some specifications writers *always* write specifications for projects that involve existing buildings exactly as they would for new work and then tack on existing-work paragraphs. That method is, after all, the most consistent. It also allows a lazy specifier to use the guides he or she already has with little additional work. It is much easier to add paragraphs than to rewrite, especially if the specifier is not working on a computer or is editing copy for someone else to keyboard. But that procedure makes no sense at all on a section where there is little or no new work involved and is absurd for projects involving historic preservation.

The single method that will work all the time is that of fully integrating the requirements for new and existing work throughout the document or specifications section. The sole reason for not advocating the integrated method as the right way is that even though the method is usually more work for the specifications writer, it often does not contribute to the construction process in any way. Neither does the integrated method produce a better or less expensive building. If that method does not do any good, why go to the trouble to use it?

Current commercial guide specifications seem to lean toward the integrated method in the few sections where they specify existing-conditions provisions.

CSI's *Manual of Practice* ignores the problem entirely, not bothering to suggest a location for paragraphs describing existing conditions.

While ease of document production is certainly important, it alone should not be the deciding factor in how a specifications writer organizes project manual documents and specifications sections. The persuasive factor should be how well the method works for the situation. So although some specifications writers insist upon using the tack-on method for everything, it is much better to write specifications that way only when the situation dictates such an approach. More often, a specifications writer should treat each section as a whole and write all the requirements at once in the integrated fashion.

Specifying Minor Items

Often, in projects where existing buildings are involved, there will be minor items that require relocation or some other limited work. When new work of a like nature is required, it is easy to include the minor work requirements in the section with the new work. Repainting an existing fan coil unit, for example, can be specified in Section 09900, ''Painting.'' Often, though, there is no related new work. Suppose, for example, it is necessary to remove an existing projection screen, store it while construction is in progress, and reinstall it later. There are no new projection screens or other audiovisual equipment. There are several optional courses of action.

It would be possible to write a Section 11302, ''Projection Screens,'' but that would probably be giving the matter more attention than it rightly deserves relative to the project as a whole. Writing separate sections for each such condition could result in bloated project manuals, unnecessary work for the specifications writer, and maybe even increased construction costs.

Another way to handle such minor conditions is to letter the requirements on the drawings. Purists will scream and some clients will not let architects put specifications on their drawings, but the possibility should not be overlooked.

The better solution is to put all such requirements in a single catch-all specifications section. *Masterformat* includes just such a section, Section 13990, ''Minor Alteration Work.'' Yes, it is there. Look in the right-hand column on the last page of Division 13, ''Special Construction.''

The only problem with using a Section 13990 is deciding whether a part of the work is sufficiently complex or extensive to warrant its own section. The first test is that of simplicity. The simplest solution is usually the best. Of course, if a project were really simple, the architect could write all the specifications requirements on the drawings and forget about a project manual altogether. And on many residential and other small projects, that is exactly what is often done.

Each complication increases the number and scope of the specifications documents. In theory, a sufficiently complex project would need all of *Masterformat*'s sections and more. There has probably never been such a project, and most likely never will be.

In general, it is probably better for most projects for an architect to use the fewest practicable number of project manual documents and specifications sections. That is certainly true, beyond a doubt, for small projects. But the ideal situation for specifications writers is just the opposite. Specifications writers would like to have a half-million or so narrowscope sections covering every imaginable condition stored in computer memory. With such a data base, there would be no editing at all, just selecting. In the real world, even if a specifications writer could generate those half-million sections, using them would result in massive project manuals and wreck the construction budget on virtually every project.

Architects tend to lean toward using more narrowscope sections, especially in project manuals for work in existing buildings. There are two reasons for that trend.

1. Fees for work in existing buildings are generally not high enough to cover the increased work involved. Architects try to cover that loss by pumping out narrowscope sections which require little editing.
2. Most projects where existing construction is involved are more complicated than are new projects. Decisions are not made as quickly and are more likely to be changed during the document production stage. Each narrowscope section requires fewer decisions than do the conglomerate broadscope sections covering the same requirements. The specifications writer does not have to wait for all the answers before beginning work. The danger of having to rewrite is reduced.

When existing construction is involved, architects tend to worry inordinately about relatively insignificant things. In a project with all new brickwork, for example, most architects would specify cleaning brickwork in Section 04200, "Unit Masonry." But when the brick to clean is existing, there is a tendency to add a section just to specify the cleaning, even when the only cleaning required is that of soiling that occurs during the work of the current contract. That is not to say that brick cleaning sections are never needed. Sometimes they are, but there is a tendency to overspecify such requirements when existing construction becomes involved.

Usually, an architect should not write a separate specifications section to cover an existing product or material unless there is no material of like kind or the work related to the existing construction is extensive. Patch a few holes in plaster cut by the contractor; no new section. Tear down a ceiling and install a new one; new section. An exception must be made, however, for work involving historic preservation, and for other cases where requirements related to existing conditions are extensive, even though the work is minimal in scope.

Simplify. Do not create a situation where a product or condition will be missed by bidders or during construction. Do not specify anything twice. Use the drawings if doing so makes sense. After all, drawing were used to specify long before there were printing presses, let alone project manuals. When it does not make sense to create a separate section and putting the information on the drawings is not a good idea, create a catch-all section. Follow *Masterformat* when doing so makes sense; ignore it when that makes more sense.

In an essay, Ralph Waldo Emerson made an often-quoted statement that fits this discussion perfectly. He said, "A foolish consistency is the hobgoblin of little minds. . . ."

The Project Manual Guide Paragraphs

The guide paragraphs in this chapter assume use of *Masterformat,* including *Masterformat's* suggestions for its own use. They also assume use of AIA documents and AIA's recommendations regarding use of those documents. The guide paragraphs follow CSI's three part section format and use an alphanumeric paragraph numbering system similar to that recommended by CSI.

AIA recommends that AIA document users not substitute their own provisions for those contained in the standard documents without expert advice. AIA says that by indiscriminately revising AIA documents, architects may unknowingly weaken either the coordinated relationship between the standard documents or within the documents themselves. Do not construe anything in this book as countermanding AIA's recommendations. And do not consider anything in this book as constituting the expert advice AIA recommends.

The guide paragraphs in this chapter are, for the most part, extracts from real projects. Some of them have been somewhat modified to make them apply more generally. Some were devised to suit particular circumstances by the owner's attorneys. Do not, under any circumstances, insert the words in these guide paragraphs directly into a project manual for a real project. They might not work for that project. They might even be harmful. They are only guides, as their name implies. Do not even use modifications of them without careful consideration of the effect of such use on the particular project at hand.

An architect who wants to modify a standard document, such as AIA Document A201, "General Conditions of the Contract for Construction," should submit the modification to the owner with a request that the owner's attorney and the owner examine and approve the modifications. If the architect is apprehensive about a modification's effect on the architect, or the architect's consultants, the architect's attorney should review the modification, too. Unfortunately, many lawyers know little about construction law. Asking an attorney who is not knowledgeable about construction law to review a standard document revision is a waste of time and money.

Some guide paragraphs in this chapter state requirements applicable also to projects with all new construction, to help put in context related paragraphs that are applicable only to projects where existing construction occurs. Most of the time, however, paragraphs that would be needed even where there was no existing construction have been omitted. The examples, therefore, do not contain every requirement necessary for an actual project.

Some of the examples contain additional paragraphs for use only with very small projects where a completely detailed project manual is inappropriate. Where the condition specified exists on a small project and a separate example has not been included, the project manual should include a detailed provision approximating the one in the example, regardless of project size. Some requirements simply do not lend themselves to abbreviation. In other cases, solely based on the architect's judgment, requirements can be abbreviated. One criteria for deciding whether to abbreviate a requirement is the relative dollar value of that requirement to the entire project. How much of a risk is there to the project of losing some control over that subject area? Often the decision is purely subjective, based on the architect's experience. It is fair to say, however, that whenever a requirement is abbreviated in a specifications section, the architect loses some control over that requirement.

Guide paragraphs in this chapter come primarily from projects with private-sector owners. This approach may seem to present a narrow point of view, one that omits much of many architects' work. But the principles represented apply to every project, regardless of who the owner is. Many bidding and contract requirements guides for government work contain provisions for existing construction. When they do not, the examples and discussion in this chapter apply. Almost always, revisions to government guide clauses related to bidding and contract requirements must have specific approval of the government in each case. Many government guides for specifications sections do not have provisions for specifying work related to existing construction, but that situation is changing.

The terms "approved," "approval," "accepted," "rejected," "reject," "accept," and similar constructs in the examples refer to actions by the architect, unless another party is named. Similarly, "satisfactory" and similar constructs mean satisfactory to the architect. The term "indicated" in the examples means shown, drawn, specified, noted, or in any other way contained in the contract documents.

As far as is practicable, the example paragraphs in this chapter follow CSI's format and language recommendations.

To use the example paragraphs, start with a good guide specifications section for projects where all the work is new. Then add paragraphs similar to those in the examples. Do not delete requirements from the original guide, unless the requirements are inapplicable to the project at hand.

For sections for which examples are not included in this book, follow the principles illustrated in the examples presented.

Guide paragraphs or comments concerning requirements are included for the following documents and sections.

Contents: Project Manual Guide Paragraphs

Bidding Requirements, Contract Forms, and Conditions of the Contract

Specifications

Division 1   *General Requirements*

01020   Allowances
01025   Measurement and Payment
01030   Alternates/Alternatives
01040   Coordination
01045   Cutting and Patching
01050   Field Engineering
01060   Regulatory Requirements
01070   Abbreviations and Symbols
01080   Identification Systems
01090   Reference Standards
01100   Special Project Procedures
01120   Alterations Project Procedures
01200   Project Meetings
01300   Submittals
01400   Quality Control
01500   Construction Facilities and Temporary Controls (Large Projects)
01500   Construction Facilities and Temporary Controls (Small Projects)
01600   Materials and Equipment
01700   Contract Closeout

Division 2 *Sitework*

02050   Demolition
02100   Clearing
02150   Shoring, Bracing, and Underpinning
02200   Earthwork
02513   Asphaltic Concrete Paving
02514   Portland Cement Concrete Paving
02515   Unit Pavers
02710   Subdrainage Systems

Divison 4 *Masonry*

04200   Unit Masonry
04400   Stone

Division 5 *Metals*

05500   Metal Fabrications

Division 6 *Wood and Plastic*

06100   Rough Carpentry
06200   Finish Carpentry

Division 7 *Thermal and Moisture Protection*

07510   Built-Up Bituminous Membrane Roofing
07600   Flashing and Sheet Metal

Division 8 *Doors and Windows*

08110 Hollow Metal Doors and Frames
08210 Wood Doors

Division 9 *Finishes*

09200 Lath and Plaster
09250 Gypsum Board Systems
09300 Tile
09500 Acoustical Treatment
09650 Resilient Flooring
09900 Painting and Finishing

Division 13 *Special Construction*

13990 Minor Alteration Work

Guide Paragraphs for Bidding Requirements, Contract Forms, and Conditions of the Contract Documents

Besides modifications aimed at adapting standard guides to cover conditions inherent in working with existing construction, other modifications to bidding requirements, contract forms, and conditions of the contract documents are usually necessary. For instance, architects often add clauses to require contractors to coordinate their activities with public utilities and government agencies, clauses to tell bidders that bonds are required, clauses that list dates, names, and addresses of the parties mentioned in the contract documents, clauses that stipulate requirements related to bidding procedures, contract time, applicable laws and regulations, taxes, subcontractor prequalification, specific insurance requirements, and a host of other requirements.

Examples

The following guide paragraphs assume that the user has written provisions to take care of requirements applicable even for projects where there is no existing construction and has otherwise done everything necessary to make the contract documents complete, except for provisions necessary solely because there is existing construction.

The number of revisions necessary in standard bidding requirements, contract forms, and conditions of the contract documents intended for use on projects where all the work is new to make them accommodate existing construction is small compared with similar revisions necessary in specifications sections (those in Divisions 1 through 16). When the contractor is selected and the contract negotiated, there are no bidding documents at all. Using preselected contractors and negotiating contracts for remodeling, renovation, and restoration projects is now widespread, especially where much existing construction occurs in a project, and especially when preparatory work, such as cleaning or reroofing, is necessary before other work can begin.

Following is a list of bidding requirements, contract forms, and conditions of the contract documents, a discussion of the provisions an architect might have to add to each to accommodate existing construction, and examples showing such provisions.

In the following list, some sections have been divided to show different methods of stating requirements between small and large projects. Definitions of the words "large" and "small" here are somewhat subjective. In general, a small project is one in which presentation of the construction documents in abbreviated form will not be harmful. All other projects are designated as large. A fairly large project in building area might be small in terms of the amount of work involved. The architect must decide whether to use the shorter or the more extensive requirements in each particular instance. Consistency is not only unnecessary, it may be undesirable. It might be quite appropriate to treat one document as if the project were small and a second document in the same project manual as though the project were large. The decision must be based on the complexity of the requirement in each case. Where no distinction is made in the following text, handle that requirement the same way, regardless of project size.

Document 00010   *Pre-Bid Information*

All Projects: Changes are not usually required in Document 00010, or in mediumscope or narrowscope documents containing pre-bid information, due solely to the involvement of existing construction. These documents should, however, notify prospective bidders that existing construction is involved.

Document 00100   *Instructions to Bidders*

All Projects: Changes are not usually required in Document 00100, or in related mediumscope Section 00120, "Supplementary Instructions to Bidders," due solely to the involvement of existing construction. Bidders should be made aware, however, that they will have to deal with existing construction.

Pre-bid conferences (Section 00130, "Pre-Bid Conference") may be held for any project, but are more likely, even for small projects, when existing construction occurs. Such pre-bid conferences are often held at the building site. In any event, Section 00100 or 00120 should notify bidders of the requirement for a pre-bid conference, and Section 01030 should state where, when, and who.

Document 00200   *Information Available to Bidders*

All Projects: Probably the most common use of this heading is to present geotechnical data, usually in mediumscope Section 00220, "Geotechnical Data," or associated narrowscope sections. If part of that data were collected during document preparation for the existing building, Section 00220 should so state, giving the source and date the data were collected in much the same manner used to identify newly collected geotechnical data.

Section 00200 could be used to convey information to bidders about other existing conditions, but what form that data should take is unclear. Imagine, for instance, issuing bidders existing building specifications as part of a bid package. Apart from the cost, the advantage of doing that is doubtful. A project's designers should become thoroughly familiar with existing conditions and should extrapolate all data needed to bid and give that data to the bidder in the bidding documents. The contractor is entitled to rely on the data presented. Giving a bidder a set of existing drawings or specifications and saying, in effect, "this is what the other architect said ought to be there, but we can't guarantee it," smacks of incompetence.

Some architects make existing building drawings and specifications available to bidders for examination, but few issue bidders copies of those documents. If an architect wanted to give bidders those documents, Section 00200 would be the place to talk about them and write the necessary disclaimers. Since the author does not approve of such a procedure, this book has no suggested paragraphs for that purpose.

Section 00300   *Bid Form*

All Projects: Since bid forms are specific to each project, existing construction would affect them, but no more so than many other factors. An architect need do nothing specific to Section 00300 solely because existing construction occurs, unless that occurrence triggers other requirements. For example, a desire for separate prices for new and existing work would affect the bid form. The very fact that there were new and existing conditions would not.

Document 00400   *Supplements to Bid Form*

All Projects: The above discussion about Section 00300 applies as well to Section 00400.

Document 00500   *Agreement Form*

All Projects: Section 00500 is the form for the project's agreement between owner and contractor. The form selected may be influenced by the fact that existing construction occurs. What the owner's lawyer writes on the form may vary a great deal to accommodate the existing construction, but the basic form will probably not change, solely due to the existing construction.

Large Projects: AIA now produces several blank agreement forms for large projects. Federal, local, and state governments also produce their own agreement forms as do some large corporations, institutions, and even a few architectural firms.

Small Projects: AIA also produces Document A107, ''Abbreviated Form of Agreement Between Owner and Contractor for Construction Projects of Limited Scope where the Basis of Payment is a Stipulated Sum.'' This form contains general conditions, which eliminates the need for Section 00700. Sometimes the complexities introduced by having to deal with an existing building will turn what might otherwise be a small project into a large project.

Document 00600   *Bonds and Certificates*

All Projects: Section 00600 contains blank forms for bonds and certificates. The requirements for bonds and certificates, even the forms for them, might vary due to several circumstances, such as multiple contract or negotiated bid arrangements, but changes in the forms themselves due solely to the presence of existing construction will probably not be required.

Document 00700   *General Conditions*

All Projects: Section 00700 contains the basic general conditions document for the project. There are, to the author's knowledge, no standard general conditions documents in general use for private-sector work that are specifically written for projects where existing construction plays a role.

Large Projects: General conditions documents in common use for large private-sector projects, such as AIA Document A201, "General Conditions of the Contract for Construction," and the 1910-8 series documents of the Engineers Joint Contract Documents Committee (EJCDC) are generally used both for new projects and for projects where existing construction occurs. Federal, local, and state governments also produce general conditions documents for large projects, as do some large corporations, institutions, and even a few architectural firms.

Small Projects: AIA Document A107, "Abbreviated Form of Agreement Between Owner and Contractor for Construction Projects of Limited Scope where the Basis of Payment is a Stipulated Sum," contains general conditions for small projects. Using A107 eliminates the need for another general conditions document. The general conditions documents developed by state, local, and federal agencies and by large corporations, institutions, and architectural firms are typically used also for small projects.

Document 00800   *Supplementary Conditions*

Large Projects: AIA Document A511, "Guide for Supplementary Conditions," suggests language a specifications writer might use to amend the requirements of AIA Document A201 or to specify requirements not included in AIA Document A201. Included are such subjects as establishing a system of precedence among the various contract documents, substitutions, who pays for permits, liquidated damages, progress payments, insurance requirements, and many others. Unfortunately, not a single one of the revisions recommended in Document A511 even mentions existing construction. AIA presents no recommendations for adding requirements to cover conditions related to existing construction.

Following are some paragraphs that have been necessary to cover existing conditions on some of the author's projects.

Definitions: General conditions documents for projects where all the work is new usually contain definitions of the work required by the contract and the project on which that work is to be done. When the basic description or definition of the work under the contract contained in the general conditions documents being used does not mention work related to existing construction and the language is such that a doubt might arise about the scope of the contractor's responsibilities related to existing construction, add a paragraph similar to the following:

> The Work under this Contract also includes demolition, cutting, and patching of existing construction where required by the Contract documents, and protection of existing construction to remain in place.

Contractor's Review of Contract Documents and Field Conditions: General conditions for large projects where all the work is new usually require the contractor to compare the contract documents and report errors, inconsistencies, and omissions. Where existing construction occurs, it is necessary to require the contractor to also examine existing conditions and report errors and discrepancies between them and the contract documents. Where the contractor is required by a general conditions document to examine and compare drawings and specifications with each other and report discrepancies found, add a requirement that the comparison be also made between drawings and specifications and existing construction at the site. Where the general conditions document contains no such requirement, add one, such as the following:

> Carefully study and compare Contract documents with existing conditions at job site. Report to Architect, at once, errors, discrepancies, inconsistencies, and omissions and materials, products, systems, procedures, and construction methods shown or specified which are incorrect, inadequate, obsolete, or unsuitable for actual field conditions discovered, or which Contractor would not warrant as required by the Contract documents. Do not proceed with Work in areas where errors, discrepancies, inconsistencies, or omissions were found, without Architect's instructions.
>
> Before ordering materials or doing Work at the site, verify dimensions and conditions affecting materials to be ordered or Work to be done, to ensure that dimensions shown on Contract drawings accurately reflect actual dimensions. Bring inconsistencies to Architect's attention and do not proceed without Architect's instructions.

Documents and Samples at the Construction Site: General conditions documents for projects where all the work is new usually require the contractor to keep at the construction site a record copy of drawings, project manual, addenda, construction change directives, change orders, and other modifications, and submittals. For projects where existing construction occurs, it is often necessary to spell out the content of documents and samples to be maintained at the site in greater detail than is stipulated in general conditions documents for projects where all the work is new. AIA recommends that such additional information be written into Division 1 Specifications Sections. But when the additional requirements are not strictly procedural, such as the three guide paragraphs that follow, specify them in Section 00800.

> Owner will furnish record copies to be marked. Contractor shall bear cost of marking changes and cost of preparing record reproducibles at Project completion as specified in Specifications Section 01700, Contract Closeout, and other specifications sections.
>
> Legibly mark Drawings and specifications to show changes to architectural, structural, plumbing, mechanical, and electrical work; changes to grades and utilities; and changes required by Change Order or made necessary by other work.
>
> Also legibly mark Drawings and specifications to record existing conditions not shown on Contract documents when such existing conditions affect the Work under this Contract, and existing conditions that differ from those shown on Contract documents in location, size, configuration, or type of

existing work-in place. Mark all such conditions, including, but not limited to, the following:
1. Depths of various elements of foundation in relation to finish First Floor datum.
2. Horizontal and vertical location of underground utilities and appurtenances, referenced to permanent surface improvements.
3. Location of interior utilities and appurtenances concealed in the construction, referenced to visible and accessible features of the structure.
4. Field changes of dimension and detail.
5. Changes made by Construction Change Directive or Change Order.
6. Details not on original Contract drawings.

Cutting and Patching: General conditions documents for projects where all the work is new usually contain clauses covering cutting and patching of work installed under that contract and the work of the owner or the owner's separate contractors. For projects where existing construction occurs, it is often necessary to modify those clauses or include additional clauses to cover cutting and patching of existing construction. The following are suggestions of paragraphs that add such requirements:

Requirements for cutting and patching new Work also apply to cutting and patching of existing construction.

Unless specified otherwise in that specifications section, Work specified in each specifications section includes cutting, fitting, and patching for that trade, including cutting, fitting, and patching to accommodate the Work of other trades, and including cutting, fitting, and patching related to existing construction.

Patches and repairs shall exactly match existing adjacent Work in all respects and shall not be obvious as patching.

Do not cut structural members until specifically approved by Architect in each case, and, where required by code, or other legal requirement, not until approved by appropriate governmental authorities.

Time: It is often necessary, particularly when parts of an existing building are to remain in use during construction, to limit the hours when the contractor may work at the site. The following is an example of one such clause:

Normal working hours and days for Contractor's Work on this Project shall be between 7 A.M. and 5 P.M., Monday through Friday, other than on federal, state, and local government holidays.

Owner may require that certain limited portions of the Work be done after normal working hours or other than on normal working days.

Confine activities within existing building and on roof to normal working days unless Owner requires or agrees to other times or days. Activities outside existing building that produce sounds audible inside existing building are similarly restricted.

Should Contractor desire to carry out portions of the Work at times other than between the hours and days stipulated in this clause, submit a written request to Owner together with specific calendar days and hours Contractor wishes to work and a description of activities Contractor proposes to carry out during those times. Construction activities will not be permitted at times other than those specified or specifically agreed to in writing by Owner. Only activities Owner specifically agrees to will be permitted during hours or on days other than those stipulated in this clause.

No extension of time will be granted and no "extra" or additional amount will be paid due to Owner's failure to approve the performing of construction activities during hours other than those stipulated as normal working hours in this clause.

Work done during hours other than normal working hours, as stipulated in this clause, shall be done at no additional costs to Owner or Architect, whether Work at other times is required by Owner or requested by Contractor and agreed to by Owner.

If necessary in order to complete the Work within the time fixed in Agreement Between Owner and Contractor, or an extension thereof, Contractor shall request Owner's agreement for Contractor to perform Work other than during normal working hours, as defined in this clause and, if Owner agrees, shall perform Work during such other times and on such other days as have been agreed to by Owner, at no additional cost to Owner or Architect. Work during such other times and on such other days shall continue only so long as is necessary to complete the Work within stipulated time period.

It is also sometimes necessary to require that certain work be done other than during normal working hours, as in the following example:

Connection, disconnection, interruption, or disruption of existing water service, electric power, fire alarm, telephone, steam, sanitary sewer, storm sewer, heating, ventilating, and air conditioning systems, or other utility or service serving existing buildings other than those within Contract limits or site areas other than that within Contract limits shall be done during daylight hours on weekends or holidays. Preparation for and cleaning up after such Work shall also be done

```
during the same overtime periods. Include the costs
of such overtime Work in the Contract Sum. Claims
for additional time or payment on account of such
overtime Work will not be honored. Coordinate the
schedule for such overtime Work with Owner and
obtain Owner's approval before proceeding with the
Work.
```

Small Projects: General conditions documents intended for use on small projects rightly contain fewer clauses than general conditions documents intended for use on large projects. The clauses that small-project general conditions documents do contain are much more abbreviated than those in large-project general conditions. Some provisions usually left out of general conditions for small projects are needed, however, when existing construction occurs. Following are some such clauses.

Definitions: General conditions documents for small projects where all the work is new usually contain definitions of the work required by the contract. When those definitions do not mention work related to existing construction and the language is such that a doubt might arise about the scope of the contractor's responsibilities related to existing construction, add a paragraph similar to the following:

```
The Work under this Contract also includes
demolition, cutting, and patching of existing
construction where required by the Contract
documents, and protection of existing construction
to remain in place.
```

Contractor's Review of Contract Documents and Field Conditions: General conditions documents for small projects where all the work is new do not always require that the contractor study and compare the contract documents and report any error, inconsistency, or omission found in them. But even for small projects, where existing construction occurs, it is necessary to require that the contractor examine existing conditions and report errors and discrepancies between those existing conditions and the contract documents. In each instance where the general conditions document requires the contractor to examine and compare drawings and specifications with each other and report discrepancies found, add a requirement that the comparison be also made between drawings and specifications and existing construction. Where the general conditions document being used contains no such requirement, add one, such as the following:

```
Carefully study and compare Contract documents with
existing conditions at job site. Report to
Architect, at once, errors, discrepancies,
inconsistencies, and omissions and materials,
products, systems, procedures, and construction
methods shown or specified which are incorrect,
inadequate, obsolete, or unsuitable for actual field
conditions, or which Contractor would not warrant as
required by Contract documents. Do not proceed with
work in areas where errors, discrepancies,
inconsistencies, or omissions are found, without
Architect's instructions.
```

Before ordering materials or doing Work at the site, verify dimensions and conditions affecting materials to be ordered or Work to be done, to ensure that dimensions shown on Contract Drawings accurately reflect actual dimensions. Bring inconsistencies to Architect's attention and do not proceed without Architect's instructions.

Documents and Samples at the Construction Site: General conditions documents for small projects do not always require that the contractor maintain a set of record documents at the construction site. Often such formalities are unnecessary. For projects where existing construction occurs, however, it is usually a good idea to require that a record copy of drawings, project manual, addenda, construction change directives, change orders, and other modifications documents and submittals be maintained at the project site and marked to show changes so that the Owner has a record of existing conditions and changes made during the course of the project. The following is an example of such a clause.

Maintain at the site, in good order, one record copy of Drawings, Project Manual, Addenda, Construction Change Directives, Change Orders, and other modifications documents, and submittals. Owner will furnish record copies of Drawings and specifications to be kept at the site. Contractor shall furnish remainder of record documents to be kept at the site.

Legibly mark Drawings and specifications currently to show changes to architectural, structural, plumbing, mechanical, and electrical Work, changes to grades and utilities, and changes required by Change Order or made necessary by other Work.

Also legibly mark Drawings and specifications currently to record existing conditions not shown on Contract documents when such existing conditions affect the Work under this Contract, and existing conditions that differ from those shown on Contract documents in location, size, configuration, or type of existing work—in place. Mark all such conditions, including, but not limited to, the following:
1. Depths of various elements of foundation in relation to finish First Floor datum.
2. Horizontal and vertical location of underground utilities and appurtenances, referenced to permanent surface improvements.
3. Location of interior utilities and appurtenances concealed in the construction, referenced to visible and accessible features of the structure.
4. Field changes of dimension and detail.
5. Changes made by Construction Change Directive or Change Order.
6. Details not on original Contract drawings.

On completion of the project, turn the marked documents over to the Architect for the Owner.

Cutting and Patching: General conditions documents for small projects do not always contain clauses covering cutting and patching of work installed under that contract or the work of the owner or separate contractors working at the site. Such clauses may not be necessary when all the work is new, since such requirements can be inferred from the other documents. For projects where existing construction occurs, however, it may be necessary to add a clause to cover cutting and patching of existing construction. The following suggested paragraphs contain those requirements.

> Contractor shall be responsible for cutting, fitting, and patching of both new and existing work as required to carry out the Work under this Contract.
>
> Unless specified otherwise in that Specifications section, work specified in each specifications section includes cutting, fitting, and patching for that trade, including cutting, fitting, and patching to accommodate the work of other trades, and including cutting, fitting, and patching related to existing construction.
>
> Patch and repair work shall exactly match existing adjacent work in all respects and shall not be obvious as patching.
>
> Cutting, fitting, and patching shall not endanger or damage Work under this Contract or existing construction, and shall not be undertaken without permission of Owner or separate contractor whose work is being cut or patched.
>
> Do not cut structural members until specifically approved by Architect in each case, and, where required by code, or other legal requirement, not until approved by appropriate governmental authorities.

Time: Even for small projects, when parts of an existing building are to remain in use during construction, it may be necessary to limit the hours when the contractor may work at the site. Since such requirements will not be less in scope due to project size, the examples given earlier in this chapter for large projects apply as well to small projects.

Existing Operating Systems: When it is necessary to keep existing services operating during the construction period, the requirements may be extensive regardless of the project's size. The example given earlier for large projects applies even for small projects.

Guide Paragraphs for Specifications

The remainder of this chapter consists of suggestions for adapting specifications sections in *Masterformat* Divisions 1 through 13 that were initially developed for use on projects where all the construction is new so that they work for projects where existing construction plays a part. The sections discussed are commonly used ones. The discussion includes example paragraphs from the author's projects.

In the following discussion and examples, some sections show different methods of stating requirements for small and large projects. Definitions of the words "large" and "small" are subjective. A small project is one in which presentation of the construction documents in abbreviated form will not be harmful. All other projects are large. An architect must decide whether to use the shorter or the more extensive requirements in each particular instance. Consistency is not only unnecessary, it may be undesirable. It might be quite appropriate to treat one document as if the project were small and a second document in the same project manual as though the project were large. The decision must be based on the complexity of the requirement in each case. Where no distinction is made in the following text, handle that requirement the same way, regardless of project size.

Some of the examples are from broadscope sections. Others were from sections *Masterformat* designates as mediumscope.

We will confine our discussion and the examples primarily to requirements made necessary solely by the involvement of existing construction. Example paragraphs that specify requirements not solely necessitated by the involvement of existing construction, have been included occasionally, however, to place in context those paragraphs that are solely related to existing construction.

Paragraph numbers in the examples are not numbers a specifier might use in a real project, because the examples usually omit paragraphs that would be needed even if all the work was new.

Most of the examples are from projects with single-contractor stipulated-sum construction contracts. This book refers to other contractual arrangements as "unconventional" as a means of identification, even though other contract forms may outnumber single-contractor stipulated-sum arrangements where existing construction plays a major role in projects. The basic principles discussed apply to all forms of construction contracts, of course, but details may vary greatly. It is not uncommon, for example, in unconventional contracts to discard entire *Masterformat* divisions, and to radically alter contract requirements normally specified for single-contractor stipulated-sum contracts.

Sometimes similar requirements are shown in more than one example because a specifications writer would write some requirements in different locations depending on the particular project. Usually it makes sense to create a separate section for each extensive requirement and to gather minor requirements into broadscope sections. The examples sometimes show a requirement in a mediumscope section and again in a broadscope section. The proper location of some requirements is controversial. When preparing an actual project manual, decide where to specify each requirement depending on the project and personal preference, carefully coordinate provisions, and do not repeat requirements. Repetition leads to errors, and requirements specified twice may be bid twice, increasing project costs.

Division 1   General Requirements

In every project, there are general requirements that apply to virtually every specifications section. *Masterformat* recommends that we specify general requirements that are contractual in nature under Bidding Requirements, Contract Forms, and Conditions of the Contract, and general requirements that are procedural in nature in Division 1.

Requirements architects specify in Bidding Requirements, Contract Forms, and Conditions of the Contract documents are mostly modifications or extensions of requirements in standard documents, such as AIA Document A201, that are applicable to the project at hand. Many, though certainly not all, requirements specified in Division 1 are modifications or extensions of the requirements specified in the Bidding Requirements, Contract Forms, and Conditions of the Contract documents.

Which requirements go in Bidding Requirements, Contract Forms, and Conditions of the Contract documents and which go in Division 1 is not always clearcut. Fortunately there are generally accepted recommendations about where to specify different types of requirements. AIA Document A521 ''Uniform Location of Subject Matter,'' which was prepared by the Engineers' Joint Contract Document Committee and is EJCDC Document No. 1910-16, is a handy listing that suggests the proper location for many requirements. Many of the requirements specified in Division 1 are not affected by whether existing construction plays a role in a project.

Section 01010   *Summary of Work*

All Projects: The broadscope Section 01010 and all the narrowscope sections that fall under the general heading ''Summary of Work'' should be specifically written for each project and may therefore be greatly affected by existing construction.

''Summary of Work'' sections usually include, as the name implies, a verbal description of the Work (a capital ''W'' as defined in AIA Document A201).

Large Projects: Use broadscope Section 10101 on large projects where the scope is easily covered in a broadscope section. Use broadscope section 01010 for projects with no requirements for work sequencing or separate contracts. When using broadscope Section 01010, include in it the same kinds of paragraphs used in the examples for mediumscope Sections 01011, 01012, 01013, 01014, 01016, 01017, and 01018.

Small Projects: The scope of the work for small projects is usually so limited that a ''Summary of Work'' section is not justified. Small projects usually will not have separate contracts in such complexity that they need more than a sentence to describe. There is seldom a need for partial occupancy by the owner. Work sequencing is not normally required. When a small project needs a ''Summary of Work'' section, use broadscope Section 01010. Since small projects seldom need a ''Summary of Work'' section, this book includes none. For guidance in developing scope of work paragraphs for those few cases where small projects need them, refer to the comments and examples for Sections 01010, 01011, 01012, 01013, 01014, 01016, 01017, and 01018.

Section 01011   *Work Covered by Contract Documents*

Large Projects: Following are example paragraphs showing ways to cover existing conditions in a ''Summary of Work'' section. The first paragraph is a disclaimer stating that the summary does not limit the work to the items covered in the summary. Such a disclaimer is essential. The architect's lawyer should review the disclaimer and modify the wording, if necessary, to suit the laws of the jurisdiction in which the architect practices. The paragraphs that follow are examples only and bear no relationship to any real project. Write the description for each project independently.

1.01 SUMMARY

A. This Project description is a summary only, is general in nature, does not include every type of Work involved in the Project, is not a complete listing of the Work required under this Contract, and does not limit Contract Work as stipulated in other parts of the Contract documents. Contractor is responsible for every part of the Work indicated in Contract documents whether or not included in the following limited summary. Refer to every part of the Contract documents for the total Work included in this Contract.

B. In general, the Work consists of:
   1. Extensive renovation in existing Building A at 142 J Street, Washington, D.C.
   2. An addition to Building A, consisting of a three level below-ground garage of about 67,000 sq. ft., a nine story building of about 148,000 sq. ft., and a penthouse of about 8,250 sq. ft.
   3. A tunnel beneath J Street connecting the addition to Building B. The tunnel is an alternate.
   4. Renovations to Building B related to the tunnel, including a new elevator and a new stairway within Building B, and other remodeling as necessary to accommodate the new connection.

C. Phasing is required. Refer to Section "Work Sequence."

D. Contract includes demolition of structures on site of Building A addition and selective demolition within Buildings A and B to accommodate new Work.

E. New construction:
   1. Addition construction: Cast-in-place concrete frame and slabs with concrete spread footings generally placed in rock. Underpinning of existing structures and shoring of new foundations are required.
   2. Tunnel construction: Cast-in-place concrete.
   3. New exterior walls of the addition are architectural precast concrete with metal stud interior liners and with concrete masonry unit back-up in some locations.
   4. Roofs of the addition are a ballasted inverted roofing system using modified bitumen composite sheet membrane.
   5. Interior partitions in the addition are gypsum board on metal studs, with CMU in some locations. New exterior walls are finished on the interior with gypsum board.
   6. Exterior soffits on the addition are either architectural precast concrete or exterior gypsum board as indicated.
   7. Other finishes in the addition are as scheduled.

    8. Sloped glazing, entrances and storefronts, and other aluminum framed glass construction is required.

    9. Wood casework and hospital equipment are required, as are plastic laminate assemblies, millwork, and other equipment.

F. Work in Existing Construction:

    1. Renovations to existing construction are required.

    2. Existing construction is generally concrete frame with concrete floor slabs with approximately one inch concrete fill over slabs.

    3. Existing partitions are plastered gypsum block and some concrete masonry units. New partitions are generally gypsum board over steel studs.

    4. Plaster patching is required.

    5. Floors are generally resilient flooring.

    6. Some areas have been previously remodeled. In those areas, walls are generally gypsum board on steel studs with plastic wall covering typical in corridors and in some public waiting areas.

    7. Some carpet exists.

    8. Existing and new ceilings are acoustical materials.

G. Sitework includes paving, walks, repairs to damaged landscaping and lawns, new landscaping, site drainage, and miscellaneous site improvements.

H. New, and revisions to existing, fire protection, heating, ventilating, air conditioning, plumbing, electrical, and related Work are required as are revisions and extensions to existing nurse call, paging, clock, and fire alarm systems in existing Building A. Only minor revisions to such systems are required in Building B to accommodate new Work.

Small Projects: See comments at Section 01010, "Summary of Work."

Section 01012 *Work by Others*

Large Projects: When specifying the contractor's responsibilities related to work to be done by persons or organizations other than the contractor, be careful to include requirements related to existing construction. It may be sufficient to mention work by others in broad terms where all the construction is new. Often, requirements stipulated in general conditions documents are adequate. But on projects where existing construction plays a major role, the owner is much more likely to employ separate contractors and to do work with the owner's own forces. When that happens, include provisions like those shown in the following example to cover the contractor's responsibilities related to those separate contractors and the owner's own forces.

```
1.03  OTHER CONTRACTS
```

A. Owner has entered into a separate contract to remove existing windows in existing building's west elevation and to install insulating glass units in same locations.

B. Owner will enter into separate contracts, or will install with own forces, Chapel pews and altar, and certain items of equipment as scheduled.

C. In addition, Owner reserves right to enter into separate contracts for other work at construction site and to do other work at construction site using Owner's own forces during the life of this Contract. Such work may include, but is not limited to, work indicated in Contract documents as not in Contract (N.I.C.).

D. It is essential that the work of the various contracts, including this one, and work by Owner's forces, be coordinated so as to create the least possible hardship to all parties involved. It is Contractor's responsibility to cooperate fully in that endeavor.

E. Major areas of concern include storage of materials, use of site, access to areas of Work, stock piles of excavated and other materials, dewatering, etc. While the various specifications sections address most foreseeable areas of conflict, they do not necessarily mention every condition requiring coordination. This Contractor shall, nevertheless, fully cooperate and coordinate the Work under this Contract with activities of Owner and other contractors working at the site, at no additional cost to Owner or Architect.

Small Projects: See comments at Section 01010, ''Summary of Work.''

Section 01013   *Future Work*

Large Projects: Requirements for accommodating future work are much more likely to be needed when all of a project's work is new. Should accommodating future work be necessary in a project where existing construction occurs, the specifications methodology would be the same as if the future work was related to a project with all new construction.

Small Projects: See comments at Section 01010, ''Summary of Work.''

Section 01014   *Work Sequence*

Large Projects: Sequencing of the work is required in some projects that have all new construction but is much more likely to occur where existing buildings are involved, particularly if those existing buildings will remain partly in use during construction of the new work. The following are example paragraphs for projects where phasing is required.

1.02 PHASING

   A. Phasing of sitework, addition construction, and alterations in existing Buildings A and B is required.

   B. The purpose of phasing is to make available to Contractor the maximum construction area at all times, while maintaining operation of Owner's facilities which remain in use during the construction period.

   C. Minimum disruption of operation of adjacent facilities and access to those facilities is required. Cooperation with Owner to minimize inconvenience is essential.

   D. Obtain Owner's approval through Architect before starting Work in any area and do not begin Work in any area until Owner has accomplished preparatory Work.

   E. Owner may require Contractor to do certain Work after normal working hours or on holidays or weekends. Refer to "Supplementary Conditions" for requirements.

   F. Work in existing pipe tunnels serving Building A may be started before July 1, 19__, but access to Owner's buildings is not permitted before July 1, 19__. Do not disrupt utilities or services serving Owner's buildings before July 1, 19__.

   G. Work required before demolition begins includes relocation of telephone services in Building B and relocation of fire alarm systems in Buildings A and B. Coordinate telephone modifications in Building B with telephone utility company.

   H. Maintain existing one-pipe heating system in Building B basement in use throughout course of construction.

   I. Maintain exit access from second, third, and fourth floors of Building B to Exit Stair No. 4, and from first floor of Building B to the street through Door No. 181, at all times until July 1, 19__. After July 1, 19__, those areas will be available solely for Contractor's operations. From beginning of work until July 1, 19__, exit lights, corridor lights, signs, and fire alarm striking stations in maintain exit access areas specified in this paragraph in fully functioning condition. During that same time, maintain Exit Stair No. 4 as a fully functioning legal exit, including access to area of refuge.

   J. Psychological Center in Building B Basement will remain occupied throughout the Work in those areas. Maintain access to exterior. Phase the Work in those areas and construct barriers and dust partitions to permit Owner's use of maximum possible area at all times.

K. Start Work on the second floor of Building A in the normal course of events in accordance with approved Construction Schedule. After starting, continue Work on the second floor without interruption until completing all second floor Work. Thereafter, Contractor is denied access to the second floor to perform Work under this Contract, except for Work Owner specifically requests.

L. Similar restrictions to those specified related to Work on the second floor of Building A also apply to Work on the fourth floor of Building A.

M. Work under this Contract includes removing existing domestic hot—water main in third floor ceiling of Building A and providing a new main. Do that Work in the following sequence:

  1. Install new hot—water main in third floor ceiling without making connections to existing risers or main. Provide valves for future connections.

  2. At a time Owner agrees to (time may be after normal working hours or on a holiday or weekend) shut down existing hot—water main for not more than 4 hours and make connections. Provide new valve in existing main downstream of new connection. Both mains will be in service temporarily.

  3. Sequentially shut down existing risers and make new connections.

  4. After making connection to last riser, close valve on existing main and remove existing main.

N. Besides doing the Work continuously at second and fourth floors of Building A, phase the Work throughout the Project so that not more than one plumbing riser group (sanitary, vent, cold water, and hot water) is out of service at any time, unless Owner otherwise specifically approves in writing.

O. Schedule Work so that no exit, exitway, passage, or fire lane is blocked or restricted in violation of any code, law, or regulation.

On a more complicated project, a detailed phasing schedule might be appropriate. When using a schedule, use the procedural paragraphs from the preceding example and add paragraphs similar to the following:

1.02 PHASING

A. Phasing of the Work under this Contract is required. Phasing shall be in accordance with the "Work Sequence Schedule" following this section.

B. Complete the various phases by the dates and within the times stipulated in the "Work Sequence Schedule," unless further modified in the Agreement Between Owner and Contractor or later modified by Change Order.

Small Projects: See comments at Section 01010, "Summary of Work."

Section 01016   *Occupancy*

Large Projects: This section includes requirements for owner occupancy of the premises during construction and for owner partial occupancy of the area within the contract limits before the date of substantial completion.

Requirements for partial occupancy by the owner of all, or parts, of the construction area before the date of substantial completion are not appreciably different whether existing construction is part of a project or not.

An owner's continued occupancy of existing buildings during construction work on them or adjacent buildings, however, by definition, occurs only on projects where existing construction plays a part. Description of such occupancy can be simple, as in the case where a new building is to be built adjacent to buildings remaining in operation. Sometimes, such descriptions become very complicated. An owner may continue to occupy not only adjacent buildings and site areas, but also parts of the building where the work is being done. The owner may occupy different parts of the existing building at different stages of the work. The following is a paragraph covering a simple case.

```
D. During the life of this Contract, Owner will
   continue to occupy and operate grounds and walkways
   everywhere on Owner's property and all existing
   building, except the actual area of construction on
   the Third Floor of the East Wing of Building A. The
   Work of this Contract shall be done and such
   temporary facilities and phasing of activities
   provided as necessary to prevent interference with
   access to existing facilities or new work areas;
   cause the least possible interference with Owner's
   activities; and protect people and property from
   harm.
```

Section 01500, "Construction Facilities and Temporary Controls" contains suggested paragraphs covering operation of existing mechanical, electrical, and plumbing systems during construction.

Small Projects: See comments at Section 01010, "Summary of Work."

Section 01017   *Pre-Ordered Products*

Section 01018   *Owner-Furnished Items*

Large Projects: Pre-ordered products and owner-furnished items sections are mostly lists. Both may be more likely to occur when existing construction plays a role in a project. Owner-furnished items may be in place at the project site. But the methods for writing the requirements are essentially the same for projects that have existing buildings involved and those that do not.

Small Projects: See comments at Section 01010, "Summary of Work."

Section 01020 *Allowances*

All Projects: Architects use allowances more often in projects where existing construction occurs because some conditions remain unknown even at contract time. Often, some demolition is necessary before conditions can be fully defined. Using allowances permits letting the contract earlier than would otherwise be possible, thus allowing the work to begin before all conditions are known.

Even though allowances are more likely in projects where existing construction plays a role, the actual writing of requirements for them is no different solely because existing construction occurs.

Section 01025 *Measurement and Payment*

All Projects: No general changes are necessary in Section 01025 solely because existing construction occurs in a project.

Section 01030 *Alternates/Alternatives*

All Projects: Existing construction may affect which parts of the work are made alternates, but the occurrence of existing construction alone does not require alternates or changes to Section 01030.

Section 01040 *Coordination*

Large Projects: Architects should use extreme care when using Section 01040 to specify requirements for coordinating the work of the general contractor's subcontractors and suppliers on projects to be built by a single general contractor. The requirement to coordinate should be a contract obligation stipulated in the agreement between the owner and the contractor and in conditions of the contract documents. The means and methods that the general contractor uses to accomplish that coordination is solely the contractor's business. Architects should be very careful when attempting to insert themselves into the relationship between contractors and their subcontractors and suppliers for fear of thereby assuming responsibility for that coordination.

For most single-contractor stipulated-sum contracts, section "01040, "Coordination" is unnecessary. Requirements for coordination of the general contractor's work with that of separate contractors and the owner's own forces can be easily covered in Section 01012, "Work by Others, and Section 01120, "Alterations Project Procedures," as the examples for those two sections illustrate.

Obviously, a project that has separate prime contractors might justify Section 01040, and some other sections as well. *Masterspec*'s Basic Version includes four guides for sections that are different from those of a more conventional single-contractor project to use for multiple-prime-contractor projects.

When using Section 01040, place in it the requirements that the discussion and examples show in Section 01012, "Work by Others," and Section 01120, "Alterations Project Procedures," and requirements specified in many other sections as well.

Small Projects: Small projects will almost never need Section 01040, "Coordination."

Section 01045 *Cutting and Patching*

All Projects: Some architects include a cutting and patching section in their project manuals and there is certainly nothing wrong in doing so. For projects where existing construction is involved, though, it makes more sense to include cutting requirements in Section 02050, "Demolition," and patching requirements in Section 13990, "Minor Alteration Work." Similar work is specified in those sections, and it seems better to place similar requirements in the same sections. Examples in those two sections cover cutting and patching requirements.

Section 01050 *Field Engineering*

All Projects: Where there is no new construction or changes to existing site works, the need for civil engineers or surveyors might not exist. As the amount of site works or new construction becomes larger, the need for survey work increases, until engineers or surveyors become essential. The only variation between "Field Engineering" when existing construction occurs and "Field Engineering" for new work, is the need to clarify that the work to be located includes both existing and new construction.

Section 01060 *Regulatory Requirements*

All Projects: No specific changes are necessary to a section listing regulatory requirements, such as building codes, solely because existing construction plays a role in a project.

Section 01070 *Abbreviations and Symbols*

All projects: Architects will use more, and different, symbols and abbreviations on projects where existing construction occurs. Refer to Chapter 3 for lists of each. It is possible to place abbreviations and symbols lists in the specifications, but they are much more likely to be referred to when placed on the drawings.

Section 01080 *Identification Systems*

All Projects: Many architects specify identification systems partly in Section 09900, "Painting," and partly in Divisions 15 or 16. Wherever the requirements are specified, the specifications writer must be careful to state how identification marking of new systems will interface with existing identification systems. Different marking systems for new and existing work can create havoc and, in a future emergency, may even be dangerous.

Section 01090 *Reference Standards*

All Projects: No specific changes are necessary in Section 01090 solely because of existing construction.

Section 01100 *Special Project Procedures*

All Projects: Sections in this heading must be fully coordinated with other sections in Division 1, such as 01045, "Cutting and Patching," sections in Division 2, such as 02050, "Demolition," and, when we are talking about alteration project procedures, Section 13990, "Minor Alteration Work" as well.

Section 01120 *Alterations Project Procedures*

Large Projects: It has never been entirely clear what the writers of *Masterformat* intended for architects to specify in Section 01020, "Alterations Project Procedures." *Masterformat* lists Hazardous Materials Procedures, such as handling asbestos, but there is a Section 02080, "Asbestos Removal." Before 1983 there was controversy among specifications writers about where to specify requirements related to work in existing buildings which do not seem to fit into any other specifications section and do not warrant their own section. But the 1983 *Masterformat* solved that with the addition of Section 13990, "Minor Alteration Work."

Using Section 01120, "Alterations Project Procedures" is a good idea when existing construction occurs. The following example shows the kinds of requirements Section 01120 might contain.

```
1.02   EXISTING CONDITIONS

    A.  Contractors Examination of Site:
        1. By executing Contracts, Contractor and
           subcontractors represent that they have:
           a. Visited the site and made due allowances for
              difficulties and contingencies;
           b. Compared Contract documents with existing
              conditions and informed themselves of
              conditions to be encountered, including work
              by others, if any, being performed; and
           c. Notified Architect of ambiguities,
              inconsistencies, and errors they have
              discovered within Contract documents or
              between Contract documents and existing
              conditions.
        2. Failure to visit the site and become familiar
           with conditions shall not relieve Contractor or a
           subcontractor from furnishing materials or
           equipment or completing the Work in accordance
           with Contract documents at no additional cost.
        3. Contractor or subcontractors will not be given
           extra payment for Work related to conditions they
           can determine by examining the site and Contract
           Documents.
        4. Contractor or subcontractors will not be given
           extra payment for work related to ambiguities,
           inconsistencies, or errors within Contract
           documents, or between Contract documents and
           existing conditions, when such ambiguities,
           inconsistencies, or errors are known to
           Contractor or subcontractor before Contract
           execution unless Contractor or subcontractor has
           notified Architect in writing of such condition
           before execution of Agreement Between Owner and
           Contractor.
        5. Interested parties must obtain telephone
           clearance from Owner before making a site visit.
```

B. Existing building will remain in use during construction period. Refer to Section "Work Sequence" and other sections for additional requirements.

C. The adjacent public school uses N Street on the north side of the construction site during school hours on school days. Do not interfere with that use or disturb the users except by specific arrangement made with school officials and all other parties concerned.

D. Space at the site is severely limited. Make use of public property and make arrangements for that use. No extra compensation will be paid due to costs associated with using public property.

E. Access by Contractor to portions of Owner's property beyond the actual area of Work under this contract is denied, except where necessary to perform the Work, and then only with specific written approval in each case. Refer to other sections for additional requirements.

F. Contractor shall accept the site and the existing building in the condition in which they exist at the time Contractor is given access to begin the Work.

G. While Work under this Contract is in progress, protect existing buildings, grounds, contents, and occupants, including those on adjacent property, whether private or public, from damage or harm due to the Work under this Contract. The existing roof at the First-Floor level has been designed to carry only its own weight and a minimum snow load. Do not use that roof for staging, product storage, or any other construction-related purpose, except to do work directly related to that roof itself.

H. During the life of this Contract, work by others may be done at the site at Owner's discretion. Refer to Section "Summary of Work." It is also possible that other contractors will occupy parts of the existing building or work in the existing building while this Contractor is still on the premises. Access to the site, and within the site to the existing building, is also required for fire-fighting equipment. Owner will continue to occupy and operate parts of the existing building and site while Work under this Contract is in progress, except areas designated otherwise in Contract documents, and will continue to use driveways, parking areas, and walkways throughout Owner's property. Areas to remain in use include access ways designated or later agreed upon by Contractor and Owner.

　　1. The Work of this Contract shall be done, and such temporary facilities and phasing of activities provided so as not to interfere with access to existing facilities to remain in use or new Work

areas, so as to cause the least possible interference with activities of other contractors and Owner's personnel, or with use of existing building by Owner's employees, students, or the public, or with use of driveways, parking areas, or walkways by Owner's employees, students, and the public, and so as to protect people and property from harm. Do not block required access ways and other access ways not required but so designated by Owner or Contract documents.

2. Do not interrupt any utility service, such as water, gas, steam, sewers, electricity, or fire protection or communication system serving a building, or part of a site, or another part of Owner's property to remain in use without prior written approval of Owner and other authorities having jurisdiction.

I. Damage caused by Contractor to existing structures, grounds plants, pavements, utilities, work by others, fixtures, or furnishings, shall be repaired by Contractor and left in as good condition as existed before the damaging, unless such existing work is shown to be removed or replaced by new Work.

J. Complete documentation of existing construction is not available. Dimensions, layouts, existing materials, and concealed conditions have not necessarily been verified and are not represented to be accurate beyond the level necessary to define the approximate scope of surface renovation and system replacement.

K. Immediately upon entering the site for purposes of beginning Work, locate general reference points and take such action as is necessary to prevent their destruction; lay out Work and be responsible for lines, elevations, and measurements, and Work executed under this Contract. Exercise proper precautions to verify figures shown on Drawings before laying out Work. See Section "Field Engineering" for additional requirements.

L. Contractor and each subcontractor, before starting work, shall verify governing dimensions at the premises, including floor elevations, floor-to-floor heights, and column locations and shall examine adjoining Work on which Contractor's or subcontractor's Work is in any way dependent. No "Extra" or additional compensation will be allowed on account of differences between actual measurements and dimensions shown. Submit differences discovered during the Work to Architect for interpretation before proceeding with associated Work.

1.03 SURVEY AND RESURVEY OF EXISTING CONDITIONS

A. After Contract award and before starting Work at the site, Contractor, Owner's representative, and Architect shall together make a thorough survey of the building and grounds where Work under this Contract will occur and areas to be used as access ways to the Work areas. Contractor shall list, and photograph if Contractor desires, existing conditions not requiring alterations, shall note discrepancies between Drawings and existing conditions, and shall designate areas of storage and routes of access agreed upon by Owner.

B. At a mutually agreed-to time before completion of the Work under this Contract, Contractor and Architect shall make a resurvey of the same areas. Contractor shall furnish a report on conditions then existing compared with conditions as first noted. Architect will sign the report of resurvey and forward it to Owner. Damage listed in the report that was caused by Contractor, or anyone employed by or under contract to Contractor shall be repaired by Contractor and left in as good condition as existed before the damaging.

1.04 PROGRESS AND COMPLETION

A. Normal working hours and normal working days for Contractor's Work on this Project shall be between 7 A.M. and 6 P.M., Monday through Friday, excluding holidays, except as otherwise specified.

B. Owner may require that part of the Work be done after normal working hours or other than on normal working days.

C. Confine activities at Project site to normal working hours and normal working days, unless Owner requires or approves other times or days.

D. Should Contractor desire to carry out part of the Work at times other than normal working hours or days, submit written request to do so to Owner together with specific calendar days and hours Contractor wishes to work and description of activities Contractor proposes to carry out during those times. Construction activities will not be permitted at times other than those specified or subsequently approved in writing by Owner. Only those activities specifically approved by Owner are permitted during hours or on days other than those stipulated as normal working days or hours.

E. No extension of time will be granted and no "extra" or additional amount will be paid due to Owner's failure to approve the performing of construction activities during other than normal working days or hours.

F. Do Work other than on normal working days and hours at no additional costs, whether Owner requires Work at such times or Contractor requests such times and Owner approves.

G. If necessary to complete Work within Contract Time, as adjusted by Change Orders, request Owner's approval to work during days or times other than those designated as normal working days or hours; and if Owner approves, perform work during such additional times and on such additional days as have been approved, at no additional cost. Work during such additional times and on such additional days shall continue only so long as is necessary to complete the Work within the stipulated time period.

1.05 EXISTING OPERATING SYSTEMS

A. Maintain operating systems, utilities, and services serving existing buildings or site in operation to serve the needs of portions of Owner's property not involved in the Work under this Contract at all times during the progress of the Work, except for such short periods as are necessary to do the Work. Such operating systems, utilities, and services include, but are not necessarily limited to, water, electric power, heating, ventilating, air conditioning, sanitary sewer, fire alarm, nurses call, clock, telephone, and communications.

B. Before interrupting, or otherwise affecting, any such operating system, utility, or service, Contractor shall consult with Owner to establish a mutually satisfactory schedule for cutover, cutoff, disruption, or other change in operation of an affected system, utility, or service. In accordance with Article 8 of the "Supplementary Conditions" and Paragraph 1.04 of this section, Owner may require that such cutover, cutoff, disruption, or change in operation be made to occur after normal working hours, or on holidays or weekends. Such agreed to times and dates shall be clearly shown in the Progress Schedule specified in Section "Submittals." Once established and agreed to, schedule of disruption of systems, utilities, and services shall be strictly adhered to, unless later changed by mutual agreement in writing between Owner and Contractor.

C. Do not sever existing pipes, conduits, or ductwork serving existing building. Cut off pipes, conduits, and ducts that are connected to portions of the building or systems to remain and seal them tightly after making bypass provisions to prevent lapses in service. Cut off, cap, and tightly seal conduits and pipes in walls, partitions, and floors to be removed; or, if their continued service is required,

move such conduits and pipes to new acceptable
locations.

D. Protect both new and existing—to—remain mechanical
and electrical equipment from injury during the
construction period. Close openings into pipes and
ducts to prevent entrance of foreign materials.

1.06   WORK AREAS AND SEQUENCE OF OPERATIONS

A. Before starting each part of the Work, consult with
Architect and Owner to establish Work areas and
sequence of operations. Refer to Section "Work
Sequence" for additional requirements.

B. Once established, clearly mark Work areas and follow
agreed operations sequence. Restrict construction
personnel and storage and stockpiling of materials
and equipment to established Work areas. Carry out
Work as rapidly as possible, at times agreed to by
Owner.

Section 01200   *Project Meetings*

All Projects: Project meetings might be held more often for a project where
existing construction occurs, and a pre-bid conference is almost a necessity; but
other than that, there is no reason to modify Section 01200 just because a project
has existing construction involved.

Figure 8-1. Existing utility lines. (Photograph by Stewart Bros.)

Section 01300   *Submittals*

Large Projects: Most requirements in Section 01300 made necessary because of existing construction can be taken care of by occasional references to existing conditions.

There are, however, at least two subjects that need expansion to handle existing construction. The first is Demolition and Alterations Schedules. Specifications writers should require a Demolition Schedule in Section 02050, "Demolition," or Section 02070, "Selective Demolition," whichever is used for the project. Such a provision might be written as follows:

```
B. Demolition Schedule: As soon as possible after
   Contract award, submit for approval a proposed
   Demolition Schedule. Coordinate Demolition Schedule
   with Phasing Schedule specified in Section "Work
   Sequence," and Alterations Schedule specified in
   Section "Minor Alteration Work." Incorporate
   approved Demolition Schedule into Construction
   Schedule specified in Section "Submittals."
```

Also require an Alterations Schedule in Secton 13990, "Minor Alteration Work." Example Section 13990 includes such a provision and a discussion of using that section to specify general alterations requirements.

In a project where existing construction is involved, include a construction schedule requirement that includes a clause similar to the following:

```
A. Progress Schedule: As soon as possible after
   approval of Phasing Schedule specified in Section
   "Work Sequence," Demolition Schedule specified in
   Section "Demolition," Alterations Schedule specified
   in Section "Minor Alterations Work," and before
   doing work at the site, submit for approval a
   Progress Schedule showing estimated starting and
   completion dates for each part of the Work. Include
   Submittal Schedule specified in this section and
   approved Phasing, Demolition, and Alterations
   Schedules. Coordinate Progress Schedule with
   approved Phasing, Demolition, and Alterations
   Schedules. Clearly show disruptions to utilities and
   services to existing building as specified in
   "Supplementary Conditions."
```

Demolishing an existing structure may be required where all the construction work is new, but demolition, especially partial demolition, is much more likely to become a factor where the work takes place in, on, or directly adjacent to existing construction that will remain in place. A separate demolition schedule, however, is not usually required when all construction work is new, even when an existing structure is being demolished.

A renovations schedule would, of course, not be required where all construction was new work.

Additional paragraphs may be needed to specify the progress schedules requirements more fully, especially if some form of CPM is required, but that is true whether the work is all new or includes existing construction.

The second area where additional requirements are necessary in Section 01300 because of existing construction is construction photographs. The following example shows how to edit part of a standard construction-photographs clause to take care of existing construction. The words in parentheses apply to projects where existing construction is involved.

```
1.16  CONSTRUCTION PHOTOGRAPHS
    A. General: Provide construction photographs taken,
       developed, printed, and mounted by a recognized
       commercial photographic studio or reputable
       photographer acceptable to Owner, in the number and
       type and at construction stages enumerated below:
       1. Before Starting Work: Have photographs taken at
          site from different points of view (both inside
          and outside the existing building), sufficient in
          number to show site (and conditions at existing
          structures) but not fewer than 30 photographs.
       2. During Progress of the Work: Have not fewer than
          10 photographs taken at least once a month from
          points of view (both inside and outside the
          existing structure), as necessary to show
          progress of construction and site development for
          each part of the Work. Coordinate taking
          photographs with utility Work and backfilling.
          Photograph each buried utility line before
          backfilling. During later stages of the Work,
          have photographs taken from suitable locations
          inside the (new and existing) building(s).
```

Small Projects: Small projects will probably not require phasing, demolition, or alterations schedules.

If photographs are required at all for a small project, the requirements will be considerably diminished from those suggested above. Where photographs are required, though, the description of their locations may not differ appreciably from that suggested above for large projects, or may be simply covered by:

```
    A. Construction Photographs: Have seven taken each
       month by a photographer acceptable to Owner, at
       locations which best show work progress. Deliver two
       8 inch by 10 inch black and white prints to
       Architect for Owner of photographs taken each month
       and negatives to Owner at Substantial Completion.
```

Section 01400   *Quality Control*

All Projects: There are no specific changes needed in sections specifying administrative requirements for testing and inspection laboratories and services due solely to the involvement in a project of existing construction.

Section 01500   *Construction Facilities and Temporary Controls (Large Projects)*

All Large Projects: The differences between project manuals for projects with all new work and project manuals for projects where existing construction occurs are manifested greatest in those sections where temporary facilities and controls are specified. The following examples paragraphs are arranged as though they were all included in a single broadscope Section 01500, "Construction Facilities and Temporary Controls." An architect might choose to divide the requirements up into mediumscope or narrowscope sections following *Masterformat*'s suggestions. The example clauses for Section 01500 are not all from the same project and therefore do not necessarily coordinate with each other.

Mobilization: Except for large and complex projects, architects seldom specify mobilization requirements. Those requirements are specific to the particular project to the extent that guidance here would not be too helpful. The occurrence of existing construction would affect a mobilization section but no more than dozens of other factors. An architect should examine all factors affecting such a section, including existing construction.

Temporary Utilities: Since a project's nature influences how temporary utilities requirements are written, we will present examples taken from two projects with different characteristics. Note the slightly different handling of each case.

Some requirements specified in the first example were also in the second example but have been deleted here for brevity.

Since requirements for temporary heat during periods when the existing heating system is not operable are much the same whether existing construction is involved or not, those requirements, though specified in each example project's project manual, have been omitted here. The specifier must add them.

The examples also omit paragraphs describing requirements that are needed even when no existing construction occurs. The specifications writer must add those requirements also.

The project in the first example was a large existing building which required extensive remodeling and to which a major addition was added. The building was not in use during construction

PART 2   PRODUCTS AND EXECUTION (PART 3 INCLUDED)

2.01   TEMPORARY LIGHT AND POWER

    A. General: Provide necessary temporary lighting and power systems.
    B. Costs:
       1. Pay connection, installation, and maintenance costs for temporary service and fees.
       2. Pay cost of energy used, regardless of source, from entry onto site to perform the Work until date of Substantial Completion.
    C. Source:
       1. Using existing electrical services and lighting in the existing building for temporary light and power for this Work where appropriate.
       2. Use new permanent electric power and lighting systems for construction operations when progress of the Work permits.

D. Service Interruptions: Temporary interruption of electric service will be necessary at certain times, such as when connections to relocated power service are made. During such power outages, be responsible for providing such auxiliary power as is needed to carry out the Work.

2.02   TEMPORARY HEATING WITH PERMANENT HEATING SYSTEMS

A. Existing System: Upon entering the site for purposes of performing Work under this Contract, assume full responsibility for the existing building. Keep the permanent heating system in use when heat is needed during the construction period. Should shutdown of the existing system be required for any reason, provide temporary heat from other sources during the period of shutdown when heat is required. Refer to paragraph titled "Temporary Heating After Enclosure, Before Permanent Heating" of this section (omitted from this example because paragraph is about portable heating devices and is the same whether existing construction is involved or not) for detailed requirements for temporary heat from other sources.

B. Source: In both existing building and addition, as soon as is practicable, after new, altered, or relocated permanent heating system components or systems are operable, provide heat from permanent heating system, under heating subcontractor's operation and supervision, until the Work is complete.

C. Costs: Pay costs of filters and operation, including fuel costs, and costs of maintaining existing and new permanent heating systems and components until date of Substantial Completion.

D. Filters: Contractor may use new permanent heating systems, new components, and altered or relocated components of existing permanent heating systems and supply and return outlets of existing permanent heating systems, in spaces where Work is being done, without diffusers and registers in place. Do not, however, operate without filters with same efficiency as those specified for permanent system.

E. Elevated Temperatures: Provide for the work of various trades as specified in individual specifications sections and to protect both existing and new work from damage.

F. Cleaning: In new permanent heating systems, and in new, and existing-to-be-altered or relocated components of existing permanent heating systems, and in areas where existing components are not to be altered or relocated but other types of work have been done, clean ducts, replace filters with new ones, correct damaged or malfunctioning parts and put the system and its components in good working condition before date of Substantial Completion.

G. Balance: Balance the entire heating system in the building, including both new and existing portions, before date of Substantial Completion.

2.03   CONSTRUCTION WATER

A. General: Provide temporary construction water to serve all trades.

B. Codes and regulations: Installation shall comply with applicable codes and regulations, including fire and safety regulations.

C. Costs: Pay cost of connection, installation, maintenance, and sewer- and water-use charges from entry onto site for purposes of performing the Work until date of Substantial Completion.

D. Source: Contractor may use existing water service for construction water but shall still be responsible for payment as specified above.

E. Service Interruptions: During certain periods it will be necessary to interrupt water service, such as when connections are being made. During interruptions of water service, provide water needed to carry out the Work.

2.04   TEMPORARY TOILETS

A. General: Provide chemical toilets in prefabricated enclosures, conforming to local health and building regulations for use by construction personnel. Do not permit construction personnel to use building toilets.

The second example is from a project that included renovating one wing of one floor of a large hospital. The remainder of the hospital building and site stayed in use during construction. Johnson Hall (not the real name) mentioned in the example was an existing building on the hospital grounds that belonged to the hospital. Johnson Hall was not occupied at the time the work was to be done, and no work in that structure was scheduled as part of the contract. The contractor was permitted to use Johnson Hall for offices and storage but no other portions of hospital property. The contractor was not asked to restore Johnson Hall to the condition that existed when the contractor's use began, since the building would require major renovation to make it usable in any case. The contract did require, however, that the contractor prevent damage to Johnson Hall's structural system and keep the building weathertight.

PART 2 PRODUCTS AND EXECUTION (PART 3 INCLUDED)

2.01 TEMPORARY LIGHT AND POWER

   A. General: Provide temporary lighting and power system to serve all trades.

   B. Sources of Power:
1. For Work Within or On Hospital Building: Use existing hospital building electrical service, subject to Owner's regulations.
2. Other Power: Use existing metered electrical services and lighting system in Johnson Hall for temporary power and light in offices and storage areas for Work in and around Johnson Hall, for site Work, and for other Work not directly associated with the hospital.

   C. Cost of Energy Used:
1. For Work Related To Hospital Building: Paid by Owner, unless Contractor abuses privilege.
2. For Other Work: Paid by Contractor. Use only power metered by Johnson Hall meter.

   D. At Completion: Remove temporary wiring and equipment when no longer needed and dispose of equipment and wiring. Repair holes left in paving, walls, and partitions, except that repair is not required inside Johnson Hall.

2.02 TEMPORARY HEATING AND COOLING WITH PERMANENT HEATING AND COOLING SYSTEM

   A. Johnson Hall: Permanent heating and cooling system is inoperative. Use portable devices for heating and ventilating. As an alternative, use existing metered natural gas service to Johnson Hall as energy source for temporary heat subject to the following:
1. Comply with requirements of this specifications section.
2. Heaters shall be approved by both Architect and Owner.
3. Pay cost of fuel used.
4. Do not use unmetered gas from Johnson Hall service.
5. Do not use hospital building's gas service as fuel source for temporary heat in Johnson Hall.

   B. Hospital:
1. Continued Operation of Hospital Systems: Owner will keep permanent heating and cooling system in use when heat or cooling is needed during construction period, without charge to Contractor, to serve building portions not involved in construction activities, and provide temporary heat and cooling source for construction activities. Coordinate connections

to existing systems and interruptions of existing system operation with Owner. Do not interrupt operation of permanent heating and cooling system operation without Owner's approval.

2. Temporary Heat and Cooling from Permanent System: As soon as practicable, after new, altered, or relocated permanent heating and cooling system components are operable, provide heat and cooling from permanent hospital heating and cooling system, under operation and supervision of heating subcontractor, until the Work is complete. Coordinate use of permanent heating and cooling system with Owner. Do not activate new system components until Owner approves such activation.

2.03   CONSTRUCTION WATER

A. Work Related to Existing Hospital Building: Use existing hospital building service. Owner will pay for construction water taken from hospital building system so long as Contractor does not abuse the privilege. Make connections at locations approved by Owner.

B. Other Work: Use existing metered service to Johnson Hall. Pay cost of water used.

Temporary Construction: Requirements for temporary bridges, decking, overpasses, and the like vary considerably from project to project. Two examples follow.

2.04   TEMPORARY DECKING

A. General: Provide temporary decking over the tunnel excavation to support vehicular and pedestrian traffic at J Street.

B. Design: Have the decking designed by a registered professional engineer to support all loads to be encountered, and to be safe and secure.

C. Codes and Regulations: Comply with laws, ordinances, regulations, and requirements of District of Columbia agencies having jurisdiction. Make required submittals, pay fees, and obtain necessary approvals.

D. Scheduling: Schedule Work so that traffic on J Street is not disrupted, except as approved by authorities having jurisdiction.

2.05   BRIDGE SAFETY NET

A. General: Provide safety netting or other acceptable method to protect persons and property from harm due to construction of the bridge over J Street.

B. Codes and Regulations: Comply with laws, ordinances, regulations, and requirements of District of

Columbia agencies having jurisdiction. Make required submittals, pay fees, and obtain necessary approvals.

C. Scheduling: Schedule work so that traffic on 22d Street is not disrupted, except as approved by authorities having jurisdiction.

Construction Aids: Both *Spectext* and *Masterspec* include paragraphs covering construction aids. Between them, they suggest basic requirements for scaffolds, staging, ladders, stairs, ramps, runways, platforms, railings, hoists, cranes, chutes, and other facilities for temporary use, wording to designate an existing stair as access way to the work area, use of existing elevators, temporary enclosures, including wall and ceiling enclosures, dewatering, enclosure of work, and other temporary support facilities. The examples here are, for the most part, more specific than clauses recommended by commercial specifications in that most of them were developed specifically for real projects.

The following example contains detailed requirements for a materials elevator. Ordinarily, an architect would not write detailed requirements for devices that are strictly for the contractor's use. In this case, however, the owner felt it necessary to dictate the device the contractor could use to gain access to the work area. Demolition work within the hospital building was extensive and would generate large amounts of debris that had to be removed from an upper floor in a building that was to remain in operation. The great potential for damage to property or injury to people and the necessity for holding noise levels down in and around the hospital were persuasive.

2.06   TEMPORARY MATERIALS ELEVATOR

A. General: Provide temporary materials elevator. Comply with applicable federal safety regulations, labor laws, and other laws, codes, and regulations of authorities having jurisdiction. Maintain material elevator until demolition and removal of debris and salvage is complete and the bulk of construction products are stored in the hospital building.

B. Type: Electrically operated. Do not use elevator operated by internal combustion engine. Equipment-generated noise level shall not exceed 85 decibels.

C. Location: Erect at exterior of hospital building B Wing in location approved by Owner.

D. Operation: Do not permit free dropping of materials, rubbish, or debris. Remove by material elevator. Do not use chutes for materials, rubbish, or debris removal unless Owner specifically approves in writing.

E. Protection: Protect building from use of material elevator to prevent damage, staining, or marring of permanent work. Brace and guy securely and provide safety devices required by codes and regulations.

F. Removal: Remove materials elevator when no longer needed and repair damage.

The following is a more general example. Even when an architect does not prescribe the device for removing trash and debris, it is sometimes better to require that chutes *not* be used. Obviously, chutes are a greater danger to existing finishes than are materials elevators. Using chutes is, of course, quite common, and often not harmful, but, while chutes are superior to dropping debris freely, they should be avoided whenever practicable because of the potential for damage to existing construction.

2.07   TEMPORARY HOISTS, CHUTES, SCAFFOLDS, CRANES, STAIRS, ETC.

   A. General: Provide temporary hoists, cranes, material elevators, chutes, derricks, scaffolds, staging, stairs, ramps, runways, ladders, platforms, railings, and similar items for proper execution of the Work. Such apparatus, equipment, construction, and use shall meet applicable requirements of labor laws, federal safety regulations, and other applicable laws, codes, and regulations of authorities having jurisdiction.

   B. Duration of Use: Maintain hoisting facilities until structure is in place and most materials have been delivered to location where they will be installed.

   C. Locations: Subject to acceptance.

   D. Do not free-drop materials, rubbish, or debris.

   E. Protection: Protect permanent construction from damage, staining, or marring due to use of chutes, hoists, cranes, material elevator, derricks, scaffolds, staging, ramps, etc. Brace and guy securely and provide safety devices required by codes and regulations.

   F. Removal: Remove and relocate scaffolds to avoid interference with other trades. Remove temporary devices when no longer needed and repair damage.

   G. Stairs: Erect permanent stairs as soon as practicable; provide temporary shaft protection until permanent railings have been installed. Protect permanently exposed surfaces from damage due to later operations.

   H. Cranes: Contractor may place crane foundations inside building lines and leave them in place if they do not interfere with proper execution of functioning of any part of the Work. Obtain Architect's approval before placing permanent or temporary crane foundations. Remove crane foundations that interfere with present or foreseeable Work or function.

Using existing stairs and elevators for construction purposes is quite common in remodeling, renovation, and restoration projects. The following clause specifies such use.

2.08   TEMPORARY USE OF EXISTING ELEVATORS AND STAIRS

   A. Elevator: Contractor may use existing Elevator No. 3 to transport construction materials, personnel, or debris, or for any other construction related purpose, subject to the following requirements.

Figure 8-2. Temporary scaffolding. (Photograph by Stewart Bros.)

1. Notify Owner of intent to use Elevator No. 3.
2. Do not use Elevator No. 3 until Owner authorizes use.
3. Submit to Architect for approval a written list of the procedures Contractor proposes to use to protect existing elevator from harm during use.
4. Comply with additional requirements, if any, conveyed to Contractor as a condition of existing elevator use.
5. Protect cab, entrances, and adjacent surfaces from damage. Satisfactorily repair damage that occurs during the construction period.
6. Prevent overloading elevator. Rated capacity is 2,500 pounds.
7. Maintenance: Assume responsibility for maintenance during use. Have elevator inspected by an elevator maintenance organization acceptable to Owner at the end of use for construction purposes. Repair damaged equipment, parts, and surfaces, or remove damaged elements and provide new, when damage was due to construction use. Thoroughly clean exposed surfaces and restore to condition existing at start of Work. Return elevator to Owner properly operating and in every way equal to condition at beginning of Contractor's use.

B. Stairs: Construction personnel may use stairs indicated in Contract documents or later designated by Owner for such use but shall maintain required exit and exit ways at all times, and permit Owner's personnel to use existing stairs at any time. Protect access ways and stairs from damage during Contractor's activities. Restore damage to condition equal to that existing before damage. Do not use stairs other than those indicated or later designated by Owner.

The following is a general clause applicable to temporary enclosures. Specifications might include more detail, even describing materials and methods to be used.

2.09   TEMPORARY ENCLOSURES

A. General: When necessary during prolonged periods of cold or inclement weather to maintain construction schedules, provide temporary enclosures of sufficient size to permit Work to continue. Provide operable openings to allow adequate ventilation for workers and heating equipment.

Figure 8-3. Condition requiring temporary enclosure. (Photograph by Stewart Bros., courtesy of Sigal Construction Corporation.)

New construction often requires the kind of major enclosure specified in the example above, but projects where existing construction occurs generally require more specific requirements to protect portions of the structure. The following clause contains such requirements. Many of the requirements specified in the following clause might also apply to new construction.

2.10   TEMPORARY BUILDING PROTECTION

A.   To Close Openings: When installation of permanent sloped glazing, doors, storefront, or permanent closure of other openings is delayed, provide temporary weathertight closures to permit use of temporary heat and to maintain suitable conditions for interior Work. Equip temporary exterior doors with padlocks. At end of each day's Work, close temporary protection and lock or otherwise secure facilities.

B.   Where Existing Construction Is Removed: Provide adequate enclosure, tarpaulin, or other temporary waterproof covers to protect against the elements where existing portions of exterior walls, doors or windows, cover over enclosed space, roofing, or other existing building shell construction or weather barrier are removed. Remove protection only when actual construction is in progress, until new construction provides weathertight seal.

C.   Protect Openings: With securely anchored and maintained boarding, case and protect sills, jambs, and soffits of new and existing finished openings used as passageways or through which materials are handled and exposed corners, spandrels, projecting features, and other existing and new work subject to damage.

D.   Finished Surfaces: Clean and free of marring or damage at time of final acceptance. At no additional cost, satisfactorily repair marred or damaged surfaces or remove them and provide new materials.

E.   Protect Existing Finished Surfaces:
1.   Place tight wood planking or plywood under materials stored on permanently exposed concrete or other finished surfaces, and before moving materials over existing or newly finished surfaces. Use wheelbarrows with rubber tires.
2.   Protect existing and new prefinished work from damage due to construction operations.
3.   Use fire-resistive building paper when using building paper for temporary protection of floors and other finished surfaces.

F.   Remove temporary protection promptly on completion of construction activities when no longer needed.

Barriers and Enclosures: In addition to the kinds of protection specified in the above clause, projects require temporary partitions and closures. Such temporary partitions and closures are more prevalent when a project includes existing construction.

2.11 TEMPORARY PARTITIONS AND CLOSURES

A. General: Where necessary to protect existing materials to remain and new Work in place, provide temporary dust-tight partitions and closures to:
   1. Separate portions of existing building where existing construction is to be demolished or altered from new Work already installed and to separate them from existing work that might be damaged during the demolition or alteration;
   2. Separate portions of existing buildings not involved in this Contract from areas where Work under this Contract will occur.

B. Location and Extent: As necessary to protect existing materials to remain, new Work, and work by Owner and other contractors from damage. Locate in cooperation with Owner and other contractors.

C. Interior Cutting Operations: Enclose to prevent dust from spreading, catch debris, and prevent injury to persons.

D. Floor Protection: Erect temporary partitions over a layer of 30-lb. asphalt felt or acceptable equivalent to protect existing floors to remain.

E. Partition Construction:
   1. Non-Fire-Resistive: Except where fire resistive construction is required by code, build temporary partitions using 2 by 4 wood studs with 1/4 inch thick plywood or tempered hardboard on one side for full height. Seal joints, including perimeter joints, to preclude passage of dust. Use accepted methods. Do not damage adjacent surfaces.
   2. Fire-Resistive: Where fire-resistive construction is required, use 2 hour construction of steel channel studs and type X gypsum board with taped joints. Seal perimeter joints to preclude dust passage. Use accepted methods. Do not damage adjacent surfaces.

F. Circulation: Where the code requires circulation through temporary partitions or enclosures, provide dust-tight, gasketed doors and frames, including hinges, and a first-quality padlock and hasp on each door, or use standard suitable hardware. Construction masterkey each lock. Refer to Section "Finish Hardware."
   1. For wood stud partitions, use either wood or hollow metal doors and frames.
   2. For fire-resistive partitions, use hollow metal doors and frames with Class B rating.

G. Removal: Relocate temporary partitions where work progress requires. Remove when no longer needed.

Protecting Trees and Plants: Technical requirements for protecting trees and other plants where existing construction is present vary little from those where no existing buildings occur, usually amounting to adding phrases such as "and at existing construction." Trees and plants around existing buildings may vary from those on virgin ground because the former were planted instead of growing naturally, but the methods used to protect them are basically the same. Lawns may not exist in natural settings and will probably require additional writing when they do, but lawn repair is usually specified in Division 2.

If a landscape section, or Section 13990, "Minor Alteration Work," specifies requirements included in the clause below, delete those requirements from the following clause.

2.12 PROTECTING EXISTING TREES, SHRUBS, AND LAWNS TO REMAIN

A. Extent:
1. Throughout Owner's property, protect existing trees and shrubs to remain. Existing trees and shrubs not shown to be removed or falling beneath new construction are to remain unless indicated otherwise. Satisfactorily repair existing trees and shrubs to remain that are damaged or destroyed during the Work under this Contract, or remove and provide new equivalent trees or shrubs at no additional cost.
2. Throughout Owner's property, protect existing lawns to remain. Existing lawns not shown to be removed or falling beneath new construction are to remain unless indicated otherwise. Remove existing lawns to remain that are damaged or destroyed during the Work under this Contract, and place new matching sod in the area of removal, at no additional cost.
3. Protect trees and shrubs to remain throughout Owner's property where subject to damage due to activities related to this Contract using means and methods specified in Section "Minor Alteration Work."

B. Protection: Avoid vehicular traffic over root zones of trees to remain and over lawns. Do not flush mortar boxes, mixers, or concrete trucks, or spill damaging materials or store materials on lawns to remain or under trees or shrubs to remain.

C. Construction Activities: Carefully supervise excavating, grading, and other construction operations to prevent damage to trees, shrubs, and lawns to remain. Do not remove trees or shrubs to simplify construction activities except with Owner's specific written approval in each case. Discard removed plants and provide new matching plants.

D. Repairs: Owner reserves the right to have damaged lawns repaired, damaged trees and shrubs removed to facilitate new construction, damaged trees and shrubs repaired or removed, and new replacement trees and shrubs installed by Owner's forces or under a separate contract, in either case, at this Contractor's expense. Should Owner elect not to do lawn or landscape work, Contractor shall hire a landscape subcontractor and do the work in accordance with requirements specified in Section "Landscaping" (Section, "Minor Alteration Work").

E. Removing Protection: Remove protection on completion of construction, or earlier, if acceptable.

F. Public Property: Be solely responsible for following laws, regulations, and requirements of authorities having jurisdiction over trees, shrubs, and lawns on public property.

G. Adjacent Properties: Be also solely responsible for actions related to adjacent properties.

Security: Security requirements can become quite extensive, especially when a construction site includes an existing structure of sensitive nature as happens in many federal government projects. Since each such project will be different, the architect must develop specific requirements in each case. Often, the government agency which is the architect's client will provide specific words to be included in the specifications.

Security requirements are normally not as stringent on private-sector projects as they are on government projects, but sometimes they are. Security requirements range from construction personnel's wearing identifications badges, sometimes with a photograph of the person, to licensing vehicles, maintaining a list of people authorized to enter the site, furnishing security clearance, excluding cameras from the site, and even installing metal detectors and geiger counters to check personnel as they enter or leave the site.

Security requirements are so specific to each project and require so much direction from the Owner that suggesting clauses here to cover them would be meaningless.

Protection of People and Property: *Masterformat* scatters protection requirements. The following clause collects those protection requirements not covered in other places into a single catch-all clause. Use such a clause to specify every needed requirement that does not fit anywhere else in the *Masterformat* system.

2.13 PROTECTION GENERAL REQUIREMENTS

A. Laws: Comply with applicable laws, ordinances, rules, regulations, and orders of authorities having jurisdiction for safety of people and protection of property from damage, injury, or loss.

B. Responsibility: Be solely responsible for initiating, maintaining, and supervising safety precautions and programs concerning Project security, but obtain Owner's approval of methods to be used and location of safeguards. Submit to Owner, through Architect, drawings and written description of methods and devices Contractor intends to use and do not begin Work at the site until such means and methods are mutually agreed on by Owner and Contractor.

C. On Public Property: In addition to other means used in the interest of safety or security, comply with the requirements of governmental agencies having jurisdiction.

D. Using J Street: Refer to Section "Alterations Project Procedures," for requirement to permit adjacent public school to use J Street. Take precautions to protect the users.

E. Protect Improvements: Throughout Owner's property, protect permanent improvements to remain, such as curbs, pavements, fences, planting, buildings, and other improvements subject to damage due to Contractor's operations. Also protect access ways outside the existing building from damage. Repair or remove and install new acceptable items where improvements are damaged during Contractor's operations. Restore surfaces damaged during construction period to condition before damage.

F. Safeguards: Erect and maintain, as required by conditions and progress of the Work, necessary safeguards, for safety and protection, including temporary fences, guards, railings, barricades, canopies, lighting, shoring, directional and danger signs, signals, and other warnings against hazards.

G. Security: Protect and secure the site, existing buildings, new addition, and new and existing materials and equipment from theft and damage by whatever reasonable means are effective. Use methods such as the following, singly or together: locks, fences, signs, patrols, radio, alarms, locked storage on-site, and off-site warehousing.

H. Wall Closures: Unless other acceptable means are provided, provide temporary closures for openings in walls along 35th, 36th, and J Streets to make the building and site secure. Secure temporary closures when Work is not in progress using suitable means such as dead bolts inaccessible from the public side or locks or padlocks construction masterkeyed in accordance with Section, "Finish Hardware."

I. Chain Link Fence: In addition to other safety and security means, erect and maintain an acceptable chain link fence to enclose the entire Johnson Hall building. In chain link fence, provide gate with lock and keep locked except when in use. Include in drawings specified in subparagraph B of this Paragraph 2.13 fencing details and a plan showing fence and gate location. Fence type and details are subject to acceptance. Do not use fence type which makes necessary the destruction of portions of walkways or pavements to remain. Do not use unacceptable fences.

J. Solid Wood Fences: In addition to other safety and security means, erect and maintain, where shown, temporary solid wood fence. Provide gates shown, with locks construction masterkeyed as specified in Section, "Finish Hardware," and keep locked except when in use. Build fence 8 feet high of 4 foot by 8 foot clear plywood panels, securely fastened to 4 by 4 pressure treated wood posts, securely set in ground. Fasten plywood panels to outside (away from Project site) and butt together evenly. Exterior plywood surfaces shall be free of dirt, stains, pitting, and splinters to permit the painting of art work on them. Leave fence unpainted.

K. Entrances: Do not block entrances to buildings to remain in use or in any way inhibit access to them. Refer to Section "Alterations Project Procedures" for additional requirements.

L. Design Live Loads: Do not permit placing materials or equipment on new or existing structures to exceed design load of structure or endanger structure or people.

M. Trenches: Do not permit trenches to remain open for prolonged periods without adequate board covering or fencing.

N. Broken Glass: Be responsible for glass broken during construction period; at completion, replace broken glass.

O. Weather Protection: During construction, provide protection against weather (rain, wind, storms, frost, or heat), and maintain work, materials, apparatus, and fixtures free from damage. At end of each work day, cover new work and exposed existing work likely to be damaged.

P. Dust: Take precautions necessary to keep Work under this Contract and adjoining property reasonably free of dust.

Q. Protection of Construction Materials: Refer to other specifications sections for specific requirements.

R. Materials Hoist: Do not permit transporting of people on materials hoisting facilities.

S. Removals:
1. Except for fences, remove temporary construction and protection specified in this section promptly when no longer needed and when removal is approved.
2. Maintain temporary fences until date of Substantial Completion, unless approval is obtained for earlier removal; then remove the temporary fence.

T. Damaged Site Improvements: Repair and restore to condition at beginning of construction, or better, existing site improvements, such as pavements, curbs, buildings, fences, lawns, plantings, and lighting which are not to be removed under this Contract but are damaged or defaced by Contractor's operations, except where new Work is required by the Contract.

U. First Aid Equipment: Provide at the site. Also provide continually available trained and qualified personnel to render first aid when needed.

V. Emergency Signs: Provide signs posted at telephones listing telephone numbers of emergency medical services, physicians, ambulance services, and hospitals.

Winter Construction: Requirements for dealing with winter weather, in those areas of the country with severe winters, presents sufficient problems to warrant its own specifications clause. It is not necessary, however, to add requirements to standard winter construction and protection clauses solely because existing construction is present.

Access Roads, Parking Areas, and Traffic Regulations: The distinction between *Masterformat*'s suggested mediumscope sections 01550, "Access Roads and Parking Areas" and Section 01570, "Traffic Regulations" has always seemed tenuous at best. We will here discuss the two as one subject.

Specific materials and construction requirements for roads, including temporary access and haul roads are more effectively covered in Division 2 sections. Materials and methods used to build permanent pavement are often applicable to temporary road construction, especially if the construction period is long. Sometimes, the beds for permanent pavement are used as temporary roadways. When that happens, specify requirements for the entire process in the specifications section where the permanent pavement is specified.

When existing roadways will be used for temporary access by construction equipment or as haul roads by large trucks and the roads will most likely suffer considerable damage, it makes sense to specify requirements for their maintenance and repair in a Division 2 paving section.

When there is no new paving and damage to existing paving is anticipated, use Section 02575, "Pavement Repair." If the anticipated damage is slight, use Section 13990, "Minor Alterations Work."

There is usually little need to control the materials and methods used to construct roads that are truly temporary. It is sufficient to state in Section 01500, "Construction Facilities and Temporary Controls" that temporary roads are required, that existing roads may be used (or may not be used, if that is appropriate), and that existing surfaces damaged shall be returned to the condition that existed before the damaging, and stop at that. If control of materials or methods is necessary, write the specific requirements in a Division 2 section.

The following examples include some typical traffic control requirements. In addition, the examples, which were taken at random from several of the author's project manuals, show other types of provisions that may be needed.

2.14 SITE ACCESS, PARKING, AND TRAFFIC REGULATIONS

    A. General: Plan and control use of site and access to site in cooperation with Owner and other contractors working at site to minimize disruption of use of other facilities; portions of buildings and site areas affected by this Contract and to remain in use; and the work of other contractors.

    B. Temporary Access Drives: Construct on the premises as necessary, and maintain in good usable condition; remove when no longer needed. Until permanent improvements have been completed, when necessary to prevent excessive dust, periodically water temporary unpaved access roads.

    C. Construction Site Access: Use most direct route from public streets as agreed to by Owner. Construction traffic elsewhere on Owner's property is prohibited.

    D. Access to Existing Building Interior: Use routes and existing doors, stairs, and elevators agreed to by Owner.

    E. Driveways Between and Around Combustible Storage

Piles: Maintain at least 15 feet wide and free of accumulation of rubbish, equipment, and materials.

F. Access for Fire-Fighting Equipment: Maintain.

G. Access: Refer to other sections for requirements to keep access to site and buildings open to Owner, other contractors, and fire-fighting equipment.

H. Use of Streets and Sidewalks on Public Property: Make arrangements with authorities having jurisdiction for use. Restrictions shall be those of the District of Columbia. Be solely responsible for adherence.

I. Roadway Closed: Owner will close the roadway south of the site to traffic during the construction period. Contractor may use that roadway as a staging area.

J. Roadways, Driveways, and Walkways: Where outside indicated Contract limit, on Owner's property and on public property, keep open to pedestrian and vehicular traffic at all times. When temporary closing of a roadway, driveway, or walkway is absolutely unavoidable, provide alternative access routes. Such temporary closings shall be approved by Owner in each case and shall be for the shortest possible time. Strictly adhere to requirements of governmental authorities having jurisdiction.

K. Parking: Owner will issue 50 temporary parking permits for use by construction personnel and will make available, at the location shown, 50 parking spaces for those bearing permits. Construction personnel shall not park in any other location on Owner's property, even when bearing permits. Access to allocated parking spaces shall be by most direct route from public streets. Construction personnel shall not drive vehicles elsewhere on Owner's property and shall take the most direct pedestrian way along walks and roadways (not on lawns) from parking lot to construction site.

L. Barricades and Signs: Should barricades or directional signs for traffic control be necessary, prepare and install such signs and barricades of approved size, color, and lettering or other markings. Remove signs when no longer needed, or at Substantial Completion, whichever is latest.

M. Restricted Use of Premises: Enforce Contract requirements, local ordinances, and Owner's instructions pertaining to signs, fires, smoking, trucking, parking, and other use of premises.

N. On-Site Storage:
1. General: Extent of Work and site area available limits amount of on-site material and equipment storage. Do not unnecessarily encumber job site with excess materials or equipment. In addition, traffic on adjacent streets and public school use of J Street may place limitations on rates and

means of delivery of materials, equipment, and supplies, removal of rubbish, and, hours during which deliveries may be made. Determine, and take into account in the Work, limitations on storage space and of times, rates, and means of deliveries to and removals from the job site whether such limitations are imposed by laws, rules, ordinances, or physical conditions. Owner will not pay extra amounts due to such limitations. Coordinate arrangements for delivery and storage of materials.

    2. Paved Areas: Do not use paved areas on Owner's property to stockpile excavated materials or to store construction materials except where shown. Use of paved areas on public property is subject to requirements of authorities having jurisdiction, and arrangements for such use are solely Contractor's responsibility.

    3. Lawns: Do not permit operations over existing lawn areas to remain, except where necessary to comply with Contract requirements. Do not use lawn areas to store materials or debris unless agreed to by Owner in each specific case.

O. Protection and Repair: Protect roadways, walks, and other permanent site improvements, and access ways subject to damage. Satisfactorily repair improvements and surfaces damaged during construction operations, or remove damaged improvements or surfaces and provide new acceptable improvements or surfaces. Except where new Work is required, return areas used for temporary access to original condition.

Temporary Controls: The following clauses contain several requirements an architect might need to include in the project manual for a project where existing construction occurs.

2.15   DAY-BY-DAY CLEANUP

A. Cleaning: Remove staining or reactive materials from new and existing surfaces immediately during course of the Work.

B. Debris: Remove hazardous accumulations of debris promptly, at least daily.

C. Dust: Confine dust producing operations during painting and finishing. Vacuum immediately after completion.

2.16   TRASH DISPOSAL

A. General: Keep new and existing buildings and site free from accumulations of waste materials.

B. Removal: Remove cartons, crates, wrappings, lunch trash, and other trash from each room daily. Provide trash receptacles on each floor of each building and in convenient locations on the site.

C. Burning: Do not burn trash or other materials on Owner's property.

2.17 EXCESS MATERIAL

A. General: Remove excess materials, including demolished materials, excess earth, and excess building materials from Owner's property and dispose of legally.

B. Clean: Keep paved drives on Owner's property and public streets and alleys clean, by cleaning daily, or more often if necessary, of earth and debris spillage from trucking involved in construction operations.

2.18 EROSION AND SEDIMENTATION CONTROL

A. General: Prevent pollution of land, air, and water; control erosion, washout, and surface runoff of earth and stockpiled materials. Preclude sedimentation in general, and especially in existing on-site and public storm-water system and public right of way.

B. Procedures: Perform erosion, sedimentation, and temporary storm-water control. Follow procedures stipulated in local laws and regulations and as shown on sitework drawings.

C. Maintenance: Maintain controls in place until permanent controls are functioning. Remove when no longer needed.

2.19 NOISE AND VIBRATION CONTROL

A. Noise and Existing Building Structure Vibration Generated by Construction Procedures, Equipment, Tools, and Operations: Keep to minimum practicable during demolition and removal from building and site, including loading and removing storage containers. Where high-noise equipment is unavoidable and permitted, confine to hours between 7 A.M. and 5 P.M., Monday through Friday. Equipment-generated noise levels shall not exceed the following in decibels:
    1. Concrete mixer: 85.
    2. Concrete pump: 82.
    3. Crane: 83.
    4. Materials elevator: 85.
    5. Pumps: 76.
    6. Generators: 78.
    7. Compressors: 81.
    8. Pneumatic tools: 86.
    9. Saws: 78.
    10. Vibrators: 76.
    11. Other tools: 85.

B. Operation of Air Hammers, Compressors, and Reciprocating Equipment: Not permitted inside existing buildings unless specifically approved in writing by Owner.

   C. Laws: Comply with applicable noise control laws, ordinances, and regulations.

   D. Acoustical Enclosures: Stationary equipment may be enclosed to produce required sound attenuation subject to continued maintenance of such enclosures to ensure that specified sound levels are not exceeded.

   E. Violations: Where field sound measurements reveal sound levels exceeding those specified, cease operating such equipment and repair or replace it with equipment that complys with the sound levels specified.

   F. Cutting and Drilling Concrete: Use only rotary or core drilling for holes through concrete. Do drilling in concrete only between 7 A.M. and 5 P.M., Monday through Friday. Do not use impact tools to cut or otherwise remove concrete or to install inserts.

   G. Power-Activated Tools: Not permitted in or immediately adjacent to existing buildings, except with Owner's written approval in each specific case, except where such use is specifically specified.

Project Signs: Existing construction may affect the locations of project identification signs or even whether such signs are permitted; but once a project identification sign is permitted or required, the requirements differ little, solely due to existing construction involvement in a project.

Other signs are more likely to be needed when existing construction occurs, however, especially when the existing construction is to remain occupied during the construction period. The following sign clauses are from one of the author's projects.

2.20 PATIENT, STUDENT, AND PUBLIC DIRECTION SIGNS

   A. General: Provide indoor and outdoor signs to direct Owner's employees, patients, students, and the public to temporarily relocated university, hospital, and clinic functions while the Work under this Contract is in progress. Integrate signs with work stages specified in Section "Work Sequence," unless later revised.

   B. Number, Design, Size, Colors, Lettering or Other Markings, and Locations: As directed by Owner.

   C. Removal: Remove signs when no longer needed, or at Substantial Completion, whichever is first.

2.21 TEMPORARY EXIT SIGNS

   A. Locations: Provide proper exit signs at temporary exits. Also provide temporary exit signs at permanent exits when existing exit signs are removed, not lighted, or otherwise not functioning.

B. Type: Temporary exit signs shall comply with the building code, laws, ordinances, and requirements of authorities having jurisdiction.

Field Offices and Sheds: Field office type and construction may not vary because existing construction occurs, but room to place offices may become a problem. Architects who work in cities are familiar with having little room for offices, storage, or staging. Even when there appears to be plenty of room, an existing building's site can become tight, for several reasons. Drives, parking areas, and access ways must be maintained. Using lawns and planting areas for storage or staging can be expensive, because those areas must be returned to their original condition sooner or later. Local contractors may not be familiar with building storage and office spaces above streets or sidewalks. Streets may be too narrow to block for construction purposes. Sidewalks may not even exist.

Sometimes, storage and office space restrictions can be relieved by using space inside the existing building.

The following clauses contain some requirements associated with office and storage at projects where existing construction occurs.

2.22   TEMPORARY FIELD OFFICES

A. Contractor's Field Office: Provide and maintain during the construction phase an adequate, heated, lighted, and weathertight office at a suitable location acceptable to Owner. Office shall be of such size and kept in such condition that it may be conveniently used for small progress meetings. Office may be a mobile unit.

B. Owner's and Architect's Field Office: Provide and maintain a separate weathertight space, structure, or trailer of not less than 120 sq. ft., near Contractor's field office for use by Owner, Architect, and their representatives. Heat properly during cold weather, cool during hot weather, and provide adequate lighting.

C. Site Limitations: On-site space is limited. It may be necessary to locate field offices off Owner's property. Should Contractor elect to locate field offices on public property, and officials having jurisdiction permit such use, such use shall be Contractor's sole responsibility. In such case, in addition to requirements of authorities having jurisdiction, do not locate a field office or trailer closer than 10 feet from an existing building. Field offices shall not encroach on adjacent properties without the consent of the adjacent property owners.

D. Space in Existing Buildings:
  1. If available, and Owner concurs, use those spaces for field offices and do not place temporary field offices on site. Comply with Owner's requirements.
  2. If space is not available inside a building at beginning of Project but becomes available later and Owner agrees, move offices and equipment inside and remove temporary facilities.

E. Maintenance, Janitorial Services, Fuel, and Power for Temporary Offices: By Contractor.

F. Access: Maintain access to temporary offices from existing street, sidewalk, or paving, and keep free of mud.

G. Relocation: Relocate offices causing interference with work of a subcontractor or other contractor. Relocate offices within buildings which interfere with work of a subcontractor or another contractor or which interfere with progress of the Work. Remove temporary office from site (including offices within buildings) promptly on Project completion.

2.24   TEMPORARY STORAGE AND STAGING

A. Facility: Storage shall be in secure, watertight buildings, or mobile units, having floors above grade, and heated to protect materials from low temperatures. Long-term, including overnight, outdoor storage of materials, or equipment not in use, is prohibited, except with Owner's written consent in each case.

B. Location: Space on the site is limited. It may be necessary to provide for storage and staging in locations not on Owner's property. Should Contractor elect to locate storage sheds or trailers on public property, and such use is permitted by officials having jurisdiction, such use shall be solely Contractor's responsibility. In such case, in addition to requirements of governmental authorities

Figure 8-4. Limited storage and office space. (Photograph by Stewart Bros.)

having jurisdiction, do not locate a temporary
building or shed or trailer closer than 10 feet from
an existing building. Storage shall not encroach on
adjacent properties without the consent of the
adjacent property owners.

C. Space Within Existing Building A: Use for storage
where Owner agrees and such use will not harm
Building A or occupants. Use space within the
addition to existing Building A for storage when
such use will not harm the addition. Do not use
space within existing Building B for storage.
Storage within buildings shall not interfere with
the progress of the Work. Refer to Section "Work
Sequence."

D. Relocation and Removal: Relocate sheds and trailers
interfering with a subcontractor's or other
contractor's work. Relocate storage within buildings
interfering with a subcontractor or another
contractor's work or with the Work progress. Remove
storage buildings and mobile units and stored
materials from within buildings when no longer
needed.

Section 01500 *Construction Facilities and Temporary Controls (Small Projects)*

All Small Projects: When existing construction is involved, construction cost is not necessarily a good gauge for estimating the number of specifications provisions needed to convey construction facilities and temporary controls requirements.

Some small remodeling, renovation, or restoration projects have requirements similar, and equal in scope, to those used in the previous examples. This is one of the problems architects face when providing services for small projects. The relationship of the new work to the existing, the owner's use of the existing building during construction, and many other factors increase the architect's work. Fees are not always high enough to cover the increased time necessary to deal with existing conditions, however. There is no such thing, in terms of specifications requirements, as a *small* remodeling, renovation, or restoration project when the project is part of an existing building which will remain in use during construction.

On the other hand, small projects consisting of buildings which will not remain in use during construction have few of the complications associated with projects that are part of larger buildings. For such projects, a broadscope construction facilities and temporary controls section might contain provisions such as those in the following examples. Where more requirements are necessary, refer to the large-projects examples for suggestions.

2.01 TEMPORARY UTILITIES

A. Light and Power: Provide temporary light and power
to each trade as needed. Comply with the National
Electrical Code, building code, and power company
requirements. Use existing service. Pay costs of
energy used. Remove temporary service when no longer
needed. Do not use temporary materials in new Work.

B. Temporary Heat: Provide temporary heat, when required, throughout the construction period.
  1. Before Permanent System: Comply with codes and regulations. Use UL-approved devices. Vent equipment to outside. Do not store fuel in building. Do not use heaters that burn fuels which produce a discharge.
  2. Using Permanent Heating System: As soon as practicable, remove temporary heaters and use permanent heating system for temporary heat. Use filters of same efficiency as those specified for permanent system when using permanent system for temporary heat.
  3. Pay all costs connected with temporary heat.
C. Temporary Telephone: Provide and pay costs for local service for use by Contractor, Owner, and Architect. Caller will pay long distance charges.
D. Construction Water: Provide temporary construction water to serve all trades. Use existing water service. Pay costs related to temporary water system.
E. Temporary Chemical Toilet: Provide. Do not use building facilities. Comply with applicable laws.
F. Temporary Fire Protection: Provide and maintain hand fire extinguishers suitable for fire hazard involved. Do not permit debris to accumulate. Store flammable or volatile liquids in open or small detached structure or trailer. Use approved safety cans. Do not store oily rags in tight permanent spaces. Store combustibles carefully to prevent fire hazard. Take other precautions suitable for fire hazard conditions at site to prevent fires and permit access for fire-fighting equipment.

Temporary Construction: Temporary construction is seldom needed for small projects. If temporary construction is needed for a small project, the discussion above for large projects applies.

2.02   CONSTRUCTION AIDS

A. Temporary Hoists, Chutes, Scaffolds, Cranes, Stairs, Etc.: Provide as needed. Comply with applicable codes, laws, and regulations. Do not free drop materials or debris. Protect permanent construction from damage by temporary devices. Relocate devices to avoid interference with other trades. Remove when no longer needed and repair damage.
B. Temporary Use of Existing Elevator: Use Elevator No. 3 for construction purposes. Submit for approval a list of the procedures proposed to protect existing elevator from harm during use. Protect cab, entrances, and adjacent surfaces from damage. Do not overload elevator. Rated capacity is 2,500 pounds. Maintain elevator during use and return to original condition at completion.

C. Existing Stairs: Construction personnel may use existing stairs for construction purposes. Protect stair and access ways and return to original condition at completion.

D. Temporary Enclosures: When necessary to maintain construction schedules, provide temporary enclosures of sufficient size to permit work to continue. Provide adequate ventilation for workers and heating equipment.

2.03 TEMPORARY BUILDING PROTECTION

A. To Close Openings: Until permanently closed, provide temporary weathertight closures when necessary to maintain suitable conditions for interior work. Equip temporary exterior doors with padlocks. At end of each day's work, close temporary protection and lock or otherwise secure facilities.

B. Where Existing Construction Is Removed: Provide adequate temporary waterproof covers to protect against the elements. Leave protection in place, except when actual construction is in progress, until new construction provides weathertight seal.

C. Protect Openings: Protect existing finished openings used as passageways or through which materials are moved and other exposed existing and new Work subject to damage.

D. Existing Finished Surfaces: Prevent damage by using suitable approved means. Leave clean and free from marring and damage at time of final acceptance.

E. Remove temporary protection promptly on completion of construction activities when no longer needed.

2.04 BARRIERS AND ENCLOSURES

A. Temporary Partitions and Closures: Where necessary to protect existing materials to remain and new Work in place, provide temporary dust-tight partitions and closures. Protect existing floors to remain from damage due to temporary partitions. Make partitions fire resistive with B-labeled doors in steel frames where fire-resistive partitions are required by code.
   1. Interior Cutting Operations: Enclose to prevent dust from spreading, catch debris, and prevent injury to persons.
   2. Removal: Relocate temporary partitions and closures when Work progress requires. Remove when no longer needed.

B. Existing Trees, Shrubs, and Lawns to Remain: Protect throughout Owner's property. Existing trees, shrubs, and lawns not shown to be removed or falling beneath new construction are to remain unless indicated otherwise. Satisfactorily repair existing trees and shrubs to remain that are damaged or destroyed during the Work under this Contract, or remove and provide new equivalent trees or shrubs at no additional cost. Remove existing lawns to remain that are damaged or destroyed during the Work under this Contract, and place new matching sod in the area of removal, at no additional cost. Have tree, shrub, and lawn work done by a specialist acceptable to Owner.

2.05   PROTECTING PEOPLE AND PROPERTY

A. Laws: Comply with applicable laws, ordinances, rules, regulations, and orders of authorities having jurisdiction for safety of people and protection of property from damage, injury, or loss.

B. Responsibility: Be solely responsible for initiating, maintaining, and supervising safety precautions and programs concerning Project security, but obtain Owner's approval of proposed methods and location of safeguards.

C. Protect Improvements: Throughout Owner's property, protect permanent improvements to remain which are subject to damage due to Contractor's operations. Repair or remove and install new acceptable items where improvements are damaged during Contractor's operations.

D. Safeguards: Erect and maintain necessary safeguards for safety and protection.

E. Security: Protect and secure site, existing buildings, new addition, and new and existing materials and equipment from theft and damage by whatever reasonable means are effective.

F. Chain Link Fence: In addition to other safety and security means, erect and maintain an acceptable chain link fence to enclose the entire site. Provide gate with lock and keep locked except when in use. Do not use fence type which makes necessary the destruction of portions of walkways or pavements to remain. Do not use unacceptable fences.

G. Entrances: Do not block entrances to buildings to remain in use or in any way inhibit access to them. Refer to Section "Alterations Project Procedures" for additional requirements.

H. Design Live Loads: Do not place materials or equipment on new or existing structures that will exceed the design load of the structure or endanger the structure or people.

I. Trenches: Do not permit trenches to remain open for prolonged periods without adequate board covering or fencing.

J. Broken Glass: Be responsible for damage during construction operations; at completion, replace broken glass.

K. Weather Protection: Provide during construction and maintain Work, materials, apparatus, and fixtures free from damage. At end of each work day, cover new Work and exposed existing work likely to be damaged.

L. Dust: Take precautions necessary to keep Work under this Contract and adjoining property reasonably free of dust.

M. Removals: Except for fences, remove temporary construction and protection promptly when no longer needed. Maintain temporary fences until date of Substantial Completion and then remove, unless Architect approves of earlier removal.

N. Damaged Site Improvements: Repair and restore to condition at beginning of construction, or better, existing site improvements which are not to be removed under this Contract but are damaged or defaced by Contractor's operations, except where Contract requires new Work.

2.06 SITE ACCESS, PARKING, AND TRAFFIC REGULATIONS

A. General: Plan and control site access and use. Cooperate with Owner and other contractors working at site to minimize disruption of use of other facilities; portions of buildings and site areas affected by this Contract and to remain in use; and the work of other contractors.

B. Temporary Access Drives: Construct on the premises as necessary, and maintain in good usable condition; remove when no longer needed. Until permanent improvements have been completed, periodically water temporary unpaved access roads when necessary to prevent excessive dust.

C. Construction Site Access: Use routes agreed to by Owner.

D. Driveways Between and Around Combustible Storage Piles: Maintain at least 15 feet wide and free of accumulation of rubbish, equipment, and materials.

E. Access for Fire-Fighting Equipment: Maintain.

F. Parking: Parking is available on the site for construction personnel at the location shown.

G. Barricades and Signs: Prepare and install of approved size, color, and lettering or other markings for traffic control. Remove signs when no longer needed, or at Substantial Completion.

H. Restricted Use of Premises: Enforce Contract requirements, local ordinances, and Owner's instructions about signs, fires, smoking, trucking, parking, and other premises use.

I. On-Site Storage: Store construction materials and equipment in temporary buildings or mobile units where shown. Do not use paved areas or lawns on Owner's property to stockpile excavated materials or for storage of construction materials, except where shown or later approved.

J. Protection and Repair: Protect permanent site improvements and access ways subject to damage. Satisfactorily repair improvements and surfaces damaged during construction operations or remove damaged improvements or surfaces and provide new acceptable improvements or surfaces. Except where Contract requires new Work, return areas used for temporary access to original condition.

2.07 TEMPORARY CONTROLS

A. Day—By—Day Cleanup: Remove staining or reactive materials from new and existing surfaces immediately. Remove hazardous accumulations of debris promptly, at least daily. Confine dust—producing operations during painting and finishing. Vacuum immediately after completion.

B. Trash Disposal: Keep new and existing buildings and site free from accumulations of waste materials. Do not burn trash or other materials on Owner's property.

C. Excess Material: Remove excess materials, including demolished materials, excess earth, and excess building materials from Owner's property and dispose of legally. Keep paved drives on Owner's property and public streets and alleys clean of earth and debris spillage from trucking involved in construction operations.

D. Erosion and Sedimentation Control: Prevent pollution of land, air, and water; control erosion, washout, and surface runoff of earth and stockpiled materials. Preclude sedimentation in general, and especially in existing storm—water system and public right of way. Follow local laws and regulations and requirements shown on sitework drawings. Maintain temporary controls until permanent controls are functioning. Remove when no longer needed.

E. Noise and Vibration Control: Keep noise and existing building structure vibration to minimum practicable. Where use of high—noise—level equipment is unavoidable, confine to hours between 7 A.M. and 5 P.M., Monday through Friday. Do not operate air hammers, compressors, or reciprocating equipment inside existing buildings unless specifically approved in writing by Owner in each case. Comply with applicable noise control laws, ordinances, and regulations. Do not use power—activated tools in or immediately adjacent to existing buildings.

2.08 FIELD OFFICES AND STORAGE

A. Contractor's Field Office:
   1. General: Provide and maintain, where shown, during the construction phase an adequate, heated, lighted, and weathertight office at a suitable location acceptable to Owner. Office shall be of such size and kept in such condition that it may be conveniently used for small progress meetings. Office may be a mobile unit. Permit Architect and Owner to use field office for construction—related activities.

2. Space In Existing Buildings: If available, use for field offices. Comply with Owner's requirements. If not available at Project start but available later, move offices and equipment inside and remove temporary offices.

B. Temporary Storage and Staging: Where shown, provide secure watertight buildings or mobile units with floor above grade and heated where necessary to protect materials from low temperatures. Use space within the existing building for storage where available, when Owner concurs. Do not interfere with Work progress. Relocate storage which interferes with a subcontractor's or other contractor's work, or Work progress. Remove storage buildings and mobile units and stored materials from within buildings when no longer needed.

Section 01600   *Materials and Equipment*

All Projects: Most requirements specified in Section 01600 do not change solely because a project involves existing construction. The following sample clause illustrates an exception.

1.06   REUSING EXISTING MATERIALS

A. Generally, use new products in this Project. Reuse products removed from the site or existing buildings only where specifically indicated. Refer to Sections "Demolition," and "Minor Alteration Work," and other specifications sections for requirements.
B. Carefully remove, handle, store, refabricate, and reinstall products indicated to be reused to ensure proper functioning of completed Work.
C. At no additional cost, arrange for transportation, storage, and handling of products that require off-site storage, restoration, or renovation.

Section 01700   *Contract Closeout*

All Projects: Most of the differences between a Section 01700 for a project with all new work and one where existing construction is involved can be handled by adding words such as "for both new and existing Work." The final-cleanup requirements, however, may need additional phrases, as illustrated by the following example.

1.05   FINAL CLEANUP

A. General: At Project completion, to the extent that such areas or surfaces were part of, or were soiled during, the Work under this Contract, give exterior and interior of new and existing buildings and site, including access ways, and office, storage, and staging areas, a thorough final cleaning. Remove temporary services, construction equipment, tools and facilities, mock-ups, temporary structures,

surplus materials, debris, and rubbish from Owner's
property. Put site in neat, orderly condition, ready
for use. Leave roof areas, pipe spaces, and other
spaces clean and free from debris. Clean to normal
"clean" condition for a first-class building
cleaning and maintenance program. Comply with
manufacturer's instructions.

Division 2   Sitework

Section 02050   *Demolition*

All Projects: It is very important to coordinate requirements specified in Section
02050, ''Demolition,'' and its mediumscope children, with requirements specified
in the remainder of the contract documents, especially with Section 01120, ''Alterations Project Procedures,'' and Section 13990, ''Minor Alteration Work.''

Each time we refer to Section 02050 here, we mean to also include the
mediumscope sections under that heading.

In the method proposed here, an architect using Section 02050 would also
use Section 13990, but not a cutting and patching section. Cutting would be
covered in 02050 and patching in 13990.

Including extensive requirements here does not imply that they are superior
to similar requirements in commercial guides, such as *Masterspec*. They are
included because everything in a demolition section is related to existing construction and because including many requirements shows how they are coordinated with other sections, especially Section 13990, ''Minor Alteration Work.''

Large Projects: The following is a compilation of several sections. Some requirements came from Section 02050, ''Demolition,'' and some from Section
02070, ''Selective Demolition.''

PART 1   GENERAL

1.01   SUMMARY

   A. Free-Standing Buildings: Owner will demolish
      existing, free-standing buildings on the site under
      a separate contract and remove demolished materials
      from the site.
   B. This Contract includes:
     1. Demolition and removal from the site of other
       existing structures found on the site.
     2. Demolition and removal from the site of the
       indicated portions of existing Building A.
     3. Selective demolition, dismantling, cutting, and
       patching on site and in portions of existing
       Building A and Building B as necessary to
       complete the Work under this Contract. Portions
       of this Work are specified in other
       specifications sections.
     4. Legal disposition of demolished materials which
       are not indicated to remain Owner's property.

C. Related Sections:
1. General Alterations Requirements: See Section "Minor Alteration Work."
2. Specific Requirements for Alterations other than Minor Work: Other specifications sections.

1.02   SUBMITTALS

A. Drawings Showing Openings: Prepare and submit for approval, drawings of the portions of the existing building where Work under this Contract will take place, showing size and location of openings to be drilled or cut in existing construction.

B. Demolition Schedule: Submit proposed schedule for demolition work in the form of a network system developed using a simplified form of Critical Path Method (CPM). Coordinate proposed Demolition Schedule with Phasing Schedule specified in Section "Work Sequence" and Alterations Schedule specified in Section "Minor Alteration Work." Incorporate approved Demolition Schedule into Construction Schedule specified in Section "Submittals."

1.03   JOB CONDITIONS

A. Disconnection of Services:
1. Notification: Notify Owner and authorities owning or controlling services affected by demolition or remodeling before beginning operations.
2. Disconnect and Cap Pipes and Services: As required by company, utility, or local authority having jurisdiction and as required for demolition work.
3. Existing Utilities to Remain: Maintain, keep in service, and protect against damage. Do not interrupt existing utilities serving occupied or used facilities, except when authorized in writing by Owner and authorities having jurisdiction. If interruption of an existing utility is necessary, provide temporary services during interruption, as acceptable to Owner and governing authorities.
4. Additional Requirements: Refer to "General Conditions" and other specifications sections for additional requirements about existing utilities and services.

B. Protection of Persons and of Property to Remain or Be Reused:
1. General: Be solely responsible for safety of persons and property. Requirements in this section supplement requirements specified in other Contract documents.

2. Means of Protection:
   a. Provide temporary barricades, fences, shoring, lights, barriers, partitions, casing of openings, chutes, closures, and other protection. Refer to the Agreement Between the Owner and the Contractor, the "General Conditions," Section "Construction Facilities and Temporary Controls," and other Contract documents for additional requirements.
   b. Ensure safe passage of people around area of demolition. Prevent injury to adjacent facilities, and to people. Erect temporary covered passageways if required by authorities having jurisdiction. Provide shoring, bracing, or support to prevent movement, settlement, or collapse of structures to be demolished and adjacent facilities to remain.
3. Waterproof Openings: Provide adequate temporary waterproof protection should it become necessary to remove parts of existing building shell to permit access to building. Leave protection in place except when openings are being used, until new construction has provided a watertight seal. Do not remove parts of existing building without Owner's written agreement.
4. Protect and support conduits, drains, pipes, and wires to remain and subject to damage by construction activities.
5. Airtight Covers: Provide for return air grills in work areas to prevent dirt and dust from entering air conditioning or ventilating systems to remain.
6. Protect Finishes:
   a. Protect finish floor coverings and other interior finishes to remain from marring and other damage. Maintain and leave protection in place until surface protected is no longer subject to damage by construction operations.
   b. Use heavy fire-retardant building paper for protection of general floor areas to remain. Cover paths of wheeled traffic, including access ways, with heavy boards or plywood.
   c. When removing portions of walls, partitions, or other vertical construction, or back-up for exterior walls in building portions which are not to be totally demolished, cover the floor on both sides of construction being demolished a distance of at least 4 feet or to the adjacent wall, whichever is the lesser distance. Where ceilings are to be removed, cover the entire floor surface.
7. Promptly repair damaged adjacent facilities to remain due to demolition operations at no additional cost.

C. Other Job Conditions:
   1. General: Do not begin demolition of indicated portions of Building A or selective demolition of portions of existing Buildings A or B until Owner has vacated those portions, discontinued their use, done necessary preparatory work in those spaces, and approved proceeding in writing.
   2. Owner's Responsibility: Owner assumes no responsibility for actual condition of site or portions of structures to be demolished. Variation from conditions at time of inspection for pricing may occur due to Owner's removal and salvage operations or for other reasons.
   3. Contractor Salvage: As Work progresses, remove from sitework and portions of buildings being demolished those items which are not to be reused in this Project, are not indicated to remain Owner's property, and which are of salvageable value to Contractor. Transport salvaged items from site as they are removed. Do not store or sell removed items on site.
   4. Explosives: Do not bring to site without written consent of Owner and authorities having jurisdiction. Written consent does not relieve Contractor of sole responsibility for injury to people or for damage to property due to blasting operations. Do permitted blasting in compliance with governing regulations.
   5. Traffic Routes: Conduct activities with minimum interference with roads, streets, alleys, walks, and other facilities. Do not obstruct streets, alleys, walks, or other occupied or used facilities without permission from authorities having jurisdiction. Provide alternative routes around obstructed traffic ways if required by governing regulations.
   6. Pest Control: Employ a certified exterminator and provide treatment in accordance with governing health regulations for rodent and insect control. Refer to Section "Construction Facilities and Temporary Controls" for additional requirements.

PART 2   PRODUCTS

2.01   SALVAGED MATERIALS AND ITEMS

   A. Materials and Items Indicated and Suitable to be Reused: Salvage for reuse. Such materials and items include, but are not necessarily limited to:
      1. Face Brick: Salvage brick removed from existing walls in sufficient quantity to fill openings in and patch existing walls.
      2. Acoustical ceilings.
      3. Doors and frames.

    4. Stair Rails: Salvage stair rails in Exit Stair No. 1 and reinstall where shown.

    5. Hardware.

    6. Medical equipment.

    7. Lighting fixtures.

    8. Other materials, devices, equipment, and items indicated to be salvaged for reuse.

B. Materials and Items that Must Be Removed to Accomplish the Work under this Contract: Also salvage for reuse, unless such materials or items are indicated to be discarded and new materials or items provided. Such materials and items may include, but are not limited to:

    1. Mechanical and plumbing equipment.

    2. Electrical lighting panels, switches, outlets, and other electrical devices.

C. Refer to Section "Minor Alteration Work" for general requirements related to reuse of removed materials and to other specifications sections for specific requirements.

2.02   OWNERSHIP OF REMOVED MATERIALS

A. Items to Be Removed by Owner: Before Contractor is permitted access into the area of each construction stage or substage, as defined in Section "Work Sequence," Owner may remove locks, locksets, latch sets, door closers, sink and lavatory fittings, and other items. Owner will also remove furnishings and portable equipment from the area of each stage or substage area of the Work under this Contract before start of Work. Refer to other parts of the Contract documents for requirements related to scheduling.

B. Items to Be Offered to Owner: Before beginning demolition, offer to Owner, for Owner's use, each material; door; window; frame; accessory; item of hardware, equipment, and furnishings; mechanical, plumbing, and electrical devices and equipment; and every other product to be removed and not reinstalled. Before demolition or removal, obtain a list of materials and items to remain Owner's property from Owner's representative. Thereafter, Owner shall retain the right to claim as Owner's property any material or item removed, even when not on the list.

C. Items Designated as Owner's Property: Removed existing fixtures, materials, equipment, doors, frames, and other items not to be reused in the Work but so selected by Owner, whether removed by Owner or Contractor, shall remain Owner's property.

D. Contractor's Property: Rubbish and debris created by demolition and alteration work, including cutting and drilling, patching and repair, and other demolished or removed materials and equipment not to be reused in the Work under this Contract, and not

indicated to remain Owner's property, or selected by
Owner to remain Owner's property, shall become
Contractor's property.

PART 3   EXECUTION

3.01   GENERAL

A. Do not begin demolition Work until Architect has
approved Construction Schedule specified in Section
"Submittals."

B. Do not cut or drill existing construction until
Architect has approved cut and drill location
drawings specified in this section.

C. Verify that spaces to remain unaltered adjacent to
areas of Work under this Contract are completely
secured and rendered dustproof before beginning such
Work.

D. Additional requirements to those specified in this
section are noted on the Contract drawings.

3.02   DEMOLITION AND REMOVAL

A. General: Execute demolition and removal carefully.
Minimize interference with existing building and
site operations, inconvenience to occupants and the
public, danger to persons, and damage to existing
materials to remain.

B. Noise and Speed: Perform demolition and removals as
quietly as practicable and with deliberate speed
once demolition work has begun.

C. Extent and Methods of Demolition: Demolish, remove
for salvage, or remove and reinstall as applicable,
all, or parts of, as indicated: sitework interfering
with new construction, masonry, concrete, walls and
partitions, floor and roof construction, roofing,
parapet construction, doors, frames, finish
hardware, plaster, gypsum board, acoustical
ceilings, suspension systems, furring, lathing,
finishes, cabinetry, ventilation items, plumbing
fixtures, mechanical and electrical equipment,
piping, lighting, and other materials and items as
necessary to do the Work under this Contract and, in
addition, where removal is indicated.

1. Use methods required to complete Work within
limitations of governing regulations.
2. Proceed systematically.
3. Demolish concrete and masonry in small sections.
4. Also demolish or remove walls and partitions in
small sections whatever the materials of
construction.
5. Breakup and removal of concrete slabs-on-grade
is specified in Section "Earthwork."
6. Remove materials so as to not impose excessive
loads to supporting walls, floors, or framing.

7. Where necessary to avoid collapse, install temporary struts, bracing, or shoring; leave in place until new Work provides adequate bracing and support.

8. Remove structural framing members and lower to ground by suitable methods. Do not allow to freefall.

9. Doors: Completely remove indicated existing doors; deliver to Owner or repair, rework, refinish, and reinstall as indicated. Note Contractor's option for reusing doors even when not scheduled for reuse.

10. Plaster: Remove only sufficient plaster, lathing, support systems, and other materials and items as is necessary to permit the Work under this Contract. Refer to Section "Lath and Plaster" ("Minor Alteration Work") for patching and repair of plaster.

11. Floors:
    a. Where existing equipment, cabinets, lockers, etc., having concrete curbs or bases are removed, also remove the concrete curbs and bases to a depth not less than 1/4 inch below the top of the adjacent concrete left in place.

Figure 8-5. Floor beyond repair. (Photograph by Stewart Bros., courtesy of Mid-City Financial Corp.)

b. When removing existing walls and partitions resting on the structural slab, also remove traces of mortar and other materials to expose structural slab beneath the location of partition or wall.

c. Except where Contract documents permit leaving existing flooring in place, completely remove existing finish flooring from locations where new finishes are scheduled. Leave top of exposed substrate completely free from materials that would interfere with bond of new materials.

d. Except where otherwise indicated, completely remove existing ceramic tile from locations where new finishes are scheduled. Leave top of exposed substrate completely free from materials that would interfere with bond of patching, topping, or finish material and not less than 1/4 inch below adjacent concrete left in place.

e. Also remove toppings where necessary to install glazed structural unit coved bases and other products. In such cases, remove topping sufficiently to properly accommodate new and reused products.

f. In addition to other removal of existing topping, also remove such amounts of topping as is necessary to allow finishing of floor surfaces level to a tolerance of 1/8 inch in each 6 feet. To accomplish specified degree of levelness, use a combination of new topping specified in Section "Cast-In-Place Concrete" and latex cementitious underlayment specified in Section "Minor Alteration Work," and grinding of existing high spots. When using concrete topping as fill, undercut existing topping along edges to provide bond. Do not use new concrete topping less than 1 inch thick.

g. When partly removing existing topping and when removing existing floor finishes, completely remove loose materials and damaged substrate materials.

h. Completely remove existing carpet from areas to receive new floor finishes. Also remove carpet cushions and all traces of adhesives.

i. Removing existing resilient flooring is specified in Section "Resilient Flooring."

j. Where Contract requires removing existing concrete slabs, also remove reinforcement. When filling openings with concrete, prepare slab edges as shown. Leave 6 inches of reinforcement exposed when filling openings with concrete.

k. Remove existing wood floors completely.

12. Ceilings:
    a. Where existing ceilings have been removed, whether under this Contract or earlier, existing hangers and hanger attachments may have been left in place. Do not remove such hangers or attachments unless so indicated. Refer to Sections "Lath and Plaster" and "Acoustical Treatment" for additional requirements.
    b. Where new acoustical panel or gypsum board ceilings are scheduled, remove existing plaster and acoustical ceilings. Where existing hangers and hanger attachments are adequate and suitable for support of the new ceilings, leave them in place and use for new ceilings. Reuse is subject to Architect's acceptance, but Contractor shall assume sole responsibility for reuse and for later failure resulting therefrom. Refer to Sections "Gypsum Board Ceilings" and "Acoustical Treatment" for additional requirements.
13. Walls:
    a. Where indicated, remove existing wall finishes and prepare surfaces to receive indicated new finishes. Leave nothing that will affect new finish. Where substrates will be exposed in the completed Work, remove every trace of old finish except paint.
    b. Remove supports for existing finishes removed under this Contract or earlier.
14. Other Materials and Items: Remove where shown to be removed or where removal is necessary to permit Work under this Contract. Remove such items and materials only to extent necessary. For requirements related to patching and repair of miscellaneous items and materials, refer to the specifications sections where such item or material is specified. When there is no related specifications section, requirements in Section "Minor Alteration Work" apply.
D. Below-Grade Construction: Removal of below-grade construction, including utilities and utility structures not indicated to remain, is specified in Section "Earthwork."
E. Pollution Controls: Use water sprinkling, temporary enclosures, and other suitable methods to limit airborne dust and dirt to lowest practical level. Comply with governing environmental protection regulations.
    1. Sprinkling is subject to Owner's approval. Cease immediately upon Owner's objection. Do not use water when it may create hazardous or objectionable conditions such as ice, flooding, or pollution.

2. Clean adjacent facilities to remain of dust, dirt, and debris due to demolition operations; comply with applicable requirements of governing authorities. Except where new Work is to occur, return adjacent areas to condition existing before start of Work.

F. Satisfactorily and promptly repair damage to existing materials and equipment to remain, or provide new equal approved products at no additional cost.

G. Remove carefully and protect items indicated to be reused. Store carefully in a safe location until reinstalled. Assume responsibility for safe storage and handling.

H. Remove carefully and protect materials and items to remain Owner's property. Move and store in a space in the building designated by Owner.

I. Debris and Items for Contractor Salvage:
1. Remove promptly from Owner's property and dispose of existing materials removed but not to be reused, or remain Owner's property. Include rubbish and debris as well as items Contractor may elect to salvage.
2. Remove wrecked and demolished material and items of Contractor salvage at frequent intervals. Do not permit rubbish to accumulate.
3. Do not burn, bury, buy, sell, or otherwise dispose of demolished materials or items on Owner's property.

J. Cutting and Drilling:
1. Cut and drill existing construction to permit the Work under this Contract. Include cutting holes and other openings for plumbing, mechanical, and electrical Work.
2. Cut by hand or with small power tools when possible. Cut holes and slots neatly to size required, with minimum disturbance of adjacent work. Cut round holes in concrete using core drills. Cut square and rectangular holes by line drilling and using chipping hammers to remove material between drill holes. Do not use large air hammers.
3. Do not operate air compressors inside building.
4. Do not drill or cut structural supporting elements without specific approval in each case, unless the element is shown on structural drawings to be drilled or cut. Do not cut existing concrete slab reinforcement.
5. Cover openings temporarily when not in use, and patch as soon as work is installed.

Small Projects: Demolition requirements for a small project will probably be fewer in number. The building, or at least the portion of it being worked on, may be unoccupied while demolition is going on. There will often be no other building on the site. Where applicable, however, the requirements specified in the previous example apply to small projects as well. It may be possible to reduce the number of words somewhat, but expect a corresponding loss of control.

Section 02100   *Clearing*

All Projects: A clearing section is often not necessary for remodeling, renovation, and restoration projects. When a clearing section is needed, the provisions it contains do not differ substantially from those in a clearing section for a project where all the work is new.

Section 02150   *Shoring, Bracing, and Underpinning*

Large Projects: An architect should never write anything that limits the contractor's sole responsibility to brace, shore, and support the work under a construction contract and to protect adjacent construction and sitework. Where existing construction is actually part of a project, however, including more requirements than are needed for a project with all new work helps prevent misunderstanding of the increased responsibilities involved. The following example contains requirements for a project where existing construction is part of the project itself.

```
PART 1  GENERAL

1.01   SUMMARY

       A. Section Includes: Requirements to provide and
          maintain sheeting, shoring, bracing, underpinning
          other supports, and related items for support of
          excavations and existing buildings footings,
          structure, walls, floors, and roofs where indicated,
          and in addition, where necessary for safety or
          protection of persons or property, and, in addition,
          where required by codes, laws, ordinances, or
          regulations of authorities having jurisdiction.
       B. Related Sections:
          1. Removal of Existing Site Structures, Portions of
             Existing Building, Houses, Including Foundations
             and Basements, and Portions of Existing Building,
             and Filling of Voids and Basements: See Section
             "Demolition." Other existing buildings will be
             removed under separate contract before Work under
             this Contract begins.
          2. Removal of Pavements, Curbs, and Other On- or
             Above-Grade Improvements; Removal of Foundations,
             Utilities, and Other Below-Grade Improvements Not
             Associated with Houses to Be Demolished; Filling
             Voids Left By Such Removals: See Section
             "Earthwork."
          3. Erosion Control; Protecting of Existing Trees,
             Shrubs, and Lawns To Remain: See Section
             "Construction Facilities and Temporary Controls."
          4. Removal of Vegetation; Stripping of Topsoil: See
             Section "Clearing."
```

5. Excavation and Other Earthwork; Drainage Matting; Continuous Drainage Boards: See Section "Earthwork."
6. Footing Drains; Under-Slab Drainage: See Section "Subdrainage Systems."
7. Utilities and Drain Lines: See Sections "Water Distribution," "Storm Sewage System," "Sanitary Sewage System," "Irrigation System," and Divisions 15 and 16.
8. Bentonite Waterproofing: See Section "Bentonite Waterproofing."

1.03   SUBMITTALS

A. Government Approval: Make submittals and obtain approvals from governmental authorities as may be required for support of excavations and existing streets and buildings. Pay costs of permits and inspections required.
B. Design Drawings: Submit design drawings for sheeting, shoring, bracing, underpinning, and other support systems, and other data prepared and sealed by a registered professional engineer acceptable to Owner. System design and calculations must be acceptable to local authorities having jurisdiction. Submittals are for information only. Architect will not check designs or calculations nor issue approvals or recommendations for approval of designs.
C. Designer's and Supervisor's Qualifications: Submit name and qualifications of licensed professional engineer who will design and specialist who will supervise construction of sheeting, shoring, bracing, underpinning, and other support work for Owner's acceptance.

1.04   QUALITY ASSURANCE

A. Laws: Do work specified in this section in accordance with laws, ordinances, codes, and regulations of federal, state, and local governments.
B. Specialist: Have shoring, support, underpinning, and bracing done under direct supervision of a specialist who is experienced in supervising the support of excavations and structures and acceptable to Owner.
C. Designer: Have shoring, support, underpinning, and bracing designed, calculated, detailed, and supervised by a licensed professional engineer selected and paid by Contractor but acceptable to Owner.
D. Contractor's Responsibility: Be solely responsible for construction means, methods, techniques, sequences, procedures, and safety precautions, including work necessary to support excavations and

existing structures. Correct, at no additional cost, damage caused by movement or settlement due to inadequate or improper supports.

1.05 JOB CONDITIONS

A. Existing Conditions Survey: Before starting work, verify governing dimensions and elevations. With Architect, jointly survey condition of adjoining properties. Take photographs, as directed by Architect, recording earlier settlement or cracking of structures, pavements, and other improvements. Prepare a list of such damages, verified by dated photographs and signed by Contractor and Architect and others conducting the investigation.

B. Establishing Benchmarks: Employ a licensed land surveyor or registered professional engineer to survey adjacent improvements, establishing elevations at fixed points to act as benchmarks. Clearly identify benchmarks and record existing elevations. Locate datum level used to establish benchmark elevations sufficiently distant so as not to be affected by movement resulting from excavation operations.

C. Resurveying Benchmarks: During excavation, have same licensed land surveyor or registered professional

Figure 8-6. Existing conditions survey photograph. (Photograph by Stewart Bros.)

engineer resurvey benchmarks weekly. Maintain accurate log of surveyed elevations for comparison with original elevations. Promptly notify Architect if changes in elevations occur or if cracks, sags, or other damage becomes evident. These survey requirements are in addition to those specified in Section "Field Engineering."

D. Existing Utilities: Protect existing active sewer, water, gas, electricity, and other utility services and structures.

E. Coordination: Coordinate shoring, underpinning, and bracing work with waterproofing requirements. Do not use a type of system or components that are incompatible with or harmful to the waterproofing.

PART 2   PRODUCTS

2.01   MATERIALS

A. General: Provide suitable sheeting, shoring, bracing, underpinning, and other support materials which will support loads imposed and also act as support for drainage matting, waterproofing, and concrete formwork. Materials need not be new but shall be in serviceable condition.

Figure 8-7. Excavation for underpinning. (Photograph by Stewart Bros., courtesy of Sigal Construction Corporation.)

B. Sheeting, Shoring, and Bracing: Steel.

C. Lagging: Pressure-treated wood.

D. Underpinning: Concrete.

E. Other Supports: Appropriate materials as indicated or required.

PART 3 EXECUTION

3.01 GENERAL

A. Extent: General extent of major foundation and earthwork shoring, and existing structure underpinning, is indicated on the structural drawings. General requirements for other earthwork and building supports may also be indicated on drawings, in the Project Manual, or in other Contract documents. Do not construe such indications as a limit of extent. Shoring, underpinning, bracing, and other support includes, but is not necessarily limited to, the following:

  1. Existing structure support: Support and prevent displacement of existing structures. Underpin existing adjacent buildings and support existing walls, floors, roofs, and other construction to remain.

  2. Excavation supports: Shoring and bracing necessary to protect existing buildings, streets, walkways, utilities, vaults, and other improvements and excavation against loss of ground, caving embankments, or other damage to adjacent improvements.

  3. Maintenance of shoring, bracing, underpinning, and supports.

  4. Remove excavation support bracing and existing structure supports, other than underpinning, as required.

B. Extra Materials: Keep sufficient quantity of sheeting, shoring, bracing, underpinning, and other support materials on hand for protection of Work and for use in emergencies.

C. Execute sheeting, shoring, bracing, underpinning, and other support Work so that structures and utilities are not damaged or disturbed, and so that access to them is not hindered.

3.02 UNDERPINNING AND SUPPORT

A. Protect existing structures from damage by use of underpinning and other support systems.

B. Underpinning and other supports shall withstand, without damage to the existing structures, loads imposed by existing and new construction activities as well as temporary construction, wind, rain, snow, traffic, vibration, and all other loads.

Figure 8-8. Supporting an existing building wall. (Photograph by Stewart Bros., courtesy of the Masonic Hall & Library Assoc., Bethesda, MD.)

3.03   SHEETING, SHORING, AND BRACING

    A. General: Protect site and adjacent properties, including public property, from caving and unacceptable soil, sidewalk, and street pavement movement. Use adequately braced sheeting and shoring. Adequately anchor and brace shoring system to resist earth and hydrostatic pressures and make ready to receive waterproofing.

    B. Shoring Shall:

        1. Retain earth and pavements under all surcharges, including weight of buildings, traffic, construction materials and equipment, temporary street decking, and other temporary construction, vibration, rainwater, and water absorption by soil.

        2. Extend at least as high as the original grade, and farther as needed to serve for forming and for berming to divert water.

      3. Be located to clear permanent footings, walls,
and other structural features, and to permit
forming, finishing, and waterproofing of concrete
surfaces.

      4. Be located to permit inspection of the
construction wherever practicable.

      5. Be ready to receive drainage matting,
waterproofing, and concrete formwork.

  C. Anchorage and Bracing: Adequately anchor and brace
sheeting and shoring to resist earth and hydrostatic
pressures.

      1. Locate bracing to clear columns, floor framing
construction, and other permanent work. If
necessary to move a brace, install new bracing
before removing original brace.

      2. Do not place bracing where it will be cast into
or included in permanent concrete work, except as
otherwise acceptable to Architect.

      3. Install internal bracing, if required, to prevent
spreading or distortion of braced frames.

3.04 MAINTENANCE AND REMOVAL

  A. Underpinning: Leave in place at completion of the
Work.

  B. Other Existing Structure Supports: Maintain as long
as necessary. Remove when permanent construction
makes temporary supports unnecessary.

  B. Sheeting, Soldier Piles, and Lagging: Leave in place
at completion of the Work, except cut down to a
level at least 3 feet below finish grade.

  C. Removing Bracing: Maintain bracing until structural
elements are rebraced or until permanent floor
construction can withstand lateral earth and
hydrostatic pressures. Remove bracing in stages to
avoid disturbing underlying soils and damage to
structures, pavements, facilities, and utilities.

  D. Damaged Work: Repair or replace, as directed by
Architect, adjacent work damaged or displaced
through installation or removal of sheeting,
shoring, bracing, underpinning, or other support
work.

Small Projects: Shoring, bracing, and underpinning are usually applicable only
to large projects. Where a small project needs such requirements, refer to the
example above for large projects for guidance.

Section 02200   *Earthwork*

All Projects: Most provisions in earthwork sections do not change because existing construction occurs in a project. Variations that are necessary can often be
handled by addition of a phrase such as ''both existing and new.''

    A few earthwork requirements, however, might require additional or modi-
fied provisions. The following examples illustrate several such cases. The examples include only additional provisions made necessary by existing construction

involvement. Paragraph numbers have been changed from those used in the source project manuals to provide continuity here.

The first example concerns rock removal. The project was an addition to a hospital. To further complicate matters, the site was adjacent to a subway station.

1.05   PROJECT CONDITIONS

   A. Rock excavation will probably require using explosives.

     1. Do not bring explosives onto site without written permission from authorities having jurisdiction.

     2. Be solely responsible for handling, storing, and using explosive materials when use is permitted, for protection of persons and property, and for damage and injury due to use of explosives. Note that proximity to existing subway tunnels and station may require unusual procedures.

     3. Be solely responsible for compliance with applicable laws, ordinances, rules, regulations, and orders of authorities having jurisdiction, including subway officials, related to transporting, handling, storing, and using explosives, including hours-of-work restrictions.

     4. Have blasting done by licensed and experienced personnel, fully and adequately covered by proper insurance and under adequate supervision.

     5. Before blasting, coordinate with Owner and Owner's consultants by testing with various intensities of charges to determine blasting level which will not interfere with critical Medical Center functions.

     6. Notify Medical Center officials at least seven working days before blasting is scheduled to occur. Include the date and approximate times of individual blasts.

     7. On the day of each blast, at least 30 minutes before the exact time of the blast, Contractor's construction supervisor shall personally notify Medical Center by telephoning 555-3321, presenting proper identification as agreed to by Owner and Contractor, and stating the exact time the blast is to occur.

        a. The communications page operator receiving the call will log the call. Operator's supervisor will be responsible for notifying Medical Center Departments, which must be notified.

        b. Should time of blast be delayed due to construction site problems, Contractor's construction supervisor shall again notify Medical Center by telephoning 555-3321 at least 30 minutes before blast is to occur. Construction supervisor shall again present proper identification and state exact time blast will occur.

8. Five minutes before exact time of each blast, Contractor's construction supervisor shall again telephone 555-3321, present proper identification, and request verification to proceed with blast, stating exact time of blast. Until specific verification to proceed is received, construction supervisor shall assume that blasting is *not* permitted and shall delay or cancel the blast until verfied permission to proceed has been granted.

9. Contractor shall cooperate with Medical Center to establish a clear means of communication between Contractor and Medical Center that will permit Medical Center to notify Contractor's construction supervisor at the site immediately if delay of a scheduled blast is mandatory due to Medical Center activity that cannot be interrupted or postponed.

The second example has to do with excavated materials storage. The requirement in the example might also apply to projects where all the work is new but is more likely to occur when existing construction is involved.

3.01   GENERAL EARTHWORK PROCEDURES

A. Site area for stockpiling excavated materials is limited and may at times be nonexistent. Where space exists, stockpile satisfactory excavated materials only in quantity needed, in an approved location. Place, grade, and shape stockpiles for proper drainage. Keep different materials separated. Locate and retain soil materials away from excavation edges; not within drip line of trees to remain.

B. Complete excavation of every description of whatever material encountered to lines and grades indicated, such as:
   1. Breaking up of existing slabs, footings, foundation walls, paving, curbs, sidewalks, and other existing on grade and underground construction to permit the Work under this Contract; removal of broken-up materials from site.
   2. Bulk excavation for new construction, paving, and site improvements and disposal of excavated material.

C. Complete other earthwork, including:
   1. Backfilling of basements of demolished buildings; dug wells; and voids left by removal of cisterns, abandoned manholes, catch basins, and inlets; and other voids left by removal of existing construction.

Figure 8-9. Doorway to the future. (Photograph by Stewart Bros.)

Section 02513 *Asphaltic Concrete Paving*

All Projects: The following example suggests some provisions related to existing asphaltic concrete paving. The project manuals from which the examples were taken referred extensively to state government requirements for pavements. An architect working in a state which does not have such requirements must work the kinds of requirements in the examples into whatever guides that architect uses. The principles remain the same.

```
PART 1  GENERAL

1.01  SUMMARY

    A. Section Includes: Providing asphaltic concrete
       paving as indicated, including new pavements,
       substrates for new brick paving, and repair and
       extensions of existing pavements.

1.04  QUALITY ASSURANCE

    A. Methods and materials used in asphaltic concrete
       paving work, including extension and patching of
       existing pavements, shall conform to current
       "Specifications for Material, Highways, Bridges and
       Incidental Structures" of the State Highway
       Administration (referred in these specifications as
       SHA "Specifications") and other local, state, and
       federal requirements and standards having
       jurisdiction.
```

PART 2   PRODUCTS

2.01   MATERIALS

    A. Paving: Use locally available materials and gradations which exhibit a satisfactory record of previous installations and meet or exceed SHA "Specifications" requirements. Materials used in patching existing paving shall match materials in existing paving. In addition to requirements indicated on sitework drawings, paving and prime and tack coats shall comply with SHA "Specifications."

PART 3   EXECUTION

3.01   SURFACE PREPARATION

    A. Remove existing asphaltic concrete pavement where indicated. Also remove existing asphaltic concrete pavement where necessary to carry out the Work under this Contract. Where indicated, and where necessary, whether indicated or not, also remove existing subbase and soil beneath subbase.

    B. When Work progress permits, patch existing asphaltic concrete and provide new asphaltic concrete pavement and new asphaltic concrete support for brick paving.

    C. Provide compacted soil subbase as specified in Section "Earthwork."

    D. Over soil subbase, provide aggregate subbase of thickness indicated on sitework drawings, but not less than the thickness required by SHA "Specifications." At existing asphaltic paving, make aggregate subbase same thickness as existing aggregate subbase. Construct aggregate subbase in accordance with the requirements of SHA "Specifications," and compact to 95 percent of the maximum density obtained at optimum moisture content as determined in accordance with AASHTO Method T99, unless a higher degree of compaction is required by SHA "Specifications."

    E. Remove loose material from compacted aggregate subbase immediately before applying prime coat.

    F. Apply prime coat to aggregate subbase when SHA "Specifications" require, at rate required by SHA "Specifications" to penetrate and seal but not flood surface. Cure and dry as long as necessary to attain penetration and evaporation of volatile.

    G. Apply tack coat to contact surfaces of previously constructed asphaltic concrete and surfaces abutting or projecting into asphaltic concrete. Distribute at rate required by SHA "Specifications," but not less than 0.15 gal. per sq. yd. of surface. Allow to dry until at proper condition to receive paving. Tack coat is not required over new asphaltic base course when surface course is applied promptly over a clean base that has been kept free of traffic.

3.02   PLACING

A. Make joints between old and new pavements, and between successive days' Work, to ensure continuous bond between adjoining Work. Make cut-out in existing asphaltic concrete pavement where new asphaltic concrete paving is placed on top of existing. Do not feather new asphaltic concrete. Construct joints to have same texture, density, and smoothness as other sections of asphaltic concrete course. Clean contact surfaces and apply tack coat.

B. Finish asphaltic concrete paving flush with abutting asphaltic concrete, Portland cement concrete, drains, and manhole covers. Grade between adjacent paving, curbs, existing pavement, and other surfaces to produce smooth surfaces which will not collect water or retain dirt. Slope to drain. Establish and maintain required lines and elevations.

3.03   PATCHING

B. Repair cuts in existing asphaltic paving in accordance with details and SHA "Specifications."

3.06   TRAFFIC AND LANE MARKINGS

A. Provide indicated painted lines and markings for asphaltic concrete paving placed under this Contract. Also provide indicated painted lines and markings for existing asphaltic concrete paving where indicated. Include where indicated:
    1. Centerlines for roadways.
    2. Parking spaces.
    3. Handicapped parking markings.
    4. Other markings if indicated.

Section 02514   *Portland Cement Concrete Paving*

All Projects: The differences between concrete paving sections for projects where all the work is new and those where existing construction occurs can be mostly handled by "match existing" phrases. Conditions where the match existing phrase is applicable include concrete materials so that color matches the existing finishes, curb and gutter configurations, joint types and widths, and concrete thickness. Sometimes it is practicable to use existing paving as the quality standard for new work in lieu of a mock-up panel. No other special provisions are required due solely to the presence of existing paving. Methods used to repair Portland cement concrete are beyond the scope of this book.

Section 02515   *Unit Pavers*

All Projects: The presence of existing unit pavers affects new pavers only if the new pavers are to match the existing. Even then, a few match existing phrases will take care of most situations. Match existing phrases may be used to specify brick size, type, color, finish, and sometimes even manufacturer and product. Match existing phrases can also apply to mortar color, joint type and width, paver pattern layout, and joint alignment.

Cleaning and repair of existing unit pavers is beyond the scope of this book. Refer to industry association guidelines, such as those produced by the Brick Institute of America, and paver producers' literature for cleaning and repair recommendations.

Section 02710 *Subdrainage Systems*

All Projects: The following example covers extending existing drain tile.

```
PART 1  GENERAL

1.01  SUMMARY

   A. Section Includes: Providing new drain tile and
      related items to extend existing drainage system as
      shown.

1.02  SUBMITTALS

   A. Certification: Submit two copies signed by
      Contractor and drainage system installer certifying
      that installed system conforms to specifications and
      that system successfully passed specified flow test.


PART 2  PRODUCTS

1.01  MATERIALS

   A. Existing Materials: Existing materials are believed
      to be as listed below. If materials are encountered
      which differ from the assumed, immediately notify
      Architect and do not proceed without instructions.
      1. Drain Tile: 4 inch size, standard strength,
         plain-ends-type, clay drain tile, in 12 inch
         lengths with fittings at corners and angles.
         Corner bends are 45 degrees.
      2. Supports: 2 by 10 pressure preservative-treated
         yellow pine or Douglas fir boards of minimum 10
         foot lengths.
      3. Joint Wrapping: 4 inch wide 16 mesh copper screen
         cloth.
      4. Joint Covering: Burlap or tarred felt.
      5. Backfill: 1 inch to 2-1/2 inch coarse gravel
         tailings.
      6. Backfill Cover: 10 mil PVC sheeting.
   B. New Materials: Match existing.


PART 3  EXECUTION

3.01  INSTALLATION

   A. Existing System: Existing drain tile is believed to
      be laid with 1/4 inch open butt joints on 2 by 10
      pressure preservative-treated boards. Joints are
      wrapped with a 4 inch wide 16-mesh copper screen
      cloth securely fastened in place with copper wire
```

and covered with burlap or tarred felt turned down sides. Backfill is deposited to width approximately 3 feet from walls and depth of 2 feet over the tile drain and covered with a layer of 10 mil PVC sheeting sloped away from wall and lapped and sealed against wall using mastic. If conditions are encountered which differ from the assumed, immediately notify Architect and do not proceed without instructions.

B. Install new tile in same manner as existing. Remove existing tile where it interferes with new construction. Extend new tile around new construction as shown. Make connections to existing tile where shown.

C. Before backfilling at new tile, flow test lines by running water through them. Remove blockages.

D. Backfill with same material used in existing construction to same width and depth.

E. Cover gravel with same material in same manner as existing fill was covered. Then fill to grade using material and methods specified in Section "Earthwork."

Division 4   Masonry

Section 04200   *Unit Masonry*

Large projects: The following example shows a method for specifying work related to some existing masonry conditions.

PART 1   GENERAL

1.01   SUMMARY

A. Section Includes:
1. Masonry, mortar, reinforcement, and accessories.
2. Patching, extending, removing and discarding, or removing and reinstalling existing masonry indicated.

B. Related Sections:
1. General Demolition Requirements: See Section "Demolition."
2. General Requirements for Minor Alterations: See Section "Minor Alteration Work."

1.02   SUBMITTALS

A. Samples:
1. For approval of materials and match with existing materials, submit samples of concrete masonry units, new face brick, and glazed structural units. Include in each set the full range of exposed colors and textures to be expected in completed Work. Submit initial face brick samples mounted as 15 inch by 20 inch by 1/2 inch panels.

2. For color selection and approval, submit cured
mortar samples in metal or plastic channels.
Include samples of mortar for use with face brick
to match existing, and mortar for use with glazed
structural units to match existing. Resubmit
until accepted.

1.03   QUALITY ASSURANCE

A. Existing brick masonry work in place shall serve as
the standard of quality for new and patching Work.

1.04   PROJECT CONDITIONS

A. Shoring, Bracing, and Underpinning of Existing
Structure Above Grade:
1. Provide temporary bracing and support of existing
masonry during masonry Work.
2. Protect existing work from damage due to new
masonry erection.
3. Be solely responsible for movement, settlement,
and other damage to existing buildings due to
masonry Work; correct damage resulting from
inadequate, improper, or careless construction
procedures or inadequate shoring, bracing,
support, or protection.
B. Should materials, systems, or conditions be
encountered in the Project that differ from those
assumed, immediately notify Architect by telephone,
followed by letter, and do not proceed without
instructions.

PART 2   PRODUCTS

2.01   BRICK

A. Salvage existing face brick for patching, extending,
and filling holes in existing face brick. Remove
mortar and clean face brick to be reused. Use only
approved face brick.
B. New Face Brick:
1. Standard, Grade, Type, Size, Texture, and Color:
Exactly match existing face brick. Use only face
brick that had been approved for use by
Architect.
2. Applications:
a. Use new face brick to patch, extend, and fill
openings in existing face brick where
acceptable salvaged face brick does not exist
in sufficient quantity to patch, extend, and
fill in openings in existing face brick walls.
b. Use in new Work where brick is exposed and
face brick is shown.
3. Product Name and Manufacturer: Same as existing
face brick.

2.02   CONCRETE MASONRY UNIT

(Here specify concrete masonry units exactly as for a project with all new work.)

B. Other Units: Should repair or replacement of existing masonry block units other than CMU be necessary, use CMU. Do not use other types of masonry block units in new Work or in extensions of existing work. Do not use other types of masonry block as bearing for new or relocated lintels, beams, or slabs.

2.03   GLAZED STRUCTURAL UNITS

A. Units: Existing units are believed to be ASTM C126, Grade S, Type I or II; sizes 8 inch by 8 inch and 5 inch by 12 inch; internal angles, square; exterior angles, bull-nosed; wainscot caps, square; bases, coved and recessed into topping.

B. Reuse salvaged units. When acceptable salvaged units are insufficient in quantity, use new units that exactly match the existing units.

2.04   MORTAR MATERIALS

A. Portland Cement: ASTM C150, Type I, except that Type III may be used for cold-weather construction.
   1. Use natural color cement for CMU.
   2. Use natural color or white cement as required to match existing mortar for face brick, glazed structural units, and precast concrete copings.

B. Masonry Cement: ASTM C91; a mixture of approximately 50 percent Portland cement and 50 percent pulverized limestone, containing an air-entraining agent to entrain not more than 15 percent by volume; match existing brick and glazed structural units mortar colors. Use only when approved when existing mortar colors cannot be matched using Portland cement mortar.

C. Hydrated Lime: ASTM C217, Type S.

D. Mortar Aggregate: ASTM C144, except that for joints less than 1/4 inch use aggregate graded with 100 percent passing the no. 16 sieve; clean, washed, and free from iron and other impurities.
   1. Where concealed, use natural colored sand.
   2. Where exposed in CMU, brick, glazed structural units, or precast coping work, use natural sand, colored manufactured sand, or a mixture of both to produce mortar to match existing mortar color.

2.05   MORTAR, PARGING, AND GROUT MIXES AND MIXING

A. Mortar for Concrete Unit Masonry, Brick, Glazed Structural Units, and Stone: Comply with ASTM C270, "Proportion Specification," for types of mortar required.

1. Except where another type mortar is indicated, use Type S mortar in setting concrete unit masonry, brick, glazed structural units, and precast concrete copings. In exposed work, match existing mortar color.
2. Use Type N masonry cement mortar in brick and in glazed structural unit work only with specific approval, where existing mortar cannot be matched using Type S Portland cement mortar.

PART 3 EXECUTION

3.01 GENERAL REQUIREMENTS FOR MASONRY WORK

A. Construct masonry used for patching and extending existing work equal to existing masonry.

3.02 BRICK WORK

A. Lay face brick in bond and coursing to match existing.
B. Make joints uniform and of type to match existing joints.
C. Cut off flush the joints on faces not exposed. Cut off flush joints where exposed and, after initial set, tool concave to match existing joints.

3.03 CONCRETE MASONRY UNITS (CMU)

A. Joints in CMU: Maintain joint widths to match existing.
B. Pattern Bond: In exposed masonry, match existing.

3.04 ANCHORAGE

A. Where masonry abuts existing concrete, anchor with structural steel angles mounted firmly to the concrete.

3.05 PARGING

A. Parge surfaces of existing masonry where not sufficiently smooth to receive properly installed gypsum board wall finish installed by laminating to existing surfaces. Refer to Section "Gypsum Board Systems."
B. Apply parging in two coats to thickness shown, but not less than 1/2 inch thick. Roughen first coat, allow to harden for 24 hours, and moisten before application of second coat. Trowel second coat to a smooth dense surface.
C. Damp cure parging for 24 hours. Protect from freezing.

Figure 8-10. Did anyone see that truck? (Photograph by Stewart Bros.)

3.06 WORK IN EXISTING MASONRY

   A. Cut, patch, and extend existing masonry as necessary for access, alterations, and new structural, plumbing, mechanical, and electrical Work. General requirements specified in Sections "Demolition" and "Minor Alteration Work" apply to Work in existing masonry.

   B. Where interior walls or partitions are extended, openings blocked up, or new openings cut, do Work and use materials matching the existing work, including jointing, reinforcement, and accessories. Cut out masonry carefully to blend new Work with old work as inconspicuously as possible. Tooth each course of exposed new masonry into existing, maintaining existing coursing and bonding. Lap new joint reinforcement 6 inches over existing where possible. Leave new masonry filling openings in existing walls and partitions in same plane as existing masonry surface. Place new masonry filling openings in existing walls and partitions to be finished with new directly applied materials, such as directly applied (laminated) gypsum board, so that new finish is in same plane as existing adjacent finished surface of wall or partition to remain.

   C. Salvage existing brick in sufficient quantity for patching and repair. Remove existing mortar; clean brick; store carefully for reuse.

Figure 8-11. Cracked brick wall. (Photograph by Stewart Bros.)

D. Use salvaged existing brick and new concrete masonry units for patching and extending existing exterior walls and for patching and filling openings in exterior walls (including temporary openings made under this Contract). Where acceptable salvaged brick is insufficient in quantity, provide new matching brick. Match coursing, joints, and mortar color exactly. Cut out existing masonry carefully and blend new Work with old work as inconspicuously as possible. Tooth each course of new masonry into existing. Lap new joint reinforcement 6 inches over existing where possible.

E. When demolishing portions of partitions built with glazed structural units, salvage glazed structural units in sufficient quantity to make repairs to, fill openings in, and make extensions of glazed structural unit surfaces. Note that glazed structural units bases are coved and recessed into existing topping. Remove carefully. Completely remove mortar from glazed structural units.

F. When patching, filling openings in, and extending glazed structural unit surfaces, use salvaged glazed structural units. Where satisfactory salvaged units do not exist in sufficient quantity, provide new matching units. Match existing colors, partition thickness and construction, joint colors and sizes, bond, and glazed structural unit shapes and sizes.

Cut using a corundum-type saw. Clean glazed structural units in the area of the Work under this Contract using a commercial detergent before installing finish floors. Do not damage glazed surfaces. Remove units damaged in the area of the Work under this Contract and install satisfactory salvaged units or provide new units.

G. Do not permit new or relocated beams, lintels, or slabs to bear on existing block units other than CMU.

   1. Remove existing block units other than CMU, and substitute CMU to the following extent:

      a. For Beam Bearing: Where new openings are cut in existing block that is not CMU, and in every other location where a new or relocated beam or lintel is installed in an existing block partition that is not CMU, remove the existing block for the entire thickness of the wall or partition 16 inches wide centered on the beam, unless a wider amount is indicated on the structural drawings, and provide a minimum of 16 inches (more if so indicated on the structural drawings) of 100 percent solid CMU the full thickness of the wall or partition from the bearing of the beam down to structural support below.

      b. For Slab Bearing: Remove the entire existing block construction as indicated.

   2. At other structural bearing conditions and in other locations indicated, remove existing hollow masonry and provide 100 percent solid masonry to the extent shown or specified earlier in this section.

H. Use CMU for blocking up openings in and extending walls and partitions of block other than CMU. Anchor CMU to existing block using veneer anchors or other approved anchors and in accordance with the building code. Provide continuous joint reinforcement in CMU. Lap new joint reinforcement 6 inches over existing where possible. Finish new masonry extending or filling openings in existing walls and partitions to be finished with new materials, in same plane as existing finished surface of wall or partition, or devise some other approved method to ensure that new finish materials finish in the same plane as adjacent, like, finish materials.

I. Work in existing masonry shall conform with requirements specified for new Work.

3.07 REPAIR, POINTING, AND CLEANING

A. Remove masonry units in the area of the Work which are loose, chipped, broken, stained, or otherwise damaged and units that do not match adjoining units.

Provide new units to match adjoining units, install in fresh mortar or grout, and point to eliminate evidence of replacement.

B. In the area of the Work, cut out defective mortar joints, refill solid with mortar, and cut flush or tool as specified. Remove nails, enlarge holes, except weep holes, and fill with mortar. Point up joints to provide a neat, uniform appearance, properly prepared for application of calking of sealant compounds.

C. Clean exposed CMU by dry brushing at the end of each day's work and after final pointing to remove mortar spots and droppings. Comply with recommendations in NCMA TEK Bulletin No. 28. Clean CMU before installing finished carpentry, finish floors, or acoustical ceilings. At patches and extensions, extend cleaning and pointing out onto existing surfaces to blend new Work with existing.

D. Clean exposed brick surfaces and mortar joints installed as part of the Work under this Contract and surfaces and joints disturbed or otherwise soiled during the Work under this Contract. Use bucket and brush hand cleaning method or high-pressure water method. Comply with BIA Technical Notes No. 20 "Cleaning Brick Masonry." Clean before mortar gets too hard; do not wait until completing

Small Projects: The extent of the requirements for a small project depends on the scope of the masonry work in the small project. Where many requirements exist but the scope of each is small, an architect might elect to specify the requirements only generally, leaving control up to the contract's general provisions. Unfortunately, a project with many conditions may not be small in terms of the number of specifications requirements needed even when the project's cost is low.

Section 04400 *Stone*

Large Projects: The following example includes some requirements for stone repair and restoration. Stone repair and restoration requirements vary considerably depending on the stone involved and the type of damage present. The example does not attempt to cover many types of stone or damage. The principles, however, apply whatever the stone or damage.

PART 1 GENERAL

1.01 SUMMARY

A. Section Includes:
   1. New limestone sills and copings.
   2. Extension of existing limestone wall with granite coping.
   3. Cleaning and repairing existing interior marble.
   4. Providing new marble to fill in openings in existing marble.

     5. Removing, cutting, reworking, repairing, refinishing storing, and reinstalling existing stone as necessary to complete the Work under this Contract.

  B. Related Sections:
    1. General Requirements for Demolition and Disposal of Materials Not to Be Reused: See Section "Demolition."
    2. General Requirements for Reconstructions: See Section "Minor Alteration Work."

1.02   SUBMITTALS

  A. Shop and Setting Drawings:
    1. Shop Drawings: Submit for approval. Show:
      a. Variations to repair procedures due to actual conditions different from those indicated.
      b. Locations and elevations of new and relocated openings; include details of sills and trim.
      c. Details and elevations of existing construction to be repaired; include each type of condition.
    2. Cutting and Setting Drawings: Submit for approval. Show dimensions, sections, and profiles of stonework units; arrangement and provisions for jointing, anchoring, fastening, supports, and other necessary details for lifting devices and reception of other work. Include elevation drawings indicating the location of each new stone unit, each refabricated stone unit, and each existing stone unit to be removed and reinstalled, marked with a number or number-letter designation corresponding to designation marked on concealed face of each unit.
    3. Do not remove stones from the buildings or deliver new stones to the site until Architect has approved specified cutting, setting, and shop drawings.
  B. Samples: Submit, for verification purposes, samples of the following:
    1. Each type of mortar for pointing and stone rebuilding and repair, in form of 6 inch long by 1/2 inch wide sample strips of mortar set in aluminum or plastic channels.
    2. On request, also submit samples of each proprietary material proposed for use in stone repair, restoration, and cleaning.
  C. Product Data:
    1. For approval, submit specifications and other data for each type of stonework. For new stone, including replacements, include certification from supplier that each complies with specified requirements and will match existing

installations. For each type of new and existing
stone, even if no new stone of that type is
required, include instructions for handling,
storage, installation, repair, cleaning, and
protection.

   2. For approval, submit manufacturers' brochures and
technical data for each mortar material, cleaning
agent, repairing compound, and other product and
material required. Include recommendations for
mixing, applying, and using and certifications
and test reports substantiating that products
comply with requirements.

1.03 QUALITY ASSURANCE

  A. Applicable Standards: Materials, fabrication,
refabrication, field cutting, finishing,
refinishing, handling, installation, and quality of
workmanship for Work specified in this section shall
comply with the building code and the
recommendations of the following as approved:
   1. Granite: National Building Granite Quarries
Association, Inc.
   2. Marble: Marble Institute of America (MIA).
   3. Limestone: Indiana Limestone Institute (ILI).

  B. Fabricator's Qualifications: Subcontract fabrication
of new stone, and refabrication of existing stone,
to a single firm which has successfully fabricated,
and refabricated, similar stone for a period of not
less than 5 years and is equipped to provide the
services needed.

  C. Compatibility Tests: Before starting each type of
Work specified in this section, test proposed
methods and materials in small inconspicuous
locations approved by Architect for compatibility
with existing materials. Do not use incompatible
materials. Do not proceed with Work until Architect
approves the tests.

  D. Allowable Tolerances: In both new and reinstalled
stone, variations shall not exceed:
   1. Variations from Plumb: For lines and surfaces of
walls and arrises, do not exceed 1/4 inch in 10
feet, 3/8 inch in a story height or 20 feet
maximum. For external corners and other
conspicuous lines, do not exceed 1/4 inch in any
story or 20 feet maximum.
   2. Variation from Level or Plane: For grades
indicated for exposed lintels, sills, parapets,
and other conspicuous lines, do not exceed 1/4
inch in any bay or 20 feet maximum, nor 3/4 inch
in 40 feet or more.
   3. Variation of Line: From existing or indicated
position in plan, do not exceed 1/2 inch in any
20 feet maximum or 3/4 inch in 40 feet or more.

4. Variation in Cross Section: From existing or indicated dimensions, do not exceed minus 1/4 inch, nor plus 1/2 inch.
5. Make junctures with existing materials flush within 1/8 inch.

E. Quality Standard: Work in place shall serve as the standard of quality required for stonework, except that inferior or deteriorated existing stonework will not be accepted as a standard for new or reconstructed work.

1.04 DELIVERY, STORAGE, AND HANDLING

A. Carefully pack, handle, and ship new and refabricated salvaged stone units and accessories strapped together in suitable packs or pallets or in heavy cartons. Unload and handle to prevent chipping and breakage.

B. Protect existing-in-place, new, and refabricated and other salvaged stone during storage and construction against moisture, soiling, staining, and physical damage.

C. Protect restoration materials during storage and construction from wetting by rain, snow, or groundwater, and from straining or intermixture with earth or other types of materials.

1.05 PROJECT CONDITIONS

A. Protect persons, motor vehicles, building surfaces, site, and surrounding areas from injury resulting from stonework.
   1. Prevent chemical cleaning solutions from coming into contact with people and surfaces they might injure.
   2. Dispose of runoff from cleaning operations by legal means. Prevent soil erosion, undermining of paving and foundations, damage to landscaping, and water penetration into building interiors.
   3. Protect adjacent surfaces from damage due to marble restoration, repair, and cleaning. Use drop cloths, polyethylene sheeting, tape, and other means necessary.

B. Clean stone surfaces only when air temperatures are 40 degrees F. and above and will remain so until stone has dried out, but for not less than 7 days after completion of cleaning.

C. Cold-Weather Protection for Installing New Stone and for Reinstalling Removed Existing Stone:
   1. Do not build on frozen work; remove existing and new stonework in the area of the Work under this Contract that has been damaged by frost or freezing; discard and provide new matching stone, except where repair of existing stone damaged by

freezing before this Contract began is
specifically approved in each specific case.

PART 2   PRODUCTS

2.01   EXISTING STONE MATERIALS

A. Where practicable, use existing stone removed from
the building to perform stonework indicated. Where
indicated, and, in addition, where necessary to
carry out the Work under this Contract, remove
existing stone from the building, protect, and store
for later reinstallation.

B. Refabricate, repair, or restore indicated existing
stone.

2.02   NEW STONE MATERIALS

A. At Contractor's option, provide new stone in lieu of
refabricating or refinishing removed existing stone.

B. Provide new stone:
   1. Where new stone is indicated.
   2. Where existing stone is to be removed and new
      stone provided.
   3. Where discarding of removed existing stone is
      approved.
   4. Where existing stone is damaged beyond repair,
      does not exist, or is insufficient in quantity to
      carry out the Work under this Contract.
   5. Where existing stone units are lost or damaged
      during the Work under this Contract.
   6. Where stone units are missing in the existing
      building.

C. Limestone: ASTM C568, with density category to match
existing limestone. Minimum compressive strength:
4000 psi per ASTM C170. Maximum absorption: 7.5
percent per ASTM C97. Limestone shall match existing
limestone in color, grade, and finish; for use in
walls and sills shall also match existing limestone
in size and profile; for copings shall be of sizes
indicated.

D. Granite: ASTM C615, Architectural Grade, and
National Building Granite Quarries Association,
Inc., for color and finish qualities; match the
existing granite coping in specie, type, color,
finish, size, shape, type of cut, and profile.

E. Marble: ASTM C503 and Marble Institute of America
(MIA); match color, finish, size, and profile of
existing marble. Abrasive hardness shall be not less
than 10 per ASTM C241.

2.03   MORTAR AND GROUT MATERIALS

A. Portland cement: ASTM C150, Type I, except use Type
III for setting stone in cold weather; complying

with the staining requirements of ASTM C91 for not more than 0.03 percent water soluble alkali. White or natural as necessary to produce visible mortar and grout colors to match existing.

B. Sand: ASTM C144, except graded with 100 percent passing a No. 16 sieve for 1/4 inch and narrower joints.
    1. For white mortar and grout, provide natural white sand or ground white stone meeting specified requirements.
    2. For colored mortar or grout, furnish sand ground from marble, granite, or other sound stone, meeting specified grading requirements for sand, as required to produce a mortar to match that existing.
    3. For pointing mortar, provide sand with rounded edges.
    4. Match size, texture, and gradation of aggregate in existing mortar as closely as possible.

C. Colored Mortar Pigment: Natural and synthetic iron oxides and chromium oxides compounded for use in mortar mixes. Use only pigments with record of satisfactory performance in stone mortars. Use only where it is impossible to match existing mortar color using natural or manufactured aggregate and white or natural cement.

D. Restoration Mortar: "M70 Stonerestauration Mortar" by Fa Jahn Restoration Techniques and Research, or approved equal; color to match stone being repaired.

E. Interior Marble Cleaning Agent: Commercial agent formulated for cleaning interior marble, recommended by specialty subcontractor who will do cleaning and approved. Agent shall not contain abrasives, acids, other caustic materials, or harsh fillers that would stain or otherwise damage the marble.

2.04 MORTAR AND GROUT MIXES AND MIXING

A. Mixes: Except where otherwise specified, use nonstaining, cement—lime mortar, complying with ASTM C270, "Proportion Specification," using specified materials.
    1. Patching and rebuilding mortar for:
        a. Limestone: Restoration mortar mixed with water.
        b. Other stone: Mix composed of white or gray cement combined with lime and selected aggregates to produce color matching existing stone. Proportion mix with 2 parts cement, 2 parts lime, and 6 parts aggregate, unless different mixes or materials are recommended by stone producer and approved. Contractor may submit for consideration a proprietary patching mortar material for each stone type, in lieu of specified Portland cement—lime mix.

2.05 ACCESSORIES, ANCHORS, AND SUPPORTS

A. Except where indicated otherwise, stonework accessories, anchors, and supports shall match those in place in the existing work. Use existing accessories, anchors, and supports when specifically approved. Provide new accessories, anchors, and supports where existing accessories are damaged or otherwise unacceptable and where new accessories are necessary to carry out the Work.

B. New Accessories, Anchors, and Supports: Of type and size indicated. Where not indicated, match existing accessories, anchors, and supports in size and type.

2.06 CLEANING MATERIALS AND EQUIPMENT

A. Water for Cleaning: Clean; potable; free of oils, acids, alkalis, salts, and organic matter. Heat warm water, if required, to temperature of 140 degrees F. to 180 degrees F.

B. Brushes: Fiber bristle only.

C. Acidic Cleaner: Manufacturer's standard strength acidic stone restoration cleaner composed of hydrofluoric acid blended with other acids, including trace of phosphoric acid, and combined with special wetting systems and inhibitors. Subject to compliance with requirements, product shall be "Sure Klean Restoration Cleaner," by ProSoCo, Inc., or approved equal. Do not use for cleaning limestone or other surfaces that product might damage.

D. Limestone Cleaner: Manufacturer's standard two-part system consisting of alkaline prewash cleaner and acidic afterwash cleaner. Subject to compliance with requirements, the product shall be "Sure Klean Limestone Prewash and Afterwash," by ProSoCo, Inc., or approved equal.

E. Liquid Strippable Masking Agent: Manufacturer's standard liquid, film-forming strippable masking material for protecting glass, metal, and polished stone surfaces from damaging effects of acidic and alkaline masonry cleaners. Subject to compliance with requirements, provide "Sure Klean Acid Stop," ProSoCo, Inc., or approved equal.

2.07 CHEMICAL CLEANING SOLUTIONS

A. General: Unless otherwise indicated, dilute chemical cleaning materials with water to produce solutions of concentration indicated but not greater than that recommended by chemical cleaner manufacturer.

B. Acidic Cleaner Solution for Unpolished Stone: Maximum hydrofluoric acid content: 3 percent. Use acidic cleaner only on unpolished granite, unpolished dolomite marbles, and siliceous sandstone.

C. Acidic Cleaner for Polished Stone: In concentration demonstrated by testing which does not etch or otherwise damage polished surface. Use acidic cleaner on only polished granites and polished dolomite marbles.

D. Alkaline Cleaner for Prewash of Limestone: In concentration recommended by chemical cleaner manufacturer. Use alkaline cleaner only on calcite limestone as prewash.

E. Acid Cleaner for Afterwash of Limestone: In concentration recommended by chemical cleaner manufacturer. Use above type only on calcite limestone as afterwash.

2.08 MISCELLANEOUS MATERIALS

A. Stone-to-Stone Adhesive: Two-part polyester resin stone adhesive with a 15- to 30-minute cure at 70 degrees F., in formulation (knife or flowing grade) recommended by adhesive manufacturer for type of stone repair needed and in color as selected by Architect from tinted or standard colors available from adhesive manufacturer. Subject to compliance with requirements, provide "Akemi" adhesives distributed by Wood and Stone, Inc., 7567 Gary Road, Manassas, VA 22110, or approved equal.

B. Mortar-to-Stone Adhesive: high-modulus high-strength moisture-insensitive epoxy adhesive with a pot life of 30 minutes at 40 degrees F. Subject to compliance with requirements, provide "Sikadur Hi-Mod Epoxy, Sikastix 370" by Sika Chemical Corporation, or approved equal.

C. Joint Fillers: Cork or other nonbituminous type to match existing.

2.09 FABRICATION

A. Cut accurately to shape and dimensions shown on final shop drawings, maintaining fabrication tolerances of applicable stone associations.
   1. Dress joints (bed and vertical) straight and at 90 degree angle to face, unless otherwise indicated.
   2. Joint Width: Exactly match existing joints.

B. Sizes and Thicknesses: Unless otherwise indicated, provide stone of thickness to match existing stone, with maximum variation from existing stone of 3/8 inches for units less than 3 inches thick and 1/2 inch for thicker units. Saw-cut back surfaces which will be concealed in finished work. Sizes shall match existing. Leave not less than 1 inch clearance between back face of units and structure framing. Clean sawn backs of rust stains and iron particles.

C. Fabricate sills to profiles and thicknesses to match existing and to dimensions needed to properly fit openings.

2.10   REFABRICATION

A. Refabricate existing stone:
   1. Where indicated.
   2. Where necessary to affect proper repairs.
   3. Where Contractor elects to use existing, unnecessary stone in a new location and such use is approved.

B. Refabricate at Project site or at a stone-producing plant, using equipment and methods appropriate to material and condition of material, and recommended in referenced standards and criteria. Cut existing stone using power masonry saws with diamond- or other special-tipped blades; create straight lines and consistent surfaces for entire depth of stone. Grind if necessary to complete joints, and refinish exposed edges. Do not spall or chip stone. Do not use refabricated stone with chipped edges.

C. Do not refabricate fractured, chipped, permanently stained, deteriorated, freeze damaged, or otherwise unacceptable stone, unless specifically approved in each case.

D. Requirements specified for fabricating new stone also apply to refabricating existing stone. Mark each refabricated stone with a number or number-letter designation identical with designation shown on cutting and setting drawings.

Figure 8-12. Split stone coping. (Photograph by Stewart Bros.)

E. Refabricate neatly to suit existing coursing and pattern. Match faces of adjacent stone units. Dress edges to follow established edges of adjacent units, including units left in place, to follow established pattern and joint size.

F. Refabricate stone back—up material from sound, approved material, shaped to engage existing coursing. Finish opening edges level and square where applicable.

G. Refit refabricated material to accommodate new Work and accept anchors, ties, flashings, supports, and accessories. Do not patch or hide defects on exposed stone faces.

PART 3   EXECUTION

3.01   EXAMINATION

A. Examine stone substrates and conditions under which stonework will be done. Do not proceed until unsatisfactory conditions have been satisfactorily corrected.

B. Should different materials, systems, or conditions occur than those assumed, immediately notify Architect. Do not proceed without instructions.

3.02   PREPARATION

A. Advise installers of other work concerning requirements for placing inserts and flashing reglets to be used for anchoring, supporting, and flashing stonework. Furnish installers of other work with drawings or templates showing location of inserts for stone anchors and supports.

B. Install steel support members to carry out the Work under this Contract. Set supports level and straight, at proper elevations, and in correct locations. Parge steel members before placing stone or flashing against them.

3.03   REMOVING AND RESETTING EXISTING MARBLE

A. Removing or resetting existing marble is not generally required. However, should marble in the area of the Work be damaged at the beginning of the Work, or damaged as a result of the Work, and the damage be too severe to satisfactorily repair, remove the damaged marble and provide new matching marble. Also, remove and reinstall loose marble in the area of the Work.

B. When removing marble, examine anchors, flashings, and accessories. Remove damaged and deteriorated items and provide new matching items. Tighten supports, level, and make ready to receive reinstalled marble coping stones.

C. Handle removed marble to prevent damage. Clean removed marble of existing mortar, sealants, and bonding materials. Completely remove existing setting beds.

D. Before reinstalling existing or installing new marble, thoroughly scrub on all sides with clean water and fiber brushes. Keep marble clean at all times.

E. Reinstall removed marble and install new marble using methods used in original installation. Leave stones in alignment and flush with adjacent stones, in proper location, and with equal-sized and open joints. Where setting beds were used in the original installation, reinstall stones in full beds of specified mortar. Fill dowel holes and anchor slots with specified mortar.

3.04 REMOVING OTHER STONE

A. Removing stone is not generally required under this Contract. Remove only stones indicated to be removed, stones that must be removed to make way for the Work under this Contract, and stones adjacent to the Work under this Contract which are found damaged or are damaged during the Work under this Contract beyond satisfactory repair.

B. Do not remove existing stone until Architect approves cutting and setting drawings specified in Paragraph "Submittals" of this Section. Verify openings sizes from approved shop drawings before removing stone.

C. Use hand methods only. Do not use jacks, saws, drills, or other power-driven devices without specific written approval in each case.

D. When removing stone, examine related anchors, flashings, and accessories. Removed damaged and deteriorated items and provide new matching items. Tighten supports, level, and otherwise make ready to receive reinstalled or new stone.

E. Prevent damage and protect existing defects from further damage. Clean removed stone, adjacent stone, and other materials left in place of all traces of existing mortar, sealants, backer rods, primers, sealers, bonding materials, paint, stains, and other discolorations. Remove existing setting beds completely. Clean removed stone and materials left in place of dust, dirt, loose material, efflorescence, and other materials that would adversely affect bonding of new mortar, repair materials, or sealants. Include removing from cracks, voids, and spalled areas embedded soiling, loose material, and previous repair material. Use tools that will not damage adjacent surfaces but which will clear cracks, voids, and spalled areas,

and slightly enlarge face opening to ensure repair
material penetration.

F. Examine each removed existing stone unit. Discard
units with deteriorated surfaces; multiple instances
of structural or edge damage; other defects which
would prevent acceptable repair, patching,
refinishing, or reinstallation; or freeze damage and
provide new acceptable units.

G. When removing stones to be reinstalled, mark each in
a concealed location with a waterproof nonstaining—
to—the—exposed—surface marker with a number or
number—letter combination identical with the
designation shown for that unit on the paving plans
or cutting and setting drawings specified in
Paragraph "Submittals" of this Section.

3.05   INSTALLING AND REINSTALLING STONE GENERAL
REQUIREMENTS

A. Provide items and do stonework indicated. In
addition, provide items and work not indicated but
necessary to ensure that new stone and existing
stone within the area of the Work under this
Contract which is indicated to be repaired,
restored, replaced, or removed and reinstalled is:
1. Complete and watertight.
2. Suitable in construction for the necessary
   function.
3. In appearance comparable with the best of the
   existing stonework. However, nothing in this
   paragraph limits other parts of the Contract
   documents.

B. Do not install or reinstall stone units which in
Architect's opinion are damaged beyond satisfactory
repair, have not been satisfactorily repaired, or
are permanently stained or improperly cleaned. Where
reinstallation of removed units is unacceptable,
regardless of the reason, provide new matching
units.

C. Where practicable, reinstall removed stone,
including loose whole units and fragments, and
refabricated stone, in same location from which
removed.

D. Where practicable, stone units removed from the
building which are not needed for reinstallation in
the location from which they were removed but are
otherwise in acceptable condition may be
refabricated and refinished and used in another
location where stone of the same type, specie, and
color is required.

E. Where using salvaged stone is not practicable,
material is declared unacceptable, or Contractor
elects to do so and the action is approved, provide
new matching stone in lieu of reinstalling removed
stone. New stone shall exactly match removed stone

in specie, type, color, shape, size, and configuration and shall be finished to match the adjacent existing stone left in place after the adjacent stone left in place has been placed in acceptable condition to comply with the requirements of this Contract.

F. Employ skilled stone fitters at the site to do necessary field cutting as stone is set.

G. Anchor stonework and bond-replacement wythes in the same manner as existing construction. Use stainless steel at least 1/8 inch thick for all added ties and anchors.

H. When installing new or salvaged stone units, butter vertical joints for full width before setting and set units in full bed of mortar, unless otherwise indicated.

I. Set stone in accordance with drawings, final shop drawings, setting drawings, and layout plans. Reconstruct stonework equal to adjacent stone areas and other similar existing installations. As the Work progresses, set and build in supports, anchors, fasteners, and other attachments shown or necessary to secure stonework in place, and accessories and flashings. Shim and adjust accessories for proper setting of stone. Completely fill holes, slots and other sinkages for anchors, dowels, fasteners, and supports with expanding grout during setting of stones.

J. Joints:
1. Provide mortar joints except where indicated otherwise. In every case, make and finish joints neatly and uniformly; make as indistinguishable as possible from existing joints left in place.
2. Keep joints uniformly similar to existing adjoining stonework but not less than 1/8 inch wide.
3. Tool joints after setting to match joints of surrounding stone.
4. Repoint new mortar joints to comply with requirements for repointing existing masonry but rake out joints before mortar sets.

3.06 INSTALLING AND REINSTALLING STONE IN WALLS

A. Cavity Construction: Where open space between back of stone units and back-up or framing exists, keep cavity open; do not fill with mortar or grout. Use cavity construction only to match existing conditions.

B. After setting and before mortar sets, rake out joints 3/4 inch deep to allow for pointing. Clean face of stone after raking. After mortar is set, wet raked joints thoroughly and force pointing mortar into joints. Tool to match existing. Use specified materials and match existing mortar.

3.07   CLEANING AND REPAIRING MARBLE

A. Clean indicated marble of dust, dirt, loose material, efflorescence, and other materials that would adversely affect bonding of patching mortar or new mortar. Include removal from cracks, voids, and spalled areas of embedded soiling, loose material, and previous repair material. Use tools that will not damage adjacent surfaces but which will clear cracks, voids, and spalled areas, and slightly enlarge face opening to ensure repair material penetration.

B. Scrub marble thoroughly using clean water and fiber brushes. Do not use wire brushes, acids, or solutions which may damage the marble or cause discoloration. If cleaning beyond normal washing with bristle brushes is necessary, obtain recommendations from the marble producer and the Marble Institute of America (MIA) and follow the more stringent of those recommendations after approval.

C. Apply patching mortar in cracks, voids, and spalled areas in cleaned marble, including both damaged locations and natural graining and other natural features of the marble surface, to produce a smooth monolithic acceptable appearance. Follow manufacturer's recommendations, as approved. Exactly match the color of the marble where exposed to view. After proper mortar cure, grind and buff repairs, using emory granules, to produce a surface texture that matches the smooth portion of existing marble surface.

D. Repairs and patches shall be virtually invisible in the completed Work.

3.08   REPAIRING OTHER STONE

A. The Contract does not require general repair of existing stone other than marble. Repair is required, however, of damaged stone immediately adjacent to the Work under this Contract and stone damaged during the Work under this Contract. Damage requiring repair is any damage that would permit water intrusion into the stone, visible discoloration or stains, surface deteriorations which affect the appearance or stability of the stone, cracks, and spalled areas.

B. Where stone repair is indicated, carefully clean and repair damaged areas using methods recommended by the organizations specified in Paragraph "Quality Assurance" of this section and patching products specified in this section. Follow manufacturer's instructions as approved and the recommendations of the organizations specified in Paragraph "Quality Assurance" of this section.

Figure 8-13. The bottom of a problem. (Photograph by Stewart Bros.)

    C. Patches shall match adjacent unpatched and undamaged stone.

    D. Where damaged areas cannot be satisfactorily repaired, remove damaged stone and provide new matching stone.

3.09 REPOINTING, SEALING, OR RESEALING STONE JOINTS

    A. The Contract requires repointing mortar joints or sealing or resealing joints with sealant, as applicable, where indicated, and where joints immediately adjacent to the area of the Work under this Contract are deteriorated, soft, spalled, popped out, disintegrated, or cracked open.

    B. Repoint joints or reseal with sealant, as applicable, where existing joints are damaged during construction operations, regardless of the circumstances, and where joints installed, pointed, repointed, sealed, or resealed under this Contract are not as specified, or have deteriorated, become soft, spalled, popped out, disintegrated, or cracked open.

    C. Repoint or reseal, as applicable, defective and unsatisfactory joints. Provide neat uniform appearance.

D. Rake out mortar from joints to depths equal to 2-1/2 times widths but not less than 3/4 inch nor less than required to expose sound unweathered mortar for joints to be repointed with mortar; to one inch for joints to receive sealant.

E. Remove mortar from stone surfaces within raked-out joints to provide reveals with square backs and to expose masonry for contact with pointing mortar or sealant. Brush, vacuum, or flush joints to remove dirt and loose debris.

F. Do not spall edges of stone units or widen joints, except where joints are less than 1/4 inch wide, widen to 1/4 inch. Discard units which become damaged and provide new units.

G. Cut out old mortar by hand with chisel and mallet, unless otherwise indicated. Do not use power tools.

H. Rinse joint surfaces with water to remove dust and mortar particles. Time rinsing application so that at time of pointing, excess water has run off or evaporated and joint surfaces are damp but free of standing water.

I. Apply first layer of pointing mortar to areas where existing mortar was removed to depths greater than surrounding areas. Apply in layers not greater than 3/8 inch until a uniform depth is formed. Compact each layer thoroughly and allow to become thumbprint hard before applying next layer. Where existing stone units have rounded edges, recess final layer slightly from face. Take care not to spread mortar over edges onto exposed masonry surfaces or to feather edge mortar.

J. When mortar is thumbprint hard, tool joints to match original appearance of joints. Remove excess mortar from edge of joint by brushing.

K. Cure mortar by maintaining in a damp condition for not less than 72 hours.

L. Where repointing work precedes cleaning of existing stone, allow mortar to harden not less than 30 days before beginning cleaning work.

3.10   ADJUSTING AND CLEANING NEW AND REINSTALLED STONE

A. Remove stone installed or reinstalled under this Contract which is broken, chipped, stained, or otherwise damaged. Also remove stone patched or rebuilt under this Contract where those units are unacceptable. Provide new stone units to replace those so removed, install as specified, and point up joints to eliminate evidence of replacement.

B. Repoint or reseal, as applicable, defective and unsatisfactory joints which were installed, reinstalled, pointed, sealed, or damaged during the Work under this Contract. Leave joints neat, uniform, and acceptable.

C. Clean stonework installed or reinstalled under this Contract not less than 6 days after completing Work. Use clean water and stiff-bristle brushes. Do not use sand blasting, wire scrapers or brushes, acid cleaning agents, or cleaning compounds with caustic or harsh fillers. Clean reinstalled stonework, including refabricated stonework, as specified in Paragraph "Cleaning Existing Stonework."

3.11   CLEANING EXISTING STONEWORK

A. The Contract does not require general stonework cleaning. Clean only those areas indicated to be cleaned.

B. Use only those cleaning methods recommended by organizations specified in Paragraph "Quality Assurance" of this section and approved. Do not spray-apply chemical cleaners.

C. Comply with recommendations of manufacturers of chemical cleaners for protecting building surfaces against damage from exposure to their products.

D. Do cleaning by methods which result in uniform coverage of all surfaces, and which produce an even effect without streaking or damage to stone surfaces.

3.12   CLEANING UP AND FINAL CLEANING

A. Leave stone installed, reinstalled, repaired, repointed, sealed, damaged, stained, or soiled during the Work under this Contract, and stone which was indicated to be cleaned under this Contract, clean and free from dirt, mortar stains, traces of cleaning compound, and other defacements.

Small Projects: The extent of the requirements for a small project depends on the scope of the stonework in the small project. Where many requirements exist but the scope of each is small, an architect might elect to specify the requirements only generally, leaving control up to the contract's general provisions, and use of cleaning and repair products up to the manufacturer's recommendations. Unfortunately, a project with many conditions may not be small in terms of the number of specifications requirements needed, even when the project's cost is low.

Division 5   Metals

Section 05500   *Metal Fabrications*

Large Projects: The following example shows a method for specifying some existing metal fabrications. Only a few conditions are included. The principles, however, apply to whatever existing metal fabrications must be altered or relocated in a project.

PART 1 GENERAL

1.01 SUMMARY

A. Section Includes:
1. Miscellaneous new metal fabrications as indicated.
2. Reworking and relocating existing metal fabrications.

PART 2 PRODUCTS

2.01 MISCELLANEOUS METAL FABRICATIONS

A. Steel Stairs:
1. Remodel and extend existing stairs and provide new stairs indicated. Join pieces by welding. Provide complete stair assemblies, including metal framing, hangers and other supports, railings, newels with cast-iron finial caps with newel-size adapters, post caps with newel-size adapters, tube standards, subrail bars, pattern bars, cast iron facings, balusters, struts, braces, framing, brackets, bearing plates, and other components necessary for support of stairs and platforms and as required to anchor and contain stairs on supporting structure and to connect new stairs to existing stairs and other existing work.
2. Fabricate stairs and platforms to details shown and approved Shop Drawings. Where not shown, match existing conditions, materials, fabrication, assembly, and installation. Assemble and reinforce to support uniformly distributed live load of 150 psi minimum.
3. Fabricate stringers of hot-rolled steel channels, or plates, as indicated. Include filler plates and clips. Provide cast ornamental moldings similar to existing. Close exposed stringer ends. Construct platforms of hot-rolled steel channels and shapes as indicated. Bolt or weld headers to stringers and framing members to strings and headers.
4. Pan-Type Platforms, Treads, and Risers: Cold-rolled carbon steel sheet risers, subtreads, and subplatforms for concrete fill and stone treads and landings; minimum thickness required to meet design live loads; reinforced by hot-rolled steel shapes. Turn treads up to form nosing at concrete-filled treads and landings.
5. Formed Steel Treads and Risers: Fabricate to configuration shown using mild steel plate of thickness required to meet specified live load requirements. Provide steel stiffeners as necessary. Provide angle clips and anchors needed for proper installation. Coat entire back surface

of treads and risers with sound-deadening
material.
6. Fabricate railing to continue beyond stairs where
indicated. Fabricate complete with tube
standards, floor flanges, continuous subrail, and
related anchors and fasteners.
7. Fabricate railings and pattern bars to parallel
stair slope, landing, or floor below as
appropriate; fabricate newels, balusters, and
tube standards to be plumb in each direction.
Weld balusters to subrail and base bar. Weld base
bar to stringers. Grind and polish welds.
8. Fabricate and join so that bolts, screws, and
other fasteners, if used, do not appear on finish
surfaces.
9. Neatly cope and weld joints. Grind sharp corners
and shop welds smooth and free from burrs, and
shop-paint all portions of stairs and railings
that are not to be embedded in concrete or
mortar.
B. Emergency Exit Walkway Enclosure:
1. Extend existing exit walkway enclosure as
indicated.
2. Fabricate to details and conditions shown. Except
where specifically indicated otherwise, use
materials, methods, and finishes which exactly
match those being extended, except that
requirements specified in this section for
materials and fabrication shall apply.
C. Decorative Turnbuckles: Carefully remove existing
turnbuckles and tie rods; store safely for
reinstallation. Adapt tie rod connection brackets
for other use where indicated. Conceal tie rod
connection brackets not to be reused in new
construction.
D. Other Fabricated Assemblies: Fabricate in accordance
with approved Shop Drawings and as required by
conditions shown, or necessary to complete the Work.
Furnish matching trim, anchors, fasteners, and other
devices for proper installation.

PART 3 EXECUTION

3.01 EXAMINATION

A. Examine existing fabrications to which new Work is
to be attached and the areas and conditions where
metal fabrications work will be done. Do not proceed
before correcting unsatisfactory conditions.

3.02 PREPARATION AND INSTALLATION

A. Steel Stairs: Remodel existing and erect new steel
stairs in accordance with details and approved Shop
Drawings to properly support design loads and to

meet smoothly with existing stairs and other construction. Conceal connections wherever possible, or use unobtrusive connections.

1. Join new stairs to existing stairs and other construction and parts of stairs, including railings components and framing, together by welding.
2. Properly support stairs temporarily during erection.
3. Continue railing beyond stairs where indicated. Anchor standards using floor flanges bolted to concrete or steel structural elements.
4. Leave railings and pattern bars parallel with stair slope, landing, or floor below as appropriate; leave newels, balusters, and tube standards plumb.
5. Stairwell cap: Install neatly without oil canning or ripple. Securely fasten in place.
6. Neatly cope and weld field joints. Grind sharp corners and field welds smooth and free from burrs.

B. Emergency Exit Walkway Enclosure: Unless specifically indicated or approved otherwise, install new elements and reinstall salvaged elements exactly as existing enclosure elements were installed, except that general installation requirements specified in this section shall apply.

C. Decorative Turnbuckles: Install in new locations indicated, using threaded steel pipe sections. Use approved end connections. Leave with turnbuckle arms aligned and with pipe supports level and securely fastened in place. Follow approved Shop Drawings. Attach to end support frames, anchor to floor structure and existing roof members. Provide intermediate suspension from roof structure as required to produce a rigid secure assembly.

D. Other Existing Metal Fabrications: Repair and restore to usable condition existing metal fabrications found to be in unusable or unacceptably unsightly condition as well as existing metal fabrications indicated to be repaired, restored, or removed and reinstalled.

1. Remove existing exterior railings and standards, including lead packing at mounting sleeves which is anchoring exterior railing standards to stone where shown or necessary to carry out the Work. When progress of the Work permits, reinstall the removed railings and standards. Fill space between sleeves and standards with molten lead to support and anchor standards. Leave railings parallel with supporting structure and standards plumb.
2. Unless otherwise shown, when working with existing metal fabrications, use materials and

methods that match the original installation.
Discard damaged metal fabrications and provide
new, acceptable metal fabrications.

Small Projects: The requirements for a small project depend on the scope of the project. Where the conditions specified in the example exist on a small project, requirements similar to those in the example are appropriate. If the amount of work involved in each metal fabrication is small, the architect might cut down the specified requirements and rely on general requirements to control quality.

Division 6 Wood and Plastic

Section 06100 *Rough Carpentry*

Large Projects: The following example shows a method for specifying some existing rough carpentry conditions. This is a section where using a separate paragraph for work related to existing conditions may make as much sense as integrating those requirements into the section as a whole. The example demonstrates that technique. It also shows requirements for minor wood framing. Handle other specific requirements in a similar way.

PART 1 GENERAL

1.01 SUMMARY

    A. Section Includes: Lumber, softwood plywood, rough
       hardware, and related items; performing rough
       carpentry work indicated.

PART 3 EXECUTION

3.01 BLOCKING, NAILERS, FURRING, GROUNDS, SUPPORTS, AND
      MISCELLANEOUS ROUGH CARPENTRY

    A. At roofs, remove existing rough wood materials where
       indicated or necessary and provide new pressure-
       preservative-treated wood nailers and blocking for
       support and anchoring of cants, roofing, curbs,
       gutters, flashings and other sheet metal, and in
       other locations where indicated or required, for
       attachment of other work.
    B. Attic Walkways: Remove existing walkways and provide
       new 3/4 inch fire-retardant-treated plywood walkway
       using 4 foot by 8 foot sheets. Loosely butt joints;
       fasten securely in place.

3.02 PATCHING AND EXTENDING EXISTING WORK

    A. General requirements for demolition are specified in
       Section "Demolition"; for alterations in Section
       "Minor Alteration Work." Requirements specified in
       those sections apply to the work specified in this
       section.
    B. Where existing rough carpentry is removed to permit
       making alterations, is unacceptably damaged, or is

noted to be removed, remove carefully; do not damage materials to remain.

C. Provide new rough carpentry to close openings in existing work, extend existing work, replace existing work that has been removed, and in other locations where indicated or necessary to complete the Work under this Contract.

D. Sizes and shapes of rough carpentry used to restore work removed to make way for the Work shall match that removed. Do not reinstall removed rough carpentry unless approved.

E. Requirements specified in this section for new Work also apply to repairs and extensions of existing rough carpentry, as do requirements shown on the Drawings. The following additional requirements also apply.

   1. Plates:
      a. On Concrete and at Roof Accessories: Use pressure-preservative-treated lumber.
      b. Anchor: To masonry, using expansion bolts into shields near each end and 48 inches o.c. between; to wood using nails; to other materials using appropriate bolts or other fasteners near each end and at 24 inches o.c. between.

   2. Framing:
      a. Use members of sizes and at spacings shown. Where framing is to replace existing, and loading has not been increased, match existing sizes and spacings.
      b. Where existing members are full dimension and finishes are directly applied, use new members of the same size as existing, or use nominal sized new members and shim to proper plane for finishes.
      c. Support ends of new framing members 1-1/2 inches when bearing on wood or metal and 3 inches when bearing or masonry or concrete, except support beams 4 inches.
      d. Lap members framing from opposite sides of support minimum 4 inches or tie opposing members together by toenailing or metal connectors.
      e. Anchor framing in an approved manner.
      f. Spike built-up members together.
      g. Provide fire stops where fire stops are removed, and where indicated or required by code.

   3. Provide other work related to existing rough carpentry where indicated or required to complete the Work.

Small Projects: The requirements in the example above apply as well to small projects.

Section 06200 *Finish Carpentry*

Large Projects: The following example shows the integrated method of specifying requirements related to existing conditions. The example shows a few conditions to indicate method. Specify other conditions similarly. This example slightly violates the *Masterformat* system by specifying wood window sash work in Section ''Finish Carpentry.'' That procedure was selected because work related to the sash was to be done by the same specialist assigned to do the frame work. It would be possible to specify window sash work in a wood windows section and frames here in ''Finish Carpentry,'' but doing so makes little sense.

```
PART 1  GENERAL

1.01  SUMMARY

   A. Section Includes:
      1. Removing existing woodwork.
      2. Providing standing and running trim, handrails,
         shelving, laminated plastic assemblies, window
         seat, AC unit enclosure, door and window frames
         and trim, window sash, and other finish carpentry
         indicated.
      3. Reworking (or replacing with new materials)
         existing interior and exterior wood door frames,
         casings, and trim; window sash, frames, casings,
         trim, stools, and aprons; paneling; and other
         finish carpentry as indicated.
      4. Installing miscellaneous equipment items,
         specialties, accessories, and furnishings
         specified in other sections where specific
         reference to installation and workmanship is not
         otherwise specified.
   B. Related Sections:
      1. General Requirements for Demolition: See Section
         "Demolition."
      2. General Requirements for Alterations: See Section
         "Minor Alteration Work."

1.02  SUBMITTALS

   A. Shop Drawings: For approval, submit Shop Drawings of
      standing and running trim; window sash, frames,
      casings, trim, stools, and aprons; door frames and
      trim; handrails and railings; shelves; plastic
      laminate assemblies; window seat; AC unit enclosure;
      and other finish carpentry items.
      1. Show proposed repair methods in each case.

1.03  QUALITY ASSURANCE

   A. Finish Carpentry Specialist: Have finish carpentry
      work done by a firm which can demonstrate successful
      experience in work similar to that for this Project,
      particularly door- and window-related work, and
      which is approved by Owner. Use only experienced
```

personnel skilled in operations necessary, and working under competent supervision. Finish carpentry specialist shall make the examinations specified in Paragraph "Examination" of this section and shall report the findings to Architect through Contractor. Do no finish carpentry work at the site until finish carpentry specialist's findings have been examined and the scope of the Work agreed on by Owner and Contractor.

B. Should conditions appear that are significantly different from those indicated, notify Architect by telephone and in writing and do not proceed without instructions.

PART 2   PRODUCTS

2.01   MATERIALS AND FABRICATION

A. General:
1. Except where indicated otherwise, materials used in repairing existing finish carpentry shall match existing materials in same assembly but shall not be lower in quality than materials specified for new Work.
2. Where indicated, and in other locations where approved, reuse existing finish carpentry items except do not reuse damaged items.
3. Except where indicated otherwise, workmanship and methods of assembly for repairing or extending existing finish carpentry shall match those in the existing assembly but shall not be lower in quality than required to meet the specified AWI quality standards.
4. Unless detailed otherwise, size and profile of units used to repair or extend existing finish carpentry shall exactly match the existing.

B. Softwood Lumber Material:
1. Stained interior frames, sash, trim, and paneling: Match existing but not of lesser quality than Ponderosa Pine, WWPA, C-Select, Clear, or better, or approved equivalent.

C. Hardwood Lumber Material:
1. Stain finish wood on First Floor and natural finish wood in other locations including standing and running trim; paneling; door frames and trim; window sash, frames, trim, stools, aprons: Oak to match existing.

D. Window Hardware: Match appearance of existing. Provide operators, tracks, locking handles, keepers, balances, sweep latches, bar hinges, push bars, pulleys, finger pulls, balances, sash weights, chains, and other hardware as appropriate for complete and correct window operation. Also provide reinforcement and fasteners.

E. Window Weather Stripping:
    a. Compression Weather Stripping: Standard, approved, nonferrous, spring metal or vinyl gasket, designed for permanently resilient sealing under bumper or wiper action, completely concealed when sash is closed.
    b. Sliding Weather Stripping: Woven pile stripping of wool, polypropylene, or nylon pile, with resin-impregnated backing fabric; comply with AAMA 701.

PART 3 EXECUTION

3.01 EXAMINATION

A. Have existing finish carpentry examined by finish carpentry specialist defined in Paragraph "Quality Assurance" of this section, who shall identify damaged finish carpentry items.

3.02 PREPARATION

A. General requirements for removals specified in Section "Demolition" apply to work specified in this section.
B. Remove portions of existing finish carpentry as follows:
    1. Where removal is indicated.
    2. Where removal is necessary to make way for the Work under this Contract.
    3. Where existing finish carpentry is damaged beyond satisfactory repair. Where part of a member is damaged beyond repair, remove the entire member.
C. Cut and remove existing finish carpentry carefully. Do not damage work to remain. When removing and reinstalling existing finish carpentry, protect against damage. Store safely until reinstalled. Do not reinstall damaged units.
D. Discard removed existing finish carpentry which is not to be reused.

3.03 INSTALLATION—GENERAL REQUIREMENTS

A. General requirements for alterations specified in Section "Minor Alterations Work" apply to the work specified in this section.
B. Rework if necessary and reinstall or relocate existing finish carpentry where indicated to be reinstalled or relocated, and where use of existing finish carpentry is permitted to extend existing work or to close openings in existing work.
C. Provide new finish carpentry to extend existing work and to close openings in existing work where no similar materials have been removed or where existing materials are insufficient in quantity or are damaged or otherwise unacceptable for reuse.

D. Patch existing finish carpentry items where indicated, where damaged at the start of the Work under this Contract, and where damaged during the Work under this Contract.

E. Rework and relocate finish carpentry, and patch, extend, and close openings in existing finish carpentry using materials and installation methods that match the existing work, except do not execute finish carpentry work using lower quality materials or methods than those indicated.

F. Make junctures between new and existing work and between relocated work and work left in place inconspicuous.

3.04 DOOR FRAMES, CASINGS, TRIM

A. Rework existing and provide new wood door frames, casings, and trim where indicated, including trim applied to metal frames and to doors. Also provide new, or rework existing, door casings and trim where existing are missing or are split, delaminated, or otherwise damaged beyond repair.

B. Fasten wood trim to metal using screws; to wood and mineral core doors using glue and screws. Apply trim to wood doors at shop or in field at Contractor's option.

C. Requirements specified for standing and running trim apply to door casings and trim.

D. Profiles shall be as indicated. Profiles not indicated shall match those existing.

3.05 WINDOWS

A. Repair existing windows as indicated. Where windows are to be repaired or removed and new windows installed, ensure that leaded-glass and other glass has been removed from the sash and properly stored or sent to shop for repair as specified in Section "Glazing." Cooperate with glazer in removal of leaded glass for protection or repair.

B. Remove existing window sash, frames, mullions, muntins, casings, tracery, sills, stools, aprons, and trim, or portions thereof, where:
   1. Indicated.
   2. Identified as damaged beyond repair during examination by finish carpentry specialist and approved.
   3. Damaged beyond repair during the Work under this Contract.

C. Repair portions of window sash, frames, mullions, casings, sills, stools, aprons, tracery, and trim using one of the following methods, as appropriate:
   1. Dry the wood, treat decayed areas with fungicide, waterproof the wood using two or three

applications of boiled linseed oil, fill cracks and holes with putty, and paint the surface in accordance with Section "Painting."

2. Build up members showing surface wear using wood putties or mixtures of sawdust and resorcinol glue, or whiting and varnish. Build up in successive layers, sand, prime, and paint.

3. Strengthen and stabilize the wood using semirigid epoxies which saturate the decayed wood and then harden. Then fill with semirigid epoxy patching compound, sand, and paint. Use epoxy compounds to build up missing or decayed parts of members; duplicate existing profiles.

4. Remove and discard damaged portion and cut and fit in a matching portion. Where window parts are damaged beyond reasonable repair, Contractor may elect to remove the entire part (such as an operating sash or an entire frame) and provide a new matching part. Where portions are removed and new portions provided, the new portion shall be the entire portion (entire bottom sash rail, for example). Do not splice members. Where entire members have been removed and new members provided, provide corner reinforcement where new and existing, or two new, members join.

D. Repair, or remove and provide new parts for, existing window operator parts such as counterbalances and sash-weight chains (or cords). New parts may match existing, except substitute chains for cords, or use modern equivalents, such as properly rated and sized, and approved, spring-balance operators.

E. Remove existing and provide new weather stripping to each window within the Contract limit line. Weather-strip each side of each operator, including meeting rails.

F. Remove existing window hardware which is deteriorated or damaged. Where existing hardware has been removed or is missing, provide new hardware, including, casement operators, tracks, locking handles, keepers, balances, sweep latches, bar hinges, push bars, pulleys, finger pulls, reinforcement, fasteners, and other hardware and devices required for proper window operation. Match appearance of existing hardware where practicable.

G. Fix operating panels in First Floor tracery but provide, or retain, acceptable existing hardware.

H. Adjust hardware and windows for easy operation.

I. At shower rooms and at private baths, install head and sill blocks, which prevent fully closing those sash and provide approximately 1/4 inch openings to allow air circulation and avoid formation of condensation.

3.06 PANELING

    A. Repair, or remove and provide new paneling for existing paneling that is damaged and identified as needing repair under this Contract or which is damaged during the Work under this Contract.

    B. Anchor new and reinstalled paneling to supporting substrate exactly as existing paneling was anchored.

    C. Make repaired, reinstalled, and new paneling match existing.

3.07 ADJUSTMENT, CLEANING, FINISHING, AND PROTECTION

    A. Repair damaged and defective finish carpentry to eliminate defects functionally and visually; where not possible to repair, remove finish carpentry and provide new, acceptable work. Adjust joinery for uniform appearance.

    B. Clean, lubricate, and adjust hardware.

    C. Clean finish carpentry on exposed and semiexposed surfaces. Touch up finishes to restore damaged or soiled areas.

    D. Finish finish carpentry work to match existing, but quality of finish shall not be less than that specified. See Section "Painting."

    E. Refinish existing surfaces in the same space with new patches, extensions, and relocated finish carpentry as specified in Section "Painting."

Small Projects: The requirements specified in the example above may well apply to a small project but might be reduced somewhat if the architect decides to rely on other contract requirements to control quality. It is always possible to reduce words at the expense of control. The judgment is subjective. For example, if there were only two or three damaged windows, the architect might simply require that the contractor repair the sash without spelling out methods.

Division 7   Thermal and Moisture Protection

Section 07510   *Built-Up Bituminous Membrane Roofing*

Large Projects: The following example shows a method for specifying existing built-up roofing repair. The methods and products used were correct for the example project. They are not appropriate for any other project. The principles, however, apply to all projects.

PART 1 GENERAL

1.01 SUMMARY

    A. Section Includes:
       1. New built-up bituminous roofing (BUR) where shown.
       2. Inspecting existing roofing to identify damage.
       3. Repairing damaged BUR, including insulation and flashings, wherever damage is discovered.
       4. Flood testing repaired roofing.
       5. Extending roof walkway at Emergency Exit Walk-Way.

1.02   QUALITY ASSURANCE

    A. BUR Specialist: Have BUR work done by a single firm with at least 5 years' successful experience in comparable work, and which is approved by Owner and roofing materials manufacturer. Use only experienced personnel skilled in operations needed, working under competent supervision. BUR specialist shall perform specified examinations and submit detailed recommendations concerning methods and materials to be used in making repairs to Architect through Contractor. Do no BUR or associated Work at the site until Architect has approved methods and materials submitted.

    B. Before starting insulation, roofing, walkways, or flashing Work, test proposed materials for compatibility with existing materials by installing each in a small area in locations representative of the damage discovered. Do not proceed until Architect approves tests.

1.03   PROJECT CONDITIONS

    A. Protect existing finishes. Do not hoist bituminous materials against building faces without adequate approved protection from grade to parapet. Protect vegetation and paving from damage due to roofing and flashing work. Completely remove bituminous materials from surfaces other than built-up roofing and bituminous flashings.

    B. Do not use incompatible materials or materials that are not compatible with existing materials.

    C. Do not uncover existing insulation until ready to do repair Work and install new insulation and covering Work.

    D. Avoid unnecessary traffic over roof areas. Use roof areas to perform Work only where unavoidable. When roof areas must be used, protect roof and flashing from damage; use temporary plywood sheets where traffic is mandatory; lay continuously at every traffic pattern and Work area.

    E. Should field conditions differ significantly from those indicated, notify Architect by telephone and in writing and do not proceed without instructions.

1.04   WARRANTY

    A. Warrant against leaks:
        1. The entire roofing and related insulation and flashing over the South Apartment Wing.
        2. Roofing, insulation, and flashing in other locations which were repaired, or removed and replaced, or otherwise worked on under this Contract.

PART 2   PRODUCTS

2.01 BITUMINOUS MATERIALS, FELTS, AND INSULATION

A. Existing roofing is a built-up bituminous system with aggregate surfacing, but exact composition of materials and system is not known. Materials listed below are intended to indicate quality of materials to be used in repairs. Materials used shall be compatible with existing, and shall be products of a single manufacturer or be furnished by the manufacturer of the roofing felts used in making repairs. If materials required are not listed below, select appropriate materials and submit data specified in Paragraph "Submittals" for additional materials required.

B. Roofing Materials: After each product name in the listing, insert "or approved equal." Repair materials are not limited to those manufactured by the listed manufacturer or even to the materials indicated. Except where otherwise indicated, weights and thicknesses shall match existing unless otherwise recommended by manufacturer for the specific use in each case and approved.
(*Here list all applicable materials.*)

C. Insulation Materials: Material, thickness, and k-value shall match existing insulation.
   1. Urethane board:
      a. Fed. Spec. HH-I-530, Type I, Grade 2.
      b. Composite type: Same, except with integrally bonded course of material to match existing.
   2. Preformed edge strips and cants: Rigid insulation units matching roof insulation, or asphalt impregnated fiber insulation units, molded to form cant strips and tapered edges to match existing or as recommended by BUR specialist and approved.

2.02 RELATED MATERIALS AND ACCESSORIES

A. Aggregate Surfacing: Reinstall removed aggregate where practicable. Where existing aggregate cannot be properly cleaned, or is insufficient in quantity, provide new aggregate surfacing. New surfacing shall be ASTM D1863-80 roofing gravel, as approved by roofing manufacturer and matching existing in type, size, and color.

B. Roof Walkway Protection Boards: Mineral-surfaced bituminous composition boards, approximately 1/4 inch thick, manufactured specifically for the purpose; match existing.

PART 3   EXECUTION

3.01   EXAMINATION

A. Have BUR on South Apartment Wing examined by BUR specialist specified in this section together with flashing specialist specified in Section "Flashing and Sheet Metal," to identify deteriorated roofing, damaged or water-logged insulation, lack of roofing bond to flashings, damaged flashing flange stripping, and damaged flashing.

3.02   PREPARATION AND REMOVALS

A. Coordinate roofing repairs with flashings and other sheet metal repair, plumbing and electrical penetrations, roof-mounted mechanical equipment, roof walkway extension, roof accessories, and other work associated, or in contact, with BUR. Inspect surfaces to receive roofing or bituminous flashings. Correct unsatisfactory conditions.

B. In each location, do not begin later Work until underlying Work and roof penetrations are approved. After rebuilding Work below roofing and substrates for base flashing, inspect surfaces and correct unsatisfactory conditions.

C. Do not remove materials to the extent that the building is subject to water intrusion without providing approved protection. Do not remove more area of existing surfaces than can be repaired in the same working day. Aggregate surfacing may be delayed, however, provided that a glaze coat of proper bitumen is applied over felts.

D. Prepare existing surfaces in accordance with approved recommendations.

1. Remove aggregate surfacing to make needed repairs, to not less than 2-1/2 feet beyond area to be repaired. Use a power scraper or other approved method. Leave roof surface smooth and free from foreign matter. Where practicable, store for future reinstallation.

2. Remove dirt and debris from area to be repaired.

3. Clean existing aggregate free of silt. If water is used, screen roof drains to prevent clogging. Permit roof to dry thoroughly before continuing.

4. Remove existing roofing indicated to be removed to the minimum extent necessary to perform the required Work. Remove existing plies in stepped layers to permit new roofing to lap existing by the specified amounts. Discard removed roofing. Do not reuse.

5. Remove insulation, cants, tapered edge strips, and nailers where recommended by BUR specialist and approved. Remove completely in full pieces.

Also remove adhesives and fasteners. Fill fastener holes. Discard removed insulation, cants, tapered edge strips, nailers, and fasteners. Do not reuse.

6. Remove existing walkway protection board only to extent necessary to perform the Work. Discard; do not reuse.

7. Remove existing base flashings and roofing felts along edges of metal flashings where felts have crawled or loosened or are damaged. Where existing bituminous materials are removed, but substrates are not removed, also remove all traces of adhesives and cements. Discard removed bituminous materials; do not reuse.

8. Remove damaged pitch pans. Where pans are intact but filler has deteriorated, remove filler only; do not damage pitch pan.

3.03 GENERAL INSTALLATION REQUIREMENTS

A. Repair BUR and associated insulation and flashings on the South Apartment Wing roof wherever damage is discovered.

B. General repair or reroofing of existing BUR, insulation, or bituminous base flashings is not required. However, where existing BUR, insulation, or flashings, or whatever type encountered, and wherever located, are damaged during the Work, and where the Work requires removing portions of existing insulation, roofing, or flashings, or new penetrations through existing insulation, roofing, or flashings, damaged or removed portions and penetrations shall be satisfactorily repaired, flashed, and otherwise made watertight and at least equal to condition when Work began. If damage cannot be satisfactorily repaired, remove damaged portion and provide new materials as appropriate. Do such Work and repairs at no additional cost. Materials, methods, and completed Work are subject to approval.

C. Protect edges, incomplete flashings, and cut existing roofing against water entry at all times. Remove cut-offs and temporary protection before resuming work.

D. Where practicable, unless otherwise recommended by BUR specialist or materials manufacturers, and approved, use materials, systems, quantities, and methods that exactly match existing. Do not, however, make repairs or new installations of lesser quality than those indicated or recommended and approved. Materials used shall be compatible with each other and with existing materials.

E. Make all repairs watertight.

3.04   INSULATION

  A. Provide new insulation, cants, tapered edge strips,
     and nailers where existing are removed and in other
     locations where indicated.
  B. Fit new insulation units snugly to each other, to
     existing units, and to vertical surfaces. Provide a
     smooth surface for roofing installation.

3.05   SPOT PATCH REPAIR OF BUR

  A. Repair disintegrated, alligatored, or weather-
     damaged felts, holes, tears, and similar defects
     using coats of bitumen, roof resaturant, and layers
     of felt as recommended by repair materials
     manufacturer and BUR specialist, and approved.
     Remove existing felt and provide new felt and
     bitumen, or leave existing felts in place and cover
     with new felts and bitumen, as recommended and
     approved.
  B. To repair splits, loosened felt edges, buckles, and
     open laps, open, dry, and embed edges in bitumen.
     Cover with bitumen and embed a ply of heavy-duty
     glass fiber mesh. Apply additional layers of
     covering felts and bitumen if recommended by repair
     materials manufacturer and approved.
  C. To repair blisters, make two cuts at right angles to
     each other, open, and turn back edges, expel
     moisture and foreign matter; allow to dry before
     repairing. Bed each layer of cut and loosened felt
     in hot bitumen and, using a roller, press turned-
     back edges into place. Expel all air. Cover with
     layers of felts and bitumen as specified above for
     splits, where recommended by manufacturer of repair
     materials and approved.
  D. Other patching methods may be used if submitted in
     accordance with the Contract documents and approved.

3.06   PLY FELT APPLICATION

  A. Provide new roofing felts where existing roofing has
     been removed and in every other location where
     indicated.
  B. Where existing roofing has been removed, apply the
     same number of plies as in the existing roofing,
     plus one ply. Where existing roofing has not been
     removed, number of new plies shall be as recommended
     by roofing materials manufacturer and BUR
     specialist, and approved.
  C. Install plies shingle fashion and uniformly cement
     with accepted bitumen to roof insulation, cant
     strips, and each other without voids.
  D. Extend first ply at least 6 inches onto surface of
     existing roof membrane left in place and each
     succeeding ply at least 6 inches beyond preceding ply,
     except extend top ply 12 inches beyond previous ply.

E. Cut off roofing felts neatly along top edge of cants.

3.07 BITUMINOUS BASE FLASHING APPLICATION

A. Provide new bituminous base flashings wherever existing have been removed, where new roof accessories are installed, and in other locations where indicated.

B. Unless otherwise recommended by roofing products manufacturer and BUR specialist, and approved, new bituminous base flashings shall match existing, but be not less than the following:
   1. Flashings shall consist of two layers of felts.
   2. First ply: Roofing felt matching the existing.
   3. Top ply: Reinforced asbestos base flashing.
   4. Extend each ply to the level of the top of the cap flashing and mechanically fasten in place.
   5. Extend bottom ply 12 inches out onto the roofing.
   6. Extend top ply out onto roofing to overlap first ply by 2 inches.
   7. Bed each ply in a trowel coat of roofing cement. Coat top coat with minimum 1/16 inch thick roofing cement.

3.08 METAL FLASHINGS

A. Set new or reinstalled metal flashings flanges on top of roofing plies in a bed of approved roofing cement and securely anchor to roof deck.

B. Unless otherwise recommended by roofing materials manufacturer and BUR specialist, and approved, strip-in metal flashings to match existing, but not less than:
   1. Use two layers of felts.
   2. First ply: Roofing felt matching the existing.
   3. Top ply: Reinforced asbestos base flashing.
   4. Extend first ply onto roofing 6 inches beyond metal flange.
   5. Extend top ply out onto roofing to overlap first ply by 2 inches.
   6. Bed each ply in a trowel coat of roofing cement. Coat top coat with 1/16-inch-thick roofing cement.

3.09 ROOF DRAINS

A. Before beginning work on or associated with BUR, remove existing roof drains in the area of the Work.

B. Install new roof drains specified in Division "Mechanical." Set at proper level in roofing cement compatible with existing and new roofing materials. Anchor securely to preservative-treated wood nailers fastened to the deck.

C. Fill clamping ring with roofing cement. Extend lead flashing specified in Section "Flashing and Sheet Metal" into clamping ring and at least 12 inches out

onto roofing. Clamp securely into ring and strip-in
as specified above for metal flashing flanges.
Provide new weeps if necessary.

3.10 PITCH PANS

A. Where pitch pans are removed, install new or
reinstall existing pitch pans in a bed of roofing
cement, except, do not reinstall damaged pitch pans.
B. Where filling material has been removed, fill pan
with hot bitumen of the type being used over a one
inch layer of approved roofing cement.
C. Where stripping-in has been removed, strip in
flanges as specified above for stripping-in new
flashing flanges.

3.11 AGGREGATE SURFACING

A. Provide surfacing in every location where surfacing
has been removed.
B. After felts are in place, apply flood coat of
bitumen at approved rate.
C. While bitumen is hot, spread and firmly embed dry
aggregate in quantity recommended by roofing
materials manufacturer and approved. Quantity of
aggregate shall not exceed design load of roof.

3.12 ROOF WALKWAY

A. Extend existing roof walkway at Emergency Exit Walk-
Way.
B. Beneath new roof walkway protection board, provide
one additional layer of roofing felt in hot bitumen
mopping, then apply flood coat and aggregate
surfacing as specified.
C. Set walkway protection board units over aggregate in
an additional pour coat of bitumen.

3.13 FLOOD TESTING

A. Stop drains and flood test repaired roofing 48 hrs.
with 2 inches of water.
B. Dry roof, repair leaks, if any, and retest until no
leaks are found.

Small Projects: Unfortunately, specifying repair of a small portion of a roof
requires just as many words as specifying the repair of a large surface. The
number of words is dictated by the number of conditions, not the quantity or
dollar value of the work involved. Reducing the above example will reduce control. It does not make sense to leave roof repair methods to a roofing subcontractor's discretion, unless the architect knows and trusts the roofing subcontractor
based on personal experience. Roof leaks are the single most common problem
owner's encounter with their buildings, even when the buildings are single-family
residences.

Section 07600 *Flashing and Sheet Metal*

Large Projects: Just as is true for roofing specifications, the number of words required to specify flashing is dependent on the number of conditions involved. The following example contains a few conditions. The principles expressed apply to many others.

PART 1 GENERAL

1.01 SUMMARY

    A. Section Includes:
      1. New flashing and sheet metal work where indicated.
      2. Examining existing flashing and sheet metal work.
      3. Repairing damaged existing flashing and sheet metal work.
    B. Related Sections:
      1. Removing Existing and Providing New Treated Wood Blocking and Nailers: See Section "Rough Carpentry."
      2. Requirements for Examining and Removing Existing, and Providing New BUR; Bituminous Base Flashings; Stripping-In of Metal Roof Flashings; Roof Insulation: See Section "Built-Up Bituminous Membrane Roofing."
      3. Requirements for Examining and Removing Existing, and Providing New Slate Shingles: See Section "Slate Shingles."
      4. General Removal Requirements: See Section "Demolition."
      5. General Requirements for Reinstallations: See Section "Minor Alteration Work."

1.02 SUBMITTALS

    A. Shop Drawings: Submit for approval for base, cap, counter, apron, ridge, valley, and vent flashing and associated receivers; pitch pans; gutters; and other flashing and sheet metal conditions where flashing or adjacent roofing Work is to be done. Include flashing details where roofing is to be repaired or new roofing is to be installed even if no related flashing work is to be done. For both existing work to be removed and reinstalled and fabricated new Work, show layout, joining, profiles, metal gages, support, anchorages, relationship to adjoining work, and other pertinent details. Produce plans and layouts at 1/4 inch scale, details at 3 inch scale.

1.03 QUALITY ASSURANCE

    A. Flashing Specialist: Have flashing Work done by a single firm with not less than 5 years of successful experience in comparable work and which is approved by Owner. Use only experienced personnel skilled in the operations necessary, and working under competent supervision. Have flashing specialist make

specified examinations and submit detailed
recommendations concerning methods and materials
proposed for making repairs to Architect through
Contractor. Do no flashing or associated Work at the
site until Architect approves proposed methods and
materials.

1.04 PROJECT CONDITIONS

A. Coordinate sheet metal Work with new and existing
adjoining work for proper installation sequencing.
Ensure best possible weather resistance and
durability of the Work and protection of materials
and finishes. Do not install sheet metal materials
before completing supporting Work.

B. Notify Architect by telephone and in writing of
field conditions that differ significantly from
those indicated. Do not proceed without instructions.

PART 3 EXECUTION

3.01 EXAMINATION

A. Flashing Associated with Built-Up Roofing (BUR):
Have examined by flashing specialist specified in
this section. At South Apartment Wing, have flashing
specialist examine flashing in the company of built-
up roofing (BUR) specialist specified in Section
"Built-Up Bituminous Roofing" to identify lack of
roofing bond to flashings, damaged flashing flange
stripping, and damaged flashing. In every other
location within the Contract limit line, and beyond
where indicated, have flashing specialist examine
existing flashings and identify deteriorated,
damaged, or missing flashings and sealants. When
damage to adjacent roofing is also present, flashing
specialist shall notify Contractor who shall notify
Architect immediately.

B. Flashing Associated with Slate Roofing within
Contract Limit Line: Have examined by flashing
specialist specified in this Section together with
slate roofing specialist specified in Section "Slate
Roofing" to identify damaged or failed flashing.

3.02 PREPARATION AND REMOVALS

A. Remove existing cap flashings where indicated, where
damaged, and where necessary to carry out the Work.
Remove cap flashing receivers only when absolutely
necessary.

B. Remove other existing flashings, and associated
accessories, where found damaged; damaged during the
Work under this Contract; indicated to be removed;
and where removal is necessary to make way for the
Work under this Contract. Carefully remove flashings
and accessories to prevent undue damage. Take
special care to not damage flashings or accessories

left in place and to be reused. Where flashings and accessories are to be reinstalled, protect and store them to prevent damage.

C. Remove existing flashing receiver sealants and other sealants in flashings where sealants are deteriorated or damaged and where existing flashing is removed. Where sealants have been removed or are missing, provide new sealants in accordance with Section "Joint Sealing."

D. Salvage for reuse only those flashings and accessories indicated to be reused or reinstalled. Do not rework removed flashings or accessories to suit new conditions. Discard existing flashings and accessories which are damaged or not in the new configuration shown and provide new flashings and accessories.

E. Completely remove existing built-in gutters and discard.

3.03 SHEET FLASHINGS AND ASSEMBLIES—GENERAL INSTALLATION REQUIREMENTS

A. General repair of flashings or reflashing is not required. However, where existing flashings of whatever type encountered and wherever located are damaged during performance of Work under this Contract, and where Work under this Contract requires removing portions of existing flashings or new penetrations through existing flashings, such damaged or removed portions and penetrations shall be satisfactorily repaired and made watertight and at least equal to the condition existing when Work under this Contract began. Remove damaged portions which cannot be satisfactorily repaired and provide new materials. Do such work and repairs at no additional cost. Materials, methods, and completed Work are subject to approval.

B. Existing flashings are believed to be copper. Flashing in contact with existing flashings and flashings used where existing flashings have been removed shall match existing in material and gage but shall have a lead coating.

C. Work related to existing flashings shall be in accordance with applicable requirements specified in this section.

D. When the state of the Work permits, reinstall acceptable removed flashings and accessories in same location from where removed. Also install new units. Reinstall existing flashing and accessories only when in like-new condition. Where flashings or accessories become damaged during the Work under this Contract, or during storage, discard such damaged units and provide new flashings and accessories exactly matching the original in metal type, gage, and configuration.

E. Repair flashings associated with built-up roofing wherever damaged. After flood test specified in Section "Built-Up Bituminous Membrane Roofing," repair discovered leaks.

F. Repair flashings associated with slate roofing wherever damaged.

G. Patch, repair, and extend existing flashings as indicated.

H. Cut, fit, drill, and do other operations to accommodate work of other trades, and make existing metal work accommodate new Work. Where necessary to cut or drill prefabricated assemblies, restore finish as recommended by manufacturer.

I. Use lead-coated copper of weight scheduled for patching and repairing existing flashings and for new gutters and flashings where other materials are not specified.

3.04   FLASHING REGLETS AND RAGGLES (CUT SLOTS)

A. General:
   1. Furnish reglets for installation in concrete, masonry, and stone to receive gutters, flashing, and other sheet metal. Reuse existing reglets where practicable.
   2. Locate reglets and raggles where shown, but in vertical locations, not less than 8 inches above roofing surface. Coordinate with other trades to ensure proper locations and installations.

B. Where raggles (cut slots) are indicated, cut raggle 1-1/2 inches deep into previously installed material.

3.05   COUNTER (CAP) FLASHING

A. Where new and reinstalled flashings are to be inserted into a receiver, insert and snap-lock upper edge of cap flashing into receiver. Lap end joints not less than 3 inches. Provide shop-fabricated soldered corners with joints at least 12 inches from angle. Fill receiver with elastomeric sealant. Bend receiver neatly and snugly to face of cap flashing. Use stepped caps at sloping roofs.

3.06   METAL BASE, APRON, AND CRICKET FLASHINGS

A. Use metal base flashings where existing base flashings are metal, where metal base flashings are indicated, and where conditions do not permit use of bituminous base flashings. Use new flashings where existing have been discarded or are missing and where new flashings are indicated.

B. At sloping roofs, provide base flashing extended up wall to same level as existing flashings, unless otherwise shown or approved. Form and install to match existing flashing, unless otherwise approved. Securely anchor in place.

C. At sloped roofing, where existing have been removed, provide apron flashing on down—slope side of vertical surface penetrations. Extend onto roofing not less than 4 inches.

D. Provide new or reinstall removed existing undamaged saddle flashing (crickets) at chimneys. Solder all joints. Turn up and out onto roof to match existing, but not less than 4 inches. Securely fasten in place.

3.07 PITCH PANS

A. Provide new pitch pans where indicated and where existing pitch pans have been removed and discarded. Reinstall existing pitch pans where removed and not discarded.

3.08 VENT PIPE FLASHING

A. Flash new vents through roofing. Reflash existing vents where flashing has been removed.

B. At abandoned vent pipes, plug opening and provide lead cap to cover top and 1 inch of pipe.

3.09 ROOF DRAIN FLASHING FLANGES

A. Provide flashing flanges for new roof drains and where existing flashings have been removed. Drains are specified in Division 15. Work related to Terrace and other nonroof drains is specified in Section "Minor Alteration Work."

3.10 VALLEY FLASHING AND RIDGE FLASHING

A. Provide valley and ridge flashing where existing flashings have been removed.

B. Fabricate and install to match existing installation, unless otherwise approved, except that fabrication and installation shall be at least equal to that recommended by the referenced standards.

3.11 GUTTERS

A. Provide new gutters where existing have been removed.

B. Provide new leader connections to gutter using 2 inch wide flanged 32—oz. copper rings brazed to copper pipe drain. Extend new pipe at least 6 inches into existing leader.

Small Projects: An architect might reduce the length of a specifications section covering flashing and sheet metal for a small project by relying on standards and not describing in the section the methods required. The requirements in the above example, however, apply to small projects as well as large ones. It takes the same number of words to describe the requirements for removing and reinstalling 4 feet of gravel stop as it does to specify removing and reinstalling 400 feet.

Division 8   Doors and Windows

Section 08110   *Hollow Metal Doors and Frames*

Large Projects: The following example shows a method for specifying work related to some existing hollow metal door and frame conditions.

PART 1   GENERAL

1.01   SUMMARY

    A. Section Includes:
       1. New hollow metal doors; door, sidelight, and borrowed light frames; and other hollow metal as indicated.
       2. Removing indicated existing doors and frames; discarding or repairing and reinstalling removed doors and frames as indicated.
    B. Related Sections:
       1. General Removal Requirements: See Section "Demolition."
       2. General Requirements for Alterations: See Section "Minor Alteration Work."

1.02   DELIVERY, STORAGE, AND HANDLING:

    A. Store new and removed existing doors and frames at building site under cover. Place units on wood sills at least 4 inches high, or otherwise store on floors in manner that will prevent rust and damage. Avoid use of unvented plastic or canvas shelters which could create humidity chamber. If cardboard wrapper on door becomes wet, remove carton immediately. Provide 1/4 inch spaces between stacked doors to promote air circulation.

PART 2   PRODUCTS

2.01   EXISTING DOORS AND FRAMES—GENERAL REQUIREMENTS

    A. During execution of the Work under this Contract, protect existing doors and frames that are not scheduled to be removed and discarded. Repair such doors or frames which become damaged during the period of this Contract to a condition at least equal to that existing before the damaging. Where repairs are not accepted, remove the damaged door or frame and provide a new acceptable door or frame. Dispose of removed doors and frames.

2.02   STEEL FRAMES

    A. Anchors:
       1. For frames set in previously placed concrete, masonry, or stone walls, provide bolts into expansion shields as indicated. Provide countersunk holes in frames for exposed bolted anchorage.

Figure 8-14. Doors beyond repair. (Photograph by Stewart Bros.)

PART 3   EXECUTION

3.01   REMOVAL AND PREPARATION

    A. Remove and discard existing doors and frames where indicated.
    B. Remove and repair existing doors and frames where indicated.
    C. Requirements specified in Section "Demolition" apply to door and frame removal.

3.02   INSTALLATION

    A. Requirements specified in Section "Minor Alterations Work" apply to existing door and frame reinstallation.
    B. Reinstall existing doors and frames removed under this Contract where indicated, but do not reinstall damaged doors or frames. Repair; or where satisfactory repairs are not possible, discard and provide new doors and frames.
    C. Paint existing hollow metal doors and frames to be left in place, or removed and reinstalled, as specified in Section "Painting."
    D. Placing Frames: Comply with provisions of SDI-105 "Recommended Erection Instructions for Steel Frames," unless otherwise indicated. Exercise care to prevent bending, twisting, or racking. Do not install damaged frames. Set frames plumb, align properly, and anchor securely.

1. Except for frames located at in-place concrete, masonry, or stone and at drywall installations, place frames before building enclosing walls and ceilings. Set frames accurately in position, plumbed, aligned, and braced securely until permanent anchors are set. After completing wall construction, remove temporary braces and spreaders, leaving surfaces smooth and undamaged.

2. At in-place concrete, stone, or masonry construction, set frames and secure to adjacent construction using not less than 3 bolts into expansion shields at each jamb. At existing openings with wood subbucks, remove the wood subbucks, and repair jamb using masonry as specified in Division 4 and allow for proper setting of mortar before securing frame to in-place construction.

Small Projects: Hollow metal door and frame specifications paragraphs for existing construction in small projects may be as abbreviated as the basic requirements specified for new work.

Section 08210   *Wood Doors*

Large Projects: The following example shows a method for specifying work related to some existing wood door conditions.

PART 1   GENERAL

1.01   SUMMARY

A. Section Includes:
1. New wood doors and related items as indicated.
2. Removing, repairing, and reinstalling existing wood doors as indicated.

B. Related Sections:
1. Removing Existing Wood Doors Not to Be Reused; General Requirements For Removals: See Section "Demolition."
2. General Requirements for Alterations and Reinstallations: See Section "Minor Alteration Work."

1.02   SUBMITTALS

A. Shop Drawings: Submit for approval. Indicate location and size of each new and existing door; elevation of each kind of door; details of construction; sizes; thicknesses; marks to be used to identify doors; location and extent of hardware blocking; fire ratings; factory priming materials and methods; methods to be used in repairing and refinishing existing doors; and other pertinent data. Use numbering and type marks used on Contract drawings.

1.03 QUALITY ASSURANCE

A. Have new doors installed and existing doors removed, repaired, and reinstalled by a specialty subcontractor who is regularly engaged in such work and by skilled workers under competent supervision.

1.04 DELIVERY, STORAGE, AND HANDLING

A. Protect new and existing wood doors during transit, storage, and handling to prevent damage, soiling, and deterioration. Comply with the "On-Site Care" recommendations of NWMA pamphlet "Care and Finishing of Wood Doors" and with manufacturer's instructions and as otherwise indicated. Package doors at factory in 10-mil polyethylene film or heavy cardboard cartons.

B. Store new and removed existing doors in fully covered, well-ventilated areas, and protect from extreme changes in temperature and humidity.

PART 2 PRODUCTS

2.01 GENERAL

A. Exposed Surfaces: Provide kind indicated. Provide same exposed surface material on both faces of each door, unless otherwise indicated.
   1. Stain Finish Doors:
      a. Veneer: Existing stain finish wood doors are believed to have premium grade oak face veneers. If other face veneers are encountered, notify Architect and await instructions. First Floor new door's face veneers shall match existing doors.
      b. Finish: Stain-finished in the field as specified in Section "Painting," to match existing door finish.

PART 3 EXECUTION

3.01 EXAMINATION

A. Examine previously installed door frames and verify that they are correct type and installed as required for proper hanging of doors; verify that existing door frames have been properly repaired and are ready to receive new or reinstalled doors. Do not install doors before correcting unsatisfactory conditions.

3.02 REMOVALS AND REPAIRS

A. Requirements specified in Section "Demolition" apply to door removal.

B. Removal of existing doors not to be reused is specified in Section "Demolition."

C. Protect existing wood doors that are not indicated to be removed and disposed of.

D. Repair, refinish, and install indicated new hardware on existing doors to remain. Remove doors as necessary to effect repairs, refinishing, and hardware installation.

E. Repair damage to existing doors using approved methods and materials. Remove portions of stile and rail doors which are damaged or deteriorated beyond satisfactory repair and provide new door portions, or, at Contractor's option, remove damaged doors and provide entire new doors matching those removed.

F. Discard doors that are damaged or deteriorated beyond satisfactory repair and provide new matching doors.

G. Where repairs or refinishing are not accepted, remove and dispose of the damaged door and provide a new completely finished and operating door of the same type and finish as that removed.

H. Replacement doors shall comply with requirements specified in this section for new doors.

I. Make repairs indistinguishable from unrepaired portions of doors.

J. Install new finish hardware as specified in Section "Finish Hardware."

3.03 INSTALLATION

A. Install wood doors in previously installed new or existing frames in accordance with NWMA recommendations, manufacturer's instructions, Contract drawings, and these specifications, so that required warranties will be effective and only after completion of other work that would raise moisture content of doors or damage door surfaces. Condition doors to average prevailing humidity in installation area before hanging. Do not hang doors in rooms where humidity is sufficiently high as to damage doors.

Small Projects: Requirements for projects where work related to existing wood doors is small need be only as detailed as the related paragraphs for new doors.

Division 9   Finishes

Section 09200   *Lath and Plaster*

Large Projects: The following example shows a method for specifying work related to some existing plaster conditions.

PART 1 GENERAL

1.01 SUMMARY

A. Section Includes: Patching and extension of existing plaster, including furring and lath.

B. Related Sections:
   1. Removing Existing Plaster Not to Be Patched: See Section "Demolition."

1.02 QUALITY ASSURANCE

A. Fire-Resistance Rating: When altering, patching, or extending fire-rated plaster, and where fire-rated plaster assemblies are shown or required by governing regulations, provide materials and installations identical with assemblies tested and listed by recognized authorities and in compliance with code requirements. Unless doing so violates the previous sentence, materials for altering, patching, or extending existing fire-rated plaster shall exactly match materials in existing assembly.

1.03 PROJECT CONDITIONS

A. Upon encountering conditions that differ substantially from those indicated, notify the Architect, and do not proceed without instructions.

PART 2   PRODUCTS

2.01 BONDING MATERIALS

A. Acid Etch Solution: Muriatic acid, mixed one part acid to 6 to 10 parts water.
B. Dash-Coat Material: 2 parts Portland cement with 3 parts fine sand mixed with water to a mushy paste.
C. Bonding Agent: ASTM C631; Larsen Products Corporation, "Plaster-Weld," or approved equal for gypsum plaster. ASTM C932; Larsen Products Corporation, "Weld-Creat," or approved equal for Portland cement plaster.
D. Bonding Additive: Acrylic based emulsion for bonding interior Portland cement plaster base coat to solid substrates. "Quick-Cure Ad-Liquid" (Finestone Corp.); "Acrylic Admix-101" (Larsen Products Corp.); "Acryl 60" (Standard Dry Wall Products); or approved equal.

2.02 GYPSUM PLASTER PROPORTIONS

A. Basecoat for Fireproofing: Mix proportions shall be in accordance with building code and not less than necessary to produce plaster to match the existing, except that proportions shall not be less than the following:
   1. Brown Coat: 2 cu. ft. perlite per 100 lbs. of gypsum neat plaster.
   2. Scratch Coat: 3 cu. ft. perlite per 100 lbs. of gypsum neat plaster.
   3. Mill-mix gypsum perlite plaster may be used if compatible with in-place materials, in

conformance with the above specified proportion requirements, and acceptable in accordance with building code.
B. Finish Coats: As specified above for scratch coat.

2.03 PORTLAND CEMENT PLASTER MIXING

A. Bonding Additive: Add to Portland cement plaster mix in amount and by method recommended by manufacturer.

PART 3 PRODUCTS

3.01 EXECUTION

A. General: Examine substrates and conditions under which plaster will be repaired. Do not proceed with plaster Work before completing Work to be concealed or made inaccessible by plaster and correcting unsatisfactory conditions.
B. Existing Ceiling Suspension Systems Left in Place: Inspect areas requiring patching. Examine hangers and attachments left in place when existing ceilings were removed. Verify adequacy and suitability of left-in-place hangers and hanger attachments for suspension system support. Remove those found to be unsuitable. Obtain Architect's approval of existing hangers and hanger attachments proposed for reuse. Remove those Architect rejects.

3.02 PREPARATION

A. Removing Existing Plaster:
1. Carefully remove:
a. Soft, deteriorated, weak, unbounded, effloresced, broken, loose, and otherwise damaged existing plaster in the area of the Work.
b. Plaster shown to be removed.
c. Plaster which must be removed to carry out the Work under this Contract.
d. Sufficient plaster, at damaged substrates, to permit repair of substrate.
2. Remove plaster back to masonry or lath and to solid adjacent plaster. Make edges straight, clean, sharp, and beveled inward.
B. Removing Existing Support Systems: Where necessary to do the Work, remove existing wall and ceiling furring and suspension systems. Also remove furring and suspension systems found to be damaged, rusted beyond repair, or otherwise unsuitable for reuse. Leave in place existing hangers and suspension systems that are sound, adequate, and suitable for reuse; or remove, clean, and store them for reuse. Reuse shall be subject to Architect's approval, but Contractor shall be solely responsible for reuse and for later failure resulting from reuse.

C. Existing Metal Lath: Where necessary, partially remove, but leave enough exposed to tie to new lath.

D. Plaster Accessories: Remove where damaged and, in addition, where necessary to carry out the Work.

E. Paint, Dirt, Oil, Grease, and Other Foreign Matter: Remove every trace from surfaces to receive new lath or plaster.

F. Cracks: Enlarge cracks 1/16 inch wide or wider. Cut back to solid substrate using carborundum-tipped saw blade. Cut perpendicular to surface and straight. Do not further enlarge cracks, except to remove soft, broken, or loose materials, or to repair backup materials. Where approved, widen cracks and install strip lath over substrate centered at location of cracking before making plaster repairs.

G. Direct Plastering: Except where metal lath is indicated, etch concrete and masonry surfaces for direct plastering. Wet surface, scrub with acid etch solution, and rinse thoroughly; repeat if necessary for adequate plaster bond.

H. Bonding Agents: Apply to every surface that will receive plaster. Surfaces to which bonding agent is to be applied shall be clean and free from substances that will affect bond. Follow bonding agent manufacturer's recommendations exactly, in every instance. Permit bonding agent to dry properly before applying plaster.

I. Cleaning and Dampening Substrates: Sweep masonry and lath clean immediately before applying plaster. Apply bonding agent. Dampen surfaces of existing Portland cement plaster, unless bonding agent manufacturer recommends otherwise.

3.03   INSTALLING METAL SUPPORT SYSTEMS

A. Ceiling Support Systems:
   1. For patching existing ceilings, use approved existing hangers and hanger attachments. Provide new hangers and attachments where existing have been removed, or are improperly placed or otherwise inappropriate, and where hangers do not exist. Do not reuse removed hangers or hanger attachments unless such reuse is approved. Attach new hangers to concrete or structural steel; not to pipes, conduits, ducts, or mechanical or electrical devices; do not use hangers so attached.
   2. Install new or reinstall approved existing furring and suspension systems where removed to do Work or make repairs.

B. Metal Furring: Provide metal wall furring where necessary to match existing conditions. Space furring members 16 inches o.c.

C. Metal Lathing:
1. Provide new metal lath where existing has been removed, and over areas to receive large plaster patches. Anchor securely. Lap over and tie to existing lath. Widen cracks and apply strip lath before patching.
2. Install metal lath to comply with referenced standards unless otherwise indicated. Lath for patching and extending existing work shall match existing installation.
D. Plastering Accessories:
1. Install new plaster accessories where existing accessories have been removed. Anchor securely to substrates. Match lines of existing accessories.

3.04 INSTALLING PLASTER

A. General:
1. Apply plaster over metal lath where existing plaster to be patched or extended is applied over metal lath.
2. Apply plaster directly to masonry or concrete where existing plaster is directly applied.
B. Terminations: Finish plaster flush with metal frames and other built-in metal items and accessories which act as a grounds, except where existing plaster is not so constructed. Where plaster does not terminate at casing beads, cut base coat free from metal frames before plaster sets and groove finish coat at the junctures with metal.
C. Thickness and Number of Coats: Apply as indicated, or as required by referenced standards. At patches and extensions, match thickness of existing plaster, and make finish of patch or extension flush with existing plaster, except that new plaster patches or extensions, including all coats, shall not be thinner than:
1. Skim Coat Plaster: 1/8 inch.
2. Gypsum Perlite Plaster: As required by code.
3. Portland Cement Plaster Over Metal Lath: 7/8 inch consisting of 3/8 inch first coat, 3/8 inch second coat, and 1/8 inch thick finish coat.
D. Build up repairs in layers.
E. Plaster Finish Textures: Repairs and extensions shall match existing finishes and be blended so that patches and extensions are indiscernible.
F. Skim Coat Plaster: Apply where necessary to match existing plaster. Use two-coat work.
G. Fireproofing: Apply gypsum perlite plaster to patch existing. Comply with code to achieve required ratings.

Small Projects: The basic requirements specified in the above example are necessary regardless of project size. For very small projects, an architect might omit product description and specify only ASTM references or trade names and rely more on the requirements contained in referenced documents to control quality.

Section 09250   *Gypsum Board Systems*

Large Projects: The following example contains paragraphs an architect might find helpful when dealing with existing gypsum board systems.

PART 1   GENERAL

1.01   SUMMARY

   A. Section Includes: Metal channel stud framing; metal wall, ceiling, soffit, and bulkhead furring; gypsum board; sound insulation; accessories; and related items as indicated. Section includes products required for patching existing gypsum board systems and for new gypsum board systems.

PART 3   EXECUTION

3.01   EXAMINATION

   A. Areas to Receive New Ceilings: Inspect and verify that existing ceilings to be removed have been removed.

   B. Existing Hangers and Attachments Left in Place: Examine areas where existing ceilings have been removed. Verify adequacy and suitability of left-in-place hangers and hanger attachments for new

Figure 8-15. A slight problem at the top. (Photograph by Stewart Bros., courtesy of Mid-City Financial Corp.)

suspension system support. Remove those found to be unsuitable. Obtain Architect's approval before using existing hangers and hanger attachments. Remove rejected hangers and attachments.

C. Concealed Work: Examine substrates and conditions under which new ceilings will be installed. Verify completion of Work above or within ceilings. Complete Work to be concealed or made inaccessible, and correct unsatisfactory conditions before proceeding with ceiling Work.

3.02   PREPARATION

A. Remove Existing Ceiling: Where new ceilings are indicated in existing spaces, remove existing ceilings. Refer to Section "Demolition" for general removal requirements.

3.03   FURRING ERECTION

A. Duct, Beam, Pipe, Conduit, and Other Furring: Where not shown enclosed with masonry or other materials, furr to conceal horizontal and vertical ducts, pipes, conduit, backs of electric panels, and other utilities and services extending below finish ceilings or occurring at walls, partitions, columns, or other locations within finished spaces, unless such utilities or services are specifically indicated to be left exposed. Electrical, mechanical, and telephone equipment rooms are not finished spaces for this requirement. This requirement also applies to existing concealed items that are permanently exposed by renovation work. Also provide furring in other locations where shown.

B. Ceiling Hangers and Hanger Attachments: For installing new ceilings in existing spaces, use approved existing hangers and hanger attachments. Provide additional hangers and attachments where existing have been removed or are improperly placed or otherwise inappropriate. Do not reuse removed hangers or hanger attachments unless reuse is approved. Attach new hangers to concrete or structural steel. Do not attach to permanent metal forms, pipes, conduit, ducts, or mechanical or electrical devices.

3.04   GYPSUM BOARD APPLICATION BY LAMINATION

A. General: Install gypsum board by lamination to existing concrete and unit masonry where indicated.

3.05   ALTERATIONS AND REPAIR WORK—ADDITIONAL REQUIREMENTS

A. Remove existing furring, suspension systems, and gypsum board where required for alterations and new mechanical or electrical Work.

B. Repair damaged existing gypsum board.

C. When repairing existing construction, use materials and methods to match those existing.
D. For extending existing work, use materials and methods specified in this section for new Work.
E. If materials, systems, or conditions differ from the assumed, immediately notify Architect and do not proceed without instructions.

Small Projects: The basic requirements specified in the above example remain necessary regardless of project size. For very small projects, an architect might rely more on the requirements contained in referenced documents to control quality.

Section 09300   *Tile*

Large Projects: The following example contains paragraphs an architect might find helpful when dealing with existing tile.

PART 1   GENERAL

1.01   SUMMARY

A. Project Includes: Ceramic and quarry tile and related items as indicated.

1.02   SUBMITTALS

A. Color Samples: Submit for selection. Promptly after tentative color selection, submit samples of each tile type, color, and texture. Mount samples on 12 inch square backing with joints grouted. Also submit samples of each type and color of base and trim shapes required. Include new tile and tile to match existing.

1.03   PROJECT CONDITIONS

A. Wall surfaces to receive tile applied using the dry-set method or the latex—Portland cement mortar method shall not vary more than 1/8 inch in 8 feet from required plane. If existing masonry walls vary more than 1/8 inch, use the conventional cement mortar method.
B. Wall surfaces to receive tile set using the conventional cement mortar method shall not vary more than 1/4 inch in 8 feet from required plane. If existing masonry walls vary more than the 1/4 inch permitted, or if mortar bed would exceed 3/4 inch thick, apply a scratch (leveling) coat to bring the surfaces within the specified tolerance.

PART 2   PRODUCTS

2.01   CERAMIC TILE

A. Tile for New Work:
(*Here specify new tile as if there were no existing tile.*)

B. Tile for Patching and Extending Existing Work: Use tile salvaged from locations where tile is indicated to be removed when salvaged tile exactly matches tile being patched or extended and is in at least as good condition as tile being patched or extended. Where matching existing tile is not available in sufficient quantity to complete patching and extensions, provide new material as follows:
   1. Tile: Type, size, color, shape, edge design, finish, features, and other characteristics to match existing tile being extended or patched.
   2. Special Pieces, Caps, Bases, Corners, Bullnoses, and Accessories: As needed; match existing special pieces in size, shape, color, design, and type.

2.02 QUARRY TILE

A. Tile for Patching and Extending Existing Work: Use salvaged tile that exactly matches tile being patched or extended, and is in at least as good condition as tile being patched or extended. Where matching existing tile is not available in sufficient quantity for patching and extensions, provide new material as follows:
   1. Tile: Type, size, color, shape, edge design, finish, features, and other characteristics to match existing tile being extended or patched.
   2. Trim: Special shapes to match existing.

PART 3 EXECUTION

3.01 PREPARATION

A. Removing Existing Materials:
   1. Remove damaged tile and setting beds, and provide new matching tile.
   2. Remove tile and setting beds indicated to be removed, and tile in areas where new tile is scheduled.
   3. Remove tile as necessary to make way for new Work. Where removal of a line or area of existing tile is necessary for new partitions, and similar conditions, remove sufficient tile to make clean continuous straight line between new and existing.
   4. Remove tile carefully. Do not mar or damage tile left in place.
   5. When removing tile, also completely remove setting beds down to solid structural concrete.
   6. Where new tile is scheduled, and the existing surface is resilient flooring, remove the existing material completely, including all traces of adhesives.

Figure 8-16. Cracked tile. (Photograph by Stewart Bros.)

    B. Preparing Existing Painted Plaster to Receive New
       Tile:
       1. Roughen surfaces that are glossy or painted or
          which have loose surface material by sanding or
          scarifying.
       2. Remove surface material that is not compatible
          with adhesive, or which would reduce or prevent
          bond.
       3. Use primer when recommended by adhesive
          manufacturer.
       4. Apply underlayment as needed; follow
          manufacturer's recommendations.
    C. Other Existing Surfaces to Receive New Tile: Prepare
       in accordance with the requirements specified or
       referenced in this section.
    D. Protection: In areas where alterations are to be
       made and existing tile floors, walls, or wainscots
       are to be extended or patched, protect existing tile
       to minimize damage. Cover floors with plywood or
       paper.

   3.02   TILE APPLICATION—GENERAL REQUIREMENTS

    A. Tile Colors, Sizes, and Types for Repair and
       Extension of Existing Tile Walls, Wainscots, and
       Floors: Match existing.

B. Reusing Removed Tile: Do not reinstall, except with Architect's specific approval. Approval will be given when existing removed tile can be salvaged in good condition and is an exact match for tile being patched or extended.

C. Installation Methods: Patch and extend existing tile using methods specified in this section that match existing conditions. Line up joints with existing. Install new tile to finish in the same plane with existing.

D. Conditions Not Specified: Notify Architect of conditions other than those specified and do not proceed without instructions. Comply with TCA recommended standards and methods for the determined condition.

E. In every case, leave existing tiled surfaces complete without voids or missing tile. Make finished surfaces uniform and in plane, with patches unnoticeable.

F. Joints: Align joints in new tile horizontally and vertically in a grid pattern unless otherwise indicated. In patching and extending existing tile, match existing joint patterns. Make joints uniform width.

3.03   CONVENTIONAL CEMENT MORTAR METHOD

A. Masonry and Concrete Walls: Use conventional cement mortar setting method for setting wall tile and tile bases on existing walls where wall surface variations exceed 1/8 inch, and in other locations where specifically indicated or required to match existing conditions.
   1. Where existing wall is unsound, coated, or a smooth material, such as ceramic tile, follow TCA Method W221 (ANSI A108.1).
   2. Where existing wall is sound, uncoated, not smooth, and is within the tolerances established by TCA, use TCA Method W211 (ANSI A108.1).

3.04   DRY-SET MORTAR METHOD

A. Walls: Use dry-set mortar method for setting ceramic wall tile and base over existing masonry that is clean, sound, dimensionally stable, reasonably smooth, and has no surface variations exceeding 1/8 inch in 8 feet.
   1. Follow TCA Method W213 (ANSI A108.5).
   2. Mortar bed shall be minimum 3/32 inch thick.
   3. Do not use dry-set mortar method over cracked or coated surfaces.

3.05   LATEX-PORTLAND CEMENT MORTAR METHOD

A. Walls and Ceramic Tile Bases:
   1. Use latex-Portland cement mortar method for

application of ceramic tile to water-resistant
gypsum board installed according to Gypsum
Association GA216, and to existing sound, smooth,
properly prepared plaster.
2. Follow TCA Method W243 (ANSI A108.5).
3. Follow TCA Method B413 at tubs and TCA Method
   B415 at showers, except use latex-Portland cement
   mortar according to ANSI A108.5.

3.06 GROUTING AND POINTING

A. Color: Uniform. Match existing in patching and
   extensions; grey for new floors, white for new walls
   and bases.

Small Projects: The basic requirements specified in the above example remain
necessary regardless of project size. For very small projects, an architect might
rely more on the requirements contained in referenced documents to control
quality. The architect might, for example, simply state which TCA requirement
applied without elaboration.

Section 09500 *Acoustical Treatment*

Large Projects: The following example contains paragraphs an architect might
find helpful when dealing with existing acoustical ceilings.

PART 1 GENERAL

1.01 SUMMARY

A. Section Contains:
   1. Removal, repair when damaged, and reinstallation
      of existing acoustical panels where indicated or
      necessary to perform the Work.
   2. New acoustical panels, suspension systems, and
      related items indicated.
   3. Panels, suspension systems, hangers, clips, tie
      wires, accessories, and related items necessary
      for proper acoustical ceiling installation or
      reinstallation.

1.02 SUBMITTALS

A. Ceiling Layout Plans: Submit of both new and
   existing acoustical ceilings to be reused.
   Coordinate with lighting fixtures and other ceiling-
   mounted equipment and devices.
B. Samples: Submit of acoustical materials and
   suspension system components. Include new materials
   and materials for patching and extending existing
   acoustical ceilings.
C. Submit manufacturer's recommendations for cleaning
   and refinishing acoustical units. Include
   precautions against materials and methods which may
   be detrimental to finishes or acoustical efficiency.

D. Furnish, and store where directed by Owner, extra material for Owner's use. Furnish not less than 3 percent of the total amount of each type of acoustical panel installed in the Project, including panels used to replace existing panels, but not less than 2 full cartons of each type.

1.03   PROJECT CONDITIONS

A. Differing Conditions: If materials, systems, or conditions are encountered which differ from the assumed, immediately notify Architect and do not proceed without instructions.

PART 2   PRODUCTS

2.01   EXISTING ACOUSTICAL MATERIALS

A. Existing Lay-In Panels: 24 inch by 24 inch mineral fiber units.
B. New Acoustical Panels for Patching and Extending Existing Acoustical Ceilings: Match existing units.

2.02   SUSPENSION SYSTEMS

A. Existing System: Suspension system for existing acoustical panels is a suspended grid complete with wall moldings, with members forming a 24 inch by 24 inch grid.
B. New Suspension Systems and their Components, for Patching Existing Acoustical Ceilings: Match existing.

PART 3   EXECUTION

3.01   EXAMINATION

A. Areas to Receive New Acoustical Ceilings: Inspect. Verify that existing ceilings have been removed.
B. Hangers and Hanger Attachments Left in Place when Existing Ceilings Were Removed: Examine. Verify adequacy and suitability for new suspension system support. Remove those found to be unsuitable. Obtain Architect's approval of existing hangers and hanger attachments proposed for use in new suspension systems. Remove those rejected.
C. Substrates and Conditions under which Acoustical Ceilings Will Be Installed: Verify completion of work above or within acoustical ceilings. Do not proceed with acoustical ceiling work before completing work to be concealed or made inaccessible and correcting unsatisfactory conditions.

3.02   PREPARATION

A. Removing Existing Acoustical Ceilings: Where existing acoustical ceilings are indicated to remain, remove acoustical units and suspension systems as necessary to perform the Work. In addition, in such areas, remove existing units that are loose or damaged beyond in-place repair. Repair removed units that can be repaired to the Architect's satisfaction. Also repair damaged units that have been left in place. Use methods recommended by unit manufacturer, and approved, including touch-up painting. Discard units that cannot be satisfactorily repaired and provide new matching units. Safely store removed units for reinstallation. Comply with requirements specified in Sections "Demolition" and "Minor Alterations Work."

3.03 INSTALLATION—GENERAL REQUIREMENTS

A. New Ceilings in Existing Spaces: Use existing hangers and hanger attachments where they have been approved. Provide new hangers and hanger attachments where existing hangers and attachments have been removed or are improperly placed or otherwise inappropriate, and where there are no existing hangers. Do not reuse removed hangers or attachments unless such reuse is approved. Attach new hangers to concrete structure. Do not attach hangers to pipes, conduits, ducts, or mechanical or electrical devices, or use existing hangers that are so attached.

3.04 EXISTING ACOUSTIC TILE CEILINGS

A. Reinstalling Removed Ceilings: Except when drawings specifically show substrates to be left exposed, and except in those locations where new ceilings are indicated, when progress of the Work permits, after completing work above existing acoustical ceilings, reinstall satisfactory salvaged ceiling systems and acoustical materials or install new matching ceiling systems and materials to make the ceilings complete. Such reinstallation or installation of new matching ceilings is required where indicated and also in the following locations:
1. Where all or portions of existing acoustical ceilings have been removed as part of the Work.
2. Where gaps or openings are present in existing acoustical ceilings at the time Work begins, in areas where Work under this Contract occurs.
3. Where gaps or openings occur in acoustical ceilings due to the Work.
4. Where existing acoustical ceilings to remain are damaged due to any activity related to this Contract.

B. Condition of Acceptable Materials: Limit reinstalled systems and materials to those that are in condition

equal to, or better than, adjacent undisturbed
ceilings.
C. New Materials in Existing Ceilings: Where patching
or extending existing acoustical ceilings is
required but acceptable materials or suspension
systems do not exist, are not acceptable, or are not
sufficient in quantity to complete the Work, provide
new acoustical materials and suspension systems. New
acoustical materials shall match existing adjacent
undisturbed (or originally installed and removed)
material in type, size, material, edge condition,
thickness, pattern, finish, and characteristics. The
new suspension system, or installation method, as
applicable, shall exactly match that existing in
similar installations or used in the original
removed ceilings or still existing in adjacent
ceilings. Repair and clean substrates as necessary
to obtain acceptable installation.
D. Limits on Reinstalling Salvaged Materials: Install
satisfactory salvaged acoustical ceiling systems and
materials subject to following limitations:
    1. Do not reinstall hangers or hanger wires, except
       where Architect agrees specifically in each case.
    2. Do not reinstall acoustical materials that were
       originally installed using staples, screws,
       nails, or similar fasteners.
    3. Do not reinstall removed materials where new
       materials are indicated.
    4. Do not reinstall removed acoustical ceiling
       systems or materials in locations other than
       those from where removed.
E. Contractor's Option: Where existing acoustical
ceilings are to be removed and patched, at
Contractor's option remove the entire acoustical
ceiling in that space and provide a new matching
acoustical ceiling.
F. Damaged Materials: Do not install damaged acoustical
materials or suspension systems. Architect will be
sole judge of satisfactory condition but will use as
a standard the condition of the adjacent acoustical
ceilings to be left in place. Where Architect
concurs, repair minor damage. Completed repairs are
subject to Architect's approvals.
G. Where existing acoustical finishes to be repaired or
extended are installed using adhesives, staples,
nails, screws, or other such fasteners, submit a
description of the methods proposed for making
repairs or extensions and manufacturer's literature
describing products proposed for use; include
installation instructions.
H. Leave ceilings complete with no voids or openings,
in same plane as existing ceiling and with joints
aligned with, and of same type as, those in existing
ceiling. Make patching and extensions as
inconspicuous as possible.

3.05 AT COMPLETION

  A. Clean soiled acoustical units installed or reinstalled under this Contract.

  B. Remove acoustical units installed or reinstalled under this Contract that are permanently stained, soiled, or otherwise damaged, and provide new acceptable units.

Small Projects: The basic requirements specified in the above example remain necessary regardless of project size. For very small projects, however, some of the conditions mentioned may not exist.

Section 09650 *Resilient Flooring*

Large Projects: The following example contains paragraphs that an architect might find helpful when dealing with existing resilient flooring.

PART 1 GENERAL

1.01 SUBMITTALS

  A. Samples:

    1. Submit selection samples of resilient materials showing range of available colors as soon as possible after award of Contract. Include new materials and materials proposed to match existing.

    2. After tentative selections, submit full size samples of each selected vinyl composition tile, 12 inch long samples of each base, and samples of vinyl sheet flooring showing a completed seam. Accepted samples shall become the standard for the work.

1.02 PROJECT CONDITIONS

  A. Sanding Existing Tile: Do not sand existing resilient flooring, backing, or lining felt.

PART 2 PRODUCTS

2.01 CLEANING AND POLISHING MATERIALS

  A. Cleaner for New Floors: Neutral chemical cleaner free from damaging alkalis and acids and free from oils and abrasives; UL—classified as to slip resistance.

  B. Cleaner for Existing Floors: A fast—acting cleaner formulated to clean tough dirt and grime, be pH—safe for resilient floors, and leave no dulling soap scum buildup.

  C. Stripping Solution: Formulated and recommended by the manufacturer for stripping discolored resilient flooring and resilient flooring with heavy wax buildup; as recommended by polishing material manufacturer, and approved.

PART 3 EXECUTION

3.01 PREPARATION

    A. Removing Existing Flooring: Where removal is indicated, and where optional, if Contractor prefers removal, completely remove existing resilient flooring. Removal of existing floor finishes other than resilient flooring is specified in Section "Demolition" or in other sections.

    B. In every case, when removing existing flooring, also remove all traces of adhesive, oil, wax, dust, paint, and other materials that would reduce bond or harm new flooring.

    C. Removal is required in the following locations:

        1. Where indicated to be removed, regardless of type of new flooring to be installed or whether existing substrates will be left exposed.

        2. Where floor finishes other than those specified in this section are to be installed in spaces having existing resilient flooring, unless existing flooring is indicated to remain in place or removal is optional.

    D. Removal Not Required: Except where removal is indicated as required, removal of existing resilient flooring is not required in areas to receive new resilient flooring or carpet. In such areas, at Contractor's option, either leave the existing resilient flooring in place and patch or repair it as specified to receive new floor finishes, providing overlayment as specified, or remove part or all existing resilient flooring. Perform removals so that new finishes are flush with adjacent like finishes and so that transitions to other finishes are acceptable.

    E. Floors to Remain as Resilient Flooring:

        1. Where existing flooring is not indicated to be removed, and where removal is optional and Contractor elects to not remove flooring completely, remove existing flooring only as necessary to perform the Work.

        2. Protect resilient flooring left in place to minimize damage; use plywood and paper as necessary.

        3. Where existing flooring is left in place, patch minor existing damage and minor damage caused by construction operations, and fill in openings in flooring, including those left by removal of existing flooring and where existing walls or partitions have been removed and those existing at the start of Work.

           a. Where such existing resilient flooring is to be left exposed, repair and patch using new resilient flooring that matches the existing in type, material, size, thickness, color, and pattern. Make patches as inconspicuous as possible.

          (1) If new material is available in type and color but not in size to match existing, make minor repairs using larger-size tile and field-cut to match existing tile.

          (2) If new material is not available to match existing, completely remove existing resilient flooring in the entire space and install new acceptable materials.

    b. Where existing resilient flooring is to be covered with carpet or another floor-covering material, patch level using new resilient flooring in material and thickness to match existing, or at Contractor's option and at no additional cost, completely remove such existing resilient flooring in lieu of patching.

  4. Where repairs are major, completely remove existing resilient flooring material in the entire space and provide new acceptable material.

F. Resilient Base:

  1. Remove existing wall base wherever it occurs in an area to be altered or remodeled under this Contract.

  2. In areas where existing base is not indicated to be removed but is damaged during the Work under this Contract, remove damaged sections of base and provide new matching base. Remove entire sections of damaged base. Do not cut base between existing joints.

  3. Where existing base is removed, unless substrate is also removed or furred for new finish, remove also all traces of adhesive, oil, wax, dust, paint, and other materials that would affect bond or harm new materials.

G. Preparation of Existing Substrates:

  1. Concrete substrates, including those exposed by removal of resilient materials:

    a. Remove all traces of paint, grease, oil, wax, mortar, oil adhesives, floor coverings, floor hardener, and other foreign substances that would reduce bond or harm new materials.

    b. Prepare uneven or rough surfaces using latex-modified cement underlayment recommended by resilient flooring manufacturer for the purpose. Leave in a condition equal to that specified for new concrete.

    c. Moisture-test existing concrete as specified for new concrete. Should moisture level exceed that recommended by manufacturers of resilient materials, underlayments, or adhesives, notify Architect and do not proceed without instructions.

        d. After underlayment has dried, properly apply
           concrete primer if recommended by resilient
           materials manufacturer.
     2. Resilient Flooring:
        a. Patch and repair as specified to the extent
           necessary to ensure a good, sound, level
           substrate for underlayment or installation of
           new finish or to provide an acceptable finish,
           as applicable.
        b. Strip existing floors to remain, including
           those to be left exposed and those to be
           covered by other materials, in areas where
           Work under this Contract occurs. Remove old
           polish buildup and existing sealers. Use
           stripping solution in accordance with
           manufacturer's recommendations. Do not damage
           flooring. Remove flooring damaged by stripping
           and provide new matching flooring, except that
           specified options still apply.
  H. Top Plane of Flooring: Adjoining surfaces to receive
     resilient materials shall be in the same plane.
     Adjacent surfaces to receive different finish floor
     materials shall be in proper planes to permit
     acceptable transitions. Use materials and methods
     specified or other acceptable materials and methods
     to produce smooth surfaces in the proper plane.
     Where proper plane cannot be achieved, so notify
     Architect and do not proceed without instructions.

Small Projects: The basic requirements specified in the above example are necessary regardless of project size. For very small projects, however, some of the conditions mentioned may not exist.

Section 09900   *Painting and Finishing*

Large Projects: The following example contains paragraphs that an architect might find helpful when specifying painting for a project where existing construction plays a part. In some cases, only a single example is given. For example, Clause 2.01 requires that natural finish on doors and cabinet work match the existing finish. There may be other surfaces where the finish is to match the existing finish. When writing a painting section, be sure to include all such conditions. Methods and techniques specified in the example were selected to work on the projects from which the example was taken. Do not assume that they are correct for any other situation. They may not work for other paint systems. They may be incorrect for other existing conditions. Check with specified products manufacturers to ensure that the methods specified are appropriate for the products specified and the conditions that exist.

PART 1   GENERAL

1.01   SUMMARY

  A. Existing surfaces to be field-painted, -finished, or

-treated include, but are not necessarily limited to:

1. Existing interior and exterior previously painted and natural finished surfaces to be exposed in the final Work, whether originally field- or factory-painted or -finished, regardless of their location, except where such surfaces are specifically indicated to remain in their present condition.

2. Existing interior and exterior previously painted and natural finished surfaces to be exposed in the final Work, whether originally field- or factory-painted or -finished, that are scratched, marred, or otherwise damaged during the Work under this Contract, regardless of their location, and even when such surfaces are indicated to remain in their present condition.

3. Existing interior and exterior surfaces that are indicated to be painted, repainted, finished, or refinished as part of the Work under this Contract, whether or not previously painted or finished.

4. Existing interior surfaces whether scheduled to be painted, repainted, finished, or refinished or not, when those surfaces are in the same plane with and adjacent to new materials (for example, where a door is removed and the opening filled or where wall material is removed and a door is added) when the new materials are painted or finished.

5. Existing concealed surfaces that are adjacent to previously painted or natural finished surfaces indicated to remain in present condition or to be repainted, or refinished, when the concealed surfaces are exposed by renovation Work and are not indicated to be otherwise finished or left unfinished.

6. Existing items not originally painted or natural finished but of same type item as new items indicated to be painted or finished, such as flashings, piping, ducts, and conduit.

B. New surfaces to be field-painted, -finished, or -treated include, but are not necessarily limited to, the following:
   (Here list all such surfaces.)

C. Field painting or field finishing is not required for the following:

   1. Surfaces indicated to remain unfinished or unpainted.

   2. Existing surfaces where new finishes (gypsum board, ceramic tile, etc.) are scheduled.

   3. Existing surfaces indicated to remain in present condition or to be cleaned only.

4. Except as otherwise scheduled, do not field-paint materials with factory-applied or integral finish, such as concrete unit pavers, paver brick, precast concrete, face brick, stone, cast stone, ceramic tile, anodized aluminum, stainless steel, laminated plastic, acoustical ceilings, baked enamel, resilient flooring, wall covering, laboratory casework, and the like.

5. Surfaces that are concealed and generally inaccessible such as inside furred areas, chases, spaces above ceilings, and shafts, and piping, equipment, and other items occurring in those spaces, unless indicated to be painted. However, repaint such spaces and items that were originally painted and are damaged during the Work.

6. Exterior cast-in-place concrete of all types, including traffic surfaces; except repaint previously painted existing concrete, where so indicated.

7. Factory-finished items, except where such items are existing and are indicated to be painted or refinished.

8. Concrete floors, stair treads, and stair risers.

9. Code-required labels, such as UL labels, and equipment identification, performance rating, name, or nomenclature plates.

10. Existing surfaces left undisturbed during the Work, unless the surfaces are indicated to be painted, finished, repainted, or refinished, or unless the surfaces are damaged during the Work.

1.02 DEFINITIONS

A. "Paint" as used in this section means all coating systems materials including primers, emulsions, enamels, stains, sealers, and fillers, and other applied materials used as prime, intermediate, or finish coats.

1.06 PROJECT CONDITIONS

A. Where conditions other than those indicated are discovered during the course of the Work, notify Architect immediately and do not proceed without instructions.

PART 2 PRODUCTS

2.01 COLORS AND FINISHES

A. Natural finish on doors and cabinetwork shall exactly match existing natural finish on existing doors and cabinetwork, unless otherwise indicated or accepted.

2.02   PAINT SYSTEMS—GENERAL

A. The following schedules do not include every item
requiring field painting, repainting, finishing, or
refinishing but are a guide to painting and
finishing systems required for painting, repainting,
finishing, and refinishing various surfaces
throughout the area of the Work.

B. Provide the indicated paint and finishing systems
for various substrates as indicated.

C. Have each painting and finishing system and product
reviewed by product manufacturers to ensure
compatibility of various coats with each other and
with existing materials, and suitability of each
coat and each system for the conditions to be
encountered. Report to Architect manufacturer's
recommendations that products or combinations of
products be used other than those scheduled
(different prime coat, for example); do not proceed
without instructions. Starting application of any
coat of a paint or finishing system shall imply
acceptance by manufacturer and applicator of system
as appropriate for conditions and of scheduled coats
as compatible with each other and substrates.

2.03   PAINT SYSTEMS

*(Here list both interior and exterior paint systems.
Include prime and each finish coat. There is no
essential difference between the form of a paint
systems list for a project where existing construction
plays a part and one where all the work is new. There
will, of course, be considerable difference in the
content. For each condition, list every coat as if that
system were to be applied to new work. Then specify in
the text the conditions under which the contractor is
to omit undercoats, primers, and first finish coats on
previously finished surfaces. The following suggested
paragraphs contain those kinds of provisions. Be sure
that the paint and finishing systems selected are
suitable for repainting or refinishing existing painted
and finished surfaces. And be careful to consider every
existing condition and material.)*

PART 3   EXECUTION

3.01   EXAMINATION

A. General: Examine areas to be painted, repainted,
finished, or refinished and conditions under which
paint or finish is to be applied. Correct
unsatisfactory conditions before proceeding. Where
existing finishes are indicated to be removed,
verify that finishes, undercoats, and adhesives have
been completely removed, exposing bare substrates
free of films or coatings.

Figure 8-17. A minor paint problem. (Photograph by Stewart Bros., courtesy of Mid-City Financial Corp.)

3.02   PREPARATION

    A. General:
        1. General Requirements for Existing Painted Surfaces:
            a. Completely remove unsound paint and prepare as for new Work.
            b. Except where otherwise indicated, where existing paint is essentially sound, remove only loose and peeling paint, rust, oil, grease, dust, soiling, and other substances which would affect bond or appearance of new paint.
        2. Removing Paint:
            a. For limited paint removal, use abrasive methods, including scraping and sanding. Use hand tools. Avoid gouging substrates. Use mechanical abrasive methods such as orbital sanders and belt sanders only with approval in each case. Do not use rotary sanders, sandblasting, or waterblasting.

Figure 8-18. Bring the big paint scraper this time. (Photograph by Stewart Bros., courtesy of Mid-City Financial Corp.)

      b. For total paint removal, use thermal methods such as electric heat plate or electric heat gun. Do not use blow torches or other flame-producing methods.

      c. Chemicals formulated for the purpose, such as solvent-based strippers and caustic strippers, may also be used for total paint removal. Use care. Follow manufacturer's directions exactly. Protect workers and others against harm, including vapor inhalation, fire, eye damage, chemical poisoning from skin contact with chemicals, and other dangers associated with use of chemicals. Dispose of lead residue and other harmful substances properly.

3. Shoulders: Grind smooth and sand as necessary to remove shoulders at edges of sound paint to prevent flaws from photographing through new paint. Where manufacturer recommends, feather paint edges using drywall joint compound or other method paint manufacturer recommends.

4. Existing Glossy Surfaces: Where existing surfaces to be painted, repainted, finished, or refinished are glossy, roughen the surface by sanding or other accepted method that will produce a surface tooth sufficient to properly receive new paint or finish.

5. Existing Surfaces Indicated to Be Cleaned but Not Painted, Finished, Repainted, or Refinished:

Remove soiling, stains, dirt, grease, oil, and other unsightly contaminants. Use detergents and cleaning compounds that are compatible with surfaces and that will not damage existing finishes. Materials and methods used are subject to approval. Refinish surfaces damaged by using incorrect products or improperly using cleaning agents, at no additional cost.

6. Scrub existing paint to be repainted using household cleaner and water. Rinse thoroughly and allow to dry before painting.

7. Water Stained Surfaces: Prime each such interior surface, and the interior finish surface applied directly to exterior walls, indicated to be painted. Use an oil base coating or paint product specifically recommended by the manufacturer to conceal water stain marks so that they will not show through scheduled paint coats. This prime coat shall be in addition to coats in Paragraph "Paint Systems."

8. Cleaning: Before starting painting, repainting, finishing, or refinishing in each area, broom-clean and remove excessive dust. After beginning operations in a given area, do not broom-clean; clean then only with commercial vacuum cleaning equipment.

9. Surfaces to be painted or finished shall be clean, dry, smooth, and free from dust and foreign matter which will adversely affect adhesion or appearance.

B. Wood:

1. Previously Painted Wood: *(Specify specific preparation the same as for new wood. No requirements for existing wood are required other than those already specified above.)*

2. Existing Natural Finish Wood Surfaces:

   a. Where surfaces to be refinished are in good condition, remove old wax and polish by wiping with mineral spirits. Change rags frequently. Sand lightly until dull; remove dust using a tack rag.

   b. Where surfaces are porous or in poor condition, and where existing finish is scratched or otherwise damaged, remove old finish completely, clean surfaces and treat as for new wood.

   c. From surfaces to be refinished, remove grease, wax, oil, and other materials which might interfere with adhesion.

C. Metals:

1. Previously Painted and Shop-Coated Ferrous, Galvanized, and Nonferrous Metal Surfaces: Remove dirt, oil, grease, defective paint, and rust using combination of scraping, sanding, wire brushing, sand blasting, and cleaning agent recommended by paint manufacturer. Wipe clean

before painting. Sand the paint shoulders if necessary to prevent telegraphing. Where necessary to produce a smooth finish, completely strip existing paint to bare metal.

2. Bare Existing Aluminum: Wash with mineral spirits, turpentine, or lacquer thinner as appropriate. Steam-clean and wire-brush to remove loose coatings, oil, dirt, grease, and other substances that would reduce bond or harm new paint and to produce a surface suitable to receive new paint.

3. Touch-Up: Touch-up existing painted surfaces and welds and abrasions to new factory- or shop-applied prime coats and shop-painted surfaces after erection and before calking and first field coat. On new surfaces, use same material as primer. On existing surfaces, use the primer listed in Paragraph "Paint Systems." Touch-up surfaces to be covered, before concealment. Sand smooth.

D. Other Surfaces—New or Existing: Prepare in accordance with paint or finishing material manufacturer's recommendations as accepted.

3.03 APPLICATION

A. Existing Surfaces:
1. Paint, repaint, finish, or refinish indicated surfaces.
2. Paint or finish previously painted, unpainted, or natural finished surfaces in accordance with detailed color schedule. Where surfaces were previously concealed and are exposed by the Work under this Contract, paint to match adjacent work in color, texture, degree of gloss, and type of paint used.
3. The extent of painting and finishing shall be:
   a. Existing Painted Surfaces Damaged during the Work under this Contract: Entire surface to natural breaks such as corners or projections.
   b. Existing Painted Surfaces Repaired, Extended, or Patched under this Contract: Entire surface to natural breaks such as corners or projections.
   c. Existing Painted and Natural Finished Surfaces Indicated to Be Repainted or Refinished: Entire surface to natural breaks such as corners or projections.
   d. Existing Natural Finish Surfaces Damaged during the Work under this Contract: Entire surface. Where surface cannot be refinished without affecting edges and projections, also refinish edges and projections.
4. Paint, repaint, finish, and refinish existing surfaces after completing patchwork, extension, or repair work and new Work in the space.

5. When applying flat finish over previously painted
   surfaces, apply all coats as scheduled for new
   Work.
6. When applying semigloss or gloss finish over
   previously painted surfaces, apply first coat
   (primer) in accordance with paint manufacturer's
   specifications and final coats as if on new Work.
7. Before painting or finishing over existing paint
   or finishes, paint or finish small inconspicuous
   locations representing each condition to test for
   compatibility. Notify Architect of
   incompatibility; do not proceed without
   instructions.

B. Number of Coats: Number indicated is minimum number
   acceptable; shall produce a fully covered,
   workmanlike, presentable job; and must be applied in
   heavy body, without improper thinning. Apply every
   coat indicated, other than primer coat, to every
   surface to be covered, including previously painted
   surfaces indicated to be painted or finished, even
   when the existing paint is sound. When stain, dirt,
   or undercoats show through final coat of paint,
   correct defects and cover surface with additional
   coats until paint or coating film is uniform finish,
   color, appearance, and coverage, at no additional
   costs.

Small Projects: The basic requirements specified in the above example remain necessary regardless of project size. For very small projects, however, some of the conditions mentioned may not exist. Where a requirement covers a material or paint system that is limited in scope, the architect may decide to omit or abbreviate the requirement and rely on the contract's general requirements to provide control.

Division 13   Special Construction

Section 13990   *Minor Alteration Work*

All Projects: Section 13990 picks up where Section 01050, ''Demolition'' leaves off. As we did for Section 01050, we have again included the entire section.

Large Projects: The following example is a compilation of several sections from the author's project manuals. Whether subjects warrant separate sections is, of course, subjective. If separate sections were used, many of the general requirements in Section 13990 would be repeated in each of those sections.

PART 1 GENERAL

1.01 SUMMARY

A. Section Includes: Patching, repair, and alterations
   not otherwise specified as indicated, or required,
   or both, to complete the Work under this Contract.
B. Application of Requirements: Requirements specified
   in this section apply to alterations work throughout
   the Work whether specified in this or other sections.

C. Related Sections:
  1. General Removal Requirements: See Section "Demolition."
  2. Refer to other sections for specific requirements for removal, alteration, and reuse of existing materials and items not specified in this section.

1.02   SUBMITTALS

A. General: When work specified in this section is required, submit descriptions of methods to be used. Include manufacturer's data fully describing each material and product, certificates certifying compliance with Contract documents, show drawings showing details of conditions to be encountered, and narrative descriptions, including industry standards, detailing methods proposed for making repairs. Provide such data, shop drawings, and descriptions whether or not materials and methods to be used are indicated in the Contract documents.
  1. Manufacturer's Data: Include a product description of each material and product proposed for use, including, but not be necessarily limited to, the following:
    a. Sod. Include seed formula and location of source.
    b. Fertilizer and lime.
    d. Materials for Concrete Repair: Include product data and instructions for proprietary products to be used as materials for concrete repairs, including bonding agents, hardeners, admixtures, curing materials, etc.
    e. Acoustical ceilings.
    f. Other products specified in this section.
  2. Certificates: Certification data and certificates substantiating that plants to be used as replacement for plants damaged during the Work exactly match those removed in every particular and have been certified by authorities having jurisdiction.
  3. Shop Drawings: Include details of each condition to be encountered, including, but not be necessarily limited to, installation and anchoring details and relationship to other work of each material and item requiring installation or reinstallation at each condition.
  4. Narrative descriptions shall include, but not be necessarily limited to, the following:
    a. Methods to be used to protect existing vegetation, paving, building walls, cabinetwork, casework, materials, equipment, accessories, and finishes to be left in place while the Work is in progress.

      b. Methods to be used to prepare existing
         surfaces for repairs.

      c. Methods proposed for sodding, and planting new
         plants to replace those removed because of
         damage. Methods submitted shall be as
         recommended by the specialist firm charged
         with planting and sodding.

      d. Methods proposed for cleaning and repairing
         acoustical ceiling and support system damaged
         or soiled during the Work under this Contract.

  B. Samples: When requested, submit for approval samples
     of materials and items proposed for use in making
     repairs and renovations. This requirement does not
     supersede submittal requirements specified in other
     sections.

  C. Alterations Schedule: Before doing any work at the
     site, submit for approval a schedule showing
     alterations required under the Contract. Coordinate
     Alterations Schedule with Phasing Schedule specified
     in Section "Work Sequence" and Demolition Schedule
     specified in section "Demolition." Incorporate
     approved Alterations Schedule into Construction
     Schedule specified in Section "Submittals."

1.03 QUALITY ASSURANCE

  A. General: Test materials to be used in making repairs
     for compatibility with existing materials. Do not
     proceed with repairs until Architect approves tests.
     Do not use incompatible materials.

  B. Plants and Sod: Planting and maintenance of plants
     and sod shall be done by an accepted single firm
     which specializes in such work.

  C. Concrete: In making concrete repairs, comply with
     applicable requirements of ACI 301, "Specifications
     for Structural Concrete Buildings," ACI 318,
     "Building Code Requirements for Reinforced
     Concrete," and the CRSI "Manual of Standard
     Practice."

  D. Acoustical Ceilings: Have reinstallation done by an
     experienced installer of such systems.

  E. Fire Performance Characteristics: Where fire-
     resistance ratings are indicated, or required in
     existing work, provide materials and construction
     identical to those of assemblies whose fire
     endurance has been determined by testing in
     compliance with ASTM E119 by a recognized testing
     and inspecting organization or by another means, as
     acceptable to the authority having jurisdiction.

1.04 DELIVERY, STORAGE, AND HANDLING

  A. Latex Cement Underlayment: Deliver in unopened
     factory containers with manufacturer's labels
     intact. Store in dry areas at temperatures above 40

degrees F. Use caution when mixing and applying to prevent irritation to worker's skin or eyes.

B. Other Cementitious Products: Deliver in manufacturers' original packages showing brand names. Store materials in unopened containers in a dry place.

C. Metal Products: Store 18 inches above ground and cover to prevent rusting and contact with soil or other materials that would destroy or reduce bond or otherwise damage the products. Do not create humid chambers under coverings.

D. Use no damaged or defective materials.

E. Do not stack materials to exceed design live loads of structure.

1.05   PROJECT CONDITIONS

A. Disconnecting Services: Notify Owner and authorities owning or controlling wires, conduits, pipes, and other services affected by renovation and repair before starting operations. Refer to General Conditions and other specifications sections for additional requirements related to existing utilities and services.

B. Protecting Property to Remain: Protection requirements specified in Section "Demolition" also apply to repair and alterations work. Protect from staining and other harm, vegetation, paving, finished surfaces, casework, cabinetwork, equipment, accessories, and devices that remain in place while the Work is being done. When removing items and surfaces to remain, in order to do the Work, protect removed items and materials from damage and staining. Satisfactorily repair damage done during the Work. Satisfactorily remove stains without damage to the stained surface. Remove and discard items with stains that cannot be satisfactorily removed and provide new matching items at no additional cost. Also remove damaged items that cannot be satisfactorily repaired and provide new matching items, at no additional cost.

C. Movement, Settlement, and Other Damage to Existing Building Due to Alterations Work: Be solely responsible for; correct damage resulting from inadequate, improper, or careless construction procedures or inadequate shoring, bracing, support, or protection.

D. Differing Conditions: Should materials, systems, or conditions be encountered that differ from those indicated, immediately notify Architect by telephone, followed by letter, and do not proceed without instructions.

E. Examine Existing Conditions: Examine surfaces to receive alterations Work and conditions under which the Work will be done. Do not proceed with the Work specified in this section before correcting unsatisfactory conditions.

PART 2   PRODUCTS

2.01   SALVAGED MATERIALS AND ITEMS

A. To the extent indicated, reuse materials and items so indicated.

B. Materials and Items to be Reused: Reinstall materials and items shown to be removed and reinstalled, or which Contractor removes to make a way to do the Work, in the same location from which removed unless indicated otherwise. Materials to be salvaged and reused in the Work include, but are not necessarily limited to, brick; concrete masonry units; acoustical ceilings; ceiling light fixtures; certain mechanical, electrical, plumbing, and drainage equipment and devices; and other materials and items indicated to be removed and reinstalled. Materials and items to be salvaged and reused in the work also include items and materials similar to those listed above that must be removed in order to accomplish the Work but that are not specifically shown or specified to be removed, if Architect approves reinstallation.

C. Materials and Items Not to Be Reused: Do not reuse in this Project materials and items removed from the existing building to make way for the Work, except with written approval, unless removed material or item is indicated to be reused or unless the Contract documents permit reuse at Contractor's option.

D. Preparing for Reuse: Clean salvaged materials and items that will be reinstalled. Clean mortar from masonry units by hand. Put operating items in proper working order. Reused materials shall be in good condition without objectionable chips, cracks, splits, checks, dents, scratches, or other defects. Operating items shall operate properly.

2.02   NEW MATERIALS

A. General:
1. Provide new materials to match existing for closing of openings, repairs, and reconstructions where suitable salvaged materials do not exist, where insufficient quantities of salvaged materials exist to complete the Work, or where reuse is not permitted. New materials to match existing shall be same types, sizes, qualities, and colors as existing adjacent materials.
2. Required new materials where similar materials do

not exist shall comply with requirements specified in other specifications sections.

B. Trees, Shrubs, Ground Covers, and Other Plants: Comply with recommendations of ANSI Z60.1, "American Standard for Nursery Stock." Exactly match removed plant in condition that existed before the damage.

C. Sod: Exactly match existing grass in type and seed mix; certified by state from which purchased; approved.

D. Fertilizer, Lime, and Other Soil Amendments; and Topsoil and Planting Soil Mix: In accordance with recommendations of specialist firm who will plant and sod, and approved.

E. Materials for Concrete Repairs:
1. Concrete: ASTM C94; 3,000 psi.
2. Bonding agent: Two component epoxy-resin grout; ASTM C881; Type I or II.
3. Curing materials: Impervious sheet of white opaque 4-mil-thick polyethylene, waterproof craft paper, or polyethylene-coated burlap.
4. Other concrete materials: As approved.

F. Latex Cement Underlayment:
1. Type: Cementitious, two-part mix consisting of milky white liquid latex and gray powder containing Portland cement; waterproof, self curing, extra high strength; designed for patching and leveling concrete preparatory to installation of resilient flooring and carpet; compatible with adhesives and flooring to be applied; capable of producing a feather edge with no crumbling or cracking; recommended by manufacturer for installations up to 1 inch thick.
2. Features: Easy mixing; delivered in premeasured portions; smooth troweling; strong in cross section; nonflammable.
3. Source: "Redy-Mastic No. 808 Latex Underlayment" by A. Z. Bogert Co. Inc., or approved equal.

G. Epoxy Grout Underlayment:
1. Type: Two-layer application; first layer (bond coat) consisting of epoxy adhesive, second layer (finish coat) consisting of a mixture of Portland cement and sand gauged with latex grout and mortar admix; compatible with substrates and flooring to be applied.
2. Source:
a. Bond Coat: "Latapoxy 210," by Laticrete International, Inc., or accepted equal.
b. Portland Cement and Sand: Type and gradation recommended by latex adhesive manufacturer.
c. Latex Admix: "Laticrete 3701," by Laticrete International, Inc., or accepted equal.

H. Acoustical Ceilings: Use existing suspension systems and acoustical materials. Should existing materials be damaged beyond satisfactory repair, use new products that exactly match those existing.

I. Other New Materials to Match Existing: Same types, sizes, qualities, and colors as existing adjacent materials for closing of openings and repairs where suitable salvaged materials do not exist, or where insufficient quantities of salvaged materials exist to complete the Work required, or where reuse of removed materials is not permitted.

J. Required new materials where similar materials do not exist shall comply with requirements specified in other specifications sections.

PART 3 EXECUTION

3.01 ALTERATIONS, PATCHING, AND REPAIRS

A. General: General repair of paving, landscaping, lawns, concrete, epoxy terrazzo, and acoustical ceilings is not required. Where cutting, alteration, removal, or repair of such existing materials is indicated as part of the Work, or is necessary to permit performing the Work, and where existing materials are damaged during the Work, patch and repair using specified products. Finish to match existing adjacent work. Patches and repairs shall not be discernible from normal viewing distance.

B. Removal and Storage Requirements: General requirements for removal are specified in Section 02050, "Demolition." Removal of some materials and items is specified in other specifications sections. Store materials and items to be reused in a safe location until reinstalled and assume responsibility for safe storage and handling.

C. Repair of Materials and Items to Be Reused: Satisfactorily repair materials and items to be reused that have become damaged during Contractor's operations, or provide new equal products at no additional cost. Provide missing parts necessary to complete each installation.

D. Patching Coordination: Coordinate patching involving various trades whether or not specifically mentioned in the Contract documents.

E. Restoring Existing Finishes:
   1. Restore floor, wall, and ceiling finishes damaged or defaced because of cutting, patching, demolition, alteration, or repair work to condition equal to that before Work under this Contract started.
   2. Where alteration, repair, or removals expose damaged or unfinished surfaces or materials, repair and finish or refinish such surfaces, or remove the damaged or unfinished surfaces or materials and provide new, acceptable, matching surfaces or materials or acceptable salvaged

materials, to make continuous areas and surfaces uniform.

F. Standards: Perform new Work and restore and refinish existing work to comply with applicable requirements of the specifications, except as follows:

1. Materials for use in repair of existing surfaces but not otherwise specified shall conform to the highest standards of the trade involved and be in accordance with approved industry standards, as required to match the existing surface.

2. Workmanship for repair of existing materials not otherwise specified shall conform to similar workmanship existing in or adjacent to space where alterations are to be made.

3. Reinstall salvaged items where no similar items exist, in accordance with the highest standards of trade involved and in accordance with approved Shop Drawings.

G. Patching Holes: Properly close and patch holes and openings in existing floor, wall, and ceiling surfaces resulting from alteration work, and those shown to be filled, to match adjacent undisturbed surfaces.

H. Repairing Cuts in Paving and Curbs:

1. Where installation of utilities or storm drainage facilities, or other parts of the Work, requires cutting of existing pavements, or curb and gutter, replace same with same type and quality of material as was removed.

2. Similarly rectify damage to pavement, curb and gutter, or other structure incurred as a result of the Work.

I. Existing Courtyard Walks and Surfaces: Protect. Repair damage to condition equal to that existing before the damage.

J. Removed or Abandoned Utilities: Cap, valve, plug, or bypass to make a complete and working installation.

K. Landscaping and Lawns: Owner will remove existing plants that Owner wishes to salvage. Protect existing lawns and plantings to remain, unless removal is necessary to carry out the Work and the plants are identified by Owner to be removed by Contractor. Owner will repair or replace plants and lawns to remain that are damaged during the Work, but Contractor shall bear cost of such repairs and replacements. Owner will provide new lawns and plantings associated with the Work.

L. Turf: Where existing turf is damaged during the Work, remove damaged turf and provide new sod. Place sod in accordance with approved narrative description of methods to be used, using approved sod, fertilizer, lime, and related materials, and during normal planting season, as approved. Sod is subject to approval in place. Maintain sod until

approved. Promptly remove rejected sod and provide
new acceptable sod.

M. Concrete Repairs:

1. Where existing concrete is cut, drilled, or
   otherwise damaged during the Work, patch and
   repair using 3,000 psi concrete. Follow approved
   narrative description of methods to be used. Bond
   new concrete to old concrete using specified
   epoxy-resin grout. Properly cure new concrete and
   finish to match existing adjacent concrete in
   color and texture.

2. Where removing existing curbs, bases, walls,
   partitions, equipment, cabinetwork, finishes, or
   topping leaves floor surface rough, depressed, or
   unlevel, patch and level to within 1/8 inch in
   each 6 feet, leaving a finish resembling that
   left by steel trowel finishing; use a combination
   of concrete topping specified in Section "Cast-
   In-Place Concrete" and latex cement underlayment.
   Tolerance applies not only within the area of
   removal but also between the area of removal and
   adjacent surfaces.

   a. Mixing latex cement underlayment: Follow
      manufacturer's instructions. Pour liquid into
      powder and mix thoroughly to proper
      consistency for Work to be done. Use material
      within one hour of mixing. If mix is too
      stiff, a small quantity of liquid latex may be
      added to aid workability.

   b. Preparation: Clean surfaces of dust, dirt,
      oil, grease, paint, and other foreign matter.
      Concrete shall be thoroughly cured, and free
      from curing compounds. If concrete is very
      dry, dampen slightly with water before
      spreading underlayment. Do not permit water to
      puddle. Brush surfaces to receive underlayment
      with a prime coat of same latex used in
      underlayment mix and allow to dry clear before
      spreading underlayment.

   c. Installation: Follow manufacturer's
      instructions. Build up thicknesses more than
      1/4 inch using multiple coats, each not more
      than 1/4 inch thick. Do not install where more
      than one inch in finished thickness.

N. Repairing Existing Epoxy Terrazzo: Where existing
   epoxy flooring material occurs in areas to receive
   new finishes, patch and level the existing epoxy
   using epoxy grout underlayment.

   1. Clean entire surface of existing epoxy floors by
      sanding or other methods. Remove wax, sealer, and
      glaze finish.

   2. Apply over the entire cleaned surface a slurry
      coat of epoxy adhesive and grout to act as a bond
      coat. Thickness of bond coat shall be
      approximately 1/16 inch.

3. Over the bond coat apply a 1/4 inch to 3/8 inch thick underlayment finish coat consisting of a mixture of Portland cement and sand gauged with latex grout and mortar admix in accordance with the admix manufacturer's latest printed specifications and instructions. Steel-trowel-finish the underlayment installation.

4. Follow admixture manufacturer's recommendations and instructions throughout mixing and application of epoxy grout underlayment system components.

O. Reinstalling Acoustical Ceilings:

1. After completing work above acoustical ceilings, examine hangers and hanger attachments that have been left in place. Verify their adequacy and suitability as support for reinstalled ceiling. Remove rejected hangers and attachments and provide new acceptable ones. Obtain approval before proceeding.

2. After approval of hangers and attachments, reinstall the existing lay-in grid and acoustical materials in the same locations from which they were removed. Do not reinstall removed acoustical ceilings in locations other than those from where removed.

3. Repair minor damage to removed acoustical ceiling components using approved methods. Should existing acoustical ceiling components become damaged beyond satisfactory repair, or should Architect reject repairs, remove such damaged components and provide new, matching, acceptable components.

4. Leave ceilings complete with no voids or openings, in the same plane as previously installed, with joints aligned, level to within 1/8 inch in 12 feet, and in every way the equal of the ceilings before removal.

5. Clean soiled reinstalled acoustical ceilings using approved methods. Remove permanently soiled or stained units and provide new matching units.

P. Existing Pipe and Duct Covering, and Existing Sprayed-on Fireproofing: Restore to their original undamaged conditions.

Q. Mechanical and Electrical Equipment and Devices: Reinstall and properly reconnect existing light fixtures; lighting panels; switches; outlets; thermostats; and other existing mechanical, electrical, and plumbing equipment and devices removed during the Work but not indicated to be removed. Reinstall only equipment and devices that are in good condition. Discard equipment and devices that are not in condition at least as good as existed before removal, and provide new equivalent equipment and devices. New equipment and devices

shall exactly match those removed in type, size,
finish, configuration, and operating
characteristics. Refer to Division 16 for
requirements.

3.02 CLEANING UP

   A. Remove periodically from site the accumulated debris
      from Work specified in this section, particularly
      from areas within building and in vicinity of
      cutting operations
   B. At completion, remove from premises scaffolding,
      equipment, excess materials, debris, rubbish, and
      packings which result from Work specified in this
      section.

Small Projects: Section 13990, by definition, covers limited conditions. Even so,
the requirements specified in our example may be too stringent or too extensive
for the conditions on a small project. When such is the case, further reduce the
technical requirements. Perhaps, if the project permits, specify only that products
match the existing, or use proprietary names without also specifying characteristics. Be careful, however, to specify procedural requirements necessary to control the quality of the completed work.

References

Advisory Council on Historic Preservation. "National Historic Preservation Act of 1966, as amended." Washington, D.C.: Advisory Council on Historic Preservation, 1981.

————. Report to the President and Congress of the United States." Washington, D.C.: Advisory Council on Historic Preservation, 1981.

American Institute of Architects. *Architect's Handbook of Professional Practice.* Washington, D.C.: The American Institute of Architects.

————. AIA Document A107, "Abbreviated Form of Agreement Between Owner and Contractor." Washington, D.C.: The American Institute of Architects, 1987.

————. AIA Document A201, "General Conditions of the Contract for Construction." Washington, D.C.: The American Institute of Architects, 1987.

————. AIA Document A511, "Guide for Supplementary Conditions." Washington, D.C.: The American Institute of Architects, 1987.

————. AIA Document A521, "Uniform Location of Subject Matter." Washington D.C.: Professional Engineers in Private Practice, a Practice Division of the National Society of Professional Engineers, American Consulting Engineers Council, American Society of Civil Engineers, The Construction Specifications Institute, The American Institute of Architects, 1981.

————. *Masterspec.* Washington, D.C.: The American Institute of Architects.

————. Ramsey/Sleeper *Architectural Graphic Standards,* 7th ed. New York: Wiley, 1981.

————. *Current Techniques in Architectural Practice.* Washington, D.C.: The American Institute of Architects and Architectural Record Books, 1976.

Brick Institute of America. *Technical Notes on Brick Construction.* McLean, Va.: Brick Institute of America.

Construction Specifications Institute. *Manual of Practice*. Alexandria, Va.: The Construction Specifications Institute.

———. Document MP-2-1, *Masterformat*. Alexandria, Va: The Construction Specifications Institute, 1983.

———. *Spectext*. Alexandria, Va: The Construction Specifications Institute.

Emerson, Ralph Waldo. *Essays: First Series,* "Self Reliance." 1841.

Heritage Conservation and Recreation Service (National Park Service), U.S. Department of the Interior. *The Secretary of the Interior's Standards for Historic Preservation Projects*. Washington, D.C.: Heritage Conservation and Recreation Service, 1979.

Kipling, Rudyard. "In the Neolithic Age."

Lewis, Jack R. *Construction Specifications*. New York: Prentice-Hall, 1975.

Meier, Hans W. *Construction Specifications Handbook, 2d ed*. New York: Prentice-Hall, 1978.

National Trust for Historic Preservation. "Summary of Preservation Tax Incentives in the Economic Recovery Tax Act of 1981," Washington, D.C.: National Trust for Historic Preservation, 1981.

O'Connell, William J. *Graphic Communications in Architecture*. Ill.: Stipes Publishing Company, 1972.

Rosen, Harold J. *Construction Specifications Writing*. New York: Wiley, 1981.

Simmons, H. Leslie. *The Specifications Writer's Book of Checklists and Forms*. New York: Wiley, 1986.

———. *The Specifications Writer's Handbook*. New York: Wiley, 1985.

Tile Council of America, Inc. "Ceramic Tile: The Installation Handbook." Princeton, N.J.: Tile Council of America, 1987.

Index